World Map, ca. 1775

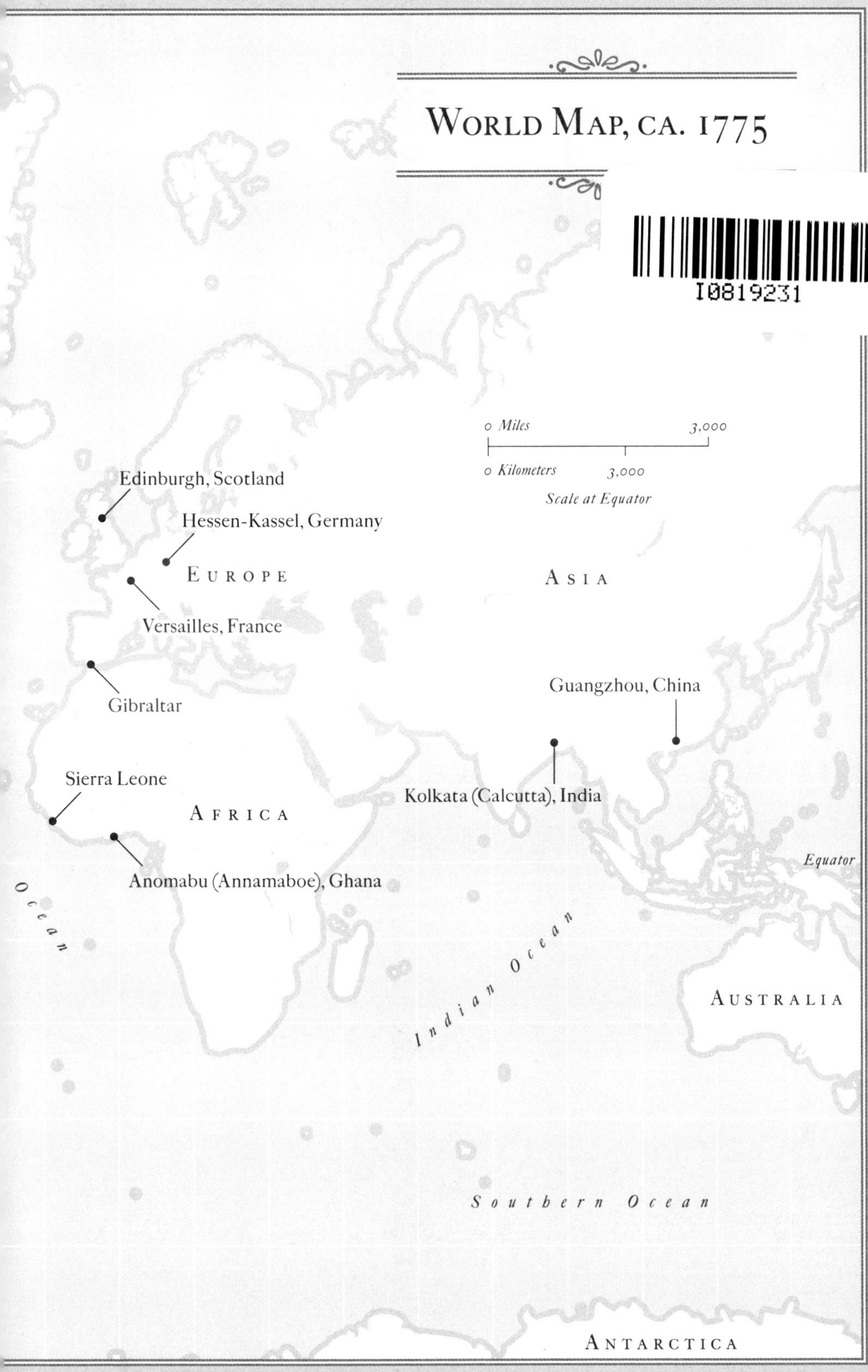

FREEDOM ROUND THE GLOBE

FREEDOM ROUND THE GLOBE

A World History of the American Revolution

Sarah M. S. Pearsall

Doubleday
New York

FIRST DOUBLEDAY HARDCOVER EDITION 2026

Published by Doubleday, a division of Penguin Random House LLC,
1745 Broadway, New York, NY 10019.

Book design by Betty Lew
Map illustrations © Jeffrey L. Ward

Library of Congress Cataloging-in-Publication Data
Names: Pearsall, Sarah M. S. author.
Title: Freedom round the globe: a world history of the American Revolution /
Sarah M. S. Pearsall.
Description: First Doubleday hardcover edition. | New York: Doubleday, 2026. |
Includes bibliographical references and index.
Identifiers: LCCN 2025042830 (print) | LCCN 2025042831 (ebook) |
ISBN 9780385548717 (hardcover) | ISBN 9780385548724 (ebook)
Subjects: LCSH: United States—History—Revolution, 1775–1783—Influence |
United States. Declaration of Independence | Social values—History—18th century.
Classification: LCC E209 .P35 2026 (print) | LCC E209 (ebook)
LC record available at https://lccn.loc.gov/2025042830
LC ebook record available at https://lccn.loc.gov/2025042831

penguinrandomhouse.com | doubleday.com

Printed in the United States of America
1st Printing

The authorized representative in the EU for product safety and compliance is
Penguin Random House Ireland, Morrison Chambers, 32 Nassau Street,
Dublin D02 YH68, Ireland, https://eu-contact.penguin.ie.

To Edward, my students,
and those whom George Washington
called the "future guardians of the
liberties of the country."[1]

Contents

Preface

In 1976, even boxes of fried chicken celebrated the American Revolution. Covered in stars and stripes, they proclaimed with cheer: HAPPY BIRTHDAY AMERICA. The form and face of George Washington—the colonies' leading American general and the first U.S. president—appeared in the shape of whiskey bottles and flower-scented Avon soaps set on crystal dishes.

The bicentennial commemoration of the American Revolution loomed large for Americans—including four-year-old me in pigtails and sneakers (like the girl on page x). Bouncing around in our pumpkin-colored station wagon in Del Mar, California (no car seats then), I gazed up at spinning blue and orange balls declaring Shell gasoline to contain "the Spirit of '76," seemingly part of the celebration. No one gave me a

This Kentucky Fried Chicken box commemorated the bicentennial of the Declaration of Independence in 1976.

At the National Museum of History and Technology (now the National Museum of American History) in Washington, D.C., Uncle Sam (John Rusk) and an unnamed child celebrate the bicentennial.

Barbie doll dressed in an eighteenth-century-style red and blue dress, with militiamen marching across the skirt, but if they had, I would have played with it. At my preschool, I cut up red, white, and blue paper. With tongue out of the side of my mouth in concentration, I glued them into the stars and stripes of the American flag and shook glitter on them with a heavy hand. In 1976, 1776 smelled floral and glistened marvelous.

A few years later, in my fifth-grade history class, we spent an entire semester summarizing pamphlets about twenty-six American Revolutionary heroes (probably an activity that had been on repeat since 1976). All twenty-six were to be assembled into a folder with an artistic cover, submitted in a crescendo of industriousness, patriotism, and colored pencils. I found writing these deferential summations so dull that I completed only three (and I never much liked decorating anything). My history report card that semester was underwhelming. I'm not proud of this behavior, but now I understand it a bit better. These Great Patriots (no Loyalists, of course) all lived Back East, most of them in places I had never even seen, like Philadelphia, some three thousand miles and two hundred years distant. I can recall only one woman: Betsy Ross, who, in her dainty little mobcap, supposedly crafted the first stars and stripes. In my dirty sneakers, racing the boys, I was not about to sew any flags. This did not seem like my world.

I am as surprised as anyone that I have written a history of the American Revolution. After teaching this material for decades, I ended up crafting the book that I wanted to read, one that covers the whole set of events—from Pontiac's War to the Constitution—and puts that American Revolution in a much richer international context. Moving beyond simple hero worship or propaganda, this capacious history aims to celebrate principles and to acknowledge complications while connecting the U.S. story with people and places all over the world. A lot has changed since 1976, more than I could have imagined, yet I still think there is a place for a new account of the American Revolution. In tumultuous times, a complex and colorful history of global resistance to tyranny has much to teach us.

These days, few of us are recognized descendants of the Sons and Daughters of the American Revolution. However, many of us would like to believe that we are Friends of Liberty, as supporters of the Revolution called themselves. Amid imperfections and intolerance, we dream of better worlds and labor in all kinds of different ways to make them a reality. This work has only become more urgent since 1976. Here, then, is my wonky celebration of the 250th anniversary of the Declaration of Independence, a grown-up version of my glittery glued-together stars and stripes. HAPPY BIRTHDAY AMERICA.

FREEDOM
ROUND THE
GLOBE

Introduction

It was a thing of beauty, though it carried death.[1] The soldier wore it into battle, close to his fast-beating heart. This 1777 powder horn was an inexpensive funnel on a strap, designed to keep gunpowder dry and at the ready to pour into a musket. European soldiers carried modern powder cartridges, as did most North American soldiers after 1777. Before then, though, striking horns like this one were crafted in their hundreds in North America from the 1740s to the 1770s.[2] Made of cattle horn, its smooth waterproof surface made it a good space for artistry. Its creator could not resist this bony canvas, carving intricate, fanciful depictions of the natural world.

A bird, wings outstretched, skims across the surface of the horn. A wide-eyed sun stares, agog, next to a regal stag and an evergreen tree. The all-seeing eye of God circles the edges, embedded in geometric designs on both ends. This creativity transformed a weapon of war into remarkable American folk art.[3] It also connected this American horn with a wider world. The artist worked in European symbols with designs found in women's embroidery and on gravestones. The patterns also evoked Native American and African motifs from pottery.[4] Other powder horns feature Indigenous warriors with feathers on their heads, great-masted ships, maps, mermaids, and even a Māori war party canoe copied from a British magazine.[5]

Words, too, marked this horn. LIBERTY read a banner clutched in the bird's beak. Other such items warned: "Steel not this Horn for Fear of Shame / For on it Is the owners Name."[6] This one read in beautiful script: "Prince Simbo his horn made at Glastenbury [Connecticut]

Nov 17 AD 1777." Simbo was a Black soldier in the Continental Army. Although some have assumed that Simbo carved the horn himself, in fact, its motifs suggest that a specialist artisan, active in the Connecticut River Valley, made it. Still, these words asserted possession and pride. Whether Simbo was enslaved or not (it is unclear), he lived in a world where every American colony included enslaved people. He carried a powder horn and a musket when many Black people were not allowed to possess firearms.[7]

What did that banner of liberty signify for Prince Simbo? He was fighting in the American Revolutionary War. Liberty had become a keyword for soldiers in that conflict in 1775. Many horns carved in 1775–77 included it.[8] It became part of a rallying cry: Liberty or death![9] This powder horn was by Simbo's side when he was stationed at Valley Forge in the dismal winter of 1777–78, when he also received a blanket.[10] Yet for a man who may have been enslaved—and very possibly had an enslaved wife or children or parents or friends or all of the above—the word had further connotations. Liberty mattered for Simbo and others because slavery was so palpable, oppressive, and ubiquitous. Flying above him like that bird, freedom was an aspiration, a fluttering dream in the distance.

What did freedom mean to other people in this era? Around the world, many people invoked it—or its opposite, slavery. In 1753, the *nawab* (ruler) of Bengal lamented that the British plundered the country and forced a "great number . . . of both sexes into slavery."[11] In 1754, Antiguans in the Caribbean condemned the impressment of men as sailors on warships as "inconsistent with Civil Liberty, and the Natural Rights of Mankind."[12] In 1762, one New England woman, pert in her anger, informed her husband: "if I am your *Wife*, I am not your *Slave*."[13] "You do not speak to us any more like brothers, but like masters, and you treat us as we treat our slaves," complained the Odawa leader, Pontiac, to settlers in the Great Lakes area in 1763.[14] In 1765, Canadian merchants grew "very uneasy with the Beginning of their Slavery."[15] That same year, at the end of a protest against the Stamp Act in Newport, Rhode Island, enslaved people and enslavers alike joined together to sing: "Britannia's Sons despise Slavery, / And dare to be nobly free!" In 1766, in the British colony of West Florida, an official fretted over "the spirit of what is . . . called Liberty" blossoming amid its white sands.[16] In 1770, a West African slave trader proclaimed himself "a friend to Liberty . . . tho I live in the Midst of Slaves & Slavery."[17] In 1771, a grieving father—devastated by the killing of his son by soldiers at a London protest meeting—pleaded with Parliament to cease "bringing destruction and slavery upon his fellow subjects."[18] In 1773, a woman transported from West Africa in chains as a girl prayed that Americans need no longer "dread the iron chain . . . meant t'enslave the land."[19] A year later, another woman in New England warned a friend that North America faced "the Same Thralldom" confronting Asians.[20] In 1775, Dubliners in Ireland toasted: "May the gates of Temple-bar be decorated with the heads of those who [employed] military force to enslave our fellow subjects in America."[21]

In other words, a refusal to be treated "like a slave"—a type of person familiar to most by then—seemed across many distinct locations to be an effective way to make a case for better treatment. The American Revolution did not provoke this shift. Rather, these demands for liberty emerged out of a wider world, sparking changes too often attributed to the political revolution in thirteen North American colonies. Of course, global claims of freedom were not new either; they had roots in classical and biblical worlds. However, they took on novel resonance in a period of accelerating rates of especially Atlantic slavery, as Prince Simbo well knew. Pulling back to view the wider world—and the range of women and men who invoked slavery and freedom—helps to clarify the meanings and purposes of those words as well as the realities behind them.

Patriots in the United States have loved to quote from Thomas Paine's 1776 independence-inspiring pamphlet *Common Sense* that the new nation would become "an asylum for mankind." They are less likely to include the section that came before it: "Every spot of the old world is overrun with oppression. Freedom hath been hunted round the Globe."[22] He meant that freedom was hunted *down*—and destroyed. Yet freedom was also hunted in the sense that people all over the world searched for it. Consciously or not, Paine was echoing an earlier wartime ode to the new empire of Britannia, with its jingoistic claim that "round the globe her conquests run."[23] Liberty and conquest were more closely linked than some liked to believe. After all, some prerogatives—to "settle" land already inhabited or to enslave people—depended on diminishing the freedom of others, a conundrum that one historian has called "freedom's dominion."[24]

Was the United States exceptional? Yes, but not necessarily in the ways people usually assume. North Americans in the thirteen colonies were not the first or only people in this era to lament their slavery or even to launch a full-scale rebellion. Plenty of other people—from rebels in Tacky's War in Jamaica in 1760 to those in the Dutch colony of Surinam in 1763 to those in St. Vincents in the early 1770s—had done so.[25] The St. Vincents insurrection resulted in the recognition of Indigenous sovereignty over part of that Caribbean island. Plenty of others around the world protested British policies, including Indigenous Americans such as Pontiac, who led a remarkably successful "war of independence against the British Empire" in the 1760s.[26]

Still, the 1776 settler rebellion ignited a flame that burned bright across many places. That it went as far as it did was astonishing, even to people at the time. What was notable was less an impulse toward resistance (shared with many) than the fact that it blossomed into a full-scale revolution; that a whole set of colonies united to declare their independence; that this event became a world war; and that rebels succeeded in starting a new nation. This process was a surprising and complicated one.

A global perspective reveals larger international movements yet also the particularities of the local. The new nation took the shape it did because of these unfolding and complex dynamics between the global and the local. One thing is clear: Rebels could never have achieved these accomplishments without the involvement of other countries. This nation may have been conceived in liberty, but it was born with the help of many midwives.

The American Revolutionary War was in fact a Russian doll of a war, with conflicts nested in other ones, far beyond the thirteen colonies. It started as an anti-imperial insurrection. It grew into "just another imperial war" (as one historian has phrased it) as well as a set of civil wars, a world war, a series of wars of settler conquest.[27] It overlapped with other conflicts: what one historian of the United States has termed the "Long War for the West" and another has called "a war for the North American continent" as well as anticolonial fights such as the First and Second Anglo-Mysore wars, led by the South Asian leaders Haidar Ali and his son, Tipu Sultan.[28] In 1780, they trounced the British in Pollilur, thanks to 26,000 cavalry and 6,000 infantry soldiers, more than the 20,000 American, French, and allied forces who succeeded at Yorktown in 1781.[29] Yet few Americans know about the help they got from the South Asian fighters who drew away British resources. If the Seven Years' War is called, rightly, the first world war, then the American Revolutionary War might be called a kind of second world war, as in 1778, an American rebellion became a global conflict. In a nod to the Seven Years' War, it might also be called the Nine Years' War (1775–84). The protean character of this war—and how and why the trajectory of the "thirteen colonies" went as it did—can be understood only across a wider canvas.

The global environment, too, shaped outcomes. Mosquitoes and viruses traveled in lethal silence over borders and boundaries, injecting the vulnerable bodies of soldiers and civilians alike with diseases like smallpox, which alone killed more than did all of the battles of the American Revolution in these same years.[30] Mexican burial records, Lakota winter counts, and agonized letters dipped in vinegar (believed to be a disinfectant) in Boston reveal the terrifying force of a smallpox pandemic in these years.[31] Hurricanes hurled wind and water over islands and mainland, destroying ships and buildings and crops and animals and people. A single hurricane in October 1780—the deadliest in recorded history and one of three that month—killed twenty-two to thirty thousand people in the Caribbean, likely more than died altogether on the American side from battles (6,800) and diseases (17,000).[32] Environmental factors mattered.[33]

The American Revolution was also bound up with modernizing processes occurring around the world, shifts in terms of cultural encounters, capitalism, communication, material lives, and what has been called the Enlightenment. Those global trends influenced its ideas, origins, and progress, a central argument here. The new nation took the shape it did because of these dynamics as well as better-known local forces.[34]

The emphasis here is on the effect of the world on the American Revolution, not the reverse (by far the more common treatment). Each chapter of this book begins outside the thirteen colonies for several reasons. First, each location holds different clues to what this meta-event of the American Revolution was, illuminating general and particular trajectories as well as graceful ideals and grim limitations. Second, this approach corrects exceptionalism, embedding the American trajectory within a larger set of transformations. Finally, starting in this way revitalizes the all-too-familiar story of the Founding Fathers—and the Declaration of Independence.

The United States commemorates the publication of the Declaration of Independence in 1776 as *the* founding event. For 250 years, people all over the world have looked to that document as an inspiration and a guide.[35] Yet what makes this event of such world historical importance is not the Declaration itself. What makes the American Revolution worth celebrating are the positive principles that informed the Declaration of Independence, including liberty. As Prince Simbo's powder horn shows us, these ideals were not restricted to Founding Fathers, to elite men in thirteen British colonies. They were not even confined to those thirteen colonies.

"How did we get here, Dr. Pearsall?" demanded my student, her face blotchy and tear-stained. I was teaching at Cambridge University. It was 2016, a year of divisive elections in both the United States and Great Britain. Since so many students expressed similar distress to me, I decided that it was time to teach a class on the origins of the United States. Like the nation it brought into the world, the American Revolution is big, beautiful, vexing, and shot through with contradictions. The Revolution celebrated the power of the people even while advancing the interests of a limited number of elite men. Its proponents included small-minded thugs as well as liberating heroes. In moments of its greatest drama, slaveholders argued for liberty and equality. Its war threatened the sovereignty of various Native American nations even as it proved their enduring power. Revolutionary thinking liberated women, yet it seemed to do little of a practical nature for them. Its events were at once local and global. I had a hunch that its global nature could help to untangle these paradoxes, or at least to illuminate them. I decided to teach a course with this larger perspective.

This California girl came to see the American Revolution in the world through my students' eyes, as they blinked in wonder at its strangeness and drama and pain. These bright, curious young people from around the world had many questions. Where, even, was Boston? And what did Bostonians have against tea? They puzzled over the hero veneration surrounding men like Thomas Jefferson, of whom some of them had never heard. For them, the American Revolution seemed naturally to be a story bigger than the thirteen colonies (which they could never list anyway). Together, we discovered extraordinary global connections far beyond what I had anticipated. Their sense of adventure inspired me to write this book.

Despite rich scholarship, popular understanding of the American Revolution too often remains trapped in events named for their settings: the Boston Massacre, the Battles of Lexington and Concord, the Yorktown surrender, the Philadelphia Convention. There are good reasons for this limited orientation. The first is pretty obvious. The American Revolution's very name presupposes that it had local relevance, having laid the foundations for the United States of America. Its victors by and large wrote the history. At the same time, scholars of the American Revolution even as late as the twentieth century tended to conceive "colonial America" narrowly, as the story of the thirteen British colonies on the eastern seaboard, with New England as the archetypal U.S. locale. In the last few decades, however, "colonial America" has burst these bounds in all kinds of ways, yet accounts of the American Revolution have not entirely caught up with this expanded geography.

As my bleary-eyed students could tell you, the history of the American Revolution is hardly an undertreated topic. There is a daunting amount of excellent work on it, much reaching beyond those thirteen colonies. Yet none of it did quite what we needed in my course. Numerous books have attended to the global dimensions of war and diplomacy.[36] Others have offered an Atlantic view considering an Anglophone empire, or the contributions of other European nations, notably France and Spain.[37] However, these books have focused on high politics and diplomacy, not necessarily accounting for a wide array of people. Historians have also narrated how the American Revolution provoked global movements of liberty, led to the migration of tens of thousands of refugees, or entrenched the workings of empire (usually related to events in France, Haiti, Latin America, or the British Empire).[38] In recent years, there has been an important and welcome move to attend to a fuller continental narrative centering Indigenous nations and mainland locations (Florida, Canada) beyond the thirteen colonies.[39] Yet few books bring all these perspectives together.

I often begin my course (now taught at Johns Hopkins) by asking students how many colonies Britain possessed in 1765. A few teenagers look at me with pity (I'm used to it) and tell me that everyone knows there were thirteen colonies. I cock my eyebrow and say: Really? Since my students are quite clever, they quickly realize that the answer is probably not the one they think it is. As I let the uncomfortable silence linger, a student might pipe up: "Canada?" In a good year, another gingerly inquires, "Weren't there colonies in, like, the Caribbean?" Yes, there were!

It has been all too easy to forget that in 1765, Britain possessed double the famous thirteen colonies in North America alone, in the Greater Caribbean (including East and West Florida) and Canada. Many other nations, Indigenous and European, vied for supremacy on the mainland continent—and elsewhere including Africa and Asia. Captain James Cook led Pacific voyages in the 1760s that fired imaginations (evident on the powder horn with the Māori warriors) and upended lives. There were also sovereign Indigenous nations near the colonies: *nations,* not simply tribes or groups awaiting removal.[40] Critical actors, their leaders engaged in international diplomacy with the British and others. In sum, as one British politician declared, "Ministers in this country, where every part of the World affects us ... should consider the *whole Globe.*"[41]

Like British politicians, the leaders of the American Revolution did consider the *whole Globe,* what they called "the powers of the earth." They wondered about their place in it, and whether and how they might deserve its plaudits. Those Founding Fathers, the statesmen and gener-

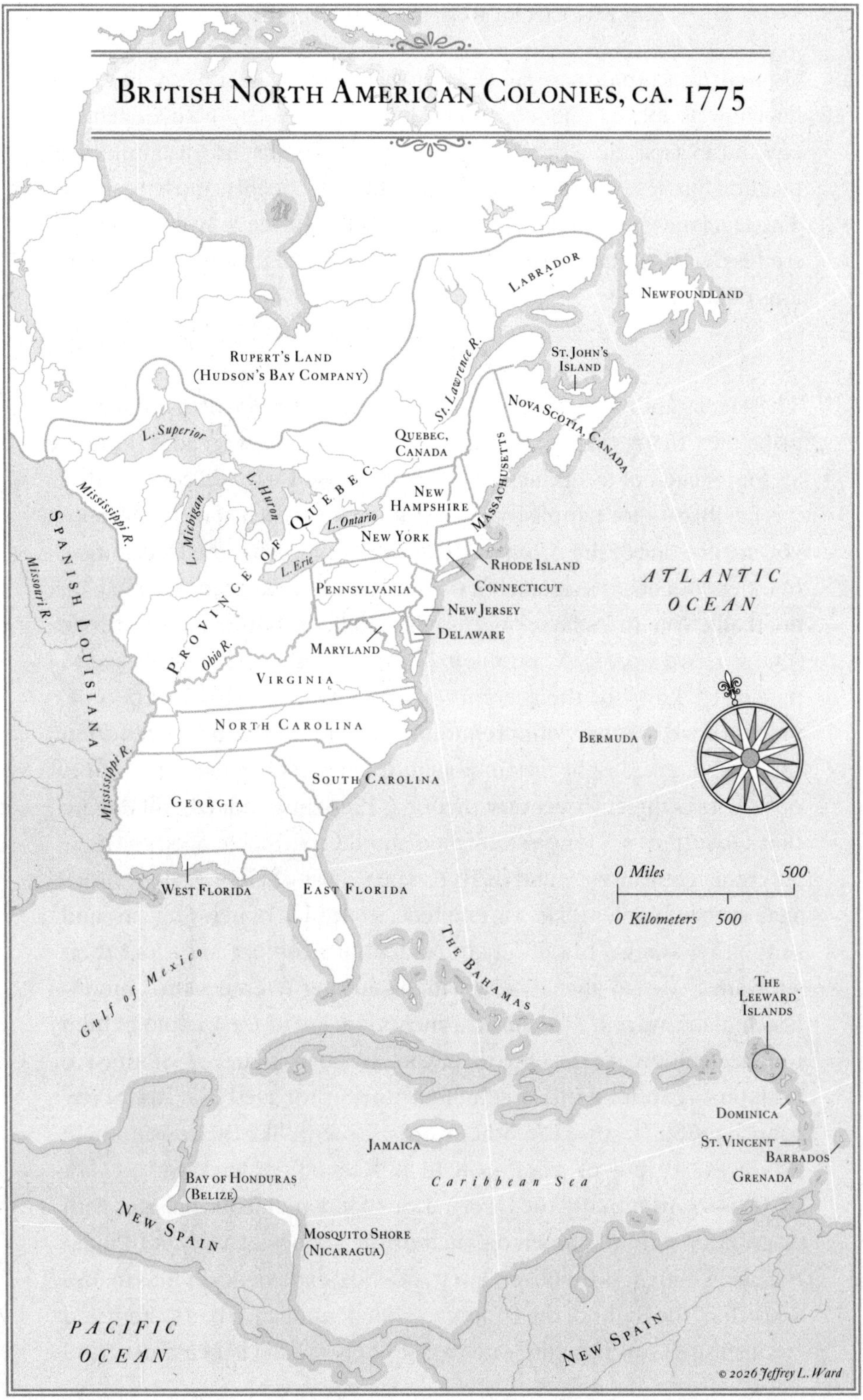

British North American Colonies, ca. 1775

Labrador
Newfoundland
Rupert's Land
(Hudson's Bay Company)
St. Lawrence R.
St. John's
Island
Nova Scotia, Canada
Quebec,
Canada
L. Superior
Massachusetts
New
Hampshire
L. Huron
Province of Quebec
L. Ontario
Mississippi R.
L. Michigan
New York
Spanish Louisiana
Missouri R.
L. Erie
Rhode Island
Connecticut
Atlantic
Ocean
Pennsylvania
New Jersey
Delaware
Maryland
Ohio R.
Virginia
North Carolina
Bermuda
Mississippi R.
South Carolina
Georgia
0 Miles 500
0 Kilometers 500
West Florida
East Florida
The Bahamas
Gulf of Mexico
The
Leeward
Islands
Dominica
Jamaica
St. Vincent
Barbados
Bay of Honduras
(Belize)
Caribbean Sea
Grenada
New Spain
Mosquito Shore
(Nicaragua)
Pacific
Ocean
New Spain

als, were far from provincial or rigidly nationalistic. They cared a great deal how people in other countries judged them. As both a clever strategy and an aspiration, they transformed a narrow dispute over imperial taxation into a set of universal claims to liberty, equality, and happiness. The Declaration of Independence reveals this process. It also demonstrates that these men had a healthy and "decent Respect to the Opinions of Mankind."

The Declaration of Independence, then, enshrines worthy universal principles. In my class on the American Revolution, we read it aloud as a group—each of us taking a section—because I have discovered that it is fatally easy for people to avoid reading it for themselves (I am sure you are not one of them, but . . .). Few need telling that the Declaration of Independence is a significant document, but actually to read it: Um, no, thank you. In its favor: its easy availability (online) and its brevity (under 1,400 words). Against it: its long sentences ("He has refused to pass other Laws for the accommodation of large districts of people, unless those people would relinquish the right of Representation in the Legislature, a right inestimable to them and formidable to tyrants only"); its eighteenth-century diction ("Prudence, indeed, will dictate that Governments long established should not be changed for light and transient causes"); and its ill-tempered list of George III's crimes against the colonies ("He has erected a multitude of new Officers, and sent hither swarms of Officers to harass our people, and eat out their substance"). Also alienating are its disturbing references to "merciless Indian savages." If we have a mental image of the people behind the Declaration, it's the elite men who signed it—many of whom were enslavers—captured in a much later portrait for the U.S. Capitol (by John Trumbull in 1819). In other words, it seems like the consummate product of a group of grumpy old men: "Get off ye olde lawn."

Or is it? Admittedly, the Declaration of Independence pulsates with disgruntlement. It enumerates the terrible actions of a tyrant to illustrate his willingness to subvert law to political expediency. It thus makes a case for "the Right of the People to alter or abolish" a bad system and "to institute Government," one "most likely to effect their Safety and

Happiness." In so doing, it shimmers with positive values. A wide range of people—what was called then "the people out of doors"—lived out those ideals.[42] They were not in the room—or even necessarily in the colonies—where it happened, but they were around: fighting, prodding, hoping, dreaming.

Still, how could I connect those people out of doors and even beyond the thirteen colonies with this made-in-America document? I had to learn how to write a different kind of history, one that connected ideas—like liberty—with the lived experience of many individuals—like Prince Simbo.[43] Those ideas were greater than that lone document, bigger even than the brilliant, eloquent, occasionally cantankerous men who wrote and edited and signed it. Even men of this era recognized that fact. In 1775, a young Alexander Hamilton proclaimed: "The sacred rights of mankind are not to be rummaged for, among old parchments, or musty records. They are written, as with a sunbeam, in the whole *volume* of human nature, by the hand of the divinity itself."[44]

To shape this complicated narrative, I plucked a positive keyword from the Declaration of Independence for each chapter and set out to show how each value prompted behavior among all kinds of people. I followed those sunbeams to words that inspire, not ones that castigate or denigrate. As definitions changed over time, people sometimes clashed over meanings, offering another avenue to understanding the period better. These keywords give us a fine entry to specific contexts of the eighteenth century, but they also point us to constructive universal ideals still capable of stirring us.

Welling out of rage and despair, these ideals celebrating liberty and equality traced out a rousing set of possibilities for people confronting oppression. In 1800, in Hartford, Connecticut, one anti-slavery speaker demanded: "Declaration of Independence! Where art thou now?"[45] In 1852, in Rochester, New York, the brilliant abolitionist orator Frederick Douglass drew "encouragement from 'the Declaration of Independence,' the great principles it contains."[46] In 1968, in Memphis, Tennessee, the civil rights leader Martin Luther King, Jr., implored his fellow citizens in his last speech: "All we say to America is, 'Be true to what you said on paper.'"[47]

I still have a creased paper printout of the Declaration of Independence. Its date stamp reads June 16, 2020, a strange moment of lockdown and contemplation. Underlines, brackets, question marks, and scrawled marginalia mark the pages in the hues of different pens over many months. For each chapter, I had to figure out the right keyword. Sometimes I chose it, began writing, and realized that it was not working. The words of the people at the time—the primary sources—guided me. When I hit on the right ideal for a chapter, I often started to see it—or versions of it—over and over in what I was reading. Then I knew I was on the right track.

Life, liberty, and happiness were obvious candidates. Others required more thought. The thirteen ideals—and places—I have chosen are not the only relevant ones, simply those that made the most sense to me in navigating the abundant, sometimes overwhelming, wealth of sources. I am not asserting that these notions were uniquely American; indeed, I am arguing the opposite. When one takes a wider view, the specific American trajectory emerges with greater clarity. Taken together, these keywords and locations furnish an argument for the importance of certain values and events.

The fireworks set off in 1776 sparked bright, boomed loud, and awed people around the world. This book lets freedom ring in unexpected ways, to unleash the wild, beautiful syncopation of global transformation and revolutionary ideals. The people climbing out of the pages here may surprise you, though some (George Washington) are familiar. A few sport wampum, glinting medals, and silken robes. They speak many languages. Even for the well-known leaders, wigs are a bit askew, breeches a little grubby. This drama reveals the origins and progress of the United States of America while it illuminates, too, the enduring challenges and laudable courage of Friends of Liberty round the *whole Globe*—including those on a river deep in the center of the North American continent.

Chapter 1

A Gallows in Bkejwanong

Unity

As her world tilted and disappeared, the last buildings she would have seen were the church, the bakery, the artillery magazine, and a few houses along Rue St. Antoine. She would also have seen the crowd. For an enslaved woman who had probably spent much of her life shrinking into the background, trying to avoid attention—a scold or a slap from a mistress, a master's unwelcome hand (or worse) in places she did not want it—it must have been disconcerting to be thrust into the spotlight. There were so many faces turned toward her. There were women like her—some Indigenous and some African—looking sorrowful in their coarse linen shifts, huddling together. Their masters stood nearby, traders in thick mantle coats with handkerchiefs wrapped round their heads, smoking and chatting in French. Red-coated soldiers, stiff and solemn, called out orders in English. The fathers, faces ruddy, prayed in Latin for her soul, black robes flapping in the wind. Mothers with babies on their backs set down their heavy baskets for a bit, soothing their children with soft words in Potawatomi. A few of the little ones chased the chickens wandering around. No one wanted to stand behind the commanding warriors, draped in blankets and furs, brass hoops in their earlobes, medals and wampum on their strong chests, silver armbands glinting in the light. The feathers on their shaved heads made them even taller, blocking the view. They probably clustered at the back, speaking low in Odawa, glowering at the dogs clothed in red.[1]

Those red-coated officials hanged the woman, but they didn't bother to record her name. That was British imperial justice in 1763. She had at least one name, probably more, but we don't know them, and probably never will. She was a daughter, likely a sister—among people for whom siblings mattered a great deal—and perhaps a mother. Yet she lacked the protection of family because her kin ties had already been broken. She was what they called a "Panis" Indian, which meant, more or less, a slave. Her fellow accused Panis had already made his escape "to the Illinois," leaving her to face the scaffold on her own. The two of them had been convicted of murdering their master, John Clapham, whose headless corpse was found floating in the river. Records include none of her words. If she gave a last dying speech, if she cried out loudly or sealed her lips tightly, it all floated away, down the straits. Yet her death helped to provoke a war that helped usher in a revolution.

The place where this hanging took place had not one but multiple names. Its Anishinaabe inhabitants called it Bkejwanong. The French had named it for the strait (*détroit*) below. The British pronounced that silent French *t* at the end: Detroit. There were many names, and just as many distinct visions of what constituted justice. Why did that death in Bkejwanong, and the murder that preceded it, matter so much? This woman's choices, and those of other Indigenous people, were interconnected. She and others of this place refused to accept coercion, making defiant bids for autonomy. They were willing to risk death for liberty.

Here is a different kind of murder mystery. What do the killing of a trader, the execution of a woman, and the war that followed have to do with the American Revolution? Solving this puzzle illuminates the central theme here: how and why diverse people forged unity in critical ways, as well as how events west of the thirteen colonies influenced the course of events elsewhere. Wars—and peace—shaped unity, pushing people together—and apart—in a complex choreography. These events in Detroit reveal an increasingly burdensome system of empire and slavery, which caused many to push back against it.

There was power in unity. Indigenous people understood this point; so did the authors of the Declaration of Independence. They called themselves the "United Colonies" and also, of course, the "thirteen united States of America" in the document's very first line. Indigenous citizens of many distinct nations, too, crafted a relatively expansive vision of unity, one nurtured by kinship, diplomacy, and religion. Anishinaabe was a designation like "European" that included many nations (such as Ojibwe and Odawa). Anishinaabe emphasis on unity and autonomy became more important as some settlers developed an increasingly narrow vision of solidarity, one excluding Indigenous people and even British and colonial officials. Both trends, stemming from wars in the 1760s, would shape the dynamics of the 1770s in profound and abiding ways.

Killing this woman rattled imperial officials. There is a whiff of anxiety in the letters that Major Henry Gladwin, in charge of the fort, exchanged with General Jeffrey Amherst, his commander, about this execution. The two men knew it hardly reflected glory on crown and country to hang a woman, especially one as powerless and seemingly inconsequential as an enslaved Indigenous woman. The assumption of British men and law in this period was that a woman criminal in a pair was merely an accomplice led astray by the man. Still, since the man had fled, these officials emphasized the necessity of executing her, even as the whole episode whispered even to them of the dangerous vulnerabilities of their colonial situation. Although "I am always Sorry to Consent to the Sending of any Unhappy Wretch out of this World," sighed Amherst, her crime was "so very heinous . . . that nothing less than her Life could Atone."[2] "This Barbarous Act," he advised, had to be punished "in the most Public Manner, as a Terror to others."[3]

British leaders like Amherst and Gladwin sought to bring terror and subjection to Indigenous people; their actions had exactly the opposite effect. Indigenous individuals did not see justice here: quite the reverse. It wouldn't be the last time that officials misread the American situation and misfired, consequences recoiling on them with devastating effect. As one observer later framed it, "at the very time we were representing the Indians to ourselves as completely subdued and perfectly obedient to our power, they were busy in planning the destruction, not only of our most insignificant and remote forts, but our most important and central settlements."[4] If British officers saw this "Unhappy Wretch" as dispensable, others did not. Her case, within a nexus of other acts of disrespect, provoked the ire of numerous Indigenous Americans, including one of the better-known of the eighteenth century, Pontiac, an Odawa leader who organized resistance against the British. Determined to assert their own vision of justice, Pontiac and others painted themselves for war, picked up their stockpiled arms, and attacked British forts, just two weeks after this hanging.

The French had founded the fort of Détroit in 1701, when they concluded a major peace with Indigenous nations in the area. In the 1730s, its French commandant drew plans of individual villages—Odawa, Potawatomi, and Wendat (or Wyandot/Huron)—clustered around the fort. Each of them had "cabins" or houses with three or four fires and two or three families.[5] Cherished by their elders, children ran free in these orderly, protective spaces. The fields extended outward from the villages. Women tilled those fields, growing the wheat, corn, and plants on which life depended, while men hunted and fished.[6] In 1750, a French missionary found Détroit's "situation . . . charming. A beautiful river runs at the foot of the fort; vast plains . . . extend beyond the sight," with villages of "Hurons and . . . Outaouas [Odawa]" across the river from the fort.[7] The Anishinaabe villages were interspersed with the French settlers' "ribbon farms," long, narrow holdings extending away from the river, each having

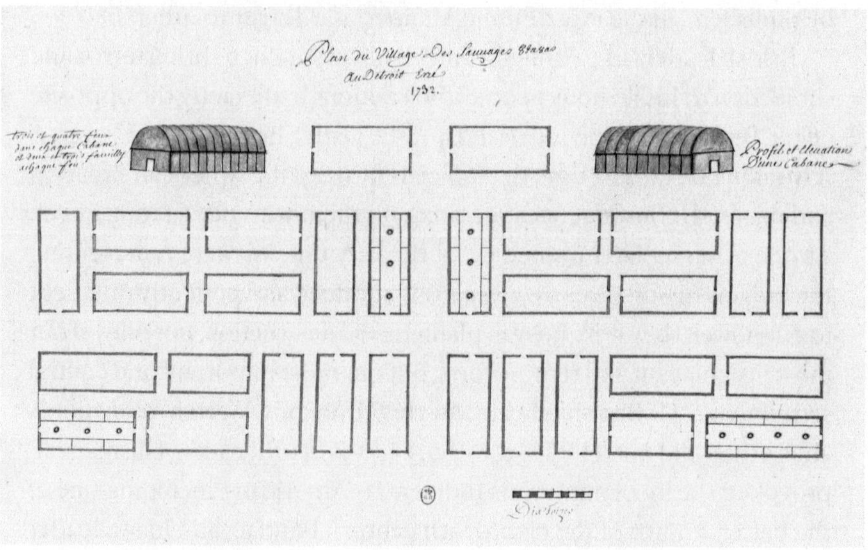

Drawn by a French officer, this 1732 plan of the Odawa village at Détroit shows longhouses of several families. Dots indicate public buildings.

a small water frontage for ease of transport. By the 1760s, whitewashed houses lined both sides of the river for five miles from the fort.[8] Soldiers arriving there in the 1760s sent reports of "this delightful spot," with rich fields of wheat, corn, and garden produce, and orchards of trees heavy in their seasons with apples, pears, and peaches.[9]

The Indigenous people who came to Detroit (as the English spelled and pronounced it) for trade identified themselves by clan and kin (and language), but they were identifiable by nation, too: Odawa, Potawatomi, Wendat, Ojibwe, Mississauga, Miami, Kickapoo, Mascouten, Lenni Lenape, Illinois, Shawnee, and even western Seneca. The Indigenous nations arrayed around Detroit had built a world together. It survived for decades. Diplomats exchanged wampum belts—a traditional item of diplomacy made of shells in alternating patterns of light and dark sewn onto leather, often made by women—in ceremonies with eloquent speeches. One Wyandot politician asserted, "All the Indians in this Country are Allies to each other as one People." While he may have been exaggerating in order to indicate that he was speaking for a group of people larger than his own, a considerable alliance had indeed been forged out of distinct communities. True, it never brought perfect

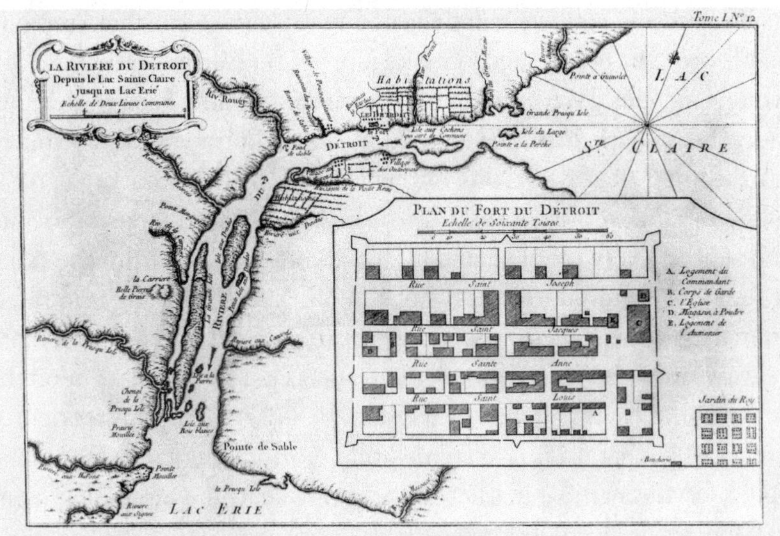

A roughly contemporaneous map of settlements at Détroit, their location on the river, and an inset plan of its French fort.

accord; some had been at war with each other in the past. Odawa and Illinois warriors had even sold Fox (Meskwaki) captives to the French at Detroit during wars earlier in the eighteenth century. Pontiac himself was both Odawa and Ojibwe, and this background helped to give him credibility with what the French termed "all the nations of the lakes and rivers of the north."[10]

Although Anishinaabe people still outnumbered Europeans in the areas around the Great Lakes, by the 1760s, this world was starting to look different. As one diplomat, Benjamin Kokhkewenaunaut, reminded the British in flattering terms in negotiations in 1764, "When the white people came first to this land They were small and we were great and we took them into our bosoms and protected them.... now the white people are become great and filled the land and you our father are a great tree under whom the Indians rest and Shade themselves."[11] The "white people" generally meant French men (and it was mostly men). The French had been traveling and living in this landscape for decades; they started small, with a few eager missionaries, some hardy settlers, and a range of sojourners called *voyageurs* and *coureurs de bois*. This latter group included French traders who exchanged goods like kettles, guns, and cloth for fur.

The fur trade underpinned the economy of these northern regions, and it brought men eager to make a profit on European demand for American skins. Beaver in particular made desirable hats. Indigenous individuals shaped this trade. Men hunted and traded, while women transformed the ponderous bodies of dead animals into that most marketable commodity: soft warm fur. That process was laborious and slow, as every bit of fat and flesh had to be scraped from the skins. It required community work, since hunting parties brought in many animals at once. The uptick in European demand in the seventeenth century reshaped the economies and societies in the areas around the St. Lawrence River and the Great Lakes, as Native Americans reoriented what had been a trading system within North America into one that could service a global market, since everyone from Dutch merchants to Chinese intellectuals longed for stylish beaver hats.[12]

Frenchmen in this area knew that Indigenous people had the knowledge and the organizational ability on which they depended. They worked to incorporate themselves into those communities, whether as traders marrying into families and doing business with them or priests baptizing the babies who came from those and other unions. Many Indigenous people converted to Catholicism, but they did not shed their identities as Odawa or Wendat. Indigenous women, used to marrying foreigners, wedded French men, too, and there was a thriving world of Amerindians, French, and what came to be called Métis, or people of shared American and European descent. The French never dominated in terms of numbers, and they often integrated into Indigenous communities. Anishinaabe and French people worked together and accommodated each other's cultures, religions, and forms of justice.[13] Out of this shared world and its cultural misunderstandings came a "middle ground"—a process, not a place—by which a new kind of world came to be, one with features of both Indigenous and French cultures and politics. Many Anishinaabe people allied with the French against what seemed to be increasing encroachment from the English-speaking settlers who "filled the land" and eyed those rich fields and orchards with envy.

In 1763, Detroit, like the rest of the region the French called *le pays d'en haut,* or the Upper Country, was a diverse and sometimes contentious community, one changing due to disease, war, and slavery. Smallpox, measles, and influenza struck with deadly force. Indigenous people died in numbers far greater than did European settlers, who had some immunities. As a French official noted of smallpox in 1756, "The Indians fear nothing so much as this disease . . . it treats them cruelly."[14] A Jesuit observed in passing in 1750 that villages of five thousand persons had been reduced to two thousand: "You may judge by this how much they have diminished in the period of sixty years."[15] Disease and war wrapped around each other in deadly embrace, as population losses drove people to look for captives by going to war, those conflicts then rendering them more vulnerable to hunger, malnutrition, and disease.

The Seven Years' War, as Europeans called it, or the French and Indian War, as colonists called it, had altered the North American landscape—and many other places—by its conclusion in 1763. It was the most significant war between enemies who fought throughout the eighteenth century: the British and the French. It started in 1754 in the British colonies, and then it moved to Europe in 1756 (the Seven Years' War actually lasted nine years in North America). The British went into debt to fight the French in North America, sending tens of thousands of British troops to join local militias in the fighting. This strategy, while costly, was effective. In September 1759, after years of conflict, the British managed to take Québec in the Battle of the Plains of Abraham. This dramatic victory effectively removed the French as major political players in the Upper Country. The British commander Captain Robert Rogers took Fort Détroit in 1760, which is why Major Henry Gladwin found himself sent there. Other officers, including Richard Montgomery, also served there. This state of affairs was confirmed by the Treaty of Paris in 1763, in which France formally ceded its mainland North American colonies to the British and Spanish. The British, exultant, now possessed an altered and enlarged empire, one technically including new kinds of people such as French Catholics and Indigenous people.

This victory for the British was costly for the French, but it was even worse for the Indigenous nations allied with them. Men like Pontiac could no longer count on the French for political alliances, though economic and social links remained important. War also devastated communities. As a Wendat leader lamented in 1760, "we are like a lost People, as we have lost many of our principal Men."[16] Some turned to alcohol to numb the pain of defeat. The demise of leaders who had offered guidance in times of crisis had pernicious effects for larger communities and for individuals left orphaned and widowed. In June 1763, another English fur trader and soldier accompanied Indigeneous people on a canoe trip from Michilimackinac down Lake Huron. Near one of the small islands, at a place of memorial, two women began to keen "to denote their grief."[17] This war, etching mourning onto the land itself, led to dreams of altering that landscape.

Slavery also came to dominate this postwar world in ever bleaker ways. Captive-taking in war had a long tradition in many Indigenous nations. Usually incorporated into communities, captives helped to rebuild populations. Their status could shift, and it did not pass on to their children. In the context of eighteenth-century world wars, this older system gave way to new forms of imperial slave trading. Indigenous captives found themselves far from home in North America and the Caribbean, enslaved for life.[18] They labored—sometimes for life—beside people of African descent in places like Detroit.[19] The degradation of the status of captives made Indigenous Americans ever more sensitive to being treated "like slaves."

With some justification, Indigenous people feared that the English planned to enslave them, or at least to treat them like slaves. Autonomy and equality were key Anishinaabe values. One Jesuit in the 1750s highlighted "the freedom in which they are reared; respect never makes them timid . . . all men seem equal to them. An Illinois would speak as boldly to the King of France as to the lowest of his subjects." To the French, this lack of hierarchy was surprising and discomfiting. This missionary was amazed that Illinois living together in their shared cabins "all live in great peace, which is due, in a great measure, to the fact that each one is allowed to do what he pleases."[20]

To many Indigenous people, the British specialized in preventing them from doing what they pleased. In 1764, Anishinaabe men expressed indignation at being stopped by British soldiers from going to their own hunting grounds.[21] A speech by an Odawa diplomat reported that the Delaware "told us this Spring, that the English sought to become Masters of all, and would put us to Death."[22] When Gladwin wrote to Amherst in April 1763, he reported that Indians had been protesting: "They say We mean to make Slaves of them."[23] When Pontiac addressed the French in 1763, he complained, "You do not speak to us any more like brothers, but like masters, and you treat us as we treat our slaves."[24] One British author and veteran of the Seven Years' War and Pontiac's War contended, "No people on the face of the earth are fuller of the idea of liberty than the North-American Indians. The very thoughts of that slavery which they were made to expect under the English, was enough to determine them to enter into every proposal the French could offer."[25]

Indigenous people who were not enslaved resented being treated like slaves (colonists felt the same). In the 1760s, several situations arose involving ordinary people navigating coercive authority that restricted mobility and autonomy. In one telling incident, a group of Indigenous women was shot at while traveling by canoe. Even in tense moments of war, a bevy of women usually signaled peaceful intentions. By custom, such women, chatting and paddling their way along the rivers, were to be left alone. The English ignored these unspoken rules. From their position on shore, British soldiers attempted to stop the canoe. In response, the women maneuvered their craft behind some brush, hiding from the soldiers gawping at them from the bank. The officer fired on the canoe, hitting the bow.

Those shots explode with that whiff of anxiety we have already witnessed, as British officers attempted to show their mastery of a situation in the face of their evident lack of it through violence toward women. The women lodged an official complaint that the British officer "had treated the Indians like Slaves." Being treated like a slave meant the threat and the reality of coercive violence, and, for women especially, sexual violence. British soldiers exchanged letters from the forts—spaces dominated by men—about Indigenous women, whom they termed "harlots," assuming easy access to at least some of them. Amherst mentioned one woman at a fort who "had entertained herself so often with the Soldiers that she was almost dying."[26] "Almost dying" does not sound much like "entertainment." Was this Indigenous woman injured by forced sex with multiple soldiers, or by their diseases? Either way, behind Amherst's disconcertingly neutral observation lies a dire situation.

The reality and threat of sexual violence may help to explain not only the canoe incident, but also the murder of John Clapham. We do not know why he was killed. All we know is that "A Cruel & Inhuman Murder" took place near Detroit in 1762, "Supposed to be Done by Two Panis Slaves... Assisted by some Indians."[27] It may be that this woman and man killed Clapham to take his goods and gain a better life. After all, the behavior of the Panis man, who made his escape without the woman, suggests that he was not necessarily the most upstanding character. Yet why would a woman have apparently helped to kill and decapitate a man, an act even the hardened Amherst denounced as "so very heinous"? Then, as now, it was rare for women to commit extreme physical violence. Those few who did so were usually desperate, having endured violence themselves. As one scholar of Indigenous slavery has observed, Panis women working for Europeans were "extremely vulnerable," routinely "made sexually available to" traders.[28] In other words, men like Clapham would have expected more than just the washing of their clothing and the preparation of their food from a Panis woman. The Panis man may have been seeking to protect her. In similar cases, the master had been directing relentless sexual violence against the woman before his death.[29]

A few women carved their rage onto bodies. After the siege of Detroit began, Gladwin sent soldiers to Niagara to obtain provisions. At daybreak, a group of hostile Wendats and Potawatomis killed and mutilated several British soldiers. One French observer reported, "Even the Indian women took a hand." The women—and only the women—did two things in particular. First, "they slashed them with knife-cuts, as we do when we want to lard beef"—a chilling description of women's brutality in a domestic register. Second, "some of the women mutilated them to the point of emasculation," or, to translate the French more bluntly, "cut off that which makes a man."[30] As with the murder of Clapham, this kind of symbolic aggression implies rage against British men as *men*. These same resentments likely erupted in the murder of Clapham and in the solidarity a great many local people felt with the Panis woman.

Violence against women provoked outrage among Indigenous women—and men. Men like Pontiac do not seem to have used sexual violence as a weapon in war, which is remarkable. So many others around the world did—and, alas, do. These men considered the loss of control that such behavior implied—an animal urge indulged by weak men lacking the courage to fight other men directly—to be shameful. Their war preparation usually curtailed even healthy sex lives, since sex was considered a dangerous distraction. In short, these Anishinaabe men did not generally use sexual violence as part of their grammar of war. They were not entirely high-minded; torture remained part of their arsenal. Yet settler violation of women registered as a strike on an entire nation. Indigenous men grieved but also fumed when women were attacked.

Sexual violence was a factor—though far from the only one—in Pontiac's resistance. One observer noted that Pontiac "under pretext of some fancied insult" from Gladwin had determined that only "members of his own nation ought to occupy this part of the world." What was the nature of this "insult"? A British soldier had struck an Indigenous man with his gun when the man attempted to protect his cousin from rape.[31] Of course, there are other explanations beyond sexual violence for Clapham's murder and Pontiac's anger. Still, this murder emerged from a setting where some people endured violence and slavery at the hands of others. The war, too, grew out of resistance to sexual violence, slavery, and coercion.

The heavy hand of British executions, offensive to Indigenous notions of reparative justice, also provoked many.[32] Indigenous justice tended to be performative and community-oriented, "covering" losses and making restitution, not instilling terror. The French had behaved differently than the British under Amherst did; the French had played by Indigenous rules. Captives, gift giving, and diplomacy could help remedy a killing that was seen as an act against a community, not just an individual. During the Seven Years' War, when two Indigenous men had murdered an allied Frenchman, they had to beg forgiveness in a highly staged ritual. They were brought bound, "naked, smeared with black paint, slave sticks in their hands." Then, performing contrition, "they prostrated themselves at the feet" of the French governor. In his scripted response, he "gave them a white shirt, advising them to have hereafter a heart as white as it was." They could then take their seats with others, "This ceremony having rehabilitated them."[33] At times, as there, the French were willing to follow local rules of punishment and rehabilitation; the British were not. Public executions—along with jails and whips, those other symbols of colonial oppression—infuriated Anishinaabe people. As one Frenchman observed, "This is and always will be their excuse for making war."[34]

In 1763, amid whips, chains, and nooses, there arose "a mountain of marvellous whiteness" and a powerful woman. They appeared in the mystical vision of Neolin, a Lenni Lenape leader, the kind of man whom the French called a conjuror, or medicine man. Neolin's dreams—linking this world and others, connecting with spirit animals, and full of symbolism—seemed to forge a path to a better world. In these moments, Neolin became the Wolf, seeking the Master of Life. The Wolf's journey began with that hill and the mysterious woman "of radiant beauty" who told him he had to climb it. No fool, the Wolf "was careful to obey the words of the woman." First, he had to bathe himself. Next, he had to ascend. As the Wolf stood facing that massive pile, "perpendicular, pathless, and smooth as ice," he "questioned this woman how one should go about climbing up." She gave him no answers, only encouragement. The Wolf figured out how to ascend; a person just had to think, to show courage, and to work for the goal. He reached villages at the top, at which point he looked down and remembered that, thanks to the bath, he was in fact stark naked.[35]

Even visionaries could have a sense of humor. Jokes taught lessons too. The Wolf's nudity could be read as a metaphor for his acceptance of his powerlessness, his willingness to listen with humility, and his purity. Despite his lack of both clothing and confidence, the Wolf eventually found his way to the Master of Life, who was also inspiring but demanding. The Master assured the Wolf of his love for the Wolf's people, but he also required reform, warning against drunkenness, fighting, polygamy, and adultery. The Master also urged political changes: "This land where you all dwell I have made for you and not for others." The Master exhorted the Wolf to "drive off your lands those dogs clothed in red who will do you nothing but harm."[36]

Pontiac and the people who supported him knew that harm firsthand. Over the nine years of the "Seven Years' War," they had lost family members, prospects, and a lot of options. It was hard to keep fighting; the costs of war were high and personal. Still, what man wanted to be a dog, or, even worse, a dog of dogs, forced to live by British rules? Domesticated, dependent, skulking around, snatching whatever food was left unguarded: Here was the miserable future painted by Neolin if the Wolf's people accepted this colonial order. Pontiac wanted to be like the Wolf: masterful and fierce, making the British cower and flee. He was not alone in this desire. If Anishinaabe could band together, and obtain enough firearms from their old allies the French, they could vanquish those dogs clothed in red. It is hard not to wonder: Was Pontiac using Neolin's visions to advance his own ambitions, or did he really believe a different world was possible? Both, probably; he wanted to ascend the mountain for himself *and* for his people. After 1763, Pontiac and many others yearned to create a strong community and to assert the independence of Indigenous nations. For some of them, it was a continuation of an old war, what one historian has called "a war for Native autonomy."[37] Unity was critical to these aims.

Donning his war belt and raising the hatchet of war aloft, Pontiac "began to chant a war-song against the English."[38] Many nations joined the chorus, chanting day after day, indicating their assent. People as diverse and dispersed as the Lenni Lenape on the East Coast and the Odawas on the Great Lakes joined the war song. They found unity, despite histories in some cases of direct conflict, especially between the Odawa and the Wendat.[39] Not everyone agreed, including one Catherine, described as an "old woman chief," who supposedly revealed Pontiac's plans to attack Fort Detroit, as well as a northern Odawa leader who "threw away" the war hatchet sent by Pontiac—or so he told the British in 1764.[40] Not everyone loved Pontiac. Yet most supported him, month after month, year after year.

The attacks Pontiac led in 1763—most of them successful—showed the hopes that thousands of people had to force the British out of their beloved homelands. As in many wars between Indigenous people and Europeans, such as King Philip's War in seventeenth-century New England, the British gave this war the name of its primary leader. Yet a name like that minimizes the solidarity of several different nations.[41] One account claimed that Pontiac was supported by "the Indians, composed of Chippewas, Potawatamies, Hurons (Wyandots), and in fact all the surrounding tribes . . . to the number of about three thousand."[42] That number, though possibly unreliable, suggests the strength of this solidarity. Indigenous forces won the Battle of Bloody Run outside Detroit in 1763, and they succeeded in taking numerous British forts in the Ohio Valley and the Great Lakes. However, they were unable to take the three largest forts: Detroit, Niagara, and Pitt.

Still, one British veteran of the Seven Years' War found it remarkable that this multinational solidarity had endured for so many months. As he phrased it, "It was a thing without precedent, for such a multitude of Indians to keep the field so long." He attributed this success to Pontiac's influence and to the ability of Pontiac's French secretary to secure supplies.[43] The provisioning of warriors suggests, though, the helping hands of Indigenous women, who grew and preserved food. They exhorted their warriors to fight well, to "exert yourselves, *and act like Men,* and true Brothers."[44] Indigenous soldiers captured numerous settlers as the British struggled to subdue this mighty alliance. They usually took women and children captive, and they killed men, sometimes torturing them first. In grave moments, they killed captives, too. In war, no one's hands stay clean.[45]

So united and powerful were these Indigenous people that some of their enemies started to get desperate, that whiff of anxiety taking on a sickening stench. For the British in North America, the war begun in 1754 had included a series of defeats, a relentless struggle against people who knew the terrain and who linked arms with the French. Men like Amherst likened the British situation in North America to previous campaigns against hardy, clever, and intractable Indigenous people that had taken centuries: the ancient Roman conquest of Britain, or the English conquest of Ireland. It seemed impossible to make headway. "We must . . . Use Every Stratagem in our power to Reduce them," Amherst decreed. The author of an anonymous manual on war found among his papers suggested one strategy: directly kidnapping Indigenous women and children in order to force their men to stop fighting, a tactic that would not have been countenanced against settler women and children. Colonel Henry Bouquet even suggested to Amherst "to make use of the Spanish Method to hunt them with English Dogs [to] extirpate or remove that Vermin."[46] Yet it was impractical to bring dogs from England to the Great Lakes, Amherst concluded.

However, British officers did have an even more deadly, if more uncontrollable, weapon at their disposal: smallpox. Amherst and Bouquet both alluded to using smallpox (which could survive for hours on textiles) "to Extirpate this Execrable Race," as Amherst phrased it. Those who survived smallpox gained a lifelong immunity to it. Therefore, it was dangerous only to those who had never had it: a great many Indigenous people and others too. Still, although this strategy was the most perilous of all, it was the one they chose. When two Lenni Lenape diplomats departed Fort Pitt after discussions, the English gave them two blankets and a handkerchief from "the Small Pox Hospital."[47]

Settler frustration underlay this biological warfare. To many settlers, including some from Northern Ireland in what is now western Pennsylvania, Pontiac's War seemed a continuation of a long, hard struggle against "French and Indian" people. After all, the great conflagration of the Seven Years' War, which killed more than a million people around the world, had also begun in such a spot. It was easy to imagine that Pontiac's War could inflame tensions elsewhere. In 1763, one Mohawk youth had planned to attend King's College (Columbia University) to train as a Christian missionary. His nation had nothing to do with Pontiac's War. However, he did not go because his friends were concerned that the war would make it difficult for him in New York City "where he can hardly be a Day without hearing his Countrymen . . . heartily cursed as deserving to be all extirpated . . . the Boys in the Street will be apt to insult him."[48]

All too many Americans did not distinguish between Indigenous allies and enemies, as at Conestoga, Pennsylvania. In 1763, during Pontiac's War, a group of peaceful allied Indigenous people took refuge there. In December of that year, a group subsequently called the Paxton Boys murdered six individuals there, setting fire to their homes in the early dawn of a snowy day. Another fourteen residents had been away at the time. The murderers followed them to Lancaster, Pennsylvania, and proceeded to kill and mutilate them, too. Of the fourteen, eight were children. Killing children in a shelter marks another attempt at "total extirpation." Yet the Paxton killers were not finished, marching on to Philadelphia in January to threaten other allied Indigenous people there. Although they were halted, no charges were ever filed against them. The killers went back to their farms and families and lived on.

Not everyone shared their vicious vision. A lot of people in Philadelphia and elsewhere denounced them. The lines drawn were not simply between British officials and frontier vigilantes. Those further east—such as Benjamin Franklin—tended to keep steadier heads and hands. Franklin was an established printer and author, an inventor (most famously of the lightning rod and also of bifocals), promoter of education (including founding the school that became the University of Pennsylvania), and civic institutions (including the Library Company of Philadelphia and the American Philosophical Society). He sympathized with Indigenous allies, producing a narrative condemning the Paxton killers.

Franklin, a consummate publicist, included the names of several of the murdered people. There was "John Smith," a Cayuga married to a woman named Peggy. There was "Betty, a harmless old Woman; and her Son Peter, a likely young Lad." There was "Sally, whose Indian Name was Wyanjoy . . . esteemed by all that knew her." He concluded: "Unhappy People! To have lived in such Times, and by such Neighbours!" He painted a vivid picture of their tragic end: "they fell on their Knees . . . in this Posture they all received the Hatchet! Men, Women and little Children—were every one inhumanly murdered!—in cold Blood!" He lamented: "the Guilt will lie on the whole Land, till Justice is done on the Murderers. The Blood of the Innocent will cry to Heaven for Vengeance." As he concluded, "*Cowards* can handle Arms . . . can wound, mangle and murder; but it belongs to *brave* Men to spare, and to protect."[49]

Ben Franklin took a lot of heat for his brave defense of Indigenous people during the Pennsylvania Assembly elections of 1764. He and members of the pacifist Society of Friends (or Quakers) such as Israel Pemberton who favored accommodation became the subject of political attacks from the kind of individuals who supported the Paxton killers. One satire rendered literal the insult of "Indian lover." On the right side of the image, Pemberton, labeled "King Wampum," is fondling the breast, spilling out of her dress, of the Indigenous woman with whom he is dancing. Her hand lingers between his thighs as she steals his watch fob. Using Quaker forms of address, she says: "Thou hast something lovely in thy Fob I must enjoy it." He replies with a leer: "Thou hast something lovely in thy countenance I must enjoy thee." On the other side, a Quaker distributes tomahawks to Indigenous men from a barrel marked IP (Israel Pemberton). Another Quaker at the table frets: "The Paxton spirit grows Stronger and Stronger." Clutching a bag of money in the center, Ben Franklin declares his desire to win the upcoming Assembly election (he did not). War far away affected local politics.

In the meantime, that war drew to an inconclusive close in 1764.

Pontiac and his allies had hoped the French would join, supplying more arms and soldiers. The French, still smarting from the Treaty of Paris, did not. Pontiac and others began negotiations with the British, who had replaced the Indian-hating Jeffrey Amherst with the more even-handed Thomas Gage. His willingness to negotiate ended the war, and gift giving and diplomacy eased the situation.

Still, distrust remained. The *Newport Mercury*, back in Rhode Island, reported in 1765 that "Pondiac and the chiefs of the other nations" had made peace with the British, but that one of them had "declared, that they had talked friendly to the English, only from their teeth out, but hated them in their hearts."[50] The British capitulation infuriated many colonists. Men like the Paxton killers envisioned an American landscape stripped of its Indigenous inhabitants, where settlers could live on their land with their wives and children in peace and prosperity. They wanted their sons and daughters to be able to move west without fear to cultivate richer farms, better lives. They blamed accommodationists like Franklin and Pemberton for tragedies in the west.

Pontiac's War also shaped British responses. They started to change tack. Facing the difficulties of managing and organizing a suddenly enlarged global empire, they did not want to launch any kind of total war against Indigenous people, whom they considered, like the French, simply another set of subject peoples, to be managed and assuaged. The British developed a plan for empire in 1764, to be rolled out over the next few years, which would have centralized authority and regulated trade, land boundaries, and justice in Anglo-Indian interactions. This "Plan for the future Management of Indian Affairs" was never enacted, and in fact one historian contends that its "utter rejection . . . may be its greatest historical relevance."[51] There are several reasons why it failed ever to take effect, but chief among them was that it was a vision of empire—with relatively even-handed treatment of Indigenous nations—unacceptable to colonists. It would also have required further taxes. What happened subsequently proved that taxation, too, could provoke resistance.

Indigenous people like Pontiac wanted to reach that shining mountain of autonomy. The residents in those villages around Detroit worked for a world without controlling British men: their stiff soldiers, their corrupt trading, their debilitating alcohol, their grasping hands. As one English soldier noted of his countrymen: "They impose on the men both in buying and selling, abuse their wives and daughters, and other female relations; and go yet greater lengths, if possible, in every other species of wickedness." He concluded: "Where is the wonder then, if we so often find the Indians on our backs, without being able to particularize the motives of their insurrection?"[52]

An enslaved Panis woman from the *pays d'en haut* died at Detroit in 1763. Her death, like her life, counted. It came out of a world of diversity and accommodation, one which started to look imperiled. After 1763, Indigenous Americans started to feel the heavy hand of British imperial justice in ways that provoked them. What was seen as the injustice of her ignominious end on the gallows was at least one factor of many that propelled a move to war.

Some have wondered: Did Indigenous Americans belong to a larger Age of Revolutions? Yes—in fact, they helped to launch it. This moment shaped profoundly all that was to follow. All kinds of people forged unity out of noble ideals (community, sovereignty, freedom) and also out of less noble ones (racial and other exclusions and fierce anti-British sentiments). In a culture of resistance to encroachments and violence, Indigenous women and men were among the first North Americans to push back hard against the British Empire. They overcame distinctions of culture, language, even histories of conflict to come together to fight for a different world. In refusing to be treated as slaves, they built solidarities on religion, kinship, and anti-British rhetoric.

A scheme for extermination, shared in different ways by Amherst and the Paxton killers, increasingly united many others in 1763, and beyond. For them, freedom meant the freedom to take Indian land, a land free of Indians. Here is the dark heart of the coming of the American Revolution, one still beating into the new republic, energizing settlers to fight, to protest, to kill, and to write declarations. In 1764, the Paxton killers complained in their *Declaration and Remonstrance* that "the Frontiers of this Province have been repeatedly attacked and ravaged by Skulking parties of the Indians, who have with the most savage Cruelty, murdered Men, Women and Children, without distinction."[53] In 1776, the Declaration of Independence condemned King George III for having "endeavoured to bring on the inhabitants of our frontiers, the merciless Indian Savages, whose known rule of warfare, is an undistinguished destruction of all ages, sexes and conditions."[54] Here is the sound of the settlers' war chant, angry words that sent musket balls flying.

In the wake of the Seven Years' War, many people in North America, Indigenous and otherwise, envisioned new worlds. Anishinaabe people dreamed of a confederation in the Great Lakes, rising like a white mountain, one that reached back to precolonial days but also looked forward to a modern and united Indigenous people. The supporters of the Paxton killers imagined instead a land cleared of the peoples who had long lived there; they were willing to do almost anything to make that happen. Others, like Franklin, wished for a new kind of empire, one in which justice prevailed.

British officials, too, had plans for a reorganized empire, one that would unite colonies from the Canadian north to the Great Lakes to Caribbean islands. Chests puffed up with victory for a time, but soon new imperial worries bent shoulders and backs. The burdens of war were heavy, and they lingered. There were debts to repay. If the British had to protect settlers, then it was reasonable that those colonists should help fund that protection. Or so it seemed to British authorities who started to enact new plans for revenue.

Chapter 2

A Tavern in St. Kitts

Consent

In October 1765, the crowd was restive and angry, ginned up on rum and righteousness. They were charging down the streets of Basseterre, the capital of St. Kitts (St. Christophers) in the Caribbean's Leeward Islands. Some Black bystanders, understandably eager to avoid a stampede of enraged White people, watched in astonishment as the Englishman William Tuckett, Distributor of Stamps, hit the ground with a thud. Amid jeers and shouts for "liberty, property, and NO STAMP TAX," Tuckett had just gotten off his horse. Someone had then shoved him down. Without pausing to consider the consequences, those helpers swept up the beleaguered Tuckett and bore him away. Tuckett informed officials in London that they had saved his life.[1]

When a government appointee highlighted that Black people had saved him from White ones in a place like St. Kitts, something was amiss.[2] He never named his rescuers, and we know little about them beyond his report. Newspaper stories in London noted only that he had been "concealed."[3] However, Tuckett's use of the plural suggests that there was a community here willing to take a major risk. After all, in these islands, if a Black man struck a White one, "the Law condemns him to loose the Hand he strikes with; and if he should happen to draw Blood, he must die for it."[4] The stakes were high. Why would they have intervened? These helpers seem to have known and felt respect or even affection for Tuckett. They may have wanted to do a favor for a man who could return it sometime. Or maybe it was a way to assert their own liberty of action even amid brutal slavery. It would not be the last time that revolutionary turmoil pushed enslaved people and British government officials into strange alliance. Whatever their motivation, no one had to ask them to perform these heroics; they just bore Tuckett away.

However, safety proved elusive for Tuckett that night. He was already feeling the unpleasant effects of that scourge of newcomers to the West Indies: malaria. He had gone to a friend's house outside the town, desperate to find bark, or quinine, to ease his fever and his aching head. In the meantime, that group of angry locals set off from Mr. Noland's tavern in the main part of town. They had stopped on the way at the house of John Hopkins, the deputy stamp collector. They ripped down the door, demanding his stamped papers. He was not home, but a woman, likely enslaved and fearful, handed them over. They built a bonfire and threw them in, cheering in the light of the flames. They then ran into Tuckett on his horse, as we have seen.

Pulled from that crowd and concealed briefly, Tuckett decided to head for his home. Unfortunately for him, so did some "500 white People." To the beat of their drums, they forced Tuckett to town. There, he endured "many gross Insults" including the threat of hanging.[5] Tuckett—sick, woozy, and fearful—had to decide what to do. Two things probably flashed through his heated brain. Thanks to close trading ties between the Leeward Islands and the mainland, he would have known that mainland stamp tax collectors (and their families) had already been attacked, their homes and property destroyed. He likely also knew the notorious fate of the last unpopular Leewards official, its governor, Daniel Parke. The "enraged populace" had beaten and shot him before "scatter[ing] his reeking limbs in the street."[6]

Perhaps unsurprisingly, then, Tuckett immediately agreed to resign his office of stamp tax collector. Even so, effigies of Tuckett and Hopkins went up in flames in Basseterre the next day. There was little chance of finding or prosecuting those involved in the "most riotous and tumultuous" mob or the fires, according to an official in neighboring Antigua. Anger was so widespread that no one would reveal anything to magistrates.[7] London newspapers claimed that St. Kitts inhabitants then moved to nearby Nevis, where, joined by locals, they threw more stamps into the fire, "sacrificed to Liberty."[8] The Leeward Islands were aflame.

1765 was a bad year to be a tax collector in the British American colonies. These men were never popular, but in that year, these mostly conservative government appointees faced rage and fires. The fury of the reaction to the Stamp Tax knocked over men like Tuckett—and the government itself. Officials had underestimated colonial opposition.

A tiny, verdant island that most people could not locate even on a map of the Caribbean seems an unlikely place to tell a story about the lead-up to the American Revolution. In fact, though, opposition to the Stamp Tax stretched from there to Canada. Major protests occurred in places that did not ultimately join the revolutionary cause. Starting in St. Kitts, rather than in the thirteen colonies, then, illustrates that protest did not lead inexorably to revolution; certain conditions had to exist for one to grow into the other.

Following in the footsteps of those irate protesters—as well as those who watched them in consternation—reveals new contours of the American Revolution. First, there is no easy or direct line from resistance in the 1760s to rebellion in the 1770s. Second, despite popular opposition on both mainland and islands, fissures started to appear between different colonies as well as between official and unofficial protesters. Unity went only so far. Third, the importance of the ideal of consent as a principle emerges with force.

Consent was seen as the foundation of a just government. The issue of consent appeared over and over in the Stamp Tax protests, as colonists began to formulate and articulate a theory of resistance hinging on their being denied the ability to consent. These notions underpinned the concept's later appearances in the Declaration of Independence. The first is in its opening: "Governments are instituted among Men, deriving their just powers from the consent of the governed." The next is about the imposition of standing armies without the consent of colonial assemblies. Finally, there was the complaint that the government had imposed "Taxes on us without our Consent."

Yet consent in a world of slavery carried ironies. A typical pamphleteer contended that "those who are governed at the will of another . . . whose Property may be taken from them by taxes . . . without their own consent . . . are in the miserable condition of slaves."[9] Many of those who emphasized consent the most were also enslavers. The Stamp Act seemed like slavery to many enslavers who were conditioned to withhold consent to those whom they enslaved.

This situation has led some to wonder: Did enslavers protest in order to protect slavery? Yes—and no. Consent took on vital importance in this era, one of rising slavery across the Atlantic world. Enslavers protected their prerogatives fiercely. They demanded the freedom to enslave and profit from slavery, yes. West Indian enslavers also had a commitment to the status quo. However, starting in the Caribbean—where enslavers did not in the end join the Revolution—complicates any simple connection between slavery and revolution. It also traces out the ways in which ideas about slavery and consent increasingly underpinned political protest in this era—as William Tuckett found out the hard way.

In the 1760s, Tuckett had joined a long line of ambitious Englishmen streaming to the Caribbean. The first English settlers had arrived in the Leewards in the 1620s, though St. Kitts did not become a British colony until 1713, after years of wrangling between the Spanish, the French, and the British. Tuckett arrived to a small (some 76 square miles) island, sugar plantations on its coasts, hills in the interior.[10] He would have heard that volcanic soil gave the sugar its distinctive taste, deemed superior even to that of the other Leeward Islands: Nevis, Antigua, and Montserrat. As an Antiguan planter conceded, the soil at St. Kitts "is the best in the known world for producing sugar in great quantity, and of the best quality."[11] People in Britain (and its mainland colonies) wanted this delicious sweetener. Since fruitful land was diverted from subsistence farming to sugar monoculture, food—from salt cod to corn—had to be imported to the islands, most frequently from places like New England and the mid-Atlantic region. This trade connected the Leewards closely with mainland colonies.[12] In the wake of the Seven Years' War, mainland and islands also shared commitments to the British Empire, Protestantism, and slavery as part of a foundational political economy. In order to avoid the long arm of imperial tariffs, smuggling was also a common practice throughout this British Atlantic world.

What would have struck Tuckett most on arrival, as for other visi-

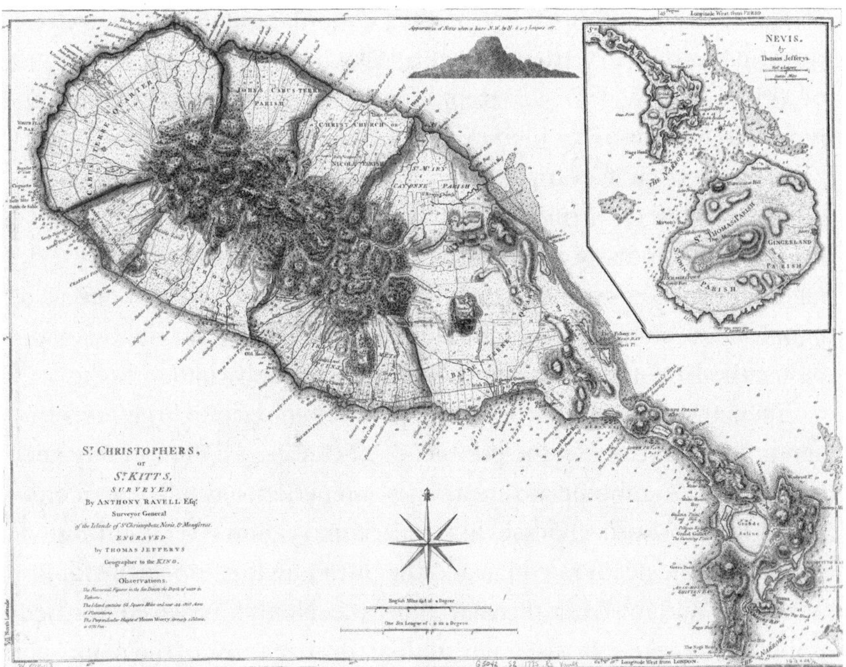

This 1775 map shows the full extent of the island of St. Christopher, or St. Kitts. Its capital, Basseterre, is on the southern coast, above and to the right of the mile marker / compass rose.

tors, was the huge number of African-descent enslaved people in St. Kitts.[13] In the Caribbean, the sugar economy went hand in hand with widespread exploitation and importation of enslaved Africans. Reliance on sugarcane, with its labor needs and its long growing season, required a considerable outlay of investment as it had to be processed onsite (in mills) into sugar, molasses, and rum. In the eighteenth-century Caribbean colonies, the rich grew richer, and the poor and middling who had a choice stopped coming, preferring mainland colonies. The rich sent their sons (and occasionally daughters) back to Britain for education, and some of them also left their West Indian estates in the hands of others in order to live in high style in Britain. Those in charge relied on bringing more enslaved Africans to work on these plantations.

West Indian islands like St. Kitts, then, became societies with extreme inequalities of wealth in highly racialized ways. Enslaved men and women did the hard labor of producing the top-quality sugar for which

St. Kitts was famous. In the 1760s, the Leewards contained about seven thousand European settlers and more than a hundred thousand persons of African descent.[14] One contemporaneous Scottish visitor to St. Kitts reported that part of her journey over its hills literally took place "on the back of Negroes" accompanied by drivers with whips. Those enslaved people exhibited horrifying scars and lived in small, windowless cabins.[15] Even their masters conceded that "During Crop-time, they work night and day almost incessantly."[16] The "incessant" labor of enslaved people made colonies like St. Kitts and Jamaica among the richest colonies in the British Empire, but this wealth was always under threat.[17]

Tuckett's malarial fever points to another major factor in eighteenth-century Caribbean life: the prevalence of disease. High mortality and low birth rates combined to create an island perpetually full of newcomers. Mosquito-borne illnesses like malaria and yellow fever contributed to keeping the death rate high and the birth rate low, especially for ill-nourished and mistreated enslaved people. Neither enslaved nor free populations were self-sustaining, unlike those in most of the mainland colonies.

As a resident of nearby Nevis observed, although the climate furnished "perpetual Spring . . . ever fresh and blooming," it was no "Paradise."[18] For enslaved people, it could be hell.[19] Threats came from nature (hurricanes, earthquakes, and volcanoes as well as diseases) and from people (invasions and rebellions). The close proximity of the French and Spanish on neighboring islands made invasion a live possibility, especially in times of war. Tuckett would have heard about events from the Seven Years' War, including a major rebellion, Tacky's War, which had rocked Jamaica in 1760–61. In this series of battles, Akan, Coromantee, and other veterans from West Africa rose up and attacked enslavers. These kinds of uprisings made those in power in the West Indies anxious about rebellion, so that they—unlike mainland colonies—generally welcomed troops stationed there.[20]

The resistance no one anticipated in the 1760s, though, was that of the stamp tax protesters. The crowd confronting Tuckett had gathered at Mr. Nolan's tavern in Basseterre. On the coast, Basseterre was the capital and center of government, but it was small, with few public buildings. So taverns housed politics—including courts and legislatures—in St. Kitts. In 1758, in a typical move, authorities waived the licensing fee for a tavern owner who "furnish[ed] the Council and Assembly with Two Convenient Rooms" and dinner.[21]

Taverns throughout the British colonies were havens for White men, places to find fraternal sympathy and to escape from the demands of bustling wives, bickering children, and awkward subordinates. In a tavern, a man could have a drink, eat a meal, peruse the newspaper, buy a saddle, hear a lecture, make a deal, find a bed for the night, even see an unusual animal like a bear. Although women, especially widows, often ran taverns and enslaved people worked in them, their sociability often excluded enslaved and Indigenous men and did not typically extend to women either. The presence of enslaved people worried authorities, who tried to prevent this kind of mingling. A woman who entered such a place on her own could feel like the bear in the cage, the uneasy subject of too many stares.[22] One Pennsylvania woman in 1759 lamented "the disadvantages a lone woman" suffered when traveling. She had trouble sleeping in a tavern since the "drinking & roaring appeared strange."[23] Taverns, like assembly politics, were open to White men from a range of backgrounds, but they were less accessible and agreeable to others.

For all the high-flown rhetoric of liberty and consent, revolutionary politics was sloshed with beer and port, dusted with snuff. In the 1770s, when George Washington and John Adams arrived in Philadelphia, they went to the City Tavern literally before doing anything else.[24] Washington was a frequent visitor to Christiana Campbell's tavern in Virginia from 1762 to 1774 (madeira was his preferred tipple).[25] In Britain and its colonies, political action often started in taverns.[26] For instance, in 1765, a group calling themselves the Sons of Liberty pledged cross-colonial solidarity against the stamp tax in a tavern in New London, Connecticut.[27] Some taxes, including the one imposed on molasses, hit drinks, too, as it was a key ingredient in small beer, the cheap, low-alcohol alternative to untreated water. Benjamin Franklin fretted that this tariff would provoke "a general Dissatisfaction."[28]

"General Dissatisfaction" sums up colonial responses to a range of revenue-raising measures enacted by the debt-ridden British government after the Seven Years' War. George Grenville, the British prime minister, was knowledgeable, energetic, astute with finances—and unbearable. His own cousin found him charmless, with a permanent "expression of peevishness and austerity." Foreign ministers so dreaded being collared by him for self-righteous harangues that they called it "being *Grenvilisé*." (George III himself grumbled about them, too.)[29] In other words, Grenville, when sure he was in the right (which he usually was), was indifferent to the reactions he provoked, an unfortunate trait in a public official. Grenville saw it as equitable that since much of the war had been fought in North America to defend the colonies, the colonists, who paid much less than Britons, should be taxed more. Also, it seemed reasonable that the colonists should contribute to their continued defense, especially in light of events like Pontiac's War.

Grenville's logic did not persuade the colonists. An early and radical protester, James Otis in Massachusetts—writing with the confident assurance of a man who had never confronted an Indigenous soldier—found it ridiculous that taxes and an army should be required against "a few ragged Indians." In his view, their British forefathers had conquered Indigenous nations without any help from a standing army.[30]

Officials in London, who had a healthy respect for Indigenous soldiers in 1765, saw a larger empire that needed reorganizing and refinancing. They felt that a plan for reform made sense, as it would shore up—and finance—the North American portion of the empire. As part of a broader imperial reorganization, then, Grenville decided to levy new taxes.

An early major initiative was the Sugar Act of 1764, increasing taxes on imported sugar and molasses. It was explicitly designed to raise revenue, as well as to ensure that mainland North Americans purchased all their sugar from British colonies rather than any others. It was a reform of the 1733 Molasses Act, to be enforced with far greater rigor. Mainland colonists viewed the Sugar Act as beneficial to the West Indians.[31] If it met with some "general Dissatisfaction," though, it did not provoke violent opposition.

At the same time, Grenville also enacted the Currency Act, which outlawed the colonial issuance of paper money. The American economy had entered a postwar contraction, so these restrictive measures fell especially hard on working people. At the same time, Grenville ordered that smuggling in the colonies, a ubiquitous and accepted practice, had to be stopped, and he enjoined customs officials to end it. As usual, he was right; smuggling was both illegal and rampant. Still, as Ben Franklin pointed out, this meant that "all Trade and Commerce, even the most legal, between Colony and Colony, was harass'd, vex'd and interrupted."[32]

Few colonists welcomed these measures, and there were petitions against them. Still, most gave grudging acquiescence. Grenville then rolled out the Stamp Tax that hit all forms of paper: newspapers, legal documents, petitions, even playing cards. Any and all papers had to carry an embossed stamp showing that the tax had been paid. It thus affected printers, publishers, merchants, and lawyers: exactly the people who could best launch an organized campaign against it. It would also have increased the price of drinks, as tavernkeepers needed to pay the tax in order to renew their licenses (to sell spirits required only a twenty-shilling stamp, but wine needed a much pricier £3 stamp).[33] To many, including Grenville, taxing tavern licenses seemed desirable, as a way to improve behavior, as in current levies on cigarettes.[34] As one British official in West Florida noted, "stamp duties are the best and most equitable mode of taxation.... They fall on the vices of mankind."[35] Few shared this view. In fact, it "alarmed the British subjects in America, [more] than any thing that had ever been done," as one opponent phrased it.[36]

Many colonists felt that the stamp tax broke two cardinal rules. The first was that colonial taxes were for regulating trade, not raising revenue. The second was that since no Members of Parliament represented colonial interests in the metropolis, colonial assemblies, which had grown in power over the course of the Seven Years' War, should be consulted. Colonists insisted that taxes should be not levied without their consent, given their rights as freeborn Englishmen. Their resistance took many forms.

Protests took place in assembly halls, as in May 1765. One French man arrived in Williamsburg, Virginia, on the day that its assembly—the

House of Burgesses—met to discuss the Stamp Act. He was struck by the "very strong Debates Concerning . . . stamp Dutys" that he heard. He listened with interest to Patrick Henry—a local lawyer—lamenting "his Countrys Dying liberty." (The governor of Virginia was less impressed, condemning "young hot and giddy members" like Henry for their "very indecent language.") The next day, the Frenchman heard more "very hot Debates" including whether consent was required for taxation. The final resolution recorded by the House of Burgesses insisted that their laws concerning "internal Polity and Taxation" were "derived from their own Consent." They informed the House of Lords that it was "a fundamental Principle of the *British* Constitution . . . that the People are not subject to any Taxes but such as are laid on them by their own Consent."[37]

"The murmurs on account of the Stamp-Duty are not confined to Virginia; all the colonies consider it as a most intolerable burthen," declared one newspaper. Soon, debates in assembly houses moved out of assemblies and into newspapers and streets. On August 14, 1765, residents of Boston woke up to a startling sight: the body of an official, Andrew Oliver, hanging from a tree. It turned out not to be an actual body, but from a distance it looked like one.[38] Such effigies were threatening, transforming impersonal impositions emanating from faraway London into threats against specific individuals who were neighbors and sometimes friends. They gave a face, a name, and a whole stuffed body, to the hated tax, and they thus allowed crowds to vent their resentment on particular individuals. In the hard postwar times of the 1760s, crowds did so with a vengeance.

Once Oliver's sinister body double had made its mark on the psyches of Boston's residents, protesters pulled it down. Yet they were not finished with it yet. A group of men carried the effigy in a mock funeral procession across Boston; they subsequently beheaded it, trod upon it, and finally burned it while a crowd shouted "Liberty and Property! No Stamp!"[39] Bostonians did to the effigy what angry residents in the Leewards had done to their governor in 1710, but in a symbolic and bloodless manner. This was progress and enlightenment—but still ominous. They also ransacked Oliver's property and his house, threatening to kill him if they found him. The message was clear.

"The noble patriotic fire which has lighted up in one place and another, of late shone so conspicuous at Boston, blazed here," too, reported an excited correspondent in Norwich, Connecticut, in early September 1765. The rebellious fire from Boston spread with reports of protests and crowd action appearing in other colonial papers over the next couple of weeks. In a typical story, one correspondent from New London, Connecticut, related that their stamp master, Jared Ingersoll, had had his effigy "hung up by the neck in the most public part of this town." His body bore the figure of a little devil on his right shoulder, and a stamp paper was pinned to his chest "under which was an inscription in praise of LIBERTY." After its time in the noose, the effigy was paraded through town "amidst the loud acclamations of some hundreds [of] people" before meeting its customary end on a bonfire.[40]

The rampaging worsened as crowds turned from demolishing effigies to destroying houses. Protesters broke into tax collectors' homes, smashing windows, burning books, emptying wine bottles, and terrifying family members. In Newport, Rhode Island, crowds tore one "House to Pieces... The Cellars... were ravaged, and the Provisions, Wine, &c destroyed." In Boston, another group "rushed onward" to the recently built house of another tax collector "and in the most savage and destructive manner broke and abused his furniture, chairs, tables, desk, glasses, china." Drunk on wine from his cellar, they also stole his money and chucked his papers and books around. The Massachusetts governor, Thomas Hutchinson, denounced how "The hellish crew fell upon my house with the Rage of devils." They left wreckage so great that "Such ruins were never seen in America," he declared. Even men who denounced the Stamp Act nevertheless observed with concern that actions against the Act had led to "inhuman cruelty & Barbarity... These mobbs, like fire once raised or kindled, cant be controwled."[41]

The Stamp Act upended life throughout the mainland colonies. News came from Charleston, South Carolina, of another protest. On coming to the house of the stamp tax collector, the crowd "broke his Windows... and consumed the Effigies [with fire], amidst the Acclamations of a large Concourse of People."[42] In West Florida, too, there was resistance. The former attorney general, in a dispute with the governor, argued that "no man can be bound to any government unless his own consent is conveyed either by himself or representative."[43] Once "the spirit of what is . . . called Liberty began to infuse itself there," many believed, "there was going to be a great revolution or rebellion" in Pensacola.[44]

Disturbances reached north, too. The only newspaper in Canada, the official *Quebec Gazette*, in which articles appeared side by side in English and French, had started publication in 1764. It ceased on the day the Stamp Tax took effect, as its printers refused to pay the stamp duty.[45] It did not appear again until the Act was repealed, with a special issue celebrating "being freed from the impositions of the grievous Stamp Act; an Act more dreadful than the icy chains of our inhospitable winter." They thanked fellow printers "in the several colonies on the Continent and West-Indies" who sent their own papers to Québec during this period.[46] This statement of printer solidarity had a wide geographic reach. Reports also arrived from Halifax, Nova Scotia, "that the Inhabitants are very uneasy with the Beginning of their Slavery."[47] Nova Scotia's stamp collector was hanged in effigy "and in the evening [was] attended by all true sons of freedom [and was] reduced to ashes."[48] On his chest was a poem that concluded: "What greater Glory can this Country see / Than a Stamp-master hanging on a Tree."[49]

On trees and streets, as well as in assemblies and newspapers, "consent" became a keyword. In September, Pennsylvanians declared: "That it is the inherent Birth-right, and indubitable Privilege, of every *British* Subject, to be taxed only by his own Consent." Maryland's colonists "Resolved Unanimously" that they had "the Right of being Governed by Laws to which they themselves have consented." Connecticut's residents pronounced, too, "That the free natural Subjects of the Great Britain . . . are to be taxed only by their own Consent." As one of them summarized, "British subjects are to be governed only agreeable to laws, to which they have some way consented."[50]

Irate about consent, many colonists agreed on the need for a formal meeting to decide next steps and to register discontent. One member of the South Carolina assembly suggested a continental congress. Another member mocked this idea: "What sort of a dish will you make?" He went on to enumerate what each colony would contribute: "New-England will throw in fish and onions. The middle colonies flax-seed and flour. Maryland and Virginia will add tobacco. North-Carolina pitch, tar and turpentine. South-Carolina rice and indigo, and Georgia will sprinkle the whole composition with sawdust." The result, he contended, would be "an absurd jumble" out of "such discordant materials as the thirteen British provinces." Another assembly member countered that "if the colonies proceeded judiciously . . . they would prepare a dish fit to be presented to any crowned head in Europe."[51]

Would the colonies be able to join together, or would they descend into "an absurd jumble"? Only time would tell. Encouragement came in the form of a broadside that was published first in New York and referenced that British unwritten constitution invoked elsewhere, *The Constitutional Courant*. It featured an old emblem: a snake cut into pieces, representing the colonies. Ben Franklin had first published this image to encourage colonial unity in 1754, during the Seven Years' War. This snake, with the motto JOIN OR DIE, encouraged unity in resistance, and the broadside was printed in Boston and Philadelphia as well as New York.[52]

In the end, those who favored a congress prevailed. Delegates from New England, New York, New Jersey, Pennsylvania, Delaware (or the Lower Counties), and South Carolina gathered in New York City, agreed that each colony should have a single vote on each matter, and commenced debates on October 8, 1765. Royal governors prevented representatives from Virginia, North Carolina, and Georgia from attending. Formal debates took place in the city hall, but many discussions occurred in taverns, coffeehouses, and homes where members were staying. After long days of meetings, men gathered in places like the City Arms Tavern, staggering back to their lodgings from late-night debates. One recorded a Monday spent "at Congress," with both mid-day dinner and evening supper at the City Arms Tavern. The next day, he dined at a different tavern and took a restorative evening off for a brisk walk around town.[53] Delegates concluded the congress by the end of October, after agreeing on petitions to be sent to London as well as a Declaration of Rights.

Although most everyone in the colonies disliked the Stamp Tax, only some colonies were prepared to represent that unhappiness officially.

JOIN OR DIE.

SATURDAY, September 21, 1765. [NUMB. I.]

The Conſtitutional COURANT:

Containing Matters intereſting to LIBERTY, and no wiſe repugnant to LOYALTY.

This 1765 "Join or Die" snake, first published by Benjamin Franklin in 1754 during the Seven Years' War, appeared above the newspaper slogan "Containing Matters interesting to LIBERTY, and no wise repugnant to LOYALTY."

None of the Caribbean or Canadian colonies sent delegates. There would be no sugar from the Caribbean or maple syrup from Canada to sweeten that colonial dish. In other words, while there was resistance in places like St. Kitts and Nova Scotia, there was no official protest. Although not all the traditional thirteen colonies were represented at the congress, most wanted to send representatives. West Indian and Canadian colonies—and also Georgia and especially East Florida—would not necessarily have done so. Although there was protest in Québec, the position of French Catholics in Canada remained uncertain, and they did not join this congress. One British official praised those in East Florida for their "very dutiful behaviour."[54]

In many (though not all) colonies, nonetheless, protests continued into late 1765 and early 1766. In Halifax, Nova Scotia, the stamp distributor remained effectively under house arrest, guarded by soldiers as "the justly enraged people, threaten[ed] his life." In December 1765, one Boston newspaper noted "the patriotic Spirit increases" in St. Kitts, where men "from the highest to the lowest . . . show [their] hearty Abhorrence of the Stamp Law." The paper continued that "on the Fifth of November . . . the Effigies of several Persons were hung up and burnt." In 1766, West Indian officials alerted the governor to the fact that "the Contagion, which has prevailed about the Stamps in Several of the Provinces in North-America, had also reached some of the Islands under Your Government." One castigated "the Madness of the People." The Jamaican stamp tax collector noted in early 1766 that he had faced "repeated Threats of Violence [and] Personal abuse."[55]

In other words, there was popular resistance even in the Caribbean and Canada, but colonial officials did not sanction it. Overall, in the

Caribbean, there was support for the British government—except in St. Kitts, which protested more vigorously than any other Caribbean colony, partly due to its long-standing trading ties with mainland colonies. Elsewhere in the Caribbean, it was a different story. Despite threats, that Jamaican stamp collector collected "a Revenue little short of £4000." In Barbados, one official observed that the taxes were "quietly submitted to. We think of the Doctrine of internal Taxations like our Brethren on the Continent but we shall only think." In other words, they, too, disagreed with the Stamp Tax, but they would not protest officially. He continued with submissiveness that Britain "is the master, my Lord, and we are a Little People, you must do as you please with us; and we have only to obey your decrees." One Barbadian official reported in early 1766 that "Near four Months are now elapsed since the Commencement of the Stamp Duty . . . all here has been Quiet & Easy." He commended "the Dutiful & Loyal Conduct of the Inhabitants of Barbados" in contrast with the "Triumphant and Rebellious Conduct" of mainland colonists.[56] Caribbean assemblies lacked "young hot and giddy" members like Patrick Henry denouncing the Stamp Act in dramatic terms. In the end, British West Indians paid 78 percent of the revenue generated by the Stamp Act and offered the least resistance.[57]

Mainland colonists drew contrasts between their own behavior and that of the settlers in the islands. John Dickinson, a Pennsylvania lawyer and writer, entered into a print dispute with the Barbados Committee of Correspondence in 1766. In response to Barbadian denunciations of the "violent spirit" of rebellion on the mainland, he derided their "unmanly timidity" and impractical "dreams of submission."[58] Other mainland colonists agreed with his assessment. In December 1765, a Boston newspaper reported "the disagreeable News of the Stamp-Act having taken place in that Island [Barbados], without any Opposition." In a January 1766 diary entry, John Adams, the Boston lawyer and intellectual, exulted that "So triumphant is the Spirit of Liberty, every where.—Such an Union was never before known in America." He noted, though, two exceptions: Canada and the West Indies. He expressed his "pitty" for his "unhappy fellow Subjects in Quebeck and Hallifax" who, as he saw it, had been prevented from protesting fully.[59] But, like John Dickinson, John Adams had no sympathy for what he saw as the submissiveness of West Indian planters. He wondered whether sufficient punishment could be devised "For their base Desertion of the Cause of Liberty? Their tame Surrender of the Rights of Britons? Their mean, timid Resignation to slavery?" He dismissed them as contemptible ("meeching" was the New England regional insult he used) "sordid, stupid Creatures, below Contempt, below Pity. They deserve to be made Slaves to their own Negroes." In fact, Adams felt that "their Negroes seem to have more of the Spirit of Liberty . . . we sometimes read of Insurrections among" them—likely a reference to Tacky's War in Jamaica, five years earlier. Elsewhere, he declared: "Our fore fathers came over here for liberty of conscience . . . and we won't be their [Britain's] negroes." The denial of consent took on new force, as it implied a future in which "freeborn Englishmen" were treated like enslaved people: a terrifying prospect.[60]

Mainland colonists like Adams threatened to withhold the sale of provisions like salt cod to the Caribbean colonies in order to pressure West Indians not to accept the stamp tax. One Boston author hoped that Barbadians would "be without provisions till the stamp act is repealed," though they continued to trade with St. Kitts. Given West Indian needs for imported food, this refusal constituted a serious challenge. A Barbadian complained to a correspondent in Philadelphia that their ships arrived "loaded with nothing but Threats of starving us." This Caribbean writer denounced patriots on the mainland, this "Sett of Men, who under the specious Name of Asserters of their Liberty" commit "the most outrageous Acts of Rebellion" even though Britain had preserved them "from the horrid Ravages of a Savage Enemy; and from the oppressive Yoke of French Tyranny."[61]

In mainland ports, Sons of Liberty burned stamped papers arriving on ships from Barbados and Antigua. One colonist, in New London, Connecticut, in March 1766, denounced the "Poor, mean spirited, Cowardly, dastardly Creoles" in the Caribbean. The author hoped no one on the continent would sell them provisions and "that they may like the Blacks, whom they now make Slaves of with Rigour, be deemed to wear the Infernal Badge of STAMPS about their Necks." Admittedly, this same newspaper issue carried another article about South Carolina Sons of Liberty refusing to sell rice to Georgia "as the inhabitants of that province had tamely received the stamps."[62] Even the mainland colonies did not have total unity.

Despite the widespread opposition to the stamp tax, only in some of the mainland colonies did assembly leaders lodge official complaints about the Stamp Tax. West Indian colonists protested in a traditional way—at a local level and at lower ranks—but they rarely did so in an institutional capacity. On the mainland, lawyers and planters used their educational and legal capital to promote a cause also supported by the kinds of men who would smash a window, chug wine from someone else's cellar, and knock down an official. That these men rubbed along together comfortably in many of the thirteen colonies is remarkable.

By starting in the West Indies and moving back to the mainland, it is possible to see just how notable mainland cross-class unity was. White men, at least, could feel more allied in the mainland thirteen colonies than they appeared to do elsewhere; they saw their struggle as a larger one uniting diverse interests. As we have already seen, one potent source of mainland unity was the shared history of recent wars against Indigenous nations. Moreover, the increasing emphasis on consent in those mainland colonies transformed what might have been dismissed as the riots of the rabble into a rather more highbrow affair.

One of those elite men, Benjamin Franklin, protested against the Stamp Act in London itself. He printed a disturbing cartoon to warn Parliament about the Stamp Act on the eve of debates about it. In early 1766, Franklin lobbied Members of the House of Commons with a satirical drawing titled "The Colonies Reduced." It depicted the figure of Britannia with her limbs (representing her colonies) cut off and lying beside her. The colonies were mainland ones: New England, New York, Pennsylvania, Virginia. Neither the more southern colonies like the Carolinas nor the West Indian colonies were included, though they were among the wealthiest, the ones on which Britannia most relied. He sent a copy to his sister Jane Mecom, explaining that "the Moral is, that the Colonies may be ruined, but that Britain would thereby be maimed."

His own caption drew attention to the "Abject Despondency" of Great Britain with "the Stumps of her mangled Arms raised towards Heaven in Vain." The caption continued: "Behold her Colonies, the Source of her Commerce, Wealth, and Glory, Separated . . . and no longer Useful." The result would be that she would end up "Sliding of[f] the World . . . No longer respected or Known among Nations."[63]

In any case, by 1766, many Members of Parliament had turned against the Stamp Tax. Clever but unpopular Grenville lost his position, thanks partly to this issue. The 1760s were an era of British ministerial instability, a quicksand morass of political infighting. In early 1766, Lord Rockingham, the new prime minister, repealed the Stamp Act. Some MPs wanted to keep the tax simply to show Americans that they would not cower before their demands. To placate those hard-liners, Rockingham pushed through the Declaratory Act, in which Parliament confirmed its right to tax the colonies with or without their consent. The stage was set for further wrangling, but for the moment, harmony apparently prevailed.

Benjamin Franklin published this cartoon in early 1766 to show Members of Parliament that the cost of the Stamp Act would be the ruination of its colonies and the dismemberment of its empire.

Word of the repeal reached the colonies that spring, prompting a wave of celebrations amid May's blossoms. Boston was "beautifully illuminated." The Sons of Liberty built a "magnificent pyramid... with 280 lamps" featuring figures of patriots "distinguished... by their love of liberty" as well as of George III. John Hancock hosted a street party "and treated the populace with... Madeira wine." As fireworks burst, "the multitudes of Gentlemen and Ladies... added much to the brilliancy of the night." New York, too, glowed. Church bells there rang, and twenty-one cannons fired a salute. The Sons of Liberty gathered at a tavern where "loyal and constitutional toasts were cheerfully drunk." By the end of the night, presumably, so were many of the drinkers. The evening wrapped up with bonfires, "harmony, and good order." Illuminations and a ball dazzled the residents of Williamsburg, Virginia, and "a large and genteel company of Ladies and Gentlemen... drank all the loyal and patriotick toasts." Similar events took place all over mainland colonies and even reached as far as Ireland, where apparently their rejoicings "were very general, as well as very great."[64] One American newspaper reported, "'PERSEVERANCE TO THE SONS OF LIBERTY IN AMERICA,' we hear, is a very common Toast in ENGLAND, SCOTLAND, and IRELAND."[65] Outside the mainland colonies, though, there were some discordant notes. Mainland newspapers sourly reported that when news of the repeal reached Barbados, "the inhabitants did not show the least sign of rejoicing."[66]

With the Declaratory Act, Parliament (and Rockingham) had confirmed their right to tax the colonies. Yet the ministerial instability of the 1760s meant that Rockingham was not long in office. In 1766, William Pitt became the prime minister. Despite opposition, his chancellor of the Exchequer, Charles Townshend, renewed attempts at revenue raising including new colonial taxes on paper, glass, and tea in 1767.

Such tariffs had been politicized by the events of 1765–66. In the later 1760s, they provoked vigorous complaints from many, including John Dickinson, in his well-known *Letters from a Pennsylvania Farmer* (1767–68). He was not exactly a farmer; he was a lawyer whose lands were tended by enslaved laborers. As we have seen, he had already been involved in print disputes with Barbadians. In the *Letters,* he summarized: "Those who are taxed without their own consent... are slaves."

Another author agreed that Britons "grant away the property of the Americans without their consent, which if yielded to . . . must fix us in the lowest bottom of slavery."[67]

Consent remained at the center of a burgeoning nonimportation movement. Its supporters refused to purchase items affected by the Townshend duties. One newspaper article encouraged nonimportation since "it is an essential right of mankind, and particularly of Englishmen, that no other person . . . may . . . take from them their property without their own consent." The author contended that it was better to wear coarse cloth and "to enjoy freedom in this state, than to be slaves in large and well glazed houses, with fine cloaths, tea, wine or punch." In February 1768, Massachusetts called on the other mainland non-Canadian colonies to refuse to import British goods, which they had all agreed to do by the end of 1769.[68]

Nonimportation offered all kinds of people an opportunity to participate in politics. Women could not vote or hold office, but they could refuse to buy imported textiles, instead producing homespun cloth. In New England, between 1768 and 1770, there were at least sixty spinning meetings involving nearly two thousand women. Ezra Stiles lauded the industry of ninety-two "daughters of Liberty" gathered for one notable meeting. As one author put it, "the industry and frugality, of American Ladies, must exalt their character in the eyes of the World," since they were ensuring "the political Salvation of a whole Continent." Virginia's House of Burgesses hosted a ball in Williamsburg attended by "the Gentlemen and Ladies . . . chiefly dressed in Virginian cloth." Homespun came to define consent. Yet much of that Virginia spinning had been done by enslaved women denied consent: Such were the ironies of this revolutionary movement.[69]

Enthusiastic crowds also celebrated the anniversary of the first major action against the Stamp Act, the August 14 destruction of the effigy of the stamp tax collector Andrew Oliver. In 1769, the Sons of Liberty in Massachusetts held a massive outdoor event to mark the date. They met under "the Liberty-Tree" at noon, where "fourteen Toasts were drank." They then proceeded to a tavern garden in Dorchester where some three hundred people dined on "three large Piggs barbecued" along with side dishes. To end the celebration, no fewer than "45 patriotic

Toasts were drank." It is little wonder that the newspaper reported that "the Company spent the afternoon in social Mirth."[70]

The Stamp Act protests of 1765–66 across a wide geography reveal clues about the meta-event that would come to be the American Revolution, though no one at the time saw it that way. Mainland protests demonstrated a burgeoning cross-class alliance—in some colonies, at least. Even lawyers and planters like John Dickinson adopted the persona of the honest farmer, in a kind of melding of elite and working-class sensibilities. Such alliances were less significant in the Caribbean. In the West Indies, demography, disease, and slavery so structured relations that such solidarities did not flourish in the same ways. West Indian wealth disparities, along with strong planter ties to Britain, joined with anxieties about demographic imbalances, low birth rates, and high mortality rates to prevent such connections from forming as strongly.

In mainland colonies, other factors came into play. Events of the 1750s and 1760s, including vigorous anti-Indian sentiment, helped to bolster the unity and confidence of the assemblies of those thirteen colonies. A shared history in which Protestant Englishmen felt that they had conquered Indigenous people and the wilderness, a history somewhat distinct from those of the West Indians and French Canadians, bolstered this unity. The mainland colonies were also literally contiguous, whereas the distances between the islands were considerable: a thousand miles separated Barbados from Jamaica.[71]

This sense of a shared colonial mainland past underpinned a new community, that of the "Sons of Liberty." These groups united men across the colonies, but they did not operate equally across all of them. The Sons of Liberty started to carve out a particular space of protest—that of the thirteen mainland colonies—thus uniting diverse colonies as well as elite and popular protest in novel ways. In particular, the Sons of Liberty often brought together masters of workshops with apprentices and servants, linking protesters across ranks.

The Sons of Liberty cast their grievances not as specific protests against tariffs, but as high-minded and universal claims to liberty. The consent of the governed was centered as the key to making a government legitimate. They looked backward, not forward, claiming that the ancient and glorious (if unwritten) British constitution gave them the right, indeed the duty, to protest this lack of consent. Some leaders in these colonies transformed material disputes largely over taxation and imperial control into something more ideological, with a lofty set of universal claims about representation and government. This tendency formed a foundation for what was to come.

Starting in the West Indies shows that the move from resistance to revolution was not straightforward. There was no clear and triumphant minuteman march from Stamp Act to independence. Instead, protest careened and ricocheted, taking sudden and startling turns. The Caribbean situation illuminates this contingency and the complications of imperial commitments. In 1766, there was fluidity in these loyalties. As we shall see, even several years later, many in the thirteen colonies continued to believe in the possibility of union with colonists in Canada and the Caribbean. Things could have gone differently.

Knocked over by protest, William Tuckett resigned his stamp tax commission. By 1772, he had had enough of St. Kitts, returning to Britain. He brought home a lifelong malarial infection, memories of a terrifying night of protest, and a "considerable fortune." He would go on to organize English political campaigns as a self-proclaimed "Friend to Liberty."[72]

Tuckett's Black helpers, also friends to liberty, probably remembered that night too, but they were likely stuck in St. Kitts. Still, they had asserted their right to action. So, in another way, did an enslaved woman called Catherine, who self-liberated, fleeing the Basseterre home of her enslaver in April 1765.[73] The runaway advertisements in virtually every colonial newspaper attest to the tens of thousands of individuals like her who offered silent, eloquent refusals of the terms of enslavement. They did not consent.

Thanks to events in the 1760s, consumer choices took on novel political meanings. The same issue of *The St. Christopher's Gazette* advertising for Catherine also included ads for "fine bohea and green tea."[74] Tea, sold from China to the American colonies by the English East India

Front and back of the Staffordshire teapot marketed to American colonial consumers upon the repeal of the Stamp Act in 1766.

Company, was soon to be at the center of new protests.[75] It was one of the goods that many mainland colonists had stopped buying as part of the nonimportation movement, substituting herbal infusions instead. A few well-heeled colonists may have steeped such concoctions in a new teapot available for sale after 1766. The vessel, made in the Staffordshire potteries in England, declared on one side NO STAMP ACT and on the other AMERICA, LIBERTY RESTORED. Here, captured in ceramic, was bright exultation at the Stamp Act's repeal. Many like Catherine knew, though, that America was hardly a land of "Liberty Restored" as she insisted on her own emancipation. For many other Friends of Liberty, the struggle was not over yet. It was only just starting to brew.

Chapter 3

A Street in Kolkata

"Baba! Baba! My Father! My Father! This affliction comes from the hands of your countrymen."[1] So called out a protester in 1770 at the window of an English official in Kolkata, or Calcutta, as it was called then. Were these his last words, using the Persian honorific "baba"? Catastrophe marked his emaciated body, just as it did his homeland. Usually green and bountiful fields now lay brown and parched. He had watched as his neighbors' bodies grew thinner, their faces more haggard. What could they do? Around him, desperate families started eating their precious livestock, where their religion allowed it. They sold their farm equipment. Then they ransomed their future, eating their seed grain, ensuring no planting the following year. Nearby, raging fires ripped through dry fields. Smallpox spread. Conditions worsened when sepoys—Indian soldiers sent to ensure government enforcement—arrived to collect the usual taxes. They stood over the people like him, demanding money. Even floggings could not always force payment, though; coffers were empty.

When this man had nothing left to give—or to lose—he walked from the fields to the streets of the growing city of Kolkata until he was outside the windows of the headquarters of the East India Company. Others went to the old capital, Murshidabad, while still others like him—but Hindu rather than Muslim—descended on Kolkata's temple of Kali, praying to the fierce goddess who protected the city to save them, too. Amid their stark vulnerability, "pestilence had broken out." Men, women, and children died in horrifying numbers. The normally bustling streets of Kolkata were nearly empty but for the dead and dying. So

This engraving from 1793, based on an earlier 1780s image, shows the river, ships, and buildings of Kolkata, visible from Fort William, built by the British.

many corpses contaminated the Hooghly River running through the city that people could not even eat its fish.

Residents stayed at home, emerging only occasionally and with fear, gagging and shielding their noses from the stench. Out of deep and infectious heaps, the hungry dead reached bony hands up to pull the living down with them: "the multitude of mangled and festering corpses at length threatened the existence of the citizens." The goddess Kali, who represented destruction as well as creation—typically depicted wearing a necklace of severed heads and hands, haunting cremation grounds, and standing astride a body—seemed to reign over the besieged city.[2]

The anguish of '76 (the year was 1176 on the Fasli [Urdu] calendar, 1770 on the English one) was unspeakable. One contemporaneous observer, Muhammad Reza Khan, could not even bring himself to "describe the misery of the people from the severe droughts and the dearness of grain." One *zemindar,* or landowner—Purtub Sing—later complained that it was "impossible to describe" so "much oppression." He blamed officials for the "desolation of the country & the oppression." One contemporary historian, Seid Gholam Hossein Khan, lamented the "innumerable multitudes swept away by famine."[3] Estimates range from one million to ten million dead; some regions lost half their population.

How had things grown so bad in this rich and storied land? And who, exactly, was to blame? Part of the answer lies in the streets of Kolkata—the new headquarters of the British in India—itself. The city had been founded in the late seventeenth century, on the site of a few villages, the crossroads of an older land-based Mughal empire and a newer maritime British one. In the middle of the eighteenth century, one *nawab,* or ruler, recounted the city's growth with disdain: "When [the British] first came to this country they petitioned the . . . government in a humble manner for . . . a spot of ground to build a factory house." No sooner had they been given permission, he continued, than "they ran up a strong fort . . . and mounted a great number of guns upon the walls . . . they rob and plunder and carry great number of the king's subjects of both sexes into slavery into their own country."[4]

Government and its stunning transformations preoccupied this thoughtful ruler—as so many in the eighteenth century. How should those in authority act? Not like this. South Asians watched in horror as the British Empire altered the terms of engagement. What had started small—a few traders here and there—had grown into a torrent of guns and threats and taxes and slavery, bolstered by those willing to do whatever it took to establish inroads in other continents. They played by different rules here.[5] Decades before the American Revolution, it was a world turned upside down.

The authors of the Declaration of Independence also claimed that their world had been turned upside down. They contended they were not the ones who had altered it. By "waging War against us," the king had "abdicated Government here." The word "government" appears over and over in the Declaration, as its authors struggled to justify the overthrow of one and the adoption of another. The word appears six times in its notable second paragraph alone:

> Governments are instituted among Men, deriving their just powers from the consent of the governed,—That whenever any Form of Government becomes destructive of these ends, it is the Right of the People to alter or to abolish it, and to institute new Government.... Prudence, indeed, will dictate that Governments long established should not be changed for light and transient causes.... But when a long train of abuses... evinces a design to reduce them under absolute Despotism, it is their right, it is their duty, to throw off such Government.... such is now the necessity which constrains [these Colonies] to alter their former Systems of Government.

Here was a central claim of this revolution, the cause of independence.

Governments were changing in the eighteenth century in part due to alterations in the extent of global trade. Americans relished Asian goods. With care, they pulled silk stockings onto their legs while adorning their bodies with bright calicoes (the word itself, like the cloth, was from India). Some elite men even adopted the banyan, an Asian style of jacket, at least in fancy portraits. The Rhode Island Congregational minister Ezra Stiles wore one in his 1756 portrait, probably a gift from the women of his congregation.[6] Umbrellas (a newfangled Asian import) shaded them from American rain and sun. Tea from China, carried by the East India Company (EIC) and others, became the daily drink of two-thirds of White Americans, with women pouring the steaming brew from teapots at specially designed tea tables. As one 1772 report on Bengal put it, "these commodities... are by custom become necessary to all nations."[7]

This global trade improved people's material lives, but it also led some to wonder whether things had gone too far. Was indulgence leading to moral and physical decline? American nonimportation movements played on this unease, emphasizing hearty homespun virtues over imported fripperies. Tea—a drink not imbibed by British ancestors, who had stuck with small beer—seemed to offer both the promise of stimulating sociability and the peril of luxury. Tea parties, an eighteenth-century rage, offered women in particular a way to participate in global consumer cultures. But maybe, some fretted, these events made women neglect their domestic duties and made the men who attended a little less vigorous.

Tea parties depended on tea.[8] Tea, whether in shiny silver pots or in dusty shipping crates, took on new political meanings for those in Asian cities, American colonies, and the halls of Parliament. Reading those tea leaves reveals global transformation, monopoly, race—and revolution.

An Asian revolution took place before the American one. These "Modern Times," as one Indian historian phrased it, wrought an *inqilab,* or an inversion of politics and society. Mughal emperors who had ruled much of India for centuries came under new pressure from increasingly militarized Maratha rulers and from European powers: the Portuguese, the Dutch, the French, and the British. In 1759, Robert Clive, the English commander in India, bragged to Prime Minister William Pitt of "the great revolution that has been effected here by the success of the English arms." In his *Memoirs of the Revolution in Bengal,* one author asserted that "the late Revolution in *Bengal* is so extraordinary . . . and of such Importance to the Nation." In 1772, a more critical writer, Alexander Dow, repeatedly condemned "the revolutions which shook and greatly depopulated the kingdom." Mughal authors across India also lamented this *inqilab,* which brought indigence to once great families. As one poet, Sauda, sighed, "Those who once lived in great mansions now eke out their lives among the ruins. . . . There is nothing to be said but this: We are living in a special kind of age."[9]

It was a special kind of age in which a small company of Englishmen became a new kind of government. The nature of society and politics in Bengal shifted in the 1750s and 1760s. In 1756, as the English fought the French across the globe, including in India, they also moved against local rulers such as the *nawab* of Bengal. Such conflicts culminated in his defeat by Clive at the Battle of Plassey in 1757. Other nawabs were deposed in 1760 and 1763. Despite violent resistance, the British emerged victorious. In the 1765 Treaty of Allahabad, the Mughal emperor granted the *diwani,* or responsibility for the civil administration of Bengal, to the English East India Company. Suddenly, this company, a private enterprise supported by 250 civil servants connected to the British government, became the de facto ruler of something like twenty million people and 150,000 square miles: an area three times larger than England. Their chief objective was not to settle or to improve Asia; it was to send profit home, whether from Indian textiles or Chinese tea. They hoped to return home rich themselves; some, now called "nabobs" (a version of *nawabs*), did.[10]

Transformations in government took place in South Asia, as elsewhere, in the eighteenth century. India—with its long and glorious history, its thriving economy, its beautiful textiles, its centralized bureaucratic state—had long attracted European traders. However, an increasingly integrated global economy transformed the nature of empire and authority. Processes begun centuries earlier accelerated, transforming daily life around the globe.

As part of this process, the British established themselves at Kolkata.[11] They built Fort William, which one 1771 arrival described as "a very handsome Fort and large Battery" near "elegant classic built houses adorned by luxurious plantations." In 1768, one English woman, Jemima Kindersley, observed that the British section was "a confusion of very superb and very shabby houses" where servants' huts intermingled with grand homes. Rank mattered. The better off traversed the muddy streets in elaborate palanquins, carriages pulled not by horses but by servants. Kindersley conceded that on account of the heat, many servants were necessary, since "the perspiration requires perpetual changes of clothes and linen; not to mention the expenses of palenqueens [palanquins], carriages, and horses." When she arrived there, she noted that the city was "daily increasing in size," thrumming with traders, workers, officials, and soldiers.[12]

This empire of pale men in palanquins rested on the sturdy shoulders of darker men. To be carried by others drew even modest English men to India, such as John Prinsep, a linen draper's apprentice whose father had died, leaving his mother and sister depending on him. He could barely scrape together the money to pay for his passage to India in steerage in 1771, arriving in Kolkata "friendless." Still, he was delighted on arrival when "a number of black men in women's frocks came to

A South Asian couple is carried in a palanquin, under the shade of an umbrella, in a drawing from 1782.

pay their Salâms and make their obeisances. I thought myself suddenly metamorphosed into a great man." Ambitious Englishmen in Kolkata relished becoming "great men." From their perches, they surveyed the landscape, dreaming of orderly cultivation and ever growing profit. They joined in "the shaking of the pagoda tree," extracting gifts and tribute from local leaders. In 1767, one such official wrote to his superior that he hoped that "The Western Junguls . . . by the encouragement of Cultivation & industry will yearly increase in value." In the meantime, he advised only "a moderate addition of revenue" as otherwise there was a risk of "rendering our Government odious & oppressive to our new Subjects by a harsh & rigorous treatment."[13]

Notwithstanding such wise advice, an unholy combination of plunder and violence characterized the EIC's brand of oppressive government in India. British power there rested on an ever increasing military presence, largely staffed by Indian soldiers, called sepoys. In 1767, this same official noted concerns from western villagers that "Seapoys... should oppress them." By the time of the famine, EIC forces included three thousand Europeans and twenty-eight thousand sepoys. Jemima Kindersley fretted for ordinary Indians under the thumb of such soldiers, stuck with only "rice and water; their miserable huts of straw... no liberty, no property, subject to the tyranny of every superior."[14]

This novel political situation was ripe for disaster, and it arrived with a vengeance on dry winds. In 1769, EIC officials noted the "very unusual Scarcity of Rain," warning London that there was "a most melancholy prospect before our Eyes of universal distress." They worried less about human misery than loss of profits: "it will occasion a very considerable Diminution in your Revenue." Yet taxation continued at its normal levels. Those at the head of revenue collection pushed those below them to continue exacting taxes despite the increasing agony of the people. Khan himself informed the EIC that "notwithstanding that a severe famine prevails... the writer has by his exertions collected as much of the revenue for the year 1176 as possible."[15]

The tragedy was unspeakable, yet protesters, including that shouting man at the window, did speak of it. They blamed the government—loudly. Officials complained that as soon as they stepped out, they were "stopped by multitudes of the poor pressing to make known their distress." A poem of the era, sung in Bengali villages, indicted those in authority: "people began to die due to scarcity of food grains. Reza Khan bought all rice from the market. Monopolization was followed by rise in price... the Famine of 1176 assumed a serious proportion." "Reza Khan" was Muhammad Reza Khan, the Naib Subahdar, or deputy *diwani,* of Bengal, appointed by the English East India Company to administer and collect taxes in the province. Yet Khan himself blamed the English. As Khan noted dryly, "It was observed at this period that the English of some rank spent their time merrily and in pleasures." Moreover, even the English admitted that as famine took hold, "the natives complained... that the English had engrossed all the rice." Indians launched a formal protest against the EIC. However, "the complaint was only laughed at and thrown out." The EIC tried to help by not allowing rice to be sold across provinces—a terrible idea, since it meant that rice could not be sold to the people who needed it most, as one official in the provinces noted. He begged his superiors to end this policy so that there was "a free & Universal Liberty . . . for the benefit of the Inhabitants."[16] They did not listen.

The government's callousness provoked outrage. Alexander Dow, critical of EIC policies, lamented in 1772 that with the famine, the situation worsened, and that as ordinary people became less and less able to pay the taxes, "the modes of collecting it became more oppressive," as the sepoys "carried terror and ruin through the country." Some of those who could not pay were "bound to stakes and whipped . . . and not a few of them expired in agonies, under the lash." "When the sources of government are corrupted," he concluded, "they poison the whole stream."[17] Just as the corpses in Kolkata polluted the Hooghly River there, so too could bad government and its violence and indifference to human suffering contaminate the whole empire.

"The ruin, which we have brought on an unfortunate country, will recoil upon ourselves," conceded one British observer. The failings of the EIC in Bengal did not pass unnoticed, in London or elsewhere in the Anglophone world. Accounts of the horror of the famine in Bengal appeared in English and American periodicals. One 1771 article in an American newspaper noted that although three hundred thousand had died in Bengal, the English still held balls and concerts there: "under . . . these places of amusement lie many dead bodies." Dogs ran through the streets with human limbs in their mouths. Another letter from an eyewitness testified: "I have beheld the hapless infant tugging at the empty breast of its mother just expiring . . . both [mother and child] have immediately been swept up amongst the dead." The suffering of mothers and children underlined the horror of the situation. People knew the EIC was partly to blame. Even before John Prinsep, that linen draper's son, had made his trip to Kolkata, a worried friend had tried to dissuade him: "Desist from a project . . . rooted in Avarice, and . . . saturated with Blood." As William Pitt the Elder phrased it in 1770, "the riches of Asia have been poured in upon us, and have brought with them not only

Asiatic luxury, but, I fear, Asiatic principles of government."[18] He meant oppressive authoritarianism—what contemporaries called tyranny.

Had a new global empire brought tyranny as well as luxury? In the 1760s and 1770s, many started to believe that it had. Oppression, enacted by soldiers inflicting violence on innocents, preoccupied many in the British Empire—from Kolkata to New York to London—in this era. Friends of liberty in those places watched, appalled, at what was happening in government. Incendiary events took place even in the capital itself in the late 1760s. In London in 1768, a radical former Member of Parliament, John Wilkes, was imprisoned for seditious libel for his satirical publication, *North Briton No. 45*, which criticized the government and the king. He had already been expelled from Parliament. On the day of the state opening of Parliament in 1768, a crowd gathered in London to protest his incarceration. One narrative recounted that a group of soldiers was brought in "to attack an unarmed giddy mob" as constables literally "read the Riot Act" to warn crowds of the law. Nevertheless, protesters posted a sign lamenting that "liberty [had been] confined with Mr. Wilkes." When constables ripped down the poster, the protests gained momentum. In the melee that followed, a soldier shot and killed a young man, William Allen. Others were killed by stray bullets or the trampling crowd. Allen's killing went to trial. The verdict was not guilty, but what one sympathetic observer called the "massacre" at St. George's Fields received wide publicity in London and beyond. William Allen's funeral attracted tens of thousands of mourners. Allen's father also launched a civil suit and petitioned Parliament for redress in a well-publicized campaign. He condemned "so barbarous and unprovoked a murder" as well as "the oppression of your petitioner" by ministers. He begged them to remedy his "unspeakable loss" so that it did not become a precedent for unfettered military violence "bringing destruction and slavery upon his fellow subjects."[19]

In New York and Boston, red-coated soldiers seemed to swarm in neighborhoods, just as they did in London and Kolkata. Troops arrived from Ireland and elsewhere in New York City and in Boston's Castle William, British headquarters, to enforce customs collection. They embedded themselves in the local landscape—and in some cases brought their families or even married local women. Yet tensions between soldiers, charged with ensuring customs collections and keeping the peace, and locals erupted in 1770.[20]

In January 1770, the same year sepoys swept the Bengali countryside, soldiers stationed in New York City were determined to pull down the Liberty Pole—a flashpoint of conflict since 1766—which led to a series of confrontations with locals. On the city's Golden Hill, a soldier "in Silk Stockings and neat Buckskin Breeches" joined with others in assailing "the Citizens with great Violence, cutting and slashing," taunting them: "Where are your Sons of Liberty now?"[21]

Sailors led the most vigorous opposition. They had long protested impressment into the British navy, developing a strong resistance to imperial power. Wherever there were crowds of protesters, there were usually sailors in it, though—not being local—they were also a convenient scapegoat for authorities. In the days that followed, British soldiers also supposedly lunged with their bayonets and swords at boys running errands as well as women on the streets, including one "coming from Market with a Bundle of Fish."[22]

Good men protected children and women. They did not swagger through city streets in silk stockings threatening them. To insult and attack vulnerable populations showed just how despicable these interlopers were. Many Bostonians reached a similar conclusion in February 1770. When a group of young men protested at the house of a merchant who had refused to join the nonimportation compact, another altercation began. A customs officer shot and killed one of the demonstrators, Christopher Seider (or Snider). He was eleven years old. Boston writers lamented "the "barbarous Murder" of this "amiable Youth . . . Victim to the Cruelty and Rage of *Oppressors*," proof that "*Innocence itself was not safe!*" A local enslaved poet, Phillis Wheatley, termed him "the first martyr for the cause."[23] He would not be the last.

The following month, on March 5, 1770, some Bostonians expressed their unhappiness with troops at the customs house by assailing them with snowballs, a few packed with stones and glass. Ignoring the orders of their commander to keep the peace, several of the exasperated soldiers responded with gunfire, killing five men—four White and one of mixed race, Crispus Attucks—and wounding several others, in what many termed "the bloody Massacre." One of the wounded was carried out by a local shoemaker, George Hewes.

The funeral of the four men killed in what came to be called the Boston Massacre—Crispus Attucks, James Caldwell, Samuel Maverick, and Samuel Gray (the fifth, Patrick Carr, died later)—brought thousands of mourners (one observer reckoned twelve thousand) to a city of fifteen thousand. Even if the attendance was exaggerated, the memorial service was a massive event. One March 1770 poem, now attributed to Phillis Wheatley, upheld the "honour'd Bier" of the slain, named individually, as a place of solidarity for those fighting "Freedom's Cause." A newspaper account contended that "Distress and Sorrow [were] visible in every Countenance." To many, this situation demonstrated "the destructive Consequences of quartering Troops . . . under a Pretense of supporting the Laws and aiding Civil Authority."[24]

Soldiers sent to local communities seemed to represent the power of tyrannical rulers eager to ignore the law, as in North Carolina in 1771 with the violent suppression of the group of reformers who called themselves Regulators. The leader of these reformers was a preacher, Herman Husband, who, like many of his followers, dreamed of a world in which Christian morality shaped economic and political choices. They clashed with the governor, William Tryon, a Friend of Government—that is, a strong supporter of government policies—and a wearer of silk stockings if ever there was one. In 1766, the Assembly voted to give Tryon a hefty £5,000 to build an elaborate mansion. Tryon refused to hire local workers, deriding their abilities to build the kind of grand and opulent complex he envisioned. He contracted with an English architect and Pennsylvanian workmen, who created an expensive and fashionable Palladian mansion. Adorned with a royal coat of arms, the building especially delighted Tryon for its council chamber, with a showy fireplace of sienna and black marble, with shiny inlaid medallions of King George and Queen Charlotte. One visitor, writing to Ezra

Stiles in Newport, described it as likely the "most magnificent edifice on the continent."[25]

At just this moment, in a weak postwar economy, North Carolina petitioners were begging Tryon to limit taxes, as poor men were selling their bedclothes and even "their Wives Petticoats" to pay them. Tryon did not send soldiers to flog those who could not pay, as happened in Kolkata. However, he also did not relent, continuing to "Drink up the Blood . . . of the Poor" who implored him to avoid "Tyranny & Oppression." Taxation levels continued high. As settlers encroached on Cherokee homelands, other conflicts arose. In keeping with British policy, Tryon, whom the Cherokees gave the honorific title of "the Great Wolf," tried to restrain settlement in order to maintain alliances with the Cherokees.[26] Many locals resented and resisted these measures. Tensions grew. The North Carolina assembly expelled Herman Husband. By late 1770, they also approved a Riot Act allowing the legal killing of rioters. The act also permitted the governor to raise militia regiments at state expense to quell any uprisings. In other words, the Assembly handed Tryon exactly what he wanted in order to crush a rising insurrection.

Tryon attacked the Regulators, who, he claimed, sought to "disturb the Public Peace of the Government." He gave orders for troops "to March . . . in Support of the Peace and Safety of the Government" as well as "to harass and distress" the Regulators. He reportedly also summoned the sheriffs, allowing them to use violence to collect taxes—just like the sepoys in Bengal. He sent eleven hundred soldiers to reduce rebels to "Obedience." Reports circulated that British regular troops had also landed in America to crush the movement, though this story proved incorrect. Still, petitioners that spring implored the governor to avoid the tragedy of sending armed men against each other. They begged him to secure "Good Government," not run roughshod over "civil liberties." Tryon remained deaf to these entreaties, ordering troops not only to confront Regulator forces, numbering some two thousand, but also to destroy the farms of the families of Regulators. Authorities arrested leaders. Pardons were offered for those who took an oath of loyalty. Most did so. However, a dozen leaders were convicted of sedition; six were hanged.[27]

The events in North Carolina divided opinion, there and elsewhere. Few adored Tryon, with his gaudy house, his arrogance, and his indifference to the plight of working people. Still, even some North Carolina Sons of Liberty saw the Regulators as "obstinate & desperate Rebels." Yet they also had their supporters. The New England Congregational minister Ezra Stiles, based in Newport, Rhode Island, sympathized with the Regulators, concluding: "What shall an injured & oppressed people do, when their Petitions, Remonstrances & Supplications are unheard & rejected . . . and Oppression & Tyranny (under the Name of Government) continued with Rigour & Egyptian Austerity!"[28] "Egyptian Austerity" invoked the Old Testament tyranny of the Pharaoh against the chosen people, even as it also evoked "Asiatic principles of government."

"Oppression & Tyranny (under the Name of Government)" summarized the problem for many, especially in mainland port towns. Everyone agreed in theory that the government had the right to collect customs revenue, but in practice, there was a tradition of Americans—as well as Britons—smuggling goods to avoid taxes and regulation. Often, officials had turned a blind eye to such practices, but now the government demanded that they take action. Few Americans welcomed officious officials. The first American use of tarring and feathering—in which an individual was publicly stripped, painted with tar, and covered with feathers—occurred against a ship's captain in Norfolk, Virginia, in 1766. Locals believed he had informed the governor that there were smuggled goods aboard a ship. They also ducked him in water, stoned him, and paraded him around the town "with two drums beating."[29]

Contraband and customs collections remained major flashpoints in the 1770s. In March 1772, the Commissioner of Customs stationed two British ships, the *Gaspee* and the *Beaver,* in Narragansett Bay near Newport, Rhode Island, to halt smuggling there. By May, the governor was complaining to the secretary of state that locals had been harassed by their crew, who stopped every single vessel in the bay. Then one June night, a group of locals, with faces blackened, possibly to look like Narragansetts, "armed with pistols, guns, and clubs," rowed a long boat out to the *Gaspee* and attacked it. Its captain, William Duddingston, jumped out of bed and appeared clad only in his undershirt "with a pistol in one hand and a hanger in the other" to deal with the marauders. They responded to this half-naked assertion of authority by shooting him in the arm and groin, after which one of them exulted: "Now you piratical rascal, we have got you." They apparently would not even let him get dressed after being wounded, so he wrapped a blanket around his waist and rested his coat on his shoulders. The marauders then forced the entire crew off and set the ship on fire. They rowed the crew away in the lights of the *Gaspee*'s flames.[30]

When officials summoned local men to testify about the attack on the *Gaspee,* they all denied it, except for one "indented"—that is, enslaved—mixed-race sixteen-year-old named Aaron. Aaron claimed he had been rowing at night and that he had been forced to board a longboat at gunpoint to participate in the event. He named several men, including John Brown, a noted slave trader and leader of the incident. Other witnesses, including others in his household, denied Aaron's testimony, but British officials took it seriously. Knowing his vulnerability, they sought to move the trial to England. In the end, however, they lacked enough evidence to pursue the case. It is unclear what happened to Aaron. However, both the reliance on this young man and the attempt to move the case to England rankled many in Rhode Island and beyond. One speaker, Richard Allen, claimed that it was shocking that the constitution and its liberties should be compromised merely "by the accusation of a negro."[31]

The testimony of a Black man, however, did alter the British constitution in 1772, in ways worrying to men like John Brown. Slavery was legal in Britain, and the British were leaders in the international slave trade in the eighteenth century. In June 1772, the judicial decision that came to be known as *Somerset* changed the legal landscape of British slavery. A Scottish customs commissioner, Charles Steuart, had bought an enslaved man, James Somerset, in Virginia. When Steuart returned to Britain, he took Somerset with him. Somerset liberated himself for some years. When he was finally recaptured, Steuart decided to sell him away to Jamaica. However, before that could happen, Somerset met

Granville Sharp, a reformer eager to end Britain's involvement in the slave trade.

Somerset, with assistance from Sharp, took his case to court. The chief justice, Lord Mansfield, ruled in Somerset's favor, declaring that a person could not be seized in England and sold abroad. Many in Britain and its colonies believed (though incorrectly) that the verdict meant that slavery had been declared illegal in England and that enslaved people would become free if taken there. Coverage of the decision appeared in at least thirteen British newspapers, several magazines, and twenty-two of twenty-four colonial newspapers.[32] To many slaveholding colonists, it also led to concerns about the British government and its willingness to support the regime of slavery on which many felt they depended.

The worrying power of the British government in these and other matters underpinned Richard Allen's sermon about the *Gaspee* incident in which he derided Aaron's claims as well as those of the government. Allen's *An Oration upon the Beauties of Liberty,* circulating widely in print in 1773, focused less on the beauties of liberty and more on the horrors of blood-soaked oppression. Its caustic dedication was to the Earl of Dartmouth, the colonial secretary, who had sought to move the trial to England. Allen painted a fearsome picture of the dangers of a bad government: an "absolute Prince is a great distress to a people." Allen defended "the government of Rhode-Island" and its legal authority. He pointed out that "the happiness, power and bulwark of Rhode-Island government" lay in its ability to execute justice in its own courts and assemblies. Otherwise, they risked becoming "a nation of slaves to ministerial power." Allen pointed to contemporaneous examples of despotism including the massacre in St. George's Field: "remember the blood of young [William] Allen cries to Heaven for vengeance." So, too, there was "a louder voice . . . still heard in Boston streets, against a bloody military power." Allen denounced Governor Tryon in North Carolina as a "cruel blood thirsty *savage,*" concluding "guard your freedom, prevent your chains; stand up as one man for your liberty."[33]

One American willing to stand up for liberty, despite her enslavement, was Phillis Wheatley, an African Christian living in Massachusetts. She was also the first Black North American, and among the first

American women, to publish anything at all: a female genius. Autumn 1773 saw the London publication of her *Poems on Various Subjects, Religious and Moral.* Her writings, inflected by her evangelical religion, had already appeared in American newspapers. She addressed 1773's political issues in a commissioned poem to the Earl of Dartmouth, the object of Allen's scorn. She praised Dartmouth for allowing "Freedom's charms [to] unfold," a subtle reference to varying kinds of freedom. Thanks to him, she continued, Americans need no longer "dread the iron chain, / Which wanton Tyranny with lawless hand / Had made."[34] Her denunciation of tyranny put her in good company in 1773.

Another enslaved woman, described as "an artful hussy," also threw off the "iron chain," though she left no words about it. Still, there was eloquence in the tap of Margaret Grant's "much worn high heeled leather shoes, with white metal buckles" on the roads that took her away—twice—from servitude. This government did not suit her. In Baltimore, Maryland, this mixed-race woman "disguised herself in a suit of mens blue cloth clothes," pretending to be the waiting boy of the English convict servant John Chambers, with whom she made her escape in 1770. She was literate and highly skilled ("a good needle woman and cook, and can wash and iron very well"). She was also well-traveled, having evidently lived in Barbados, Antigua, Grenada, Philadelphia, and the Carolinas. She had learned a lot. Still, her 1770 bid for freedom did not succeed. She tried again in 1773, from Baltimore County, "big with child," wearing a "white Holland Jacket" and a petticoat full of holes.[35] A heavily pregnant woman on her own would have struggled to make her way across a hostile landscape. Still, the child in her belly may have inspired her to reject oppressive government—yet again. Their fate is unknown.[36]

On the other side of the world, crates of Chinese tea were growing stale in warehouses. By 1773, the situation of the EIC had gone from bad to worse. The company had purchased huge amounts of tea from merchants in Guangzhou, increasing its debt load to intolerable levels. When the troubled state of the company came under Parliament's scrutiny, its stock price plummeted. However, Parliament deemed the EIC too big to fail; its collapse would have pulled too many others down with it. Parliament was not without its private concerns: by the 1760s, something close to one-quarter of MPs held stock in the EIC.[37] Today, this might be called a conflict of interest; in 1773, it was business as usual.

Parliament took the fateful decision to bail out the EIC in 1773. These plans included altering its structure and selling off that surplus tea. Parliament passed three acts in the spring of 1773 to right the listing ship of the EIC. Among these was one allowing the direct sale of tea to American merchants through EIC-appointed representatives for the next five years. The tariffs on tea were lowered so as to expedite its sale to Americans. Members of Parliament anticipated that this reduced tea tax would benefit the EIC, the British government, and American tea drinkers. They assumed Americans would welcome these changes. As it turns out, many did not.

Why did so many Americans care so much about the 1773 tea tax? It had little to do with taxes, and even less to do with tea. Most Americans adored tea. Although the act would have lowered the price on EIC tea, most Americans drank tea smuggled by the Dutch anyway, so the lower price seemed to offer little. The Townshend Acts had included a tax on tea, but it became an even more problematic commodity in 1773 because of the EIC. EIC tea, imported from China and exported to Americans, came to symbolize the toxic nature of global monopoly and oppression. One Boston newspaper in 1773 called tea "a slow poison," deleterious to health. John Adams, too, derided it as "political Poison," while one doctor lectured on the "ill Effects of Tea" on the body.[38]

The cost of doing business with the EIC, particularly of drinking its tea, seemed perilously high. Patriots sounded the "Alarm," as one series of pamphlets published in New York was called. These publications painted a dark history of the East India Company, returning again and again to the image of slavery to summarize the relations of the colonists to the EIC. It condemned "the relentless Barbarity" exercised toward Asians. The author alleged that the EIC starved South Asians by monopolizing food so that "thousands perished by this black, sordid, and cruel Avarice." "Cruel tyrants," they also exacted taxes through torture. Its author castigated the EIC for its failures of government and business in both Asia and Britain. At the end of the series, the author concluded that the company men "have poisoned the Constitution at home" and were now trying to extend this corruption to North America. The EIC had to be stopped in order to halt the "tyrannical spirit" that had already sunk "Government so low."[39]

Another pamphlet, aimed at workingmen, warned that the EIC intended "to enslave the *American* Colonies, and to plunder them of their Property, and, what is more, their *Birth-right* LIBERTY," since the Company was already "well versed in TYRANNY, PLUNDER, OPPRESSION, and BLOODSHED." A Boston newspaper in early December 1773 warned of the impending arrival of EIC ships bringing tea "for the purpose of *enslaving* and poisoning all the Americans," sent out by "the ministry of Great Britain and their auxiliaries, the East-India slave-makers." It also asserted that "we are neither to be frightened, or cajoled out, of our Liberty, by Nabobs [or] Ministers." Yet this very same issue carried more than one advertisement for businesses selling "India GOODS." Mercy Otis Warren, a supporter of resistance and a wearer of silk and calico, warned her radical English friend Catharine Macaulay of "A System of Despotism that should Reach beyond the Atlantic, & involve this Extensive Continent in the Same Thralldom that Awaits the Miserable Asiatic."[40]

John Dickinson, who had risen to prominence for his *Letters from a Pennsylvania Farmer* in the late 1760s, joined the chorus of critics, connecting the disastrous situation in India with America's possible ruin. In his "Two Letters on the Tea Tax," from November 1773, he rejected the tea tax in no uncertain terms. He fretted that the EIC ships were on their way "to *establish a Monopoly* for the *East-India Company* . . . and . . . repair their broken Fortunes by the Ruin of *American* freedom and Liberty!" Dickinson asserted that the EIC was part of the ministry's plan to enslave Americans. It was thus little wonder that "the Minds of the People are exasperated" almost to madness. Dickinson summarized the EIC's history of bad government in India thus: "they have levied War, excited Rebellions, dethroned lawful Princes, and sacrificed Millions for the Sake of Gain"; moreover, "they have, by the most unparalleled Barbarities, Extortions, and Monopolies, stripped the miserable

Inhabitants of their Property, and reduced whole Provinces to Indigence and Ruin." Here was the grim possibility that awaited Americans if they allowed the EIC to hold sway.[41]

Dickinson connected this terrifying future with racial subjection, emphasizing that Americans, unlike Indians, were "British subjects." EIC officials having squandered their profits, Dickinson continued, they now "cast their Eyes on *America,* as a new Theatre, whereon to exercise Talents of Rapine, Oppression and Cruelty." Dickinson saw the whole plan to sell EIC tea more cheaply in America as a means to force Americans down to the low point to which Kolkata had fallen in the last few years. He evinced solidarity with Indians—but only up to a point. Dickinson refused to accept the EIC's plan, but in language designed to establish that Americans were not like South Asians: "But thank GOD, we are not Sea Poys [sepoys, or soldiers], nor Marattas [Maratha imperial rulers], but *British Subjects,* who are born to Liberty, who know its Worth, and who prize it high." In their refusal to act like sepoys and marathas—both hierarchical military figures—Dickinson reinforced the notion that freeborn White Americans did not behave in the inegalitarian manner of those of "Asiatic governments."[42] Even as he expressed sympathy with the Indians, he was also making cultural and racial claims here, that Americans deserved to be treated better than South Asians.

Seven ships loaded with tea made their way across the Atlantic in 1773. They were headed to Charles Town (now Charleston), South Carolina; Philadelphia, Pennsylvania; New York, New York; and Boston, Massachusetts. "Friends of Government," handpicked consignees, were supposed to unload the tea for sale. Things did not go as intended. One ship ended up wrecking off Cape Cod. Another, bound for New York, also blew off course, spending the winter in Antigua. The two intended for South Carolina and Pennsylvania did not land their cargo as planned. Under pressure from locals, the consignees refused the tea and either put it into storage or sent the still-loaded ship back to England.[43]

However, three of the ships reached Boston, where that great Friend of Government, Governor Thomas Hutchinson, whose sons were among the consignees, insisted that the ships be unloaded. Just before the expiration of this demand, on December 17, something else happened. On the night of December 16, 1773, a group of men, faces blackened and dressed as "Mohawks," boarded the ships, used hatchets and what they called "tomahawks" to break into the wooden chests of tea; they then threw it all overboard. As George Hewes, a participant who had also carried one of the injured men after the Boston Massacre in 1770, recalled years later, "In about three hours from the time we went on board, we had thus broken and thrown overboard every tea chest to be found in the ship; while those in the other ships were dispossessing of the tea in the same way, at the same time."[44]

Dressing like "Mohawks" was a kind of minstrel show, undeniably cultural appropriation. It was a disguise, but it also exploited longstanding connections between Indigenous Americans and violence. It claimed an American identity, since Native Americans were symbolic of the land. Yet, as with Dickinson's refusal to accept a role as sepoy or maratha, it was also a way to indicate distance from non-White people. The participants "played Indian" in order to assert a vigorous White masculinity.[45]

Protests had involved destruction of private property before, as Thomas Hutchinson could attest. Yet this episode was different. Those smashed windows and emptied wine bottles of 1765 were, at least in theory, the result of a "lawless mob." This destruction of private property—belonging to a corporation, the English East India Company, not to the government—was encouraged and organized by the leading patriots of the town, the kind of well-heeled men, like John Hancock, who were not supposed to condone mob violence.

This event in December 1773 was a calculated and radical destruction of private property. It was only decades later that it received a much more benign name: tea party. It was no party. The men who broke the chests open and dumped the tea into the harbor did so silently and soberly, getting on with the job at hand. It was all performed "without the least Damage done to the Ships or any other Property." This organized devastation—and the willingness of even colonial elites to condone it—shocked people on both sides of the Atlantic. Even some critics of the government thought these actions had gone too far. One Massachusetts man confided in his diary, "I am Sincerely Sorry for the Event." Even other towns in Massachusetts passed resolutions against it: "we abhor, detest, and forever bear our Testimony against the Proceedings . . . being so very contrary to the Spirit of our Laws and the Liberty of the People."[46] British ministers and officials, as well as many ordinary Britons, found this strategic and systematic attack on private property detestable.

Still, the sodden tea leaves in Boston Harbor indicated a firm rejection of the EIC and its government. The destruction was neither wanton nor self-serving. When some shipwrecked tea washed ashore in chests elsewhere, it led to a considerable debate about what to do with it. When one Boston participant in the destruction of the tea put a few leaves in his pocket, others "raised the cry of an *East Indian*!" Having marked him through their language, in a somewhat garbled way, they then proceeded to grab the tea, to rip his coat, and to kick him "in the rear."[47] When others found bits of tea in their boots when they got home, they threw it into the fire rather than scrape it into a teapot. For many, to imbibe this tea was to digest the poison of the EIC and the corruption of empire. Tea had gone from being a welcome stimulant to a toxin to be avoided at all costs.

"We are living in a special kind of age." Plenty of Americans would have agreed with this sentiment from a Mughal poet, even before the shocking spectacle of hundreds of pounds of tea in Boston Harbor. "Oppression & Tyranny (under the Name of Government)" worried many in this era, whether in Kolkata or London or Boston. Soldiers and sepoys enacted the will of officials and ministers, risking "rendering our Government odious & oppressive . . . by a harsh & rigorous treatment."[48] The EIC seemed to represent the worst excesses of an overreaching empire, a love of gain, and a willingness to sacrifice ordinary people for profit and power. The dire situation of Kolkata in the early 1770s was proof, if any further was required, of the horrors likely to ensue from allowing the EIC more power in the American colonies. Bostonians and many other Americans rejected being treated like Indians.

To many Americans, the EIC appeared in league with the forces of evil, as in an American cartoon from early 1774. On the left side, an "East Indian [Company] Director," proclaims: "I wish we may be able to establish our Monopoly in America." Standing nearby is "Belzebub the Prince of Devils" as well as William Tryon, now governor of New York, eager to "cram the Tea down the throat of the New Yorkers." Crates marked with Chinese characters are labeled TEA FOR AMERICA and PLAN FOR AN INDIA WAREHOUSE IN AMERICA. Here were global capitalism and monopoly, linking nations through avaricious business practices. Above them is Britannia, who laments that the "conduct of those my degenerate Sons will break my heart." The "Sons of Liberty," clad as Indigenous soldiers, emerge on the other side, under the command of an Indigenous queen. "We will secure our Freedom, or die in the Attempt," they claim. On their side is the Goddess of Liberty, with the pole and cap of Liberty.

Yet for all their mockery and radicalism, Americans still wanted the goods sold by the East India Company: the bright calico, the soft silk, the reviving tea. Despite boycotts and smuggling, between 1770 and 1773, colonists paid duties on 787,000 pounds of company tea. In early 1771, John Adams recorded going to John Hancock's house and drinking tea "from Holland I hope, but don't know." While he hoped the tea was smuggled by the Dutch, he did not inquire too closely into its origins. A few months later, Thomas Jefferson ordered "India cotton stockings," silk stockings, and "a large Umbrella with brass ribs covered with green silk."[49] However, Adams, Jefferson, and others remained dubious about the marriage of corporation and government, a new kind of imperial alliance. Would luxury and indulgence lead inexorably to famine and death?

Protesters from Kolkata to Boston pushed their governments to behave differently: to avoid violence against citizens, to exact taxation in a reasonable way, to punish soldiers who exerted undue force. When governments did not do so, they forfeited the loyalties of those whom they governed. The shouting man outside the bedroom of the EIC official made it into the historical record only because of the letter of an English official published in Britain and its American colonies. The letter itself served to underline the need to reject oppression, even as it seemed to participate in that very subjugation.[50] The toxic stream flowing past this official's window would soon envelop many.

Famine and plenty both haunted a world altered by global trade and empire. They were two sides of the same coin. Two magnificent goddesses—Kali and Liberty—witnessed greed, tragedy, and the worst of governments in the 1770s. One sported the cap of Liberty; the other wore a necklace of heads. "Liberty or death": it was the choice of the era. In this dreadful dilemma, where was happiness to be found?

Chapter 4

A Society in Edinburgh

Happiness

"Ten Ladies" listened "with unusual attention" to the speakers debating the proposition in soft Scottish brogues: "Is a Nation in a State of Barbarity or a nation in a State of Luxury and refined manners the happiest?" By contrast, the gentlemen were likely a little distracted that cold night in January 1775, sneaking glances and shifting a little in their seats as they adjusted themselves to the rustle of petticoats and the hint of perfume. This debate was the very first one to which women had been admitted at the previously all-male Pantheon Society in Edinburgh, Scotland's capital city. The clerk did not record whether the women sat together, but in any case, the hall was filled almost entirely with men. The presence of women at such events was controversial; it required pluck for the women to show up. Yet Edinburgh's gentlemen prided themselves on their gallantry in allowing women in these audiences. At the end of the exciting night, everyone listening voted on the proposal.[1]

Did happiness lie in refinement or in barbarism? The answer, like the debate itself, opens up a central concern of the age. Happiness became a preoccupation across a broad swath of the English-speaking world in this period—for men and also for women. Its connections to ideas of refinement, community, freedom, and equality can seem slippery now, but they were more apparent to people at the time. Understanding what happiness meant—and why it had radical potential—helps us to understand the American Revolution as well as the wider landscape from which it emerged. That world was a busy, chattering one, lively and loud with meetings and minutes, debates and declarations, crowds and chuckles and catcalls.

With its nonsensical debate topic—"How far is it from the 1st of August to the foot of Westminster Bridge?"—this 1783 cartoon lampooned the kinds of debates that took place in this era. Note the absence of women in the audience.

Happiness has long prompted debate. The concept can seem so anodyne, so vague. In the nineteenth century, "the pursuit of happiness" was even called one of the "glittering generalities" of the Declaration of Independence. Now happiness seems so elusive, floating away in the smoke of a scented spa candle. It's easy to miss the audacity of the concept in the 1770s. Theorists of this era drew on classical understandings of *eudaimonia,* or human flourishing: substantial happiness that came from a good and moral life, from community and connection. This substantive happiness was not about mere pleasures of the flesh or simple amusement. Yet as John Locke argued in the late seventeenth century, people could take different routes to happiness: "This variety of pursuits shews, that every one does not place his happiness in the same thing, or chuse the same way to it."[2]

Chasing happiness on the streets of a city in the midst of transformation—Edinburgh—reveals that what has been dismissed as mere "glittering generality" carried significant bite in this era. Nowadays we see something small and personal in happiness. In those days they saw something big and important. There were both "private Happiness" and the "Happiness of Mankind," related to sensibility, equality, and virtue. Some of those individuals centering new understandings of human happiness were luminaries of what has been called the Scottish Enlightenment, intellectuals like David Hume, Lord Kames, and James Boswell. Yet unnamed and unsung folk—including those ten women—who showed up for debates also took risks to advance new possibilities. It was not only American patriots who pursued happiness—or who shifted the nature of public deliberations in the 1770s.

In December 1773, just as some men in Boston joined together to lob tea off ships, men in Edinburgh founded the Pantheon Society to discuss current events. It was a new kind of institution, giving men a chance to leave their houses of an evening to join in reasoned consideration of matters of public interest. Many similar clubs sprang up in the urban landscape of Britain, Ireland, and British North America; one scholar estimates some twenty-five thousand over the course of the century. The oldest student society still in existence—the College Historical Society at Trinity College, Dublin—was founded in 1770 in order to allow its young men to debate one another formally.[3] The Pantheon Society, the College Historical Society, the Sons of Liberty, and continental congresses all offered a way for men to forge new paths together. "To be happy, the passion must be benign and social," declared one.[4]

Men had long been able to frequent taverns and alehouses for conversation (and of course they still could). Elite men also had clubs, which required permanent paid membership and the approval of a committee. However, in innovative institutions like the Pantheon, no committee decided on admittance, no annual fees were due. Any man who could afford a ticket could join for the night to participate in enlightened disputations. The men who founded the Pantheon were more open to newfangled ideas—like allowing women to attend public debates.

Edinburgh was a city in transition in the 1770s. Most Pantheon Society debates in these years took place in St. Mary's Chapel. Despite its religious-sounding name, the chapel was part of the Masonic Lodge, another sociable all-male institution thriving in this era. It was then in Old Town, off the Royal Mile, on a narrow lane near Edinburgh's hulking castle. People listened to speakers in Old Town. Elsewhere in Edinburgh, they heard digging and hammering, as the city's New Town was then being built. Edinburgh developers capitalized on residents' desire for a more commodious capital city befitting its literary and philosophical luminaries. New Town, with its wide, graceful crescents, was to encapsulate ideals of enlightened living. Eventually, the Masonic Lodge and many other institutions would move there (where they still exist). Men—and then women—assembled in these spaces.

For all its pretensions to enlightened sociability, though, Edinburgh remained medieval at its heart. In its narrow lanes, a local pedestrian, on hearing the cry of "Gardyloo!" from a high window, knew that the reeking contents of a chamber pot were about to be flung onto the street (and possibly onto unsuspecting heads) from an upper floor. By midcentury, things had gotten so bad that locals petitioned magistrates to do something about those "emptying and throwing their foul Water, and other Filth and Nastiness, on the Streets." In response, in 1749, the

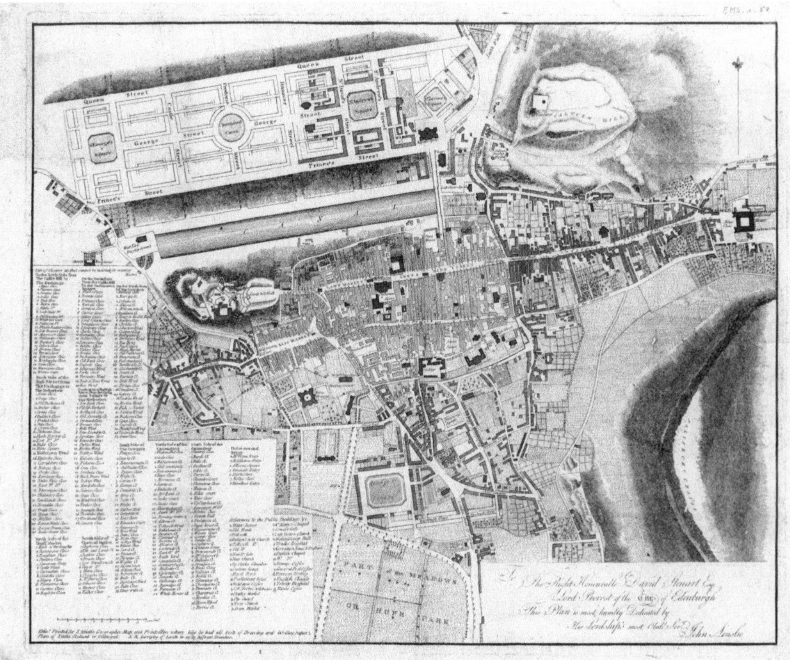

The orderly grid and squares of New Town appear at the top left of this 1780 map of Edinburgh, with what is now known as Old Town in the center.

Council passed what became known as the Nastiness Act to restrict this practice to the hours of darkness.[5] In other words, in Edinburgh as in many places, dirt and poverty still sullied a world of rising refinement and cultural capital. Women and men who strolled and rode in carriages in Edinburgh's dirty streets conversing about current events and big ideas hoped for a cleaner, more wholesome city. They also imagined a better, happier world altogether, one guided by polished moral sentiments, free from the horrors of despotism, superstition, and barbarity as well as of cascading excrement.

The kind of people who gathered at the Pantheon Society seem as though they would have been the types to agree with major Scottish thinkers such as David Hume and Henry Home, Lord Kames, both of whom argued that happiness lay in refinement. Hume had published an essay contending "that the ages of refinement are both the happiest and most virtuous." That debate in January 1775 was likely a nod to this essay and this claim. Kames agreed: "We refine upon the pleasures of society, because our happiness consists chiefly in social intercourse."[6]

Did refinement win the debate in January 1775? It did—but only with the women. When questioned for their views, every single woman in attendance voted for refinement. That women chose refinement as the path to happiness is not a shock. A few years later, another Scottish theorist would publish a global history of women arguing that "every savage people" in the world began their journey to civilization first with "the barbarous custom of enslaving and treating with the utmost severity" women.[7] For women, barbarism seemed especially problematic. Did every woman genuinely support refinement? It is hard to say. Maybe even if a polite lady yearned occasionally for a broad-shouldered barbarian, she was not about to admit it in a public forum in Edinburgh in the 1770s.

In fact, though, barbarism won the debate as a whole: a surprise. Evidently, the majority of men dreamed of (being) broad-shouldered barbarians, too. Men—and men alone—thought national happiness lay there, not in refinement and luxury. Why? Were they imps of the perverse, voting for barbarism on the very first night they allowed women to attend debates at the Pantheon Society? Was it a way of thumbing their noses at the constraints of having ladies present? The men presumably saw something more vigorous and exciting, maybe even liberating, in raw masculine barbarism than in effeminizing luxury. Perhaps they thought that barbarians would be more likely to enjoy certain privileges—like easy access to women, or the chance to live free.

One of the pale and weedy debaters that night likely raised a key question: What did "happiness" even mean? It was surely not the first time that the question had been asked in St. Mary's Chapel. Happiness was an enduring preoccupation at the Pantheon Society. In April 1774, they enquired whether "a Married or a single State [was] most Conducive to Private Happiness." Only two men were willing to speak publicly in favor of being single. "Married" won by a landslide. Marriage remained a key topic. A December 1774 debate—on whether a spouse should be chosen for love or money—attracted a large and lively crowd. It was an "entertaining" evening. This fact may help to explain why a meeting then took place at which it was "Unanimously agreed to admit Ladies to hear the debates of the Society." Women did not speak publicly; Edinburgh's gentlemen found it unseemly for a lady to address a crowd. However, the women were there, and they voted on resolutions: a significant alteration of custom. Other debates pondered "Whether does knowledge or ignorance conduce most to the happiness of Mankind?" (knowledge won "by a small majority") and "Whether does the Happiness of the Marriage State depend most on the Husband or Wife?" (most agreed on the wife).[8]

"Happiness" had many meanings. It connected to refinement, to sociability, and, most important, to equality. An observation by David Hume might strike us as uncontroversial. He argued that objects did not have worth in themselves apart from the feelings they created in people. If they generated strong positive feelings, then "the person is happy. It cannot reasonably be doubted, but a little miss, dressed in a new gown for a dancing-school ball, receives as compleat enjoyment as the greatest orator, who triumphs in the spendor of his eloquence." While there was of course a patronizing quality in his account of a young woman in a new dress, there was also an equality here: she was just as happy as the most impressive speaker who swayed an entire assembly. In his view, substantial happiness was not reserved for distinguished men.[9]

Others of Hume's day deemed such views to be extreme and fringe.

Another Edinburgh resident, James Boswell, mentioned to the great intellectual Samuel Johnson "Hume's notion, that all who are happy are equally happy; a little miss with a new gown at a dancing-school ball, a general at the head of a victorious army, and an orator, after having made an eloquent speech in a great assembly." Johnson disagreed with Hume: "Sir, that all who are happy, are equally happy, is not true. A peasant and a philosopher may be equally satisfied, but not equally happy. Happiness consists in the multiplicity of agreeable consciousness. A peasant has not capacity for having equal happiness with a philosopher."[10] In other words, basic animal satisfactions could be equal for peasants and philosophers, but happiness required a more sophisticated sensitivity: that "multiplicity of agreeable consciousness." A young woman would find merely a basic pleasure in her pretty dress; a peasant could obtain but rough satisfaction from a good crop. Their joy in their own abilities and successes could never equal the significant happiness of the learned orator or philosopher. For men like Johnson and Boswell, only elite White men of refined sensibility could experience true happiness; others—by dint of rank, race, or gender—could not even aspire to it.

To claim happiness, then, could be a radical act of equality in the 1770s, whether in Edinburgh or Boston. In this period, many individuals came to believe in their own ability to achieve happiness, even in the face of imperial punishment, domestic disappointments, and tough separations. Yet what did they mean by "happiness"? Let's follow a few individuals as they pursued happiness in order to understand this ideal—and the events of 1774 in the aftermath of the destruction of the tea—better. From a series of small acts of personal defiance on the road to happiness grew tumult, protest, and, ultimately, revolution.

The snow fell softly upon Boston in late January 1774, on streets and churchyards, soldiers and citizens. As shivering locals rubbed their hands over crackling fires and cupped mugs of steaming herbal brews, they commiserated and fretted over what was to come. They knew there was going to be a strong reaction from the British government, but they did not know what form it would take. People were on edge in the winter of 1773–74.

Yet the snow had its pleasures, as one lucky boy with a sled knew as he rushed downhill in icy joy. Careless as children in a hurry sometimes are, he ran his sled into the feet of one of the more cantankerous people to tread those streets: John Malcolm. The startled boy looked up into the disapproving face of this dour customs official, an avid supporter of the crown and its ministers. Earlier in the decade, Malcolm had even traveled to North Carolina to fight the Regulators, and disgruntled sailors had already tarred and feathered him in New Hampshire for seizing a ship on absurdly narrow technical grounds. Malcolm may have been unsettled or even slightly injured by the sled; his fine leather shoes and silk stockings had almost certainly been splashed with dirty snow.

Still, this little scuffle was not a major incident—at least not until this irascible Friend of Government made it into one. He towered over the boy with a cane tipped in metal. In this era, men occasionally carried heavy canes they could wield in self-defense (a few were even "loaded" with molten metal on the inside, which could prove lethal).[11] Given Malcolm's position, personality, and history, it would not be surprising if he felt himself in need of a walking stick that doubled as a weapon, and he was not shy about using it.

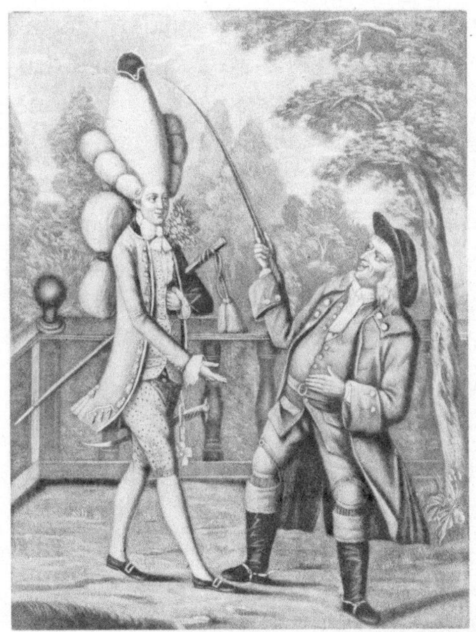

In this 1774 cartoon, a young modern "macaroni" in silk stockings and outlandish wig carries a metal-tipped and tasseled cane as well as a sword in his belt, in contrast with his honest farmer father.

As Malcolm cursed and threatened, arm poised to strike, the boy remained "perfectly quiet." In that tense moment, a civic-minded bystander happened by. It was none other than George Hewes, the shoemaker who had carried off one of the injured men in the shooting in King Street in 1770 and who had helped destroy tea in 1773. A father of three himself, he interposed himself between the two, cautioning Malcolm with quiet menace: "I hope you are not going to strike this boy with that stick." Malcolm spluttered that Hewes was an "impertinent rascal," demanding to know how he dared to "speak to a gentleman" like that. Hewes retorted that he was no rascal, and his credit was as good as any man's (Hewes had served time in debtors' prison a few years earlier, so he may have been especially sensitive on this point). In any case, Hewes added, "*I* never was tarred and feathered anyhow." At that, Malcolm struck Hewes on the head with the cane, causing him to lose consciousness. He survived, but Hewes carried the indentation of that cane in his skull for the rest of his very long life.[12]

By this time, a crowd was starting to gather, and a messy street fight followed in the slippery snow. Malcolm wielded not just his cane but also his sword so that he "graz'd one man." On being informed of this event, magistrates issued a warrant for Malcolm's arrest for breach of peace. Malcolm, who had returned home by then, pleaded that he was afraid to come out of his house as the people of Boston were too threatening. The magistrates agreed to return the next day. In the meantime, word of the brawl electrified Boston, and a furious crowd surrounded Malcolm's house. After various insults and shouts were slung, a few people, jeering, broke into his house and seized him.

The tarring and feathering Malcolm had received in New Hampshire was a gentle rehearsal for the "modern jacket" (as contemporaries called tarring and feathering) he got in Boston that night. In New Hampshire, they had left his clothes on, and the proceedings had been quick. In Boston, on that frigid January night, they "tore his clothes off, and tarr'd his head and body, and feathered him," carting him down King Street "amidst the huzzas of thousands" to the Liberty Tree. Once there, amid "a vast concourse of people," the leaders "whipped him, beat him with sticks and threatened to hang him." They made him toast member after member of the royal family with tea, forcing the liquid down his throat until he retched and vomited. "Several gentlemen" tried to stop this activity, but to no avail. Most thought Malcolm would not survive the torments (he did, though much of his skin peeled off in gruesome strips).[13]

Malcolm's misery on Boston's streets divided opinion. An account sympathetic with Bostonians argued that Malcolm had "behaved in the most capricious, insulting, and daringly abusive manner." In this view, Malcolm had destroyed the happiness and peace of a larger community and so deserved what he got. This account concluded: "See reader, the effects of a government in which the people have no confidence." In other words, the whole sorry episode was the fault of bad government. By contrast, an English woman sympathetic with Malcolm saw in this episode a "poor Old Man" who had suffered "inhuman treatment." For her, the torture showed "the abject State of Governm[ent] & the licentiousness & barbarism of the times."[14] Even some of the most avid protesters against British policies were ashamed of what had happened, and they sought to disavow Malcolm's mistreatment. In fact, this event so shook local sensibilities that no one was tarred and feathered in Boston again. Yet tensions remained high.

Even before news of this shocking event reached Britain, orators of all stripes had been arguing over how to deal with the unruly colonies. In 1774, the Pantheon Society "Carried by a great Majority that Britain has a right to Tax her Colonies." Many in Britain agreed—but how to punish those who had destroyed the tea in Boston Harbor? In the House of Commons, debates grew so heated that at points MPs could not even hear the speakers. Lord North and the British government presumed that the colonists in Boston would apologize. As North phrased it in debates, Boston was guilty of "outrages" and had set a disgraceful "example from one end of the continent to the other." One MP declared that "the town of Boston is almost in a state of nature," inhabited by barbarians.[15] If Bostonians would not voluntarily make restitution to the East India Company for the tea, then Massachusetts should be punished—or so ministers like North decided.

Even at the center of power, though, other voices urged restraint.

Rose Fuller, an MP and absentee Jamaican plantation owner and enslaver, was sympathetic with Americans. He argued that harsh punishment of the colonists would result in "the total destruction of this country." He suggested that instead of closing the port of Boston, as had been proposed, the government simply levy a large fine on the colony of Massachusetts. No one took up this proposition. Another MP argued for reparations to the EIC. Still, he fretted that "the people out of doors" in America—by which he meant ordinary folk as distinct from their leaders—lacked respect for Parliament. He croaked, Cassandra-like: "I feel the storm is rising."[16]

That storm was indeed rising. Newspapers tracked it. A single issue of the (London) *Morning Post* included one writer who advised stern measures against Americans, suggesting that if they then still resisted, at least it would be clear that "the sword must be drawn." A different author in the same issue, using the pseudonym Amor Patriae (Love of Country), urged ministers instead to act like gentle fathers: "Treat America as you would do a *disobedient* child; strive to reclaim her, not by menaces and violence, or the terror of your arms, but by the more gentle and effectual means of persuasion, and mild measures." This writer advised that the British government might otherwise end up "driving the Americans into a state of *desperation*" by "acts of *oppression*" which would permanently alienate them.[17]

Such warnings against draconian punishments went unheeded. The British government brandished a heavy cudgel over Bostonians in four harsh Parliamentary acts in the spring of 1774. The first two, the Boston Port Act and the Massachusetts Government Act, took direct aim at that colony, closing the port of Boston until full restitution had been made to the East India Company. Such a policy seemed unfair to many since it punished everyone indiscriminately, even those who had opposed the action. The second of these acts altered the government structure in Massachusetts, diminishing the power of the popular assembly which had passed "many dangerous . . . resolves." Henceforth, meetings would require the written permission of the governor or his lieutenant.[18] The other two acts—the Impartial Administration of Justice Act and the Quartering Act—allowed for the moving of trials away from hotspots (thus protecting people like Aaron in the *Gaspee* incident) and also enabled a commander to requisition local housing for troops. North appointed a new governor of Massachusetts, Thomas Gage; he was also the commander of the British forces in North America. Since these roles were usually separate appointments, making one man both governor and general sent a message. He arrived in Massachusetts flanked by several regiments to back up his authority. Here seemed to be the tyranny in red coats long feared.

This legislation—denounced by many colonists as the Intolerable Acts—sought to press Massachusetts—and any other unruly colonies—into behaving differently. A circular letter of the Boston Committee of Correspondence exclaimed that the Boston Port Act "fills the inhabitants with indignation." Even those who had not agreed with the destruction of the tea, the letter continued, concurred that such an act was "not to have been expected even from a barbarous state."[19]

At the same time, another significant piece of legislation, the Quebec Act, passed. It had taken several years to negotiate the place of French colonists in newly British Canada. It allowed French Canadians to practice their religion, even permitting them to serve on the government council, whose membership was expanded by the act. It was a major victory for French Canadians—and for tolerance more generally. It did not replace French with British law, instead allowing a hybrid of French and English law. It expanded the boundaries of Canada far to the west, into the Ohio Valley and the Great Lakes area, which angered speculators and others in the lower colonies who saw this area as theirs. The Quebec Act was not part of the punitive legislation, but many colonists saw it as such, thanks to its timing and provisions. Shortly thereafter, Guy Carleton, the Irish governor who had advocated for the act, arrived with his wife—fluent in French—to the considerable acclaim of locals in Québec in September 1774. Carleton informed the secretary of state that "'All Ranks of People amongst them vied with each other in testifying their Gratitude and Respect" for the Quebec Act and his arrival.[20] French Catholics were pleased. New England Protestants were not.

Many in the lower colonies saw the Quebec Act as a dangerous threat to British Protestantism. Newspapers portrayed the legislation as a means of establishing Catholicism (or popery or papistry, as it was called) in the lower colonies. Women in South Carolina complained that the "schemes" of the British government "smell strong of Popery." In Newport, newspapers included lurid and false stories of the British government's plans "to raise an Army of Canadian Papists" in order to massacre New Englanders. Friends of Liberty toasted each other "No Popish Army in a Protestant country." One of Newport's residents, the Reverend Ezra Stiles, fretted that the act not only enlarged the Province of Québec but also "established the Romish Church & IDOLATRY." He found it "astonishing" that Parliament and king would "establish Popery over three Quarters of their Empire": overstatement indicative of his troubled state.[21]

The Quebec Act, together with the punitive legislation, constituted foul medicine for many Americans to choke down, a sentiment captured in 1774's satirical drawing "The Able Doctor, or America Swallowing the Bitter Draught." Lord North, with the "Boston Port Bill" in his pocket, forces tea down the throat of yet another topless Indigenous woman representing America, who is nevertheless simultaneously spewing the tea into North's face. Lord Mansfield, the chief justice, holds her

This British cartoon mocked the severity of what many colonists called the Intolerable Acts of 1774.

arms behind her as Lord Sandwich, known for his lewd conduct toward women, peers under her skirt. On the left, a Frenchman and a Spaniard confer over this situation. On the right stands the unpopular Lord Bute, in a kilt, holding a sword labeled MILITARY LAW. In the distance behind them lies "Boston cannonaded," while in the foreground lie the tatters of a Boston petition. Britannia face-palms, too horrified to watch.

In the summer of 1774, America gathered herself up, shoved the ministers off, and stood up. Resolve in the thirteen colonies stiffened, and calls came for a general meeting. Far from isolating Boston, as British officials had imagined, they had driven many other colonists to rally around Massachusetts, seeing in Boston's plight what might happen to all of them. To avoid that future, they looked to the past. In June, a New York printer repurposed that twenty-year-old emblem, the segmented colonial snake first used by Franklin in 1754 and then republished in the Stamp Act crisis of 1765–66. He put it on a newspaper masthead: UNITE OR DIE. Other printers, in Boston and Philadelphia, soon followed.[22]

Several colonies sent money to demonstrate their support for what Carolinians called "our suffering brethren" in Boston. A meeting in Maryland announced "that the town of *Boston* is now suffering in the common cause of *America,* and that it is the duty of every Colony in *America* to unite." Even some residents of Québec—"in compassion" over "the present unhappy discord"—collected wheat to be sent to Boston. In reply, Bostonians thanked "our brethren in Canada," promising "Whilst we stand compact, like a band of brothers, no proud invaders will be able to subdue us." George Washington made an impressive speech, promising to pay for and raise a regiment of a thousand men, with himself at the head, to march for Boston's relief. John Dickinson

[THURSDAY, JUNE 23, 1774. THE [NUMBER 1642.]

NEW-YORK JOURNAL OR, THE GENERAL ADVERTISER.

Containing the freshest ADVICES, both FOREIGN and DOMESTIC.

PRINTED AND PUBLISHED BY JOHN HOLT, NEAR THE COFFEE-HOUSE.

Here in 1774 was the third appearance of the disjointed American snake, published previously in 1754 and 1765.

assured a Massachusetts friend that the thirteen mainland colonies "are very unanimous" about holding a congress. Sympathetic with Massachusetts, they pledged unity: "What never happened before," he concluded, "has happened now."[23]

What happened was the first meeting of the Continental Congress in Philadelphia in September 1774. This group sought to ensure that both the American colonies and Britain could find "happiness and prosperity."[24] Happiness was a substantive political project. The designation of this group as the Continental Congress signaled inclusion—it was meant to span the continent—while it also reveals exclusion, in that it did not include the Caribbean islands. There were still hopes of including Canada as well as West and East Florida. Even in a time of considerable unity, though, not everyone answered the call.

Bringing diverse colonies together was a challenge. In August, one delegate from Massachusetts, John Adams, made his way to Philadelphia. Left at home, his wife, Abigail, expressed "The great anxiety I feel for my Country . . . The Rocks and quick Sands appear upon every Side." John reassured her that "I have the strongest Hopes, that We shall yet see a clearer Sky, and better Times." He was touched by the sympathy that even Pennsylvania Quakers—pacifists—showed for the scrappy Boston fighters. In the meantime, though, he, too, narrated the difficulties of congressional unity: "Fifty Gentlemen meeting together, all Strangers, are not acquainted with Each others Language, Ideas, Views, Designs. . . . fearfull, timid, skittish." He joked that even if the proposal put before the Congress was a simple equation—2+3=5—it would take two full days of tedious speeches full of "Logick and Rhetorick, Law, History, Politicks and Mathematicks" before they would vote their approval.[25] Wrangling politicians has never been easy. For Americans unused to cross-colonial collaboration, it proved especially tricky. Yet there was sufficient anger about British policies to knit many together.

Despite the challenges of the first of these Continental Congresses, the delegates ultimately agreed on the adoption of the Suffolk Resolves, denouncing the recent acts of Parliament. The Intolerable Acts were deemed "gross infractions" of American rights, to be "rejected as the attempts of a wicked administration to enslave America." The Quebec Act was denounced as "dangerous in an extreme degree to the Protestant religion and to the civil rights and liberties of all America." The final declaration of the Congress asserted, using language from the seventeenth-century philosopher John Locke, "That they are entitled to life, liberty and property: and they have never ceded to any foreign power whatever, a right to dispose of either without their consent." In the end, the colonists agreed to boycott British goods.[26]

Not everyone heeded the call to resistance. Tarring and feathering—imagined or actual—were the predictable result. In October, just as the Congress declared a general nonimportation plan beyond the more local ones already enacted (such as those on tea and textiles), one merchant, Anthony Stewart, decided to try to land tea at Annapolis in Maryland. After facing the fury of locals, he decided that the wisest course of action was to set fire to the ship. With that, the *Peggy Stewart* blazed in Annapolis Harbor. As one disapproving account had it, this burning "saved Mr. *Stewart,* if not from death and destruction, at least from ruin, tar, and feathers."[27]

Tarring and feathering continued to capture the British imagination, as in the October 1774 print by Carrington Bowles, "A New Method of MACARONY MAKING, as practised at BOSTON." It was a garbled representation, implying in its caption that Malcolm was tarred and feathered due to his landing tea. Two cretinous colonists—one on the right wearing a Sons of Liberty cockade and holding a cudgel and the other on the left sporting a hat reading "45," a reference both to a defender of liberty, John Wilkes, and to the 1745 Scottish Jacobite Rebellion—force a teapot on the feathered Malcolm, gallows looming in the background. The title, referring to the male archetype of the "macaroni," or dandy, plays on the idea of masculine frippery, here rendered political and covered in feathers.

Not all tar and feathers remained imaginary, though some incidents bordered on the absurd. One New Jersey meeting condemned Samuel Seabury's anti-congressional screed by ordering that the book itself be tarred and feathered. "The pamphlet was then, in its gorgeous attire, nailed up firmly to the pillory-post, there to remain as a monument of the indignation of a free and loyal people." When a Scottish woman

This 1774 British cartoon mocked the destruction of the tea and the tarring and feathering of men like the colonial customs official John Malcolm.

visited North Carolina, she said she found it difficult to look at local men "without connecting the idea of tar and feather." Fearful of "the fury of an ignorant zeal," she noted of one anti-American letter she sent home: "I risk tar and feather was it to be seen." (In fact, no woman was tarred and feathered.) By November 1774, one man, sympathetic with the British, fretted that "the seeds of rebellion are already sown, and have taken very deep root."[28] Boycotts gathered force.

Surveying this rising tide of popular protest with gloom was Virginia's royal governor, John Murray, the fourth Earl of Dunmore. He was a Scot determined to prove his loyalty to the crown. His father had been convicted of treason in the Jacobite Rebellion for supporting the Scottish claimant to the throne, Charles Edward Stuart, known as Bonnie Prince Charlie. The son, though from Scotland, was determined not to make the same mistake. He served first as governor of New York before moving to Virginia in the autumn of 1771. Lord Dunmore's Scottish origins did not endear him to many Virginians. Numerous Scottish merchants traded Virginia's tobacco, and to many of their neighbors, they seemed too successful, too aggressive in pursuing debt, and too inclined to band together as Scots.

Dunmore determined on two plans to bolster his limited popularity. The first was to bring his wife and children to join him in Williamsburg. This decision may have had more intimate motivations, but it was also publicized widely. The *Virginia Gazette* reported in March 1774 that Lady Charlotte and their six children had arrived in Williamsburg "to the great joy of the inhabitants." People in the town illuminated their houses, and the town fired the cannon and let off fireworks. In the paper, an anonymous "lady" offered a poem to Lady Charlotte on the imagined domestic bliss of reunion: "And in his arms you meet your fond reward. / Your lovely offspring croud to his embrace." The worthies of Williamsburg also gave a public address praising Lord Dunmore's "many private virtues."[29]

In addition to spending more time with his wife and family, Dunmore also employed more ruthless, yet equally time-honored, strategies to win friends in Virginia. What better way for an unpopular leader to change the narrative than by stirring up a war on the frontier, so that Virginians could turn their angry gaze toward Indigenous nations and away from the imperial crisis? Virginia and Pennsylvania had been sparring for years over these western lands, but they agreed that the Indigenous nations there were not the ones who deserved to possess it. Speculators were especially eager to gain access to these lands. Dunmore's agents began spreading rumors of an impending attack by Shawnees and Western Seneca, who were still recovering from the aftershocks of Pontiac's War. As Pennsylvanians observed with cynicism, "the scheming party in Virginia are making a tool of their Governor," using him, and his desire to ingratiate himself with locals, to help them in a takeover of Indigenous homelands.[30] Although the Shawnee leader, Cornstalk, managed to soothe his own people, especially young men eager for revenge against settlers, colonists were not so easily assuaged.

Following false rumors of an Indian attack, many settlers fled east, while others joined forces mobilized by Dunmore. One officer, drumming up recruits, promised that Indigenous people would be forced off "their Country. Their Townes may be plundered & Burned [to] prevent them from giving us any future Trouble." In September 1774, Dunmore himself marched to Fort Pitt to lead Virginia militia forces of twenty-four hundred men in an offensive against the Shawnee and allied Lenni Lenape, Western Seneca, and other nations. One Virginia planter and patriot, James Madison, reported that "The loss of the Indians was considerable . . . they immediately sued for peace as the only method to save themselves & their *Towns* from destruction."[31] Despite this surrender, their lands came under intense pressure, leading to the movements of settlers, including Daniel Boone, across the Cumberland Gap and into what became Kentucky.

In the end, Dunmore's strategy, so costly for the Shawnee and other nations, did little to divert Virginians' attention from the imperial crisis. In that same letter, James Madison noted that "A spirit of Liberty & Patriotism animates all degrees and denominations of men. Many publickly declare themselves ready to join the Bostonians." At the same time, Madison fretted, "If America & Britain should come to an hostile rupture I am afraid an Insurrection among the slaves may & will be promoted."[32] How far would this "spirit of Liberty" go? At this time, one New England newspaper started to outline an "independent state" composed of the current colonies and offering alliance to other nations (a thinly veiled allusion to France).[33]

That same New England paper of October 1774 was full of news about Canada. There was a report of a planned Jesuit college in Québec. The Jesuits were among the most loathed bogeymen of the Anglophone Protestant imagination, and the newspaper considered it shocking that such "enemies of Christianity" would "find an asylum in the dominions of a Protestant Prince." The paper also detailed a plan to appoint a Catholic bishop of Québec, a horror for New Englanders who saw such men as villainous foreign agents of the pope himself.

Yet there remained hopes for a Canadian alliance. There was news of "considerable commotion in Halifax [Nova Scotia], concerning tea," the kind of protests seen in the other mainland colonies. There was also a letter from the "Sons of New-England," addressed "To the Canadians." It called Canadians their "brethren" and assured them that they wanted religious and other freedoms for them and everyone else. It hoped they would join the common cause, and that Canadians would be willing to "risk every thing for the defence of AMERICAN LIBERTY."[34]

AMERICAN LIBERTY—often tied to happiness—filled American newspapers in 1774. In one mock newspaper ad, an aggrieved husband, *Loyalty,* complains that his wife, *American Liberty,* has been behaving "in a very licentious manner," warning creditors not to trust her. She had run away, seeking her own happiness at his cost. A counteradvertisement from *American Liberty* asserted that *Loyalty* was a tyrant who had "behaved in an arbitrary and cruel manner," allowing his servants "to direct and insult me."[35] This political satire was riffing on a familiar kind of advertisement in these newspapers: those between separated spouses. Unhappily married couples, who had no legal right to divorce, sometimes took to local newspapers to air their grievances. Since a wife who left a marriage could still draw on her husband's credit, a husband could use a local newspaper to warn people that he would not honor credit extended to his wife. Occasionally, aggrieved wives (like *American Liberty* here) responded, publicly justifying having left a no-good husband.

Happiness was increasingly upheld as an ideal even in these sparring ads. Claiming the importance of happiness in marriage was a radical act in an era in which the legal right to divorce (even for abuse or adultery) was extremely limited. Unhappiness in marriage now began to seem to many a valid reason for separation. One husband, Samuel Pettibone in Litchfield, Connecticut, in 1771, started his ad in large letters: "I am so unhappy in my last marriage" that he was placing an ad to complain that his wife, Mary, had fled and run him into debt. Mary's unhappiness provoked his. That same issue of the *Connecticut Courant* also saw several other ads from husbands and wives airing their marital disappointments.[36] Such notices demonstrate that happiness was an increasingly important ideal for marriage, and that its absence was felt to justify ending a marriage, for women as well as men.

In October 1774, other kinds of happiness engaged the attention of a group of southern political activists. They met in a genteel home in Edenton, North Carolina, in October 1774.[37] Like many staunch Friends of Liberty, they decided to form an association to support the boycott of tea. What made this group "memorable," as subsequent coverage had it, is that all the participants were women. Noting their desire for "the peace and happiness of our country," they deemed it their duty, not only for their families but for themselves, to "do every thing as far as it lies in our power" to maintain the nonimportation of tea. They drank an herbal infusion instead. The women signed the pledge with their own names, which was unusual in itself: Penelope Barker, for instance, and Elizabeth Johnston. Then they persuaded other women, often linked by family ties, to do so as well, for a total of fifty-one signatures. This text and all their names appeared in the *Virginia Gazette*. In early 1775, more than one London newspaper picked up this story; one even included all the signatories, with the opening paragraph noting that the "ladies of this province have determined to give a memorable proof of their patriotism."[38] The full names of ladies did not generally appear in the press, so to include them was in this case likely a mark of derision.

This mocking notice of the Edenton gathering caught the attention of one North Carolinian living in London, Arthur Iredell, who wrote his brother, James, about it in January 1775. He noted that he saw the name Johnston, the birth name of his sister-in-law. He wondered whether it was a relation, and he continued, tongue in cheek, asking: "Is there a female Congress at Edenton, too?" He hoped not, since "we Englishmen" were already "afraid of the male Congress," a reference to the Continental Congress. Yet he argued that female patriots were far more fearsome: since "Amazonian" times, they had proved to be the "most formidable enemies." In a typical claim of the era, he highlighted female powers of attraction, noting that "the more we strike to conquer them, the more [we] are conquered!" He comforted himself with the humorous observation that at least "there are few places in America which possess so much female artillery as Edenton."[39]

The Edenton Friends of Liberty provoked mockery in other quarters as well. A satirical cartoon published in London in March 1775 depicts the event itself in unflattering terms. It was a useful two-for-one image for conservative British audiences, deriding both the colonial cause and the political organizing of women. The drawing portrays a chaotic gathering of women, some putting together the pledge, others in the background emptying tea canisters. The image subverted what in fact had been an orderly and organized petition campaign by elite women. Those presiding here mostly look either vacant and submissive (one such woman is in the embrace of a man in a red coat) or harsh (like the one who holds the gavel). Two of the women at the center have fashionable powdered "high roll" hair. One woman drinks punch directly from a bowl in an uncouth manner. The pledge promises that the women will avoid "that Pernicious Custom of Drinking Tea, or . . . ye wear of Manufacture from England until such time that all Acts which tend to Enslave this our Native Country shall be Repealed." One woman is leaning over the pledge in a way rarely shown in portraits, with her posterior, not her face, in the center of the image. On the floor under the table, a peeing dog licks the face of a neglected child to indicate that these mothers are ignoring their domestic duties in favor of unfeminine political activity. Holding a tray with quill and ink is an enslaved woman, a reminder to London viewers that supporters of colonial liberty who worried over the "enslavement" of their country were themselves slaveholders. The cartoon was accurate on this point, since doubtless the labor of unnamed enslaved women and men made possible the political organizing of other women and men in every single one of the North American colonies.

Newspapers highlighted the bids for freedom by the Edenton women; historians have commemorated them too.[40] Less celebrated was another woman in Edenton who also sought to secure happiness. An advertisement seeking her return appeared as far away as Virginia in early 1775. A Black woman called Road (similar to Rhoda), born in New England and apparently speaking in that "dialect," liberated herself from slavery in Edenton. Road had already shown her pluck, her refusal to be kept down. Her hair was combed into the same kind of fashionable high roll of those in the Edenton satire, and she reveled in what was described with disapproval as "gaiety in dress." She made her escape in a striped jacket—of fashionable homespun—as well as a chintz gown, and, most striking of all, a red petticoat. This outfit was topped and tailed with silk hat, black cloak, and leather high heels. It's hard to walk a long, bumpy path in heels, but Road did, likely with a forged freedom pass.[41] Perhaps she wanted to return to her people in New England. Maybe she came from the same circles as Phillis Wheatley.

Following Road down the winding path to self-liberation demonstrates that pursuing happiness could be a political act for all kinds of people. Road, along with Phillis Wheatley, lived in a world in which newspapers—the very New England ones that carried poems penned by Wheatley—also carried ads like this one: "TO BE SOLD, A Healthy Negro Girl, about twenty three years old, born in this country.—LIKEWISE—A serviceable MARE, which goes well in a Carriage."[42] This kind of dehumanizing advertisement indicated the dangerous assumptions that underpinned theories about happiness and what was then called "sensibility," that is, sensitivity and the capacity for refined sentiments. For enslaved women to make claims about feelings and happiness was to undermine these pernicious assumptions.

Such sensibility animated Wheatley's *Collected Poems*. The collection revolves around death and ill health. Yet Wheatley asserted her power as a poet to transform mourning into joy. Dead preachers became "thrice happy saints." Even a five-year-old who had died became a "happy babe" on a "blissful shore." An African painter whose work the poet admired was also "thrice happy." She also linked happiness and freedom, as in her 1773 ode to the Earl of Dartmouth: "HAIL, happy day, when, smiling like the morn, / Fair Freedom rose New-England to adorn." In this ingeniously anti-slavery poem, Wheatley allowed "Freedom's charms [to] unfold" for the reader. She addressed America's political situation and its endurance of "wanton Tyranny," moving on to account for her own "love of Freedom." She recounted her own history of enslavement—"snatch'd from Afric's fancy'd happy seat." Her love of liberty sprang from domestic happiness and African origins.[43]

Choosing happiness took pluck. Phillis Wheatley, like Road, knew that chasing that dream was a terrifying, exhilarating prospect, full of threats and obstructions at every turn. Road's escape—perhaps back to her people—shows that joy and justice called to all kinds of women—and men—in the 1770s. Whether in Edinburgh or Edenton, at the tea table or in assembly or in church, "Fair Freedom" beckoned. Like *American Liberty* and the little miss in her dancing frock, Road, flashing her saucy red petticoat, stepped out and pursued happiness. Still, all of them found themselves on a rocky path, one growing only stonier as 1775 wore on.

Chapter 5

A Castle in Anomabu

People whispered that those in charge wore shoes made from human skin. Their menacing footwear was quiet, unlike their incomprehensible shouts and the clank of their chains. Even if such links did not literally encircle his own young neck, the boy later called Newport was still weighed down by the heavy knowledge of the drastic alteration in his life.

What were his origins? Was he with his friends near his home when he was taken, as one contemporary, Ottobah Cugoano, had been, stolen in the woods by "several great ruffians" wielding cutlasses? Was he a war captive, transported by exultant soldiers and sold to local slave traders? Was he paying a family debt? Was he passed from one trader to another, as many were? Did he have any family with him? What language did he speak? What was his real name? There are so many questions about his life, and so few answers. Records suggest that he was sold at Cape Grand Mount, in what is now Liberia, and then taken to Anomabu in what is now Ghana.[1]

Anomabu (or Annamaboe) Castle on West Africa's Gold Coast brought all kinds of people together; it was a cosmopolitan and multilingual place. "Castle" meant it was larger than a fortress. In 1752, the African Company described it as "'the Key to the Whole Trade of the Gold Coast." When this boy was there, it was a building site, with a more substantial fort going up. It became a central hub of the rising and extensive British slave trade, a holding place for thousands of enslaved people destined to be transported to the Americas. Built at the same time was a grand house called Castle Brew, at the northwestern corner

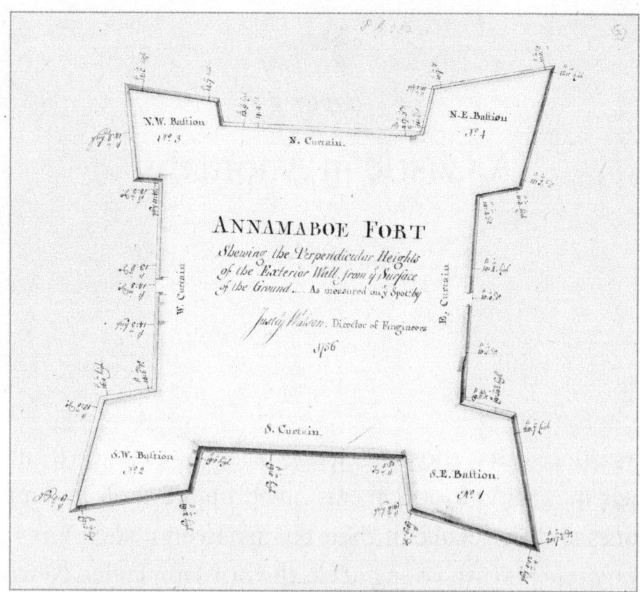

This 1756 drawing shows the plan for the new British castle at the older fort of Anomabu.

of the fort. It was in the latest Palladian style, with large windows and a black-and-white marble walk.[2]

The owner of this house, Richard Brew, was one of the two most powerful men at Anomabu in this era. He was married to the daughter of the other: an African *caboceer*, or commander, called John Corrantee, a diplomat and merchant. Corrantee courted alliances with both Francophone and Anglophone traders. He sent one son to be educated in France, and another—William Ansah Sessarakoo—to England, where his portrait was painted.[3] Striding across marble walkways, Corrantee and Brew both managed to navigate complicated politics with high stakes. So eventually would that terrified boy curled up in a dark corner of a slave ship.

The call for liberty in the Declaration of Independence and elsewhere by American enslavers like Thomas Jefferson, George Washington, and others has been called the "American paradox." A wider view, one starting in West Africa, reveals that this "American paradox" was hardly exclusively American. Richard Brew at Anomabu—who, according to his leading historian, "sent more slaves off the coast than any other individual"—declared in 1770: "I am a friend to Liberty. . . . I Mortally hate logs & Chains, tho I live in the Midst of Slaves & Slavery." (A "log" here referred to a punishment of attaching a heavy piece of wood to a person "to impede movement.") Those enslavers—African and American and British—who called themselves, seemingly without irony or apology, Friends of Liberty saw no inconsistency in their holding others in slavery. From today's vantage point we see nothing *but* inconsistencies, not to say hypocrisy.[4]

If we start not with Thomas Jefferson and George Washington but instead with people in Anomabu like Brew, Corrantee, and Newport, though, we start to see that it was in fact in this era that slavery—which seemed natural to so many in Africa and Europe and in the Americas before then—started to seem incompatible with being a Friend of Liberty. In a sense, what we are witnessing are the origins of our contemporary understandings. The American Revolution did not exactly cause this shift, though its tumult and challenges advanced it. Rather, these redefinitions of liberty emerged out of a wider world that generated changes too often attributed solely to the American Revolution.

Two preconditions were necessary for new understandings to emerge. The first was the establishment of ever more dismal forms of slavery in the eighteenth century, affording many people with a crystal-clear sense of what being "treated like a slave" was like. In Anomabu and many places around the world—including, as we have seen, places as disparate as Detroit on the Great Lakes and Kolkata on the Hooghly in India—new forts established innovative forms of daunting power. That expanded fort at Anomabu in the 1750s symbolized a fortified imperialism and slave trade.

The second precondition was that people started to push back not just against individual exploitation but against the entire system of oppressive authority. We have already seen that process at work in places like Detroit with Pontiac's War; it also took place on West Africa's Gold Coast and eventually in those thirteen American colonies. Africans, too, protested slavery in the American colonies. The chaos of the American Revolution may actually have impeded a budding transatlantic anti-slavery alliance. In the long term, though, the wider recasting of liberty remains our inheritance, which is why we now register the inconsistencies so profoundly. Starting in West Africa with one lost boy reveals the foundational nature of Atlantic slavery—and liberty.

The boy was one of a million people forced out of Africa into Atlantic slavery in the eighteenth century, with one-quarter of them taken by the British from West Africa. More enslaved people went from Anomabu than from any other British West African fort, including the better-known Cape Coast Castle. Slavery on an industrial scale reshaped Africa and the Americas. The transatlantic slave trade had metastasized both war and slavery in West Africa in the eighteenth century.[5] Wars secured captives to be sold across the Atlantic, in exchange for more arms for more wars: a vicious and transformative circle of conflict and slavery. In what is now southern Ghana, the Asante Kingdom fought for, and won, territory, establishing ties with the Dutch at nearby Elmina Castle in 1744. Elsewhere, there coalesced what one scholar has called a Coastal Coalition, becoming what contemporaries called the Fante Nation, unified through a pervasive military culture as well as shared language and religious worship. A 1772 governmental council at Cape Coast Castle reported that "the Ashantes intend to come down upon the Fantees... in a hostile manner." The Council provided guns and gunpowder to the Fantes, whom they termed "pretty much civilized," to use against the "Ashantees... a rude and unpolished set of Men, governed by a despotic tyrannical Prince." Gunpowder, guns, rum, and tobacco were "much wanted all along the Gold Coast."[6] The "Big Men"—like Corrantee and Brew—who controlled the flow of these goods flourished in new ways in this era. Europeans depended on fragile relations brokered with local leaders. As one British official put it, "it is necessary from our present Weakness to keep Black Men of Power in our Pay, that through their Influence, we may live in peace and Amity."[7]

At Anomabu, that boy would have seen men of power; he knew that they enjoyed a life he was now denied. Emerging out of this pernicious combination of West African war and slavery, liberty took on new significance. Another child taken a few years later, in 1761, also first formulated ideas about liberty and slavery in West Africa. Phillis Wheatley came from an area north of the Gold Coast, on a slaving ship, the *Phillis*, in 1761. Since Phillis Wheatley became a published poet, we know more about her sense of liberty than about that of most others of her time. In her adult life, she was sardonic about calls for liberty by enslavers, commenting to a sympathetic Mohegan minister, Samson Occom, on its "strange Absurdity." She continued: "How well the cry for Liberty, and the reverse Disposition for the exercise of oppressive Power over others agree,—I humbly think it does not require the Penetration of a Philosopher to determine." Her cry for Liberty began not in America, but in "the Land of Africa" amid what she, like the Reverend Ezra Stiles, termed "Egyptian slavery."[8]

But what did liberty mean to that boy at Anomabu? It must have seemed impossibly distant. Africans did not agree on its definitions any more than Americans did. Would it have looked like escape and flight from slavery? Would it have looked like a return to the soft arms of his mother, the house of his family, the village life he had in fact lost forever? Would it have looked like a chance to make his own choices, read religious books, carry a gun and fight? He could manage none of those things.[9]

Here is what slavery meant for him: a bleak transatlantic voyage with a hundred fellow captives. The ship was the *Venus*, captained by William Pinnegar out of Rhode Island. As even one British observer, sympathetic to slave traders, framed it, "what a scene of misery and distress is a fully slaved ship. . . . The clanking of chains, the groans of the sick, and the stench of the whole is scarce supportable." What now lay around the boy was a deep and terrifying ocean. The boy survived the seventy-six-day journey to the West Indies, unlike seven others. Once in Jamaica in late March 1757, nearly all of those enslaved on board were sold. One-fifth were children. This boy would have watched, aghast, as others he had come to know well over that dreadful journey together—at least a few of whom could perhaps be counted as family and almost certainly as friends—were taken off the ship, leaving him behind. In fact, they were swallowed up in the voracious maw of Jamaican plantation slavery.[10]

Having been among the first onto the ship, the boy must have been in disbelief to find himself still on it when almost everyone else was gone. Would he ever get off that horrific vessel? Captain Pinnegar didn't linger in Jamaica, loading the ship with molasses and sugar as he hurried on to the final leg of what came to be called "the triangle trade," from Jamaica to Rhode Island. On arrival to Newport, Pinnegar brought the boy to the town minister, Ezra Stiles, who had already paid for him with a barrel of rum the year before.[11]

Here was a world where a man, even a thoughtful New England minister and Yale graduate like Ezra Stiles who loved liberty, could—and did—exchange a barrel of rum for a child to keep as a slave for life. We have met Stiles before, denouncing "Egyptian tyranny." (He later became president of Yale University, and he helped found Brown University.) He named the boy Newport, for his new home, a center of the slave trade—just as Phillis Wheatley had been named for the ship that carried her into American slavery. Marked in their names by the locations of their grim fates, both Phillis and Newport would come to transcend them.

From the 1750s to the 1770s, Newport changed. The boy, who learned English and Congregationalism and how to survive in a New England household, became a man. The town, too, grew larger. Its share of the Atlantic slave trade increased. Rhode Island "rum-men"—so called because captains like Pinnegar carried large quantities of rum, distilled in New England from West Indian molasses and sugar—dominated the American trade. In 1770, Newport's merchants accounted for 70 percent of the American slave trade. By 1774, there were some twelve hundred Black people in Newport, about 14 percent of its population. Like Newport, 87 percent of them were enslaved.[12] The Black community in Newport created networks, forged in places like Anomabu, on slaving ships, at prayer meetings led by a Christian named Sarah Osborn, and around two Congregational churches, the First (led by the Reverend Samuel Hopkins) and Second (by the Reverend Ezra Stiles).[13]

Some of Newport's most devout Christians hailed from Anomabu. Like John Corrantee's sons, John Quamino (also spelled Quamine or Quaum) had been sent from Anomabu for education in the 1750s, with a Rhode Island captain who had illegally sold him.[14] Unredeemed and stuck in slavery, he attended those meetings at Sarah Osborn's house.[15] The Reverend Samuel Hopkins baptized him at the First Congregational Church in 1765. In 1769, John Quamino married a woman called Duchess Channing, described in one Rhode Island memoir as "the daughter of an African prince [with] the bearing of royalty."[16] Duchess lived in slavery in the household of the Newport trader and distiller John Channing. Between 1770 and 1773, Ezra Stiles baptized three children of John and Duchess Quamino.[17] Bristol Yamma married a woman named Phillis, enslaved in another household; they also had children. Another member of the Newport Black community was Obour Tanner. Baptized by Hopkins in 1768, she had likely been on the *Phillis* with Phillis Wheatley; the two formed an enduring friendship.[18]

For John Quamino and Bristol Yamma, liberty was a winning lottery ticket—literally. Lotteries were common in the eighteenth-century Anglophone landscape, and Newport had its share.[19] In the 1770s, these young men had managed to scrape their little cash together to buy a ticket. To their delighted amazement, they won. With their winnings, Quamino bought himself freedom, and with the help of an additional loan, Yamma did too. By August 1773, they were both free, though their wives remained enslaved.[20] With support from Hopkins and Stiles, John Quamino and Bristol Yamma decided to return to West Africa as missionaries. They had good reason to praise the Lord, and they still dreamed of returning home. In preparation, they studied at Princeton under the guidance of its president, John Witherspoon. They were ready to go in 1774.

In 1774, the enslaved man Newport—now close to thirty years old and a member of Stiles's Newport household for nearly two decades—witnessed resistance and war rolling onto the American landscape, just as they had transformed his homelands. He did not leave a diary; Stiles did. With that, and sources from other observers, we can watch events unfold in real time. In the tense winter of 1774–75, in North America, Newport and Ezra Stiles, along with thousands of others, braced themselves for war's arrival. In the aftermath of the first Continental Congress and the Intolerable Acts in 1774, colonists expected word from London of what was going to happen next.

Rumors about guns and powder and troops filled the void; weaponry changed the game on both sides of the Atlantic. Stiles noted in December that governors of every colony had been ordered "to seize all powder & Arms." Stiles also reported as fact (which it was not) that the British had approached French Canadians and the Six Nations Haudenosaunee (or Iroquois) "to joyn the Kings Troops against the Colonies." Worrying news arrived from New York, where its assembly, under the leadership of Tories—supporters of the British government—had supposedly rejected the agreement of the Continental Congress. Stiles stewed over reports that "the Tories are highly elated & laugh & say the *Snake is broken*," a reference to Benjamin Franklin's 1754 snake-of-union emblem that had adorned colonial newspapers in 1765 and again in 1774–75.[21]

Another literate enslaver, this one in South Carolina, Henry Laurens, anticipated that "there will follow infinite trouble & distress throughout the Colonies of North America." He was not wrong. He reported that some of his compatriots were "Red-hot & foolishly talk of Arms." He concluded: "Good God, what are we to do? Nothing less than to destroy each other." His son, John, writing from London, warned his father: "More troops are preparing for America. . . . We should train our Men throughout the Continent to Arms, secure a Retreat for the Old and Weak, and make ready for the worst."[22] The Laurens family committed to the side of protest, with the father eventually becoming the president of the Continental Congress in the 1770s.

As they readied for the worst, colonists awaited word from the king himself, and for the reports of a speech he gave to Parliament in November 1774. As Henry Laurens put it, "I begin to wish with an anxiety not usually intruding upon my peace, for the Kings Speech." This news finally hit the colonies at the end of January 1775. In no uncertain terms, the king condemned the "most daring Spirit of Resistance and Disobedience" and "fresh Violences of a very criminal Nature" in Massachusetts, which had been "countenanced and encouraged" in the other colonies. Parliament affirmed its agreement with this assessment, warning of "all the calamities of a civil war."[23]

With the king's speech, "the die was cast," pronounced Abigail Adams. In a letter to her friend and fellow American political observer Mercy Otis Warren, she contended that George III's speech would "stain with everlasting infamy" his entire reign. Although she confided herself, as a mother and wife, to have "a Heart tremblingly anxious," she also asserted, "We know too well the blessings of freedom, to tamely resign it." "The Sword is now our only, yet dreadful alternative," she concluded. "Sword" was metaphor. What colonists had to have—just like the Fante on the West African coast—were guns and gunpowder. Although Henry Laurens acknowledged a variety of reactions to the king's speech, many thought it foretold conflict. He claimed that "people here are determined never to lose their Liberty but by downright force.— . . . 10,000 will not conquer the Wills of the people." When Americans chose resistance, "then we Shall be applauded by Englishmen & by the Impartial World."[24] Ezra Stiles declared, upon hearing of the speech, "the spirit of the p[eo]ple, instead of being dampt. Rises into determinate Resolution for Resistance."[25]

Buoyed by this rising "Resolution for Resistance," Stiles compiled cheering, if somewhat misleading, stories of other colonies joining the cause. News had broken of the petition to the king, approved by the Jamaica Assembly at the end of December 1774, pointing out that Jamaican leaders had "with deep and silent sorrow, lamented this unrestrained exercise of legislative power," fearful, like their mainland compatriots, of "being reduced to an abject state of slavery, by having an arbitrary Government established in the Colonies."[26] The elite enslavers of the Jamaica Assembly knew well how abject the state of slavery could be. The assembly begged the king to intervene to avert a disastrous war; they were desperate to avoid any problems affecting the import of vital food provisions from the mainland colonies. They also emphasized that they would agree to be bound only by laws to which they had assented. This was a controversial statement, and many in both the West Indies and Britain did not welcome it. Still, in February 1775, Stiles reported with puzzled delight that despite Jamaica's two hundred thousand enslaved people, "Unexpectedly the Politics of Jamaica are altered & they are coming over to the side of American Liberty."[27] Good—if equally suspect—news came from the north, too. Stiles scribbled that inhabitants of Québec had sent a petition to the crown seeking repeal of the Quebec Act.

In 1775, it was still possible for a well-informed person such as Stiles to believe in an alternative geography of resistance, an unruly and unexpected snake of union: one slithering through Jamaica and Québec but not New York. Even by 1775, there was still fluidity regarding which colonies might join this rebellion.

Stiles then offered extraordinary considerations on liberty. He wondered at the refusal of the crown to accept the authority of the Continental Congress. He claimed that "the King must know, the British Parl[iamen]t must know, for the World will know it, that the American Continental Congress of Sept. last was a regular legal patriotic Body." After declaring that the Continental Congress was not just legal but exemplary, Stiles continued: "It holds up Light to Engl[and], to Europe, to the World, to shew to all the enslaved Empires around the Globe, How they may put their Lives in their Hands, & from orderly & regular Congresses for Petitions to Tyrants the Higher Powers, rise into a System of irresistible Vindication & Liberty."[28] Stiles offered a global vision in which all kinds of "enslaved Empires"—that is, those in which oppression prevailed—would be inspired to seize agency and to seek liberty. He saw salvation in "orderly & regular Congresses." The colonies' was to be an organized pursuit of liberty. He also linked two concepts not usually paired: "vindication" (with overtones of justification) and liberty, emphasizing both as religious concepts.

In other words, liberty had Christian connotations, for Stiles and others. Stiles had celebrated the expansion of the British Empire in 1760's Canadian conquest, assuming it would bring "more Liberty, the Liberty of Men and Christians—civil and religious." In 1766, upon the Stamp Act's repeal, the Christian teacher Sarah Osborn had celebrated "precious Liberty . . . used for the Glory of God."[29] Liberty could mean the right to choose a church and a pathway to God.

Meanwhile, amid slavery, Newport sought ways to put his life in his own hands. The very next day, Stiles recorded that he had admitted "my

Negro Servant Newport" into full membership of the Second Congregational Church. In 1775, Newport found Christian liberty and vindication, if not other sorts.

In that mild but nerve-racking winter of 1774–75, Newport, Stiles, and others continued to measure the rise of hostilities. In March 1775, "the News flew like Lightning" that British troops "on a secret Expedition" had landed in radical-leaning Marblehead, Massachusetts, to face a "vast Multitude" of angry locals, with warning guns firing continuously and the soldiers taunting residents by poking them with their bayonets. In this tense atmosphere, the town of Newport did not mark the anniversary of the repeal of the Stamp Act as usual: a "few Boys jingled the Bells a little, but were soon stopt."[30]

"The sword is drawn here," warned an Englishman in April 1775. He encouraged Americans to fight to avoid "submission and slavery," contending that a year of war was worth "the very existence of liberty on the face of this earth."[31] English newspapers reported on the formation of colonial militia units and the movement of British regiments from Ireland to North America.[32] In early April, Stiles witnessed the mustering of the Newport militia, with hundreds cheering them on. On news from Parliament that Americans could be considered "rebellious," "the Friends of Liberty are hereby exasperated & declared themselves ready for the Combat."[33] They did not have to wait long.

On the morning of April 19, 1775, members of the Massachusetts Committee of Safety—the self-appointed group of citizens acting as the local government—alerted "all Friends of American Liberty" to the march of one thousand royal troops to Lexington, where they intended to seize gunpowder. The troops ran into a company of American militia who refused to disperse. Locals said the British fired first; as one soldier testified to the Provincial Congress of Massachusetts: "I heard . . . an officer, say, 'damn them, we will have them,' and with that shots were fired."[34] However, as usual, others disputed this claim.[35] The rebels, aware of British plans to march, had already removed the powder. Eight militiamen were killed in Lexington before troops moved on to Concord. As British troops retreated to Boston, they came under fire from many directions. As the result of skirmishes at Lexington and Concord, 273 men were wounded or killed or went missing.[36]

Vulnerable populations were among the first casualties. Supposedly, houses on the route of the British march were plundered and burned. Soldiers were said to have driven women in childbirth out into the streets and shot old men in their homes. As one witness concluded, such behavior would "disgrace the annals of the most uncivilized Nation."[37] The British commander, Thomas Gage, investigated these accusations, claiming that the soldiers had acted with "tenderness" to young and old with "no vestige of cruelty or barbarity." Somewhat undermining his contention, however, was the admission that "old people, women or children, may have suffered" when troops had fired into houses. However, he defended their actions by asserting that locals had shot at them first.[38]

The British in Massachusetts denounced the conduct of residents during the hostilities. They complained of shots coming from houses, indicating the participation of civilians like women, children, and old men. One British soldier reported (with obvious exaggeration) that five thousand locals fired on them between Concord and Charlestown. Even a woman nursing a baby, he related in disgust, "was seen to fire a Blunderbus . . . from their Windows."[39] He was not impressed with this multitasking mother. Other soldiers reported on the underhanded tactics of the Americans: "they did not fight us like a regular Army, only like Savages, behind Trees and Stone Walls. . . . These People are . . . full as bad as the Indians."[40]

By April 20, reports arrived in Newport that British troops "are now actually engaged in butchering & destroying our Brethren." Stiles declared: "The Town was thrown into Alarm and all went into preparation." Threats came from a British ship in the harbor that Newport would be laid "in ashes" if any local men joined the rebels. On April 21, Stiles noted, "This has been a day of universal Anxiety. . . . All Business is laid aside."[41] That Sunday, he preached on Psalms 79 and 80, lamentations on the horrors of war:

> The dead bodies of thy servants have they given to
> be meat unto the fowls of the heaven, the flesh of

> thy saints unto the beasts of the earth.
> Their blood have they shed like water round about
> Jerusalem; and there was none to bury them.[42]

His mind tormented by images of corpses and a blood-soaked land, he laid down his quill that evening after writing in his diary, "The Times are very affecting."[43]

Even ardent Friends of Liberty stepped gingerly into war; it was fearsome territory. As both Newport and Stiles could have told you, there were plenty of "enslaved Empires" around the globe, yet none of those had taken their lives into their hands quite like this. While there had been plenty of resistance in the early modern era, including in Ireland and Scotland, no British colonies had ever entered into armed conflict with the government in quite this way. The British, and the British American settlers, knew their own history of seventeenth-century revolutions; they also knew that those had not ended well. They knew other wars—like the Seven Years' War—on even more familiar terms. Yet no one in 1775 had any clear guidance or strategy for people who claimed their rights as freeborn Englishmen fighting against His Majesty's troops. To many, it seemed little short of unnatural. Many Friends of Government—called Tories or, later, Loyalists—were not eager to go to war either. Even General Gage waited almost a month after Lexington and Concord to declare military law.[44]

Events in the middle of 1775 propelled further conflict. In May, Lord Dunmore in Virginia tried to seize munitions at Williamsburg; when this attempt failed, Dunmore took refuge on a British ship there.[45] In June, when he reported this event, Ezra Stiles also took delight in the news that every member of the Virginia House of Burgesses had appeared for the meeting wearing homespun, with the slogan LIBERTY OR DEATH either embroidered or painted on their clothing. Women, including enslaved ones, had likely both spun the cloth for the suits and embroidered or painted the motto. Here was a powerful and unheard-of statement of unity, literally worn on the chests of lawmakers. Stiles exulted: "There is a grand & noble Spirit in Virginia!"[46]

In Massachusetts, British generals such as William Howe pushed for further assaults, one of which was attempted at Breed's Hill—near Bunker Hill, for which the battle became known—in June 1775. It was a disaster for the British, and the conflict settled into a grim stalemate.

Meanwhile, the Second Continental Congress had already begun meeting in May 1775. Its members were busy. First, they worked to win friends among Indigenous nations. They even tried to translate their Anglo-American style into language that would resonate among these hoped-for allies. These ham-fisted efforts probably registered as laughable, even offensive, to their intended audiences, but they did try. In April 1775, the Provincial Congress of Massachusetts met with what they called the "Stockbridge Indians," Mohicans represented by a sachem, or leader, Solomon Uhhaunauwaunmut. An experienced diplomat, he had traveled to London in 1766 to seek recognition—which did not come—of Indigenous land rights. Disaffected with British politicians, these Mohicans were more willing to throw in their lot with the Americans. Uhhaunauwaunmut commiserated: "Brothers: I am sorry to hear of this great quarrel between you and Old England." He promised that he and his community would stand with those fighting for freedom, though he warned them that his nation would do so only in their "own Indian way."[47] By June, the Provincial Congress of Massachusetts was asking these communities to send warriors and to help broker alliances with other Indigenous peoples to the west (especially the Six Nation Haudenosaunee, or Iroquois). The Americans used language meant to mirror the stirring eloquence of Native American diplomatic speeches: "We have now made our hatchets, and all our instruments of war, sharp and bright. All the chief counsellors . . . are sitting in the Grand Council-House in *Philadelphia*"—that is, at the Continental Congress.[48]

The Second Continental Congress may have sat in their Grand Council-House, but their overtures also reached beyond Philadelphia to French Canadians. A committee of the First Continental Congress, headed by John Dickinson, had already written a letter to Québec's inhabitants. It explained in patronizing terms how the English government worked, explicating its safeguards (trial by jury, habeas corpus, freedom of the press), which they presumed the French did not enjoy—or maybe even understand. They pointed out that "The injuries of Boston have roused and associated every colony, from Nova-Scotia to Georgia. Your province is the only link wanting to compleat the bright and strong chain of union." They acknowledged that there were religious differences with French Catholics but expressed confidence that the "transcendent nature of liberty" could overcome such distinctions.[49] They commissioned its translation into French, by Pierre Eugène Du Simitière, a Swiss-born American artist and patriot, and its publication by Fleury Mesplet, a French printer then in Philadelphia. They ordered a thousand copies for Canadian distribution.

By early 1775, Québec's governor, Guy Carleton (described by one visiting American as "a man of sour, morose temper"), complained that the letter from the Continental Congress was stirring up the population, by planting dangerous doubts about British imperial authority.[50] On May 1, 1775, the day the Quebec Act took effect, the life-size marble statue of George III in Montréal—erected in gratitude for his assistance following a fire—was vandalized. His face was blackened, and his neck was festooned with mock rosary beads made from potatoes and a sign: LE PAPE DE CANADA OU LE SOT ANGLOIS (The Pope of Canada or the English Fool). Some assumed it had been done to provoke local animosity against the English.[51]

Efforts to win over French Canadians took on greater urgency in the Second Continental Congress. There is a note of desperation in the second letter, drafted by John Jay, Samuel Adams, and Silas Deane, again translated and published by Du Simitière and Mesplet, with a thousand copies printed in French. "We yet entertain hopes of your uniting with us in the defence of our common liberty," pleaded the Continental Congress. They informed Canadians that they all suffered under "tyranny, you and your wives and children are made slaves." The Continental Congress again acknowledged religious differences—"we perceived the fate of the protestant and catholic colonies to be strongly linked"—and urged the Canadians to reject "the fetters of slavery, however artfully polished." They also warned Canadians that if the French joined the war, they would soon be sending their own sons to die in West Indian battles. Finally, they attempted to shame the Canadians into joining:

"We can never believe that the present race of Canadians are so degenerated as to possess neither the spirit, the gallantry, nor the courage of their ancestors." Signed by "Jean Hancock," le "Président du Congrès," this missive prompted discussions in Canada, though it is unclear how effective it was.[52]

Still, in November 1775, George Washington thought that it would be "political" both to invite Canadians to send members to the Continental Congress and to "raise a Regiment or two of Cannadions."[53] If they refused to join, American leaders imagined an easy conquest of Canada, one in which military victory would also "persuade" Canadians and allied Native Americans to join the cause. Canada and its people would become part of the new political union.

The Second Continental Congress also hoped to win at least neutrality from the Haudenosaunee. Its commissioners framed the dispute with Britain in familial terms: "You Indians know how things are proportioned in a family between the father and the son." They painted a picture of "a family quarrel between us and old England . . . We desire you to remain at home, and not join either side." A Mohawk leader, Little Abraham, agreed, taking the opportunity to renew the "friendship chain." The commissioners promised Haudenosaunee representatives that their general, Philip Schuyler, would never "pluck one hair from an Indian's head, or spill one drop of Indian blood." They assured the negotiators that "whatever may happen between us and our enemies, we will never injure or disturb the peace of the *Six Nations*."[54] Americans made a lot of promises in those days—a strategy that would long continue.

The Second Continental Congress also reached out to the Irish. A committee consisting of James Duane, William Livingston, Samuel Adams, and John Adams drafted a letter asserting that the British were bribing "wild and barbarous savages" to kill "innocent and defenceless women and children." They alleged that the British were inciting "domestic insurrections," meaning slave rebellions. They acknowledged that the Irish had their own grievances against the British: "We sympathize with you in your distress." They concluded with a prayer that "iniquitous schemes" of eradicating liberty across the British Empire would soon be defeated.[55] The Irish, who knew British tactics well, were generally sympathetic to the American cause, though they could not send much in the way of practical support. Still, in July 1775, Dubliners apparently toasted: "May the gates of Temple-bar be decorated with the heads of those who advised the employing a military force to enslave our fellow subjects in America."[56]

Encouraged by the Jamaica Assembly's 1774 statement of sympathy, the Second Continental Congress also sought to bring Jamaicans into the fold. They appointed yet another committee—William Hooper, James Wilson, and Thomas Lynch. Their missive recognized that "the peculiar situation of your Island forbids your assistance," by which they meant its enormous population of enslaved people and its vulnerable Caribbean location. Conceding that their own nonexportation of provisions had led to food shortages, they advised Jamaicans to convert their "sugar plantations into fields of grain"—an impracticable solution. Still, they continued: "But why should we make any apology to the patriotic Assembly of Jamaica, who know so well the value of Liberty; . . . and who foresee how certainly the destruction of ours must be followed by the destruction of their own?" They pointed out to Jamaicans enduring a shortage of provisions that authorities had permitted the famine in Bengal, sacrificing "the lives of millions to the gratification of their insatiable avarice and lust of power." Jamaicans did not find this letter terribly persuasive.[57]

The Continental Congress also established the Continental Army to transform a disparate set of militias into a single fighting force. To lead this army, the congress chose a man with considerable military experience (during the Seven Years' War) who was also intelligent, charming, and tall (a favored attribute among military leaders): George Washington. From Virginia—a location deemed necessary to convey the "Continental" aspect to New Englanders already fighting—he was also rich enough from plantations worked by enslaved people not to require compensation, thereby clinching the deal. He turned out to have other advantages, including a lifelong immunity to smallpox conferred by an earlier infection.[58] Even as Washington accepted congratulations from colleagues on becoming the commander of the Continental Army, he must already have been dreading composing the letter to his wife, Martha, knowing that she would hardly welcome the news that he would not be home for dinner for quite some time. In a note gift-wrapped in "the prettiest Muslin" (for two new outfits for her) and soothing words, he assured her that "so far from seeking this appointment I have used every endeavour in my power to avoid it." A master of self-deprecation, he fretted whether he was equal to the task. He encouraged her "to summon your whole fortitude & Resolution" to endure their time apart.[59] It would turn out to be a lot longer than either of them anticipated in July 1775.

To accompany George Washington on his trip to Massachusetts, the Continental Congress generated another document to convey to the British the "Causes and Necessity of their taking up Arms." Yet another committee—John Rutledge, John Dickinson, and Thomas Jefferson—formulated it, complaining once again of the tyranny imposed on the colonies. They contended that Governor Carleton was stirring up Canadians and Native American allies to attack them. They argued that they had to turn to arms because the British had already done so in order "to effect their cruel and impolitic purpose of enslaving these Colonies by violence."[60] There had already been rumblings in Virginia about the possibility of the British inciting enslaved people, with a report in the House of Burgesses that there was "A Scheme, the most diabolical ... to offer Freedom to our Slaves, and to turn them against their Masters."[61]

At the same time, though, the Continental Congress hedged its bets by also formulating the "Olive Branch Petition," seeking peace. An additional committee—John Dickinson, the lead author, along with John Jay, Benjamin Franklin, Thomas Johnson, and John Rutledge—drafted this statement. They pointed to the enduring loyalty of the colonists even though they had been grumbling about their treatment since 1763. They emphasized their love for the monarchy. They hoped the king, like a good father, would interpose himself between Parliament and the colonists so as to effect "a happy and permanent reconciliation."[62] By the time this statement reached ministers in London, the king had already issued a royal proclamation that the mainland colonies were in "open and avowed Rebellion" and should be treated as traitors. Therefore, he refused the petition, although it was subsequently published in London newspapers. Opinion was hardening on both sides of the Atlantic. That same summer, one British observer near Fort Pitt wrote with dismay that locals were "Liberty mad, nothing but War is thought of."[63]

In 1775, many Americans were preparing for war by seeking to prevent rebellions on the part of enslaved people. In June, Henry Laurens in South Carolina informed his son, John, that he had assembled enslaved people to warn them "to behave with great circumspection in these dangerous times."[64] Looking for subversion and possible insurrection, enslavers like Laurens tended to find it, with an alleged "design & attempt to encourage our Negroes to Rebellion & joining the King's Troops."[65] The leader of this supposed plot was Thomas Jeremiah, an established pilot and fisherman who had lived in Charles Town for decades.[66] He was also one of the richest free Black men there. Henry Laurens described him as "a forward fellow, puffed up by prosperity, ruined by Luxury & debauchery & grown to an amazing pitch of vanity & ambition & withal a very Silly Coxcomb." Coxcomb was another word for fop, the kind of man who wore bright waistcoats and carried a fancy cane. "Ruined by debauchery" held a whiff of sexual impropriety. In other words, Jeremiah was a sharp dresser and a popular man about town, as well as an astute businessman and a vigorous defender of his rights. None of these qualities endeared him to Laurens and many others of his class. Indeed, men like Laurens had literally given a sentence of castration to a Black man accused of attempting "to ravish a white Woman" in Virginia in June of that same year.[67]

On the basis of flimsy evidence and witness statements subsequently retracted, Thomas Jeremiah was convicted of planning an insurrection. He had prominent defenders, including clergymen and even the attorney general, who argued that his status as a free Black should protect him. As Henry Laurens wrote in disgust, "one of them threw Magna Carta in the Faces of the people," apparently seeking to present Jeremiah's rights in the hallowed English tradition of resistance to overweening authority. Even South Carolina's royal governor, William Campbell—an ambitious Scot unpopular with locals—intervened to try to save Jeremiah. After threats of violence, though, Campbell backed down, writing in frustrated despair: "I find I cannot save him."[68] In August, Jeremiah was executed. News of this episode did not help the patriot cause in England. Even Henry Laurens's own son, John, then living in London, reported that people there were appalled at the colonists' lack of "justice and humanity."[69]

Another ambitious Scottish governor provoked even more ire among enslavers in 1775. On November 7, Lord Dunmore finally did what he had earlier threatened to do: offer liberty to enslaved or indentured men "that are able and willing to bear arms, they joining his Majesty's troops."[70] Dunmore founded the Ethiopian Regiment, comprising Black men who had fled slavery. The reference to Ethiopia invoked a long and proud tradition of African Christianity and wisdom.[71]

In offering to arm enslaved men, Dunmore punched enslavers squarely in the gut. In the *Pennsylvania Journal,* Dunmore's proclamation appeared after a poem stating there was no "devil more damn'd" than Dunmore. George Washington wished him dead: "the World would be happily rid of a Monster without any person sustaining a loss."[72] Such is the language of fury, from a leader known for his calm. Ezra Stiles, an enslaver, noted that Dunmore had recruited more than two thousand soldiers into a "Black Regiment with the Inscription on their Breasts LIBERTY TO SLAVES." Here was the startling sartorial counterpoint to the Virginia assembly members appearing with LIBERTY OR DEATH. This time, Stiles did not rejoice in the "grand and noble spirit" of liberty in Virginia; he recorded no comment.

Enslaved Africans with liberty on their chests and minds pushed men like Stiles to think harder about freedom. It is possible to see this process at work in terms of his Congregational colleague in Connecticut, the Reverend Levi Hart. Hart had helped to train John Quamino and Bristol Yamma for their West African mission. Shortly after their departure from his home, Hart delivered and published a sermon, *Liberty: Described and Recommended,* on a verse from Isaiah (61:1): "The Spirit of the Lord God is upon me, because he hath anointed me—to proclaim Liberty to the Captives."[73] Hart defined liberty as "a power of action . . . and a freedom from force."[74] He delineated four types of liberty: civil, religious, ecclesiastical, and spiritual. So far there is nothing exceptional here, but then Hart pivoted, moving in for the kill. He challenged his listeners: If they rejoiced in living in "this land of liberty where the spirit of freedom glows," how, then, could they participate in the "*horrible slave-trade*?"[75] He advised: "let us for once put ourselves in the place of the unhappy Negroes,"[76] concluding: "Who can count us the true friends of liberty as long as we . . . publicly connive at slavery?"[77]

"Unhappy" enslaved people themselves—Quamino, Yamma, and also local people—had prompted Hart to argue against slavery. In the very autumn that Hart delivered this stinging rebuke of a sermon, enslaved people wrote the first petition against slavery to the Sons of Liberty in Connecticut. They opened: "Your characters, as *sons of* liberty, oblige us to think *you* the most zealous assertors of the *natural* rights and liberties of mankind . . . which encourages us, poor unhappy Africans." They continued that they knew that "LIBERTY . . . is as necessary to the happiness of an African, as it is to . . . an Englishman."[78]

John Quamino and Bristol Yamma also influenced Hart's friend, the Reverend Samuel Hopkins in Newport. Like Hart, Hopkins started to question the inconsistency of slavery in a land of liberty. He even wrote to the Continental Congress to win funding for the West African mission and to argue against slavery.[79] Although Quamino and Yamma had received further training from the Princeton president and Scottish minister John Witherspoon, politics intervened to scuttle the mission. Although the West African enterprise had received money and "good encouragement in England and Scotland," the war had halted communication and funding. Hopkins sought support from Congress instead, arguing that "Africans have as good a Right to defend their Liberty as we have." He denounced the inconsistencies of so-called Friends of Liberty, contending that the slave trade and slavery were "inconsistent with . . . our struggle for liberty." He argued that Americans had enjoyed "almost miraculous . . . success" because of divine approval of "their opposition to unrighteousness and tyranny, and struggle for liberty."[80] Despite Hopkins's pleas, Congress never offered its support for the West African mission.

Still, other Africans began advocating for liberty in print. "Thy Power, O Liberty, makes strong the weak / And . . . Ethiopians speak," declared Phillis Wheatley. Liberty could strengthen the voice of even the marginalized. Similar themes animate the frontispiece of her book of poems, likely based on a rendering by the notable Black artist Scipio Moor-

In this rare visual portrayal of an African woman in the eighteenth century—the frontispiece to her 1773 book of poems—Phillis Wheatley, depicted holding a pen and composing a poem, evinces wisdom, thoughtfulness, and decorum.

head.[81] Depicted as a female genius, Wheatley in modest clothing with a black ribbon around her neck ponders her thoughts, with quill, ink, paper, and book before her. We have already seen how she linked her "love of Freedom" with her origins in "Afric's fancy'd happy seat." In a letter to the Mohegan Reverend Samson Occom, published in 1774, she asserted: "God has implanted a Principle, which we call Love of Freedom; it is impatient of Oppression and pants for Deliverance."[82]

Even as they literally wore it on their chests, though, people of this era fumbled and lurched toward liberty. It had many meanings. One headstrong sixteen-year-old, Baikia Harvey, had decided to leave the remote Orkney Islands off the north coast of Scotland to "seek a better way of living," coming as an indentured servant to the American colonies. Unlike Newport and others, he had had a choice, but by 1775, he regretted the one he had made, writing to his godfather back in Scotland, "I am vere sorry that I did not take your Advice and stay at home." Finding his indenture intolerable, he had run away, joining the American army "against a sett of people they call Torrys." He noted that some of his fellow soldiers were "Little Boys not Bigger than my Self... & all their Cry is Liberty or Death." He hardly understood what this phrase, or this war, meant. His main takeaway was to warn his godfather not to let any other Scots come over "for the Americans will Kill them Like Deer in the Woods." What did liberty mean for Harvey? To him, it seemed simply a war whoop for boys, a vacuous motto for a prejudiced and hostile people. Harvey's story did not end well; he was killed fighting in South Carolina in 1779, at age twenty-one, in a war he seems to have only dimly understood.[83]

In personal writings, some women also pondered whether liberty applied to them. "I can't help exclaiming now and then, dreadful fruits of Liberty," declared Margaret Livingston in a 1776 letter to her sister. Unlike men with their "romantic notions" of the goddess Liberty, Livingston contended, women were unlikely to gain much since "our Sex are *doomed* to be obedient in every stage of life."[84] Others were equally sardonic. One woman, Grace Growden Galloway, enduring an unhappy marriage, penned a ditty:

> never get Tyed to a Man
> for when once you are yoked
> 'Tis all a Mere Joke
> of seeing your freedom again.[85]

The yoke connecting the couple could be a heavy burden, especially when it was almost impossible to obtain a legal divorce. Growden connected autonomy with being single. She was neither the first nor the last person to see freedom in intimate terms.

"I am a Friend to American Liberty," Ezra Stiles declared. What exactly did he mean? People like Stiles struggled to understand how liberty operated, and whether and how some forms of slavery (including racial slavery) could be compatible with liberty. There was no single voice on this issue in this era. Men like Henry Laurens found little incompatibility in being both pro-liberty and pro-slavery. Yet even Henry's own son, John, had quite different views, increasingly seeing the system of slavery as inconsistent with liberty. In 1773, Stiles was sanguine that the cause of American liberty would eventually prevail, though he did not know how, exactly. Still, he proclaimed, "I have perfect Confidence that the future Millions of America will emancipate themselves from all foreign Oppression."[86]

Other men beyond the American rebels sought liberty, joining the Ethiopian Regiment. The costs were high. Without adequately preparing the new regiment, Dunmore attacked Virginia militiamen at Great Bridge, the route to Norfolk, on December 9, 1775, with five hundred "volunteers and blacks." They sustained heavy losses, resulting in a "vast effusion of blood on the bridge."[87] Lord Dunmore and the Ethiopian Regiment captured the attention of many, including the Reverend Samuel Hopkins. He did not agree with Dunmore's politics, but he did think the enslaved should be freed. In December 1775, he informed the Continental Congress: "the conduct of Lord Dunmore . . . in . . . promising . . . liberty" showed that the only way to defeat the British was by "granting freedom . . . ourselves."[88]

In the meantime, John Quamino, finally free after decades of slavery, gave up on going to West Africa as a missionary. Instead he volunteered for military service to support the American rebellion. He wanted to show his commitment to liberty, and he probably also wanted to earn the money to buy his wife's—and his children's—freedom.[89] Even for free people, liberty could be dear and slow in coming. To win their freedom, he left his wife and children and went off to fight.

For all that its cry has been "Liberty or Death," Americans have long struggled to comprehend and to enact freedom for all—as the enslaved man Newport well knew. As he had done for decades, Newport worked to build community in the town of Newport, his presence—and perhaps his conversations—forcing Stiles and others to start to consider the moral quandaries of slavery. Although he was now a full member of the Second Congregational Church, and an equal in Christian liberty, this young man, rising from the dark corner of a slave ship, remained enslaved in Stiles's household throughout 1775. The cry of "Liberty" would continue to sound throughout a wider Atlantic world, echoing north to Canada.

Chapter 6

A Wall in Québec

"The weather is very severe indeed!" acknowledged even a Canadian on the last short, dark day of December 1775.[1] Soldiers fumbled to get their frozen fingers on the triggers of their muskets, firing into the dark. Pelted with wet, heavy snow, men struggled to keep their powder dry as they loaded their muskets from powder horns.[2] "Snowing and blowing very hard" recorded a laconic Continental Army soldier, Jeremiah Greenman.[3] Continental Army forces had been besieging the city of Québec for some weeks, with a "hot cannonading" in the chill.[4] Today was to be the final assault. Before dawn, he and other men crept toward the city, "with hearts unda[u]nted to scale the wals." They were a motley crew, this young army, wearing mismatched clothing, including, somewhat confusingly, old British military uniforms from the Seven Years' War.[5] Pinned to their random assortment of hats, pulled low over their cold ears, were scrawled handmade signs proclaiming LIBERTY OR DEATH.[6] Some of Greenman's comrades were trying to ignore blisters caused by new boots rubbing on feet that had been bare for months. Others felt a little woozy, trying to swallow away the telltale scratchiness building in their throats. Under the cover of that blizzard, and despite the challenges, these Continental Army soldiers looked forward to taking Québec.

In 1775, Québec carried heavy symbolic freight for colonists. Greenman, born in May 1758, was likely only just toddling on tiny feet when red-coated soldiers had conquered the city in September 1759 during the Seven Years' War. That month, forces under British General James Wolfe—himself shot and killed in the fighting, thus becoming a celebrated martyr for Britain and Protestantism—won the Battle of the Plains of Abraham just outside the city. The Greenmans likely exulted over the news, as most British colonists did.[7] The British had taken Canada.

Growing up in Newport, Rhode Island, Jeremiah Greenman would have heard about this monumental victory and the death of Wolfe, which may have fired his decision to enlist at seventeen; maybe his options were also limited. Joining up offered this young man—educated, but not very well—a chance to earn money and to work toward independence. He seems to have been orphaned early, which made everything harder.[8] The ambition of a man like him was personal independence—making money, marrying, supporting a family. As daunting as war was, he threw his shoulders back, stood up straight, and marched. He was eager to prove himself and to bring home glory (and wages). Traversing the northern wilderness that russet autumn of 1775, the first of this war, these eager young soldiers dreamed of becoming heroes in the sequel to 1759's epic drama. Men are so often fighting the last war (and, in some cases, wearing its moth-eaten uniforms).

Independence remained in the distance in late 1775. By July 4, there

This 1760 image shows the British victory at the Plains of Abraham outside the city of Québec in 1759.

would be a declaration, asserting in its final paragraph that the "United Colonies" (thirteen of them) were now "Free and Independent States" (a phrase that appears twice in that important last paragraph). Canada appeared there as a "neighbouring Province" that served as a dangerous example of "Arbitrary government" for the abolition of "the free System of English laws." In late 1775, however, Canada looked less like a neighbo(u)r and more like a friend, soon to be part of a fuller United Colonies. Much changed in the following six months.

To leaders like George Washington, in late 1775, Québec seemed the key to strengthening those United Colonies and perhaps ending the fighting. In the autumn of 1775, Richard Henry Lee predicted to his friend Catharine Macaulay that Congress would soon add Canadian delegates to "complete the union of 14 provinces."[9] In 1775, some Canadians, too, saw a future in which they would be united with the lower colonies. One innkeeper held meetings in 1775 "to foster the spirit of rebellion" in his Canadian parish, speaking "scornfully of royalist leaders."[10] Washington and others assumed that the French and Indigenous people of Canada—so recently and awkwardly integrated into the British Empire—would rush to join the cause of liberty against the British.

Strange to say, U.S. independence had origins in what is now Canada. That last short day of 1775 shaped 1776—and beyond. Two nations emerged amid the frigid darkness of revolution and war, as the momentum toward independence rolled forward like a snowball. Things could have gone so differently. What happened in Québec in 1775–76 mattered—for what became Canada and for what became the United States of America.

A charming Irishman led the Continental campaign in Canada in 1775. A veteran of both the Seven Years' War and Pontiac's War, Richard Montgomery had abruptly resigned his British military commission and moved to New York in the 1770s, volunteering his services when fighting began in 1775. His second-in-command was the energetic and irrepressible Benedict Arnold. Arnold assured the Continental Congress in June 1775 that a force of only two thousand men could "very easily" conquer both Montréal and Québec. He argued that such a victory would help "to discourage the enemies of American liberty... restoring that solid peace and harmony between Great Britain and her Colonies."[11] Others at this time imagined that Indigenous First Nations in Canada would also join the French in fighting the British so that "Quebeck will be taken."[12] Canada's Irish governor (and veteran of the battle of the Plains of Abraham)—Sir Guy Carleton—appeared to have few soldiers at his command. The British ministry was slow in sending reinforcements.

"Quebeck in its present defenceless State must fall into [Arnold's] Hands an easy Prey," agreed George Washington in a letter to the Continental Congress in September 1775. He informed the congress that since both Canadian and Indigenous allies had urged this American conquest, he had sent Arnold and one thousand men to conquer the city.[13] Ezra Stiles also believed that Canadians themselves had requested this plan.[14] It was a pincer strategy. Montgomery moved his troops from Lake Champlain up the St. Lawrence to Québec while Arnold marched his men, including Greenman, up to the Chaudière River through the heavy woods of what is now Maine. Along the way, Montgomery and his troops managed to take St. John and then, an even greater coup, Montréal at the end of November.

The monarchy looked to be toppling in Canada. That marble sculpture of George III, vandalized earlier in Montréal in 1775, was now beheaded altogether, to the cheers of the soldiers stationed there.[15] Hailing "our colonial brothers," one local lawyer (on behalf of many) informed Montgomery that "our chains are broken, and a happy freedom restores us to ourselves—a freedom which we have long desired."[16] The next step was to join forces at Québec to take that city and thus the province.

What became Québec City, in Québec Province, had been among the first places founded as part of the colony of New France in 1608. In 1775, the entire settler population of the province was 70,000, with about 110,000 in what is now Canada as a whole. (By way of comparison, Connecticut alone had 200,000 settlers, so the population disparity was considerable.)[17] It was a diverse population, with *habitants* (farmers), *coureurs de bois* (traders), and Indigenous people of diverse nations (see photo section page 1). Most of its inhabitants were Francophone

Catholics. It had become part of the British Empire only in 1759–60; it remained French in character. The Upper Town was surrounded on several sides by steep ground; stone walls protected the other sides. The Lower Town, isolated on a tip of land, consisted of a narrow strip of houses, with a couple of streets running along the St. Lawrence River. Paths between them wound up the rocky hillside.

Scaling the walls of Québec City was a challenging prospect, especially in winter. In December 1775, the Lower Town was well defended "by the quantitys of ice and snow heaped up." One Friend of Government there envisioned the Continental Army invaders on ladders failing to take Québec, with the government's forces looking down on them with arms folded, smirking and smug: "It will be a fatal attempt for them; they'll never scale the walls."[18] Montgomery and Arnold believed otherwise; they knew that liberty and strong soldiers could surmount mere walls. The plan was for Montgomery's forces to take the Upper Town, while Arnold's forces would conquer the Lower. They imagined that grateful *habitants* would emerge to hail the Continental Army as liberators, with the province joining the common cause.

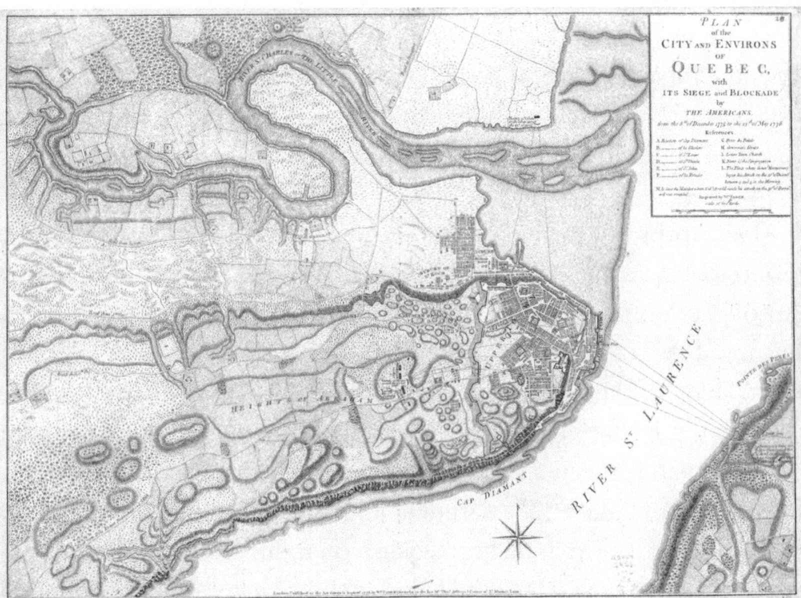

This plan of Québec City and its environs shows the attempted—and failed—conquest of the city by Continental Army forces in 1775–76.

There was every reason for American optimism. There had already been those campaigns by the First and Second Continental Congress to woo French Canadians. Its *habitants* were assumed to resent the British government, as just about everyone else—including the French in France itself—did. Québec residents had sent wheat to support *les Bostonnais* when their port was closed in 1774. Americans such as John Hancock imagined that French Canadians and Indigenous Americans—still smarting from the Seven Years' War and Pontiac's War—would be delighted to throw off the yoke of the British Empire, hailing the Continental troops as heroes. He thought early Canadian victories showed that the "Smiles of Providence" shone over their cause.[19] Guy Carleton claimed to be able to rally ten thousand troops, but one New York major scoffed that Carleton would be lucky to find "10 *willing* men in all Canada."[20] One Boston newspaper proclaimed: "from the friendly disposition of the Canadians and the Savages, joined to the intrepidity of the Continental Army, there is a fair prospect of the speedy reduction of the metropolis of Canada to the obedience of the United Colonies."[21] It was a cheering if thoroughly jumbled message: Canada a metropolis? Friendly First Nation and French Catholic enemies? Allies reduced to obedience? Nothing here quite made sense, but no one wanted to think too hard about it. The point was: Everything was looking good in late 1775.

This optimism turned out to be misplaced, given the state of the Continental Army. After a grueling trip north, the soldiers under Arnold's command were far from fighting fit. They lacked food, clothing, and blankets. Even in September, George Washington, knowing that "Many of the Men have been without Blankets," worried "to see the Winter, fast approaching upon a naked Army."[22] One soldier on Arnold's march, the nineteen-year-old Aaron Burr, described his transformation from bookish law student into "shirtman"—and his odd array of donated attire—in light-hearted fashion to his sister. His outfit consisted of boots, coarse wool trousers, a short jacket, a fringed hunting shirt "from a Southern Gentleman," and an outlandish hat topped with a foxtail and feather that made the five-foot-six Burr look taller—"the

Donor I suppose meant to help my Deficiency in Point of Size." There was one indispensable item: "My Blanket is slung on my Back, as that's a thing I never trust [away] from me." He concluded: "add a Tommahawk, Gun, Bayonet, &c. and you have your brother Aaron—And pray how do you like him?"[23]

The lack of winter clothing, especially boots, in the face of the impending Canadian winter was no joke, though. Despite his eccentric outfit, Burr was one of the more fortunate soldiers. By late November, one recruit complained, "Our army [is] almost barefooted," noting that they had to take the day at a standstill so that the few shoemakers among them could cobble together shoes with leather stolen from the British.[24] Montgomery worried to his wife that Arnold's men were "half-starved and half-naked."[25] In early December, as a *douceur* (or inducement), he ordered a suit of clothes and a dollar for each soldier.[26]

Continental Army supply problems went beyond textiles. The soldiers were hungry. On the march north, they were reduced to foraging—and worse. By November, one soldier lamented, "Set out weak and faint, having nothing at all to eat; the ground covered with snow. . . . Eat part of hind quarter of a dog for supper; we are in a pitiful condition."[27] Jeremiah Greenman—an urban kid and "certainly not an experienced woodsman," as the editors of his diary phrased it—recorded being dropped "up to our arm pits in water and very cold," clambering up muddy hills in rain and snow, and being forced to eat squirrel, candle wicks, and, yes, dogs.[28] The soldiers' emaciated bodies, pale faces, and thick "monstrous" beards—very much *not* the fashion in the 1770s—alarmed some locals along the route.[29] However, they could not slow down to wait for supplies (or razors) or even to hunt or fish. Washington and the other leaders knew that the term of service for the first enlistees was expiring at the end of calendar year 1775, so time was of the essence. Washington also knew that pay was running short and so "the greater Part of the Troops are in a State not far from Mutiny."[30]

Other disasters awaited, sly and unseen. Malnourished and crowded into camps with rudimentary facilities, soldiers were supremely vulnerable to the worst scourge of the era. "The small pox very [rife] among our troops," recorded Greenman in December 1775.[31] Just before the battle, one soldier, Caleb Haskell, stricken with smallpox himself, noted that one of the men in his room died, and that "all of the houses in the neighborhood are full of our soldiers with the small-pox." Soldiers were not inoculated against it at this stage. At least Richard Montgomery had already had smallpox, so he was able to lead the forces into battle.

In the end, though, in 1775, the Americans matched the British in Québec in 1759 in only one important respect: They got a martyr too. The weather was "inconceivably" cold. "This is no wall scaling weather," crowed one loyal Canadian.[32] Before Montgomery's men could even reach those walls on December 31, though, they came under heavy fire, "cannon roaring like thunder and musket balls flying like hail."[33] Carleton and his men were ready for them. There was little cover, and the conditions made it almost impossible even to see far in front of their faces. Things went from bad to worse quite quickly when Montgomery and one of his aides-de-camp were shot and killed. His men retreated in confusion. Arnold's forces were left "to fight for our Selvs," as Greenman wrote in consternation.[34] They did not last long. Arnold was wounded and carried off the field. Caleb Haskell, too ill to fight, heard that "Every Captain in Colonel Arnold's party was killed or taken."[35] Once the high command was decimated, it was a mess. To Carleton's fewer than twenty casualties, there were more than eighty on the American side, and one-third of their forces, some four hundred soldiers including Jeremiah Greenman, taken prisoner.[36]

1776 opened in misery for the Continental soldiers. Even hardy New Englanders such as Caleb Haskell found "the weather almost unendurable by reason of the cold."[37] The snow lay thickly drifted, blanketing the horrors. British soldiers located the corpse of Montgomery, his hand, frozen, above the bank of snow, his bayonet beside him.[38] They did their best to give this distinguished veteran of so many British battles—a "genteel man and an agreeable companion," as even his enemies conceded—a proper burial, despite the difficulty of digging out the hard earth.[39]

Confined to close quarters, the smallpox continued to run rampant among the POWs, squeezed into the Jesuit ("Jessewit," as Greenman wrote) College. He lamented, "we have no room. Not a nuf to lay down to sleep."[40] Close to one hundred of them apparently renounced the rebellion and took an oath of loyalty to the king, or so Canadians reported.[41] Since the service term for many like Haskell had expired, in theory, they could leave. In practice, they often could not. When Haskell, recovered from smallpox, along with others in his company, refused to join another company, since they were "freemen," they were court-martialed for disobedience.[42]

Altogether, the attack on Québec was a dismal failure for the Continental Army due to smallpox, disorganization, poor supplies, and the folly of attempting a Canadian siege in winter. There was a reason that the Battle of the Plains of Abraham had taken place in September. As one Pennsylvania newspaper put it, "who but enthusiasts for Liberty could carry on a siege [there] at such a season of the year?"[43] In the eighteenth century, "enthusiasts" was generally an insult, like calling them maniacs for liberty. There were other, subtler reasons for this lack of success. Although Guy Carleton was a somewhat "sour" man, he was no fool. He knew the challenges of a direct assault on the city. The British had fought the French in 1759 on the fields outside the city—the Plains of Abraham—because of the difficulty of attacking the city itself. In fact, when the French attempted to besiege and retake the city in 1760, the British held it.

Carleton and others also worked hard to counteract what he described as "the Consequences of an Infection" with "the Minds of the People poisoned" thanks to radical southerners.[44] Those who imagined Canadian sympathies with the common cause were not wrong. In 1775, there were plenty of *habitants* along the St. Lawrence and the Chaudière rivers who sympathized with *les Bostonnais* (as locals called all those of the lower colonies). One official in the parish of Sainte Marie admitted that instead of arresting spies, he had helped them on their way, "and several had even slept in his house." Authorities blamed his misbehavior on the fact that he had been "corrupted by his wife," who had "made a thousand disparaging remarks about the priests" and other government supporters in the parish.[45] On the Ile d'Orléans, an island north of Québec, there were others who "made trouble." Two cousins were identified as "the most dangerous men in this parish." However, in fact, the most terrifying rebel there was apparently a woman, Madame Chabot. "With her subversive spirit," she went door to door to drum up support for the common cause. This Canadian Friend of Liberty had "perverted almost all the people" in her parish.

However, Canadian supporters of the revolutionary cause did not gain the upper hand. There were Friends of Government among both the French and the English. The Catholic Church, a powerful voice, urged parishioners to support the government. The Quebec Act had done a great deal to placate many French Canadians since it allowed them to practice Catholicism and to retain French laws and some offices. The Americans were a more uncertain prospect, as Friends of Government—especially the priests—emphasized.[46] The government-sponsored *Quebec Gazette* warned Canadians not to be "seduced and intimidated by wicked men and rebels" who would not allow Catholics to practice "the religion professed by your ancestors."[47]

What does not explain the lack of success in Canada are the most common explanations: that locals were passive, wedded to social order, or simply opportunistic. Men like John Adams were contemptuous at the time of Canadian ability to explain and understand political processes. Even the congressional addresses, though translated into French, assumed a patronizing tone. They explained their aims s-l-o-w-l-y and LOUDLY in hopes these foreigners would understand their lofty ambitions and their vision of liberty.

Friends of Government in Québec could be equally contemptuous of ordinary folk, portraying the rebels as "propagating false news to intimidate the Country people, who . . . swallow any ridiculous tale."[48] This same officer noted that once the Americans had been vanquished by the spring of 1776, "The peasants come sneaking in with a few eggs, or a pat of butter [to sell]—conscious of their disloyal conduct, they are meanly submissive—ask any of them the price of what he has, 'Oh my dear sir, it's for you to name the price—I am content with whatever pleases you.'"[49]

Historians have tended to echo these kinds of assessments, assuming passivity or at least a tendency toward "social order and loyalty" among *les habitants*, with one account declaring: "There were no enlightened leaders in the Province of Quebec."[50] That is not the case. There were women like Madame Chabot, energetic and "subversive," anticlerical and pro-rebellion. There were men like "Jeremiah Duggan lately a hair dresser in this place, [who] has the title of Major and heads five Hundred Canadian rebels."[51] Some Friends of Government apparently had more dread of some of their "fellow Citizens than of the declared rebels."[52]

What, then, *does* explain the lack of Canadian support? The short answer is the behavior of the Continental Army and the lack of financial credit on the part of the United Colonies. The soldiers' unruly behavior confirmed the suspicions of many French Canadians that they had more to fear from Protestant New Englanders than from the British. Even before the attack on Québec in December 1775, Continental soldiers had already set fire to several houses and "killed a french woman," as Greenman casually recorded.[53] This kind of collateral damage had an effect. One anonymous notice posted in Montréal in January 1776 asked "what Benefit they cou'd Expect to reap from so mobby a Banditry . . . without money without Arms without Discipline without Clothes and without Credit."[54] As Continental troops occupied Montréal and other areas into the spring, things went from bad to worse. Continental soldiers, unpaid and still largely unfed, pillaged local farms and houses.[55] By April, Major General Philip Schuyler lamented "the Licentiousness of our Troops in Canada" who indulged in "scandalous Excesses."[56]

The lack of supplies among Continental soldiers gave locals pause. It seemed unlikely that these poorly provisioned people could successfully achieve their goals. By May 1776, many there assumed Congress had "not Credit enough" to procure goods.[57] In Madame Chabot's parish, for instance, three *habitants* had joined the Continental Army with enthusiasm. They had returned disaffected after four months' service, having received no pay at all beyond a pair of shoes.[58] In another town, Ursuline nuns tended wounded Continental soldiers. When their attorney sought reimbursement for food and medicine, an officer advised him to tell the nuns "to have patience and they will be paid." The lawyer replied with acerbic wit: "I am going to tell these Ladies to feed your soldiers patience; we'll see how fat they'll be." The sisters were still seeking restitution for these costs many years after the war.[59]

Indigenous allies of the French were also skeptical of claims of friendship. British officials in Canada noted that they were able to muster close to fifteen hundred Indigenous soldiers in October 1775. They alleged that if the British marched against the rebels, "Late as the Season is, they will joyn them."[60] Meanwhile, the rebels were losing support among the Haudenosaunee (Six Nations, or Iroquois). A Mohawk leader, Thayendanegea (Joseph Brant), reported to Lord George Germain, the British secretary of state for the colonies, that "The Disturbances in America give great Trouble to all our Nations." He reported that "many strange stories have been told to us by the people in that country." Such tales worried Indigenous allies. Winter conflicts between Indigenous soldiers and rebels in Canada had resulted in the death and wounding of many of the strongest Indigenous men. According to Thayendanegea, "no White people" had shown up to support their efforts, resulting in losses that disproportionately affected the Six Nations.[61]

"Strange stories" and grim realities of conflict, misunderstandings, and lack of payment all contributed to turn potential Indigenous, French, and English allies in Canada against the American rebels. Even a begging letter from the Continental Congress in early 1776—in which they informed Canadians that "your liberty, your honor and your happiness are essentially and necessarily connected with the unhappy contest" and thanked them for services to "the common cause"—had little effect.[62] An ineffectual diplomatic mission in the spring of 1776, led by an ailing Benjamin Franklin and including awkward Maryland Catholics such as Charles Carroll of Carrollton, did little to restore Canadian confidence in American promises.[63] As Carroll recorded in May 1776, "we found all things in much confusion, extreme disorder, and negligence, our credit sunk."[64] The commissioners reported, "Our Enemies take the advantage of this Distress, to make Us look contemptible in the Eyes of the Canadians." The behavior of the Continental Army had apparently "contributed much to Changing their good Dispositions towards Us into Enmity." The commissioners recommended that if more money could not be sent immediately, it would be better to withdraw from Canada altogether.[65]

In other words, Americans fumbled both war and diplomacy in Canada. They squandered the goodwill and high hopes of rebels like Madame Chabot and Jeremiah Duggan. As one of Schuyler's underlings in Montréal informed him in the spring of 1776, "we have bro't about ourselves by Mismanagement what Governor Carlton himself could never effect": the near-complete loss of support among Canadians.[66]

Meanwhile, in the lower colonies, "Melancholy Tidings!" of the defeat and death of Montgomery reached *les Bostonnais* in January 1776.[67] In Cambridge, Massachusetts, George Washington received the "melancholy account of the unfortunate attack on the City of Quebec, attended with the fall of General Montgomery" on January 17.[68] That same month, an English writer published a broadside in Philadelphia, dedicating half of the profits from sales "for mittens for the troops that were going to Quebec."[69] That would have been a lot of mittens, because the publication was the best-selling pamphlet of eighteenth-century North America: *Common Sense.*

Thomas Paine did not use *Common Sense* merely to vandalize the marble monarchy, to which many Americans still felt an attachment. Instead, with swift, sure strokes, he beheaded it altogether. With vigor, Paine argued for "independence," invoking it more than thirty times. Stating that "I[ndependence] is the only Bond that can tye and keep us together," he offered several arguments in its favor. He asserted that independence from Britain was the only way to settle American affairs, to avoid civil wars, to avert tyranny, to improve finances, and to be taken seriously on the world stage. On this last point, he reminded his readers that at that moment, as colonies, they had no international standing. Only "by an Independence" could Americans "rank with other nations." He acknowledged that people had "fear respecting Independence" because they could not imagine a new form of government; "men do not see their way out." He disputed the idea that "the infant state of the Colonies" was a concern, asserting that this youthful energy was actually "an argument in favour of Independence." Paine pushed Americans to avoid procrastination, because "until an Independence is declared, the Continent will feel itself like a man who continues putting off some unpleasant business from day to day, yet knows it must be done." Such action, however unpleasant, was overdue. The king's speech had "prepared a way for the manly principles of Independence," and really "the

Independency of America" had already started, with 1775's first shots. In short, for Paine, "the Independency of this continent" was inevitable.[70]

Given the glum mood after the defeat in Québec, Paine's arguments landed squarely in the public mind. "A masterly irresistible performance," pronounced Major General Charles Lee in a letter to George Washington. Much of its success had to do with timing. As Lee put it, "Poor Brave Montgomery! But it is not a time to cry but to revenge."[71] One British official in Jamaica condemned *Common Sense* as "a most traitorous libel . . . expressive of the intentions of the North Americans from the beginning."[72] This curmudgeon had a point: Most of Paine's contentions had been in circulation for some time. Still, no one had put them together with such brio, making them so accessible at just this critical moment. Another critic denounced it as "One of the vilest things that ever was published," ruing that after its appearance, "Nothing but Independence will go down. The Devil is in the people."[73]

Paine proffered a sword to cut the ties with Britain. Many like Lee, smarting from the humiliation of defeat in Canada and the untimely death of Montgomery, snatched it out of his hands, ready to rush into battle. As early as 1768, one European visitor had contended that there was "such a great spirit of independence" in the colonies that with better communication and organization, the colonists would easily be able to form an independent nation.[74] They were now ready to take up the challenge.

The United States of America was starting to take shape. One military administrator, Stephen Moylan—from Ireland, with experience in Portugal and France—hoped in a January 1776 letter that he could become its ambassador: "I should Like vastly to go with full and ample powers from the United States of America, to Spain."[75] The use by this cosmopolitan Irishman of the phrase "United States of America" appears to be its first occurrence in writing.

Not everyone was entirely convinced. William Smith—the man given the commission to preach Montgomery's funeral oration in February 1776—included in it a public wish for reconciliation. He lauded Montgomery for having recognized that "the sword of civil destruction, once drawn, is not easily sheathed."[76] He had a point. Still, this sermon irked so many in the Continental Congress that they refused to print it.

The death of an Irishman in Canada propelled many other Americans to agree, though, that independence was the right path. Montgomery was the man of the hour, forming the focus for a nation uncertain of next steps in the wake of this unexpected defeat. Smith lauded him for his "tender regard towards his own army," and one poet, Ann Eliza Bleecker, praised "the softer virtues in his bosom."[77] Altogether, his death provoked an outpouring of heartfelt, if mostly mediocre, poetry, orations, and stories, including an acrostic poem in a Maryland newspaper, spelling out RICHARD MONTGOMERY down the page with lines on the order of

> O truly great! In courage thus t'excel,
> Montcalm and Wolfe, who likewise nobly fell!
> Each brave American laments thy fate.[78]

(Marylanders showed their adoration by naming Montgomery County for him.) Smith, too, linked Montgomery and Wolfe, finding them "animated with a kindred spirit."[79] Bleecker compared him to "gallant Wolfe."

Few of these authors acknowledged that Wolfe's death in Québec came amid victory while Montgomery fell leading his men into defeat. The comparisons allowed many to connect to a nobler past without dwelling on their stunning ability to snatch defeat from the jaws of victory. No one mentioned this discomfiting point in their poems and orations—no one, that is, except Tom Paine, who lingered on the defeat and noted that Montgomery did not "expire like the brave General Wolfe, in the arms of victory."[80]

In fact, Paine capitalized on the momentum for independence by publishing a dialogue between the ghost of Richard Montgomery and an American delegate in February 1776. Montgomery's apparition mouthed many of *Common Sense*'s arguments for independence: "I am sent here . . . to warn you against listening to terms of accommodation." Montgomery's ghost used his bayonet to poke and prod Americans toward independence, declaring that the connection with Britain was "unnatural and unnecessary," its "monarchy and aristocracy . . . vehicles of slavery."[81]

The grave loss in Canada precipitated the Declaration of Independence, created with an eye to France and Spain as allies. The Continental Army had lost friends and made enemies in a place where they should have done better. The Canadian disaster reinforced the inadequacies of the current system of supply. One anxious letter from Charles Lee to John Hancock in April 1776 had noted that all the soldiers and officers were competent "but horribly deficient in arms, shoes, and blankets." He knew that it was impossible to get arms, but he had implored Hancock for blankets in hopes that "a multitude of lives would be saved."[82]

To obtain the help it needed, the newly named United States of America had to become an independent nation. Few nations would intervene in a colonial rebellion against another nation, but they might be willing to join a war waged by an independent nation against the hated British. As Robert Livingston, Richard Montgomery's brother-in-law, observed, France was a good prospect for "foreign aid."[83] Sam Adams agreed that France would "openly lend her Aid... if America would declare herself free and independent."[84] As James Warren, a New England Friend of Liberty, wrote in a late 1775 letter to John Adams, they could not "Admit of foreign powers while you Continue to Acknowledge A dependency on Britain." James's wife, Mercy Otis Warren, a writer, was blunter. She advised Adams that the rebels "should no longer piddle at the Threshold. It is Time to Leap."[85]

Many rebels were ready to leap. In 1775, even before fighting began and certainly after, there was a time where it seemed that independence *could* happen. By early 1776, after Paine's *Common Sense,* it seemed to many that it *should* happen. By the spring of that year, with the disgrace of the failure to take Canada and the desperate need for supplies, it seemed that it *must* happen.

Still, there were endless disagreements about what form a new nation should take. No one had a clear sense of what would work best. Newspapers ran all kinds of articles about the advantages and dangers of independence. Many repeated the concerns raised and refuted by Paine, but there were others. "Is it Common Sense, or common Nonsense?" inquired one author in April 1776, arguing against a formal declaration of independence. This writer focused on the two likeliest allies: Spain and France, questioning how useful Spain would be when "the government of her own unwieldy Colonies is already a weight which she can hardly bear." The Spanish would worry over "our seducing her own American subjects," leading to future revolts. France was yet more dangerous, likely to want Canada back and also prone to "bloody massacres, the revocation of sacred edicts, and the most unrelenting persecutions." After all, the French were "strangers to Liberty."[86] Another author, arguing for independence, assumed that some in the audience would think that "France will be for invading Canada or the Floridas, and thus we shall forever be involved in war."[87]

There were many counterarguments for independence, some verging on the ridiculous. One Virginia writer in 1776 denounced "this squeamishness about independence" and exhorted those in the "United States of America" to choose the right path. Nothing surprising here, except that this was the first appearance in print of the phrase "the United States of America," only recently coined in private letters. Another pro-independence author assumed that France "seems prepared to give [assistance]; and, if she does, England must desist from her cruel plan of enslaving the Colonies."[88] Others painted grim if far-fetched pictures of what reconciliation might bring: "Great Britain may convert her African into an American Company of Slave-traders, and send her ships to carry her white negroes to the West-Indies to work her sugar plantations."[89] Here was an extreme version of the common claim that Britain sought to enslave America. Others denounced Britain as "a prodigious mass of corruption." This same author contended that if they remained linked, Britain would never make financial restitution for losses already incurred, and so the "credit of our paper money will sink, and we shall be beggared and ruined. Independence is the only thing that can save us." The author concluded, "let us assert Independence and Freedom with an open and manly boldness."[90] Another pro-independence writer advised that the Continental Congress should take a recess in order "to consult their constituents about that important question," since "Congress should . . . only echo back the sentiments of the people. This can only be done through the medium of Committees and Conventions."[91]

"Committees and Conventions": it might be the least thrilling revolutionary rallying cry ever. Such phrases indicated something important about the nature of this revolution, and its transatlantic origins in the kind of solidarities that created the Pantheon Society in Edinburgh as well as many civic institutions. This national declaration, it was suggested, should be built on the local and state declarations that had preceded it, in turn coming out of local meetings and drafts.[92]

As they groped their way to a new nation, revolutionary Americans could be so earnest. These were no French *sans-culottes* (wearing workers' trousers rather than gentlemen's breeches), full of spit and fire. These men very much had their elegant culottes—or breeches—on when they attended those consultations. Their commitment to meetings and yet more meetings, to correspondence and consultations, was second to none in 1775–76. Here was a group endeavor, orderly and legalistic and accessible—at least to those wearing the culottes. Among that particular segment of the population, it allowed for a cross-section of participants, so that most every committee had someone from New England and the mid-Atlantic and the South; this range of representation was important. They were taking their lives into their hands, yes, but in a measured and thoughtful and balanced way. Here was the image Americans loved to project to the world, and it was a major aspect of this Revolution—but not the only one.

Independence became an offer that could not be refused. The elite men writing newspaper articles and filling the Continental Congress wanted it all to appear reasonable, universal, and enlightened. Yet the engine thrumming away under the rubric of Committees and Conventions was the brutal partisan violence we have already seen, the threats, the beatings, the tarrings and featherings. The fact that this machine ran powerfully on its own allowed these elite men to disavow violence even while benefiting from it. They did not need to mob and threaten. The people "out of doors" did it for them. These same months saw ordinary folk—a milkman in New York, for instance—threatened and imprisoned for supporting the crown—simply by drinking the traditional toasts to King George when tipsy at a tavern.[93]

When the Declaration of Independence came, it emerged, of course, out of Committees and Conventions, pushed to the top of the full agenda by a series of events outside those thirteen colonies. In May, the Second Continental Congress voted for the creation of a new American government, a move forwarded by John Adams. As this welter of state building began, news from other countries tipped the balance in favor of moving to the full and formal independence of what was becoming the United States of America.

The Canadian situation remained discouraging. Even in January, George Washington had predicted to Benedict Arnold that the course of the war in 1776 hinged on Canada: "to whomsoever It belongs . . . will the Ballance turn." He predicted that if his forces did not take Canada, "the contest at best, will be doubtfull, hazardous and bloody."[94] In April, Robert Morris worried that if Canada should go to the British, "they will soon raise a Nest of Hornets on our backs that will Sting us to the quick."[95]

Yet members of the Second Continental Congress remained hopeful—about Canada, the military, and Indigenous allies. A mustering of troops in Philadelphia in May 1776 buoyed flagging spirits. Members of the congress, along with Washington and other officers, reviewed several battalions, three companies of artillery, and the light horse brigade. In addition, "21 Indians of the Six Nations . . . gave the Congress a War-dance," a performance suggesting Haudenosaunee solidarity.[96] As Schuyler had observed to Washington in April, "I am perfectly in Sentiment with you my dear General that we ought to engage the Indians to co-operate with us; but I fear it will be a difficult . . . Task to accomplish, unless Canada should be entirely in our possession."[97]

Then news arrived that the British government was contracting with foreign mercenary soldiers. On June 7, 1776, at the Continental Congress, Richard Henry Lee introduced a resolution for a formal declaration of independence: "That these United Colonies are, and of right ought to be, free and independent States."[98] Such a move was vital "for forming foreign Alliances." He explained in a letter to another Virginia planter his reasoning for bringing this motion forward: "our enemies are determined upon the absolute conquest and subduction of N. America. It is not choice then but necessity that calls for Independence, as the only means by which Foreign Alliance can be obtained." A note on the letter by its recipient summarized it thus: "our Independence is by compulsion."[99]

Not everyone at the congress—or elsewhere—agreed that this leap was advisable. John Dickinson, that Pennsylvania lawyer who had advocated for resistance in 1767–68 and 1773–74, did not think formal independence was the right move. He thought it would be better to ensure foreign aid first. He contended, with a certain degree of justification, that a declaration would hold little meaning, since "foreign Powers will not rely on Words." He argued that they should await help from the French, as otherwise they would have "Destroy[ed] a House before We have got an[other] [for] the Winter." He also warned that the war unleashed might be severe, with burning of towns and the "Sett[ing] Loose [of] Ind[ians] on our Frontiers." Despite Dickinson's not unreasonable concerns, the momentum was for independence. He abstained from the vote, and he continued to serve the new nation.[100]

Independence brought excitement—and of course more committees. Once the resolution for independence had passed (agreed to by all but New York—though they later voted in favor), three separate committees were appointed. One was to draft the declaration. A second was to work on foreign alliances. A third was to figure out the best plan for confederation. The first committee included John Adams, who had been pushing for independence for months; Thomas Jefferson, well known as an author of a radical pamphlet in 1774; Benjamin Franklin from Philadelphia, brilliant but at this stage not very well; a Connecticut lawyer, Roger Sherman; and the New York lawyer, Robert Livingston. While Thomas Jefferson was the lead author, his was not the only voice here; the declaration went through a committee with several important edits from Adams. On July 2, Congress voted formally to declare independence. They then spent the next two days altering and shortening the committee's draft. They cut about one-quarter of the original text, to ensure a pithy statement that would fit into a single-page broadside for wide publication. They cut a long passage excoriating George III for entering into the African slave trade and encouraging enslaved people to rise up (a dig at the dastardly Dunmore). They also shortened a section berating the king for sending over "foreign mercenaries."

What did they keep? They retained the opening paragraph assuring the other "Powers of the Earth" that they had "a decent Respect to the Opinions of Mankind." It was critical to position the United States not as a set of rebellious colonies but as a nation assuming its "separate and equal" station. They asserted their commitment to the notion that "all Men are created equal, that they are endowed by their Creator with certain unalienable Rights, that among these are Life, Liberty, and the Pursuit of Happiness." They submitted the "facts" of the tyranny of George III "to a candid World." "Candid" was a pleasing word choice. It meant fair, but it also implied, as a notable eighteenth-century dictionary had it, "free from malice; not desirous to find faults."[101] They put their case before a world they assumed would be not just impartial but well disposed toward them; once again, earnest American optimism shines.

The Declaration included that long list of grievances against the king, circling around his skirting of the law and his willingness to wage war against his own colonies and highlighting his "cutting off our Trade with all Parts of the World." They evinced horror at his decision to bring "large Armies of foreign Mercenaries" to America and to encourage "merciless Indian Savages" to attack settlers. They asserted the right, indeed the absolute necessity, to transform themselves from "these United Colonies" to "FREE AND INDEPENDENT STATES."[102]

Even once independence was declared—published as a broadside on July 4, 1776, by the Philadelphia printer John Dunlap—these committee men in their culottes remained busy. The second committee, for foreign relations, had its origins in an earlier Committee of Secret Correspondence including John Dickinson, Benjamin Franklin, Benjamin Harrison, John Jay, and Thomas Johnson. Silas Deane, a New England merchant, had already been sent on a secret mission to France in March 1776, to purchase *matériel.* Franklin, Dickinson, and Harrison remained on the committee, joined by John Adams and Robert Morris, the financial genius of the new nation. Adams drafted the treaty with France that, with the Declaration of Independence, formed what one historian has called "mutually interlocking foreign policy documents."[103]

In fact, though, the very first nations to recognize the United States formally were Indigenous ones: the "St Johns and Micmack Tribes of Indians" concluded "A Treaty of Alliance and Friendship" with the new United States of America on July 19, 1776.[104]

With one member from each of the thirteen colonies—now states—the third committee produced the Articles of Confederation. Their work proved the most protracted and contentious; the Articles were not accepted until 1777 and not ratified until 1781. This document also dealt, though more obliquely, with foreign powers. John Dickinson was the lead author here. His vision—shared by some but not, as it turned out, by all—treated the Haudenosaunee and other Indigenous nations as significant political and diplomatic players. He imagined a system in which the United States, rather than individual states, regulated trade and diplomacy with Indigenous nations, as with any other sovereign foreign power. The early draft of the Articles called for "a perpetual alliance offensive & defensive" with the Six Nations with "their lands to be Secured to them and not Encroached on." This plan included federal Indian agents and protections for Indian trade and land. This draft would have required congressional consent to go to war with an Indigenous nation. An exception was made if Indigenous nations invaded a state, at which point a state could go to war—but only in the event of actual invasion.[105]

In the final version, these provisions ensuring that Indigenous nations were treated as such by the new American one were subsequently excised or watered down, so that states became the main arbiters of negotiations with Indigenous nations. It also allowed states to go to war on the mere report of an impending attack by Indians (but only by Indians—states could not go to war due to an attack by any other foreign power) rather than an actual invasion. By the final version of the Articles, there were only two mentions of Indigenous nations, neither of which acknowledged their sovereignty.

By contrast, the Articles, in both draft and final forms, acknowledged explicitly that Canada could join the union. In fact, in November 1777, the Continental Congress ordered that the Articles be translated into French and efforts be launched toward "conciliating the affections of the Canadians towards these United States."[106] This new United States of America was more willing to see a settler nation like Canada brought into the fold than an Indigenous one, and the Six Nations—long major political players—went unmentioned in the final version. This bifurcation between two groups often linked in 1775–76 was significant. The shape of this independent nation was starting to solidify in particular ways.

In May 1776, Jeremiah Greenman turned eighteen. He should now have been on the road to personal independence. Instead, he remained broke and forlorn, stuck in a Québec prison "very discontented and quite out of hope of ever being" released. He rejoiced when a captain visited and "gave me a Coupel of Shirts & a pair of Trowses [trousers] with Sum Sugar & tea." These gifts sweetened the last month or so of Greenman's time as a prisoner of war in Canada. He would not be freed until August, still "without Shoes." He recorded nothing about the Declaration of Independence in 1776, though in September he did note with relief "I got me a pair of Shoes"—a first step to one kind of independence.[107] Independence mattered at both a personal and a national level. It could be unnerving, though.[108] Both kinds of independence could also be illusory, since individuals and nations remained connected in complex webs of interdependence.[109]

In the meantime, though, in Greenman's hometown, Newport, there was a celebration of national independence. The Rhode Island Assembly endorsed the Declaration, reading it aloud, followed by the firing of thirteen cannon and thirteen musket volleys.[110] The town turned out for the celebrations. Rhode Island's own version of the Declaration had already appeared in the newspaper in June.[111]

On July 9, 1776, Washington himself read the national Declaration of Independence to the huzzahs of his troops. In these same days, though, tens of thousands of British and other soldiers and sailors were landing in New York. Amid the optimism of that week, Washington may have recalled a moment of pessimism, his own words from January 1776, about what would happen if that new United States of America did not manage to conquer Canada. Whether he remembered them or not, Washington and those who cheered that Declaration—including those in Newport—soon found that this contest would indeed turn out to be "doubtfull, hazardous and bloody."

Chapter 7

A Village in Hessen-Kassel

Grim tales emerged from the villages of this blood-soaked land. Despite some happy endings, the stories—many still familiar—were bleak. One girl, Cinderella, endures menial labor, harsh commands from her stepmother, and the cruel taunts of her stepsisters, who later cut parts of their own feet off in order to jam them, bleeding, into the elegant glass slipper proffered by a prince. A scheming stepmother—an evil witch disguised as a comely queen—plots the murder of an innocent daughter, Snow White, by poisonous apple. The impoverished parents of two hapless children, Hansel and Gretel, send them into the forest knowing full well that a child-eating witch lives there in an enticing gingerbread house. In the sagas from Hessen-Kassel in what is now Germany, unfit protectors propelled vulnerable young people to make their own uncertain way across a menacing landscape.

Spangenberg Castle in Hesse, perched on a wooded hill, looked like the perfect setting for a prince holding a glass slipper. It dominated the timbered town of Spangenberg and thus the youth of Andreas Wiederhold, who became one of the "Hessian mercenaries" so feared and despised by the Americans. Growing up in that town, Wiederhold probably heard the fairy tales. In one such story, now little known, a father makes a bad deal with the devil that sees him forced to hand over his beloved twelve-year-old son. The boy survives a series of misadventures—including falling in love with a talking snake who turns out to be a princess—to become the king of the Golden Mountain. When he returns home to his parents, though, they do not recognize him. How had their sweet little boy become the deep-voiced, hairy,

This seventeenth-century depiction of Spangenberg shows the castle on the hill to the left overlooking the main part of the town.

strapping fighter now standing in front of them? To show them the truth, he is obliged to give up the trappings of a king as well as the safety of his own royal wife and son, and to endure several further challenges. He proves himself, but it costs him dearly. When he finally stumbles home, armed only with a magic sword wrested from giants, he finds his wife about to marry another. Fury possesses him. He dispenses with civility and turns to unrestrained violence, beheading his wife and everyone else in the kingdom. The story concluded: "All at once they all lay there in blood, and he was once again King of the Golden Mountain."[1] Power came at a high and bloody cost.

Unexpected as it may seem, wars—including the American Revolutionary War—thrum in the background of at least a few fairy tales. They speak of the particular pain of the eighteenth century, when beloved boys from Hessen-Kassel were forced to become fierce, unrecognizable soldiers. The vulnerability of these boys and their families can be traced in more obvious places such as records of the military, petitions to authorities, and payouts to princes. Yet they surface, too, in tales collected by the Brothers Grimm, published in the early nineteenth century. The Grimm brothers grew up in Hessen-Kassel, where they were inspired to record these narratives, related by older women—including one who had lost her husband in the American campaigns.[2]

In the United States in 1776, locals also told tales of betrayal and brutality. "He is at this time transporting large Armies of foreign Mercenaries to compleat the works of death, desolation, and tyranny," wrote the authors of the Declaration of Independence of King George III. Indeed, this unfit protector was guilty of "Cruelty & perfidy scarcely paralleled in the most barbarous ages." Such actions were "totally unworthy the Head of a civilized nation." Even in war, leaders were supposed to be practitioners of civility.

The American Revolutionary War transformed boys into men. Sometimes it also made them into monsters. The importance of civility emanates from invocations of its opposites: cruelty, barbarity, brutality. One Friend of Liberty reported that both Hessian and British troops had behaved with "savage Barbarity."[3] Another blamed the fire that engulfed New York City in 1776 on the "ungovernable Brutality [of] those Men monsters the Hessians."[4] "We shall have a severe trial this summer," fretted another in May 1776, "with Britons, Hessians, Hanoverians, Indians, negroes and every other butcher the gracious King of Britain can hire against us."[5] Here were the bogeymen of Revolutionary America, a motley and terrifying crew.

Civility was a complicated issue. Some forms of violence could be enacted by civilized people, but other forms—especially as directed at civilians, above all at women and children—also influenced the course of the Revolutionary War. In recent years, historians have emphasized brutality in this war.[6] Yet distinctions here are important. Some violations were sporadic, committed by individual soldiers in the heat of the moment. Others were systematic, ordered by officers. Some enemies were treated with respect as "brothers" while others counted as "barbarians" against whom violence could legitimately be unleashed.[7]

Americans imagined that the Hessians, hired by the king, ignored dictates of civility, law, and decency. The Hessians—and the British—believed the same of Americans, who fired on the British and Germans "like savages" in guerrilla warfare. People on each side told tales about the other, denouncing their way of conducting war by redefining them as uncivilized villains. One Hessian prisoner of war in 1777 recorded that locals who had heard stories about these "Men monsters" came in droves to view them but left disappointed: "They had come to see strange animals and found to their disgust that we looked like human beings."[8]

The human beings of Hessen-Kassel, including Andreas Wiederhold, knew the agonies of war firsthand. Several battles of the Seven Years' War were fought there, as had happened in the War of Spanish Succession of the 1740s. In fact, the French—fighting the British and their German-speaking allies—had captured Spangenberg Castle in 1758. In 1759, the same year the British prevailed against the French at the Plains of Abraham in Québec, the French had a much more major victory at the tiny village of Bergen, near Frankfurt, in Hessen. Compared even to the most significant North American battles, such as that of the Plains of Abraham—involving eight thousand troops altogether from both sides—numbers involved in the Battle of Bergen are staggering. The combined forces of allied troops from Hessen, Hanover, Brunswick, and Britain amounted to at least 24,000, with 2,500 casualties, against French forces of 30,000, with 1,800 casualties.[9] Imagine tens of thousands of soldiers, many on horseback, massed in the fields and woods and hills around this little place; the locals were overrun. That was even before more than four thousand men and boys "all lay there in blood."

Hessian soldiers exemplified a severe military culture, exploited for international deals. By 1775–76, there was one soldier for every four households there.[10] People even in other German regions considered Hessians "barbarians," reported Andreas Wiederhold as he traveled from Hesse through Hanover to North America.[11] Frederick, the landgrave, or ruler, of Hessen-Kassel, decided to deploy Hessian soldiers by offering them to George III. In late 1775, the landgrave negotiated a treaty with Great Britain to provide soldiers for pay, knowing that many of them, a few still children, would be wounded or killed thousands of miles from home. Although mercenaries had long served in Europe, no one had ever sent them across the Atlantic. Even the British diplomats who negotiated the treaty conceded "that the Service is new in its Nature, & at a Great Distance," and the soldiers would require "some Encouragement to engage cheerfully."[12]

Between 1776 and 1783, Britain offered encouragement to the leaders of Hessen-Kassel to the tune of £3,000,000.[13] They also brokered deals with several other rulers. In most of these agreements, troops received pay and provisions equivalent to those of their British coun-

This 1778 drawing captures how a Hessian grenadier with his distinctive miter-shaped metal helmet and boots looked to Americans in the 1770s.

terparts, but with "blood money" clauses, giving the ruler an additional payment, for instance, for each three men wounded and for each one killed.[14]

Like the king of the Golden Mountain, then, the landgrave Frederick had blood on his soft hands, and it seeps into the stories the people there told. Even a fellow ruler, Frederick the Great of Prussia, condemned the uncivil behavior of the other Frederick who had "sold his subjects to the English, as one sells cattle to be slaughtered.... I pity those poor Hessians who will terminate their careers unfortunately as well as unnecessarily in America."[15] Englishmen, too, viewed this arrangement with dismay. Frederick Bull, an MP sympathetic to the American cause, gave an impassioned speech to Parliament in 1776: "The war you are now waging is an unjust one... founded in oppression, and its end will be distress and disgrace." He concluded: "Let not the historian be obliged to say that... the German slave was hired to subdue the sons of Englishmen and of freemen."[16]

"Those poor Hessians" were in service for neither liberty nor loyalty. They were there to make money for a prince and the region—although also for themselves and their families. Boys and men were often forced into military service, at which time they had to leave their families and take an oath of obedience to the landgrave. High-ranking leaders favored tall recruits and often bartered to obtain men of greater height.[17] Although they were all called Hessians, these soldiers—close to thirty thousand by the end of the war—in fact came from six German-speaking regions: Hessen-Kassel, Hessen-Hanau, Braunschweig-Wolfenbüttel, Anhalt-Zerbst, Ansbach-Bayreuth, and Waldec.[18]

In Hessen-Kassel, authorities used conscription. Sons expecting to inherit property were exempt, so the burden fell on poorer men, labeled "available" or even "expendable" (*abkömmlich* or *entbehrlich*), a chilling description of a human being. Authorities opted where possible to conscript foreigners (*Ausländer*) instead of natives (*Landeskinder*). Such decisions meant that not all the soldiers from a particular area were actually from that region; one-quarter of troops sent from Hessen were not from Hessen. They mostly came from other German-speaking areas, but a few came from places farther afield such as Ireland, Portugal, and Russia.[19]

Rules—often ignored—stipulated that conscripted soldiers should be between seventeen and forty-five and above five feet three *zoll* (about five feet four inches, or 164 cm), so they could handle the long ramrod of their musket, with sufficient teeth strong enough to tear open powder cartridges.[20] However, since officials had quotas to fill, older men missing teeth and boys not yet at full height were ground in the gears of this war machine. One British officer wrinkled his nose at the group of Hessian conscripts sent to him whom he described as "a very unequal Body of Men, a great many very old & very exceptionable [that is, objectionable], a larger number very young who will not grow better."[21] Still, they bolstered British numbers considerably, leading many to hope for a swift end to the war.

A few German-speaking officers went voluntarily, if not with joy, viewing American service as a chance for heroism—and promotion. One was Colonel Friedrich Adolf von Riedesel, Baron of Eisenbach, soon promoted to major general, tasked with commanding the first contingent of German-speaking troops sent over. He left his wife, pregnant with their fifth child, declaring that his "heart was broken" but advising her that "we must... not complain." Still, since officers sometimes brought their wives and families abroad, this couple decided that she should join him in North America. Once the baroness had given birth to their third surviving child, she bundled up their four-year-old, two-year-old, and ten-week-old for the long voyage across the Atlantic, which, as she noted, "took all my courage."[22]

Before Riedesel departed, people helpfully recounted disturbing tales of lost travelers, storms at sea, shipwrecks, hungry cannibals, and toothy, terrifying Americans who, she was warned with breathless certainty, "ate horsemeat and cats." A calm pragmatist, she was most concerned about "going into a strange country where I did not understand the language." She needed all her serenity even before she left Europe. She faced chilly nights at remote taverns with "suspicious-looking" hosts and rooms full of weapons. While they were riding through a Dutch forest at dusk, a heavy object crashed onto the top of her carriage. When she reached out a cautious hand, she felt the scratchy woolen stocking on the cold leg of a hanged man. While out walking in Bristol, England, sporting a fashionable Continental chintz dress with green taffeta, sailors surrounded her, laughing and jeering "French whore." She rushed into a nearby shop to shake off the hostile, leering crowd of men. She went home and promptly gave the dress away

An engraving of a portrait of the baroness at the time of her marriage (in 1762) to Baron von Riedesel.

"although it was still quite new." It was only after sixteen months of such misadventures—involving friends who turned treacherous, challenging living arrangements, depleted finances, and a slow journey—that she was reunited with her husband in Canada.[23]

In 1776, two English brothers also experienced a series of misadventures in North America. They were the commanders of British forces: Admiral Richard Howe, the leader of the British naval fleet in North America, and General William Howe, head of the British armed forces there. Both were also Members of Parliament. Even as they spearheaded Britain's war effort, they were hopeful about the prospects for peace. Richard and William had served during the Seven Years' War (William had fought at the Battle of the Plains of Abraham in 1759, during which he had led forces scaling the Heights of Abraham).[24] Richard was serious and blessed with equanimity, William was livelier. When the ship carrying Richard Howe to North America ran into a dreadful storm and began to heave and rock on the waves, everyone else, panicking, "reeled to & fro" almost at "their Wits end." Before Howe's secretary, Ambrose Serle, went to cower under his bedclothes "to prepare . . . for Death," he observed in amazement that amid the bedlam, Howe "possessed himself with great Composure."[25]

The Howe brothers may have been resolute, but neither was especially hawkish. In fact, William had opposed the Coercive Acts in 1774.[26] However, they were prepared to do their duty by king and country. They were keen to act both as peace commissioners and military leaders; they hoped to beat the rebels but also to offer generous terms to terminate once and for all this unnatural war. They imagined that many, if not most, Americans favored loyalty. They expected that in New York, they would find many loyal subjects who would help them quell the rebellion. In the meantime, they would bring the might of the British Empire to bear.

Since 1776 had opened with news of the resounding defeat of the Americans at Québec, many Britons including the Howe brothers assumed that it would not take long to finish the job. By summer 1776, British and German forces by the thousands were heading to North

America, where their momentum seemed unstoppable. With no little smugness, the Earl of Sandwich congratulated the Earl of Suffolk on obtaining the German mercenaries: "I am persuaded [they] will have the desired effect, and convince the colonists at last that we are in earnest."[27]

In late June 1776, New Yorkers witnessed a remarkable sight: more than one hundred British ships arriving en masse. Under the command of General William Howe, they were carrying nine thousand British troops. Shortly thereafter, on July 12, another 150 ships arrived there, too, under the command of his brother. They carried another eleven thousand troops as well as ten thousand sailors. Altogether, it was the largest set of British forces ever assembled in mainland North America, with two-thirds of its army, almost half the navy, and an additional eight thousand Hessian troops.[28] Among them was one of the recruits at the upper end of the age limit: Andreas Wiederhold, in his mid-forties.[29]

The arrival of these ships was an extraordinary show of British force, under the command of these two brothers. These British and German forces (thirty-eight thousand) exceeded the entire population of Philadelphia, the largest city in North America (thirty thousand). These regiments had been well drilled and supplied, and they were ready to fight. The Continental Army had only nineteen thousand troops, badly supplied.

The Hessians themselves relished the prospect of victory. One Hessian soldier in harbor, eager to make landfall, dreamed of "fighting for honor, country, meat, and vegetables." He rubbed his hands together as he registered the cannon fire they could already hear from the ship: "it is certain that terror and discord are among them."[30] Andreas Wiederhold exalted in the four hundred ships in the bay: "One cannot describe how terrifying this looks." He used a little English for a sardonic observation: "I think that *Mister* Wassington [i.e., General Washington], who is the commander in New York, must have a bit of a headache."[31]

"*Mister* Wassington" soon had more than a headache, as the two armies met in ominous silence on Long Island on August 27, 1776. On a "cool clear & pleasant" morning, each side assembled troops in battle formation: a display of military strength. The rebels "with Colors flying" lined up on a ridge. For nearly an hour, each side "stood looking at each other, almost without a Shot."[32] Yet, as one woman observed, "seventeen thousand Men have not landed to look at one another."[33] Washington had nine thousand troops there, a sizable proportion of his army, but not all of it (he thought the first attack would be on Manhattan). Howe started with fifteen thousand, soon twenty thousand, men, and he added recently arrived Hessians. Each side awaited the order to fire. When it came, it did so with a bang—and a British feint, as Howe and his forces took a back route to attack from behind as well.

The Battle of Long Island was a disaster for the Continental Army. Washington managed to survive and escape, informing John Hancock that he had been riding for close to forty-eight hours "and never closed my eyes" and was even now "much hurried & Engaged."[34] He reported the loss of a thousand men (against fewer than four hundred for the British) and the capture of Generals Sullivan and Stirling.[35] Wiederhold wrote home that "the dead and wounded are impossible to report, because they are still lying all over the woods."[36] After this, it was a mere matter of days before the British took New York City, which they did after the Battle of Kip's Bay in the middle of September. They held it for the entirety of the Revolutionary War.

Wiederhold reflected on civility in a letter he sent about the Battle of Long Island. He reported that he had taken nineteen American soldiers as prisoners. The men had fallen on their knees before him, at which point he made them "beg the king for mercy and pardon." After that, though, he carried the wounded to the surgeon, gave them bread and rum, and "treated them humanely." Apparently, the men were surprised but grateful, and they did not want to leave him. According to Wiederhold, their officers had warned them that they could expect no such humane treatment from the monstrous Hessians, who would "scalp them, mutilate all their limbs, and whatever other such atrocities there are." Wiederhold, indignant, observed, "these are the acts of monsters and barbarians . . . not of civilized regular troops like we were."[37] The well-trained Hessians saw themselves as practitioners of regular and formal civility, whatever Americans claimed of them. Actually, even George Washington admitted "that our people who have been prisoners generally agree that they rec[eive]d much kinder treatment from [the Hessians] than from the British Officers."[38] Yet others saw it differently—even those on the same side.

"These People make War like Savages," complained Ambrose Serle, Howe's secretary, of the Americans.[39] Many Britons likely agreed, as in a spicy 1776 satire titled "The Female Combatants." It depicted the war between Britannia and America as a brawl between a mother and a daughter, with bright feathers on their heads, punching each other's lights out. Stylish, sour-faced Britannia in wig and pearls threatens: "I'll force you to Obedience you Rebellious Slut," while a wild and topless [Native] America, body painted like a fierce ancient Pict, hair flowing free, hollers, "Liberty Liberty for ever Mother while I exist." Britannia's shield appears with a withering tree, America's with a thriving one topped with a liberty cap.

Yet there were serious repercussions to "fighting like savages." Serle, himself a father, related how the small son of a British officer was playing on the Jersey shore a few days before the Battle of Long Island. According to Serle, rebels shot and killed him, cheering and retreating. Invoking that classic figure of tyranny in eighteenth-century European thinking, Serle fulminated, even "a Turk would detest so dirty an action. This is not War . . . but Murder; and, upon a defenceless innocent Child." He also related how enslaved people fled to the British military, seeking freedom. "In America itself," he muttered, "there is nothing to be heard but the sound of Liberty, and nothing to be felt but the most detestable Slavery."[40] In his view, American slavery of various kinds signified their lack of civility.

Still, Serle had to admit that incivilities occurred on both sides: "the main Body of the Hessians . . . committed already several Depredations." Serle wished that they could have avoided the use of these foreign troops. He lamented the "Devastations" that Hessians had wrought on fine houses. They had smashed windows, doors, and furniture. Moreover, Serle continued, they had deposited "Filth" (that is, feces) in the fine houses of Long Island and elsewhere so that it was unbearable to enter them. Serle also walked the landscape, shocked and horrified by the many "putrid dead Bodies" strewn on the ground: too many for the military to bury at once. Some months later, he reported on the movement of two thousand rebels, "almost naked and the poorest Wretches that can be conceived." Having taken to his bed during that storm at sea, he felt sympathy for soldiers lacking such retreats: "'Tis a hard unpleasant Life this of a Soldier's, which is passed in a little paltry Tent which will neither keep out Wind, or Rain, or Vermin."[41]

Soldiers indeed endured "a hard unpleasant Life" in the American Revolutionary War. When the comrades of one Continental Army private, Ezra Tilden, became ill in the summer of 1776, he scribbled in his diary "Oh, it is Exceeding bad being in tents here, when Sick, to Lie in ye Rain & die. . . . Far from friends, & Relations, & from ye Comforts of Life."[42] Tilden carried all the "Comforts of Life" he could on his person. He relished making lists (towns passed through; items bought and sold; guard duty rota). Perhaps for this reason, or in fear that he would lose some of it, he recorded every single item in his possession, thereby allowing us the unusual opportunity to poke around in an ordinary soldier's pack.

A well-prepared soldier's burden was heavy. Tilden carried vital items: a blanket, a gun, a cartouche (cartridge) box, a hatchet, and a powder horn (perhaps carved like Prince Simbo's). Then there was food and drink: a loaf of bread, a bottle of ground coffee, a pound and a half of drinking chocolate, a bag of plums (probably dried), three and a half pounds of sugar, and a "New milk Cheese" weighing five pounds. To go with the food, there was a wooden plate, a spoon, a fork, a jackknife, and a pewter bowl. There was clothing: three shirts (one woolen, one cotton and linen, another striped); three pairs of stockings (white, blue, and gray); garters (to hold the stockings up); long trousers; two underjackets, a short coat; a great coat; a pair of arm strings; a pair of leather breeches; a pair of cloth breeches; a frock (probably for sleeping); a hat; a cap; a pair of boots, two pairs of shoes; knee buckles; and shoe buckles. Even with this full set of clothing, there would have been a need for laundry; the number of undergarments was decidedly limited.[43] That, combined with not infrequent bouts of illness, made for a continuous need for washing. Then there were other things: sewing items (thread, needles, yarn); writing items (a quill, paper, sealing wax, a penknife); toiletries (soap, a comb, a mirror); a snuffbox "full of Snuff"; a couple of handkerchiefs; a leather strap; and a cod line (rope).[44]

Despite his full pack, Tilden endured hunger, severe illness, and trauma. "Had I known as much Before I came," he admitted, "I should not hardly have ventur'd from home, for any money, whatsoever." That double negative added emphasis. Still, Tilden was among the more fortunate. When he watched the arrival of the defeated troops from Canada, like the shoeless Greenman whom we have already met, "what disheartened & Discouraged me most of all, was . . . to see so many Poor Soldiers a going home, that Look'd like death almost, Like walking Ghosts, or Skeliton's." "God Bless ye Soldiers," he declared.[45]

Tilden's experience, though better than many, was typical. In August 1776, with the bread, cheese, and plums long gone, he longed for "Corn, Green-Beans & pease, new-Potatoes, Cucumbers, Butter, Cheese, molasses, spoon-victuals, pudding &c &c &c . . . But I cannot get any of them, not at all, at all, at all." That repetition at the end echoed like his empty belly. A few weeks later, he declared, with another emphatic double negative, "I was Exceeding hungry; never so hungry, hardly, in my Life before." The connection between hunger and illness could be obvious. After heating up some bits of old corn in "lake water" in desperation in November, he related "great Pain in my Bowels & a Smart purging [diarrhea] followed."[46]

Such incidents were minor, though, compared to what others suffered. Tilden had *heard* about the horrors of war, he related after one skirmish, "but much worse . . . to See & feel ye horrors of War . . . I Saw a Sight Was Shocking indeed; a good many, both of our men, & ye Enemy, Lye dead." To see so many corpses shocked this young man. Yet even more dreadful were the desperate moans of the wounded. Others nearby were "very badly wounded just dying. . . . Some shot almost thro, & Crying to God, to Jesus, &c to take away their lives. Poor Miserable Creatures Indeed!"[47]

Soldiers were on the front line of "ye horrors of War," but those terrors affected civilians too. No one denied there were incivilities. One Friend of Liberty alerted Thomas Jefferson in 1776, "these damn'd Invaders . . . play the very Devil with the Girls and even old Women to satisfy their libidinous appetites."[48] In September 1776, in Long Island, two British soldiers, John Dunn and John Lusty, raped Elizabeth Johnstone in her house as her four-year-old daughter "stood by crying" and her baby lay in the bed next to her (at one point, they made Johnstone nurse the baby to stop the crying). One soldier held her while the other assaulted her, and then they changed places. When confronted, Dunn and Lusty denied it. However, they added that even if they had done it, "she was a Yankee whore or a Yankee bitch, and it was no great matter." The soldiers used their words to dismiss her with a shrug, her anguish of no importance. Their words show what war can do: it transforms terrified mothers of sobbing children into "rebellious sluts" deserving of violence.[49]

This wartime rape case, though, also reveals heroics. There were two other women in the house with Johnstone when the soldiers arrived and demanded hospitality, drink, and, finally, sex. One was Hannah, a Black woman turned out of the house by Dunn and Lusty. She was likely familiar with the threat of sexual coercion. She ran to the nearest house, a quarter of a mile away, seeking help, but the neighbors said they could not leave their own house. Even after the event, her heroics continued; she testified on Johnstone's behalf. The British military court did something that colonial civil authorities would not generally have done: they allowed her testimony as evidence. She reported that when they ejected her from the house, that "Lusty followed her, and swore . . . that he would knock her brains out." When Elizabeth Johnstone appeared at the door, Dunn and Lusty turned their attention to her, dragging her inside. Hannah also informed the court that Elizabeth Johnstone was a war widow whose husband had been killed in Montréal. The other witness in the house was an old woman, bedridden, named Freelove Hollowbird. One of the men threatened to rape her, too, but she cried out "Murder." In the end, again, the men focused on Johnstone. Still, Hollowbird was near enough to the event that she "sat up in her bed and saw it all; she remembers seeing the tall man's private parts."[50]

Despite the clarity and precision of this testimony, in this era, the words of these three women—one the survivor, one Black, and one elderly and disabled—were not in and of themselves sufficient to achieve a conviction against White men in a rape case. However, at least one of the men to whom Elizabeth Johnstone had turned after the incident supported her narrative. He testified that when she came to them, "she seemed to be in the greatest distress and confusion." It was he who reported that Dunn and Lusty had called her a whore; he does not seem to have approved.

However, matters soon started to stack up badly for Johnstone. While she maintained that she had resisted continually, she bore no physical marks of struggle.[51] The highest-ranking witness, whose testimony would have been accorded the most significance—the surgeon to whom Johnstone reported the rape—was quite measured in his statements, not especially supportive. When asked whether Johnstone, on rushing to him for help after the assault, had been "in that violent agitation of Spirits, that a Modest Woman might be supposed to be in" after such an event, the surgeon declared that he did not think she was, despite her tears. She had in fact managed to tell her story "plainly": damning testimony. Evidently, if equanimity was considered a laudable quality in a general, it was not so in a woman who had been violated.

The surgeon also claimed that the soldiers, on being apprehended, "did not appear to be alarmed," but merely "very drunk." When asked whether such intoxicated men could actually have perpetrated this rape, he allowed that it was possible, "but it was a mere possibility."[52] When they took the stand, Dunn and Lusty both denied any wrongdoing. They contended they had simply been seeking cider, and if anything untoward had happened, they were not the perpetrators. They proclaimed their innocence in no uncertain terms.[53]

The court sided with Dunn and Lusty. Such a verdict is exactly what we would expect in this era, when rape convictions against White men were exceedingly rare.[54] A careful examination of the original trial records, though, reveals something extremely unusual: a change of verdict owing to the intervention of no less than General William Howe himself. Howe insisted on a new verdict, one in which Dunn and Lusty were found guilty. The court reported that "His Excellency" had "signified his disapprobation of the said Sentence" in this case and another heard at the same time. In this era, commanding officers had the power to shape the outcome in military courts; soldiers had no right of appeal. The Court had assembled again "in order to revise their proceedings."[55]

Howe ordered that the court change its verdicts in both cases to punish miscreants with rigor. At the same time as the rape case, there were also cases for theft and pillage from private homes. After Howe's directive, the court found the ringleader of the theft guilty and sentenced him to "one thousand lashes on his bare back with a Cat of nine tails." In the altered verdict, Dunn and Lusty were sentenced to hang. This new set of verdicts, recorded along with all the testimony, received a literal sign-off from General Howe.[56]

Why did Howe intervene in these sentences? It is unlikely that his involvement can be attributed to his concern for Johnstone. In fact, these cases were a public relations disaster. It is worth observing that had the men raped Hannah, the Black woman, it is highly unlikely that the verdict would have gone this way, if the case had even come before the court. Rather, these particular events—violation of a White war widow and mother and pillage perpetrated against middling folk by British soldiers—made the British look uncivilized, monstrous. Howe flogged and hanged soldiers for plunder again in August 1777.[57]

Tales of incivilities had political power. In Howe's later testimony before the House of Commons, he observed that stories of plunder and rape by British troops appeared in American newspapers "to irritate and enrage the people . . . the British soldiers were represented as a race of men more inhuman than savages."[58] The Howe brothers, therefore, keen to broker peace, tried to ensure that uncivil behavior was punished. If violence against a woman like Johnstone took place, it had to be seen as sporadic and punished by authorities, rather than ordered or condoned by them.

The result of this emphasis on civility and power was one of the very rare eighteenth-century court decisions in a rape survivor's favor.

Beyond these legal interventions, the Howe brothers followed up their success in taking New York City with several victories, including one at White Plains in October 1776. They also took Forts Washington and Lee. By December, the British also occupied Newport, Rhode Island. The Continental Army was struggling. Many soldiers had not been paid, which hardly encouraged them to reenlist; terms of service usually terminated at the end of the calendar year. In September 1776, one Black soldier, Sezor [Caesar] Phelps, wrote home requesting help with getting his wages.[59]

George Washington fretted in letter after letter about the problems of enlistments and supplies. In a long, glum letter to John Hancock on December 20, 1776, he denounced "short inlistments" as "the Origin of all our misfortunes."[60] The next day, he declared that he was "led to despair" by the impending loss of soldiers.[61] The day after that, he declared in frustration, "you may as well attempt to stop the Winds, from blowing . . . as the Regiments from going when their term is expired."[62] Washington also worried about clothing: "The Cloathing of the Troops is a matter of infinite importance . . . many of 'em being entirely naked & most so thinly clad as to be unfit for service."[63] The lack of arms was of such a serious nature that Benjamin Franklin made his way to France in 1776 to negotiate a treaty in order to obtain them.[64] The paucity of food and clothing was an issue, too, since it dented recruitment and retention of soldiers. Washington reminded Robert Morris, whose money raising (including from secret French loans) underpinned the Continental Army, that "nothing will contribute more to facilitate the recruiting Service than warm & comfortable Cloathing."[65]

Loyalties started to wither. Were supporters of rebellion losing enthusiasm and switching to the British? Washington worried that "the Enemy are daily gathering strength from the disaffected; This strength, like a Snowball by rolling, will increase."[66] He assumed that the British were waiting for the river to freeze over so that they could take Philadelphia. The Continental Congress was so alarmed at this prospect that it decamped to Baltimore, Maryland, in December 1776.

Given the stunning debacle of Québec of the previous winter—due partly to year-end terms of service and to lack of supplies—the sensible choice for Washington would have been to keep his powder dry and wait out the worst of the winter. Such was Howe's prudent course of action. No general relished leading troops into battle in deep winter. Frozen rivers were treacherous; troops were pale and unhealthy; and battles were tougher in the cold. Moreover, he was up against a formidable opponent, a Hessian colonel, Johann Rall, who had been in service since age fourteen. He had fought in the War of Austrian Succession in the 1740s, the Jacobite Rebellion in 1745, the Seven Years' War, and the Turko-Russian War in the early 1770s.[67]

But Washington was desperate. The American cause—and Washington's pride—hung in the balance. He was about to lose thousands of soldiers at year's end. Moreover, he worried about the British gaining unstoppable momentum by taking Philadelphia. As he summarized it, he behaved with boldness—not to say recklessness—because he had "A character to loose—an Estate to forfeit—the inestimable blessing of liberty at Stake."[68] After trying to choose between his limited options, on Christmas Eve, he determined on an attack, ordering that soldiers be given blankets and three days' worth of cooked food to see them through.[69]

The assault on Trenton began early on the morning of December 26, 1776. With troops divided between the high and low roads into town, the Continental Army was able quickly to surround the Hessians, who, recognizing the impossibility of their situation, surrendered: "23 Officers and 886 Men" while only four Continental Army soldiers were wounded.[70] Somehow, Washington landed what he later termed "our late lucky Blow."[71]

The Trenton victory was a late Christmas gift for the American forces. How had it happened? The most common story—that Hessians were too hungover from Christmas revelries to resist the attack—is an enjoyable one, but there is little evidence to support it. There have been claims since the battle itself that Rall was arrogant and careless. However, these contentions need to be taken with a grain of salt, as many of them originated with those eager to exonerate themselves for this failure. Certainly, Rall assumed that he would be able to fight the Americans on a battlefield. The rules of civility called for such tactics. Rall was not expecting a surprise attack on his garrison the morning after Christmas. He may have had a certain amount of arrogance, since it did seem unlikely that the Continental Army would attempt it. As another Hessian officer put it, "we had a very poor opinion of the rebels, who previously had never successfully opposed us."[72] Rall paid dearly for whatever his mistakes were, dying at Trenton that day.

In the deep winter of 1776–77, the very name of Trenton gladdened the hearts of Friends of Liberty. So thrilled was the Continental Congress in Baltimore that they immediately ordered that Washington's letter about the victory there be published as a broadside by the local printer, Mary Katherine Goddard.[73] Washington followed up the triumph at Trenton with another at Princeton in early 1777. Things seemed to be looking up for the common cause: "Our Affairs at present are in a prosperous way.... Recruiting goes on well—& a Beleif [*sic*] prevails that the Enemy are afraid of Us."[74] In early 1777, Washington rejoiced that "The year 1776 is over." Far from hoping it would be marked with celebrations, he prayed that the nation would never "be plagued with such another."[75]

"Thus had the times changed!" declared the Hessian officer Johann Ewald after the attack on Trenton. In his view, they had underestimated the Continental Army and thus lost their advantage. He felt that many of his countrymen "had become completely disheartened by the disasters of Trenton and Princetown."[76] Thousands of Hessians were marched down to Virginia as prisoners of war; a few, including Andreas Wiederhold, kept diaries or sent letters, giving us a chance to see the American landscape from their perspective. Wiederhold reported that settlers along the Susquehanna River greeted them by pelting their wagon with "filth" (feces). In Lancaster, populated by many Germans, he praised the "good beer," but not the locals, who had evidently lost any positive German qualities.[77] Another officer agreed that these German American settlers were "the most ill-natured people in the world."[78] Wiederhold recounted a tale in which a "drunken German rabble" attacked and threatened to hang him. However, "just at the moment of greatest tumult," an American captain, "very polite and courteous," came to his rescue. "Therefore I was not hanged although insulted and thoroughly shaken."[79]

For all that Americans condemned Hessians, German soldiers were not always so thrilled with the United States, either. The heat and insects plagued elaborately dressed men unaccustomed to such conditions. In 1777, several members of one German regiment, marching through Virginia, died of heatstroke thanks to their heavy uniforms, high leather boots, and cumbersome sword hilts.[80] Other soldiers endured "vast swarms" of mosquitoes and infestations of wood lice, which could "crawl into the ears, biting inward so fast that it causes the most intense pain" and hearing loss.[81]

Europeans were also sometimes dismayed by American waste, greed, and cruelty. Wiederhold had been struck by American plenty on arrival: "Livestock in abundance! Wheat, corn, and every possible grain of the best sorts . . . Fruit, chestnuts, some other nuts, cherries, apricots, peaches."[82] Yet he was pained by local treatment of natural resources: "The Americans are very wasteful with their wood. If they continue in this way, and America becomes more populated . . . wood will become rare and expensive." He also viewed Philadelphia as a modern Sodom and Gomorrah, full of "depravities."[83] Another soldier complained of one village that "You cannot imagine any people more mean and malicious than the inhabitants here."[84] Another soldier observed, "If any people worships money, it is the Americans."[85] Johann Ewald reported that Americans had hanged fathers in front of their families for letting their sons escape to join the British: "The friends of the revolution excuse this tyranny by saying that liberty for all must be forced on a few by despotism."[86]

German soldiers were also horrified by American slavery. One lamented that enslaved people had to "do all the housework."[87] Wiederhold denounced the system altogether: "It is a shame on all humanity how barbaric some people treat [enslaved people], and it causes a shudder to see the Americans . . . understand nothing about them." He summarized in disgust: "Animals are treated better in Germany." He contended that Black people "all have a better character than the whites" and would flourish if allowed to pursue education.[88]

Wiederhold was also chagrined by American treatment of Indigenous people. In 1777, Wiederhold, himself a POW, met another POW, a Lenni Lenape leader, who was incarcerated. The fact that this Indigenous man was held in prison suggests some of the distinctions in the treatment of prisoners of war between those considered brothers and those considered barbarians. Wiederhold was never put in a jail. He was amazed and delighted to meet this fellow captive, though. He described the leader's strong body tattooed with snakes, "which identified their tribe from others." He then recounted how this Indigenous gentleman shook their hands and welcomed them cordially as allies. There was civility in these encounters between two groups both dismissed by Friends of Liberty as barbarians and monsters. The local interpreter for the Germans wanted the Lenni Lenape leader to show them traditional war dances, which, ever gracious, he was willing to do. However, the Germans stopped this proceeding, as "it grieved us that a man sitting in jail should dance."[89]

In the spring and summer of 1777, as these German captives were being marched in their heavy wool uniforms down to Virginia, the Continental Army gained new momentum. The British appointed a new general, John Burgoyne, who brought forces down from Canada through upstate New York on a northern campaign. Along with German-speaking auxiliaries, there were also Haudenosaunee warriors allied with the British. Burgoyne had some success as he and his forces swept south, including at Fort Ticonderoga in early July. Many locals were especially disturbed that the British side included Indigenous allies, and these tensions erupted when a settler, Jane McCrea, was killed by two of them on her way to meet her Loyalist fiancé. The death of McCrea served excellent propaganda purposes, as those fighting against the British deployed it as evidence of the unholy alliance of British, Loyalists, Hessians, and Native Americans.[90]

These tensions also erupted at the small but fierce battle near the Oneida village of Oriska in early August 1777. In what came to be called the Battle of Oriskanay, both sides mainly fielded native-born troops: Loyalists, Mohawks, and Senecas against Patriots and Oneida allies. One such ally was Nia-man-rigounant (or Akiatonharónkweni or Colonel Joseph Louis Cook), who had fought at Québec (depicted in Trumbull's painting of General Montgomery). The battle was a major loss for American forces, with limited gains for the British. As one Seneca warrior, Tah-won-ne-ahs [Théwonyas], or Chainbreaker (also called Governor Blacksnake), recalled in sorrow decades later, it was "the most Dead Bodies" he had ever seen at once with "the Blood Shed a Stream Running Down."[91]

The British—with German-speaking and allied Indigenous soldiers—continued to try to press their advantage in this area in the late summer and autumn of 1777. It was an ongoing struggle for dominance. The British succeeded in taking Philadelphia in September 1777, a major victory.[92] Still, that same month, the Americans established themselves at Freeman's Farm. They secured a strong position with an overlook, Bemis Heights near Saratoga, and a noted Polish officer and engineer, Tadeusz Kościuszko, fortified their position. In September, General Burgoyne launched his attack against the Continental forces under General Horatio Gates.

"I was filled with fear and anguish and shivered whenever a shot was fired," declared Baroness Riedesel as she watched from a safe distance her husband leading his regiment in battle in Saratoga.[93] The Continental Army held their position, thanks in part to the fortification secured by Kościuszko. In October, Burgoyne attempted another attack; it failed. He capitulated. Altogether, he had lost more than eleven hundred men, and another six thousand either fled or were taken as prisoners of war.[94] One Black soldier, Agrippa Hull, who would later serve with Kościuszko, subsequently recalled that the American band played "Yankee Doodle" as the thousands of POWs were marched off.[95] It was a stunning blow.

The effects of Saratoga were diverse but significant. For a few lucky ones, it brought reunion. After the capitulation on October 17, Baroness Riedesel and her children drove through the American camp with trepidation to meet her husband, who had come through unharmed. However, no one insulted them; some "even looked with pity to see a woman with small children there." When they arrived, one "very handsome man" lifted the children out of her carriage, hugged them, and "with tears in his eyes, helped me out. 'You are trembling,' he said, 'Don't be afraid.'" She said that his kind treatment of her little girls gave her courage. He then invited her to bring the children to dinner. "Surely, you are a husband and father, because you are so good to me," she told him. She was not wrong. Major General Philip Schuyler of the Continental Army had a wife and seven living children. He served her a delicious meal including steak, potatoes, and "good bread and butter. No dinner had ever tasted better to me."[96] Officers could treat the wives and children of other officers, even enemy ones, well.

Schuyler's civility continued; he offered to let her stay in his house, near Albany. On her way there, two days' ride away, she was to stay the night in a house where a French doctor was tending a wounded German officer. The doctor, charmed by her sudden appearance and her ability to speak French, proceeded to make advances, saying "all sorts of sweet things and impertinences," including that "it would be better to stay with victors than with the defeated," and offering to share his bed with her that night. She was horrified by these overtures, but too nervous to express it "because I was without protection." At that moment, to her considerable relief, her husband and his aide walked in, and the doctor scuttled off. She did spend the night in his bed—with her husband.[97]

Others who had experienced the battles at Saratoga were less fortunate. A few of the wounded English and German soldiers were brought to this house to recuperate. One of them, who had been shot in the leg, turned out to be the nephew of the couple with whom Riedesel had stayed in England. Although he never complained, she heard his moans through the wall and during her frequent visits. Determined to keep his limbs, and worried about becoming a burden to his family, he refused to have his leg amputated, praying and hoping it would be all right. Yet gangrene set in. Despite his earlier objections, doctors performed an emergency amputation, in hopes of saving his life. "But it was too late, and he died a few days later."[98]

British soldiers suffered; so did German ones. Baroness Riedesel recounted meeting one wounded Hessian so haunted by war that he had been driven "mad" and was being cared for by Ursuline nuns in Canada. He was overcome with terrible visions—perhaps of bayonets, lost friends, or even talking snakes. Hearing her speak German, he dashed into the corridor, shouting: "Be my rescuer! Help me to die so that I may return to Germany!"[99] If he returned to his homeland, it would likely be only in dreams—or in death. One-third of German-speaking soldiers never did return, though some stayed by choice.[100] Like this despairing veteran, though, too many other men in the American Revolutionary War died far from home, "Poor Miserable Creatures," never to be fully restored or reunited.

The men who survived battles at Saratoga and elsewhere wore the agonies of war on their shattered bodies: smallpox scars on their faces, bodies disfigured by musket balls, missing limbs amputated to save their lives. Yet even those who were physically whole endured the memories of the roar of cannons in their ears, the shouts of "Fire," the desperate pleas—in English, Mohawk, French, German, and other languages—of dying men. One German officer recorded on an "extraordinarily dark and silent night" that he could hear not just the barking of dogs and the calls from the sentries, but "the mournful voices of the wounded who had remained on the field, crying for help." Even though they were enemy soldiers, he still "felt sorry that I could not help them."[101] One Seneca warrior, devastated by the killing he had himself done at places like Oriska, agonized over how "it is Bad . . . to Spill the human Blood," even as he acknowledged it was to "protect . . . our own Country."[102]

Leaders often made choices to protect their countries, but they were supposed to do so in ways appropriate to the "Head of a civilized nation." Individual soldiers might do despicable things, but the "Head" was supposed to behave with greater civility. It did not always work like that, though. Many of those who paid the price were soldiers themselves, who sometimes wondered at their own uncivil behavior in these terrible circumstances. They knew better than anyone else that power came at a high and bloody cost.

Stories of incivilities also influenced the course of the war. The caricatures of the Hessian "Men-Monsters" transported from German lands to kill Americans motivated many Americans to fight. Yet those Hessians had their own tales, even if there was no happily ever after. No one thanked them for their service. The Hessian officer Johann Ewald rued that there was not even a real homecoming: "all services performed were forgotten. . . . We became agitated, muttered in our beards, [and] cursed our fate."[103]

Also cursing his fate, Andreas Wiederhold remained in the new United States until 1784. Even other Germans did not welcome him and other Hessians home when he was finally able to return. Hanoverians, still sniffy about the barbaric Hessians ("Hanoverians behaving like Hanoverians"—*die hannöverischen Hannoveranen*—as Wiederhold complained), would not allow the Hessians—eager to get home—to cross overland. The humiliating termination of Wiederhold's epic eight-year odyssey fighting and nearly dying in the American Revolution was to be crowded with rank-and-file soldiers loaded onto a barge, fighting the current, for a slow, dispiriting trip home on the river Weser.[104] It was no fairy-tale ending.

Still, by late 1777, fate seemed at last to be smiling on the American rebels. In his residence at Passy, outside Paris, one American—Benjamin Franklin—received dispatches from home informing him of the victory at Saratoga.[105] So thrilled was Franklin that—ever the publicist but lacking any printing capacity—he and his fellow diplomats began copying by hand an announcement to inform the French that in October, General Burgoyne had been "obliged to lay down his arms, 9200 men killed or taken prisoner." Franklin also sent a copy to the French foreign minister, the Comte de Vergennes. News of this American victory soon electrified France—including the court at Versailles.[106]

Chapter 8

A Hall in Versailles

In 1777, at the royal court of Versailles near Paris, the bright flames of crystal chandeliers reflected off ornate candelabras and pale gleaming marble. In some rooms, those flickering lights caught the shiny floral silk of armchairs and the polished mahogany of writing tables as well as the gilt tooling adorning popular books of the era, including dictionaries and treatises on enlightened living. The golden emblems of Louis XIV, some representing him as the Sun King, shone on doors, an ever-present mark of that long-dead monarch's enduring power.[1]

The courtiers there wanted to sparkle, too, so that they could catch

This 1745 engraving shows the busy scene of a royal masquerade ball at Versailles illuminated by glowing chandeliers and candelabras.

Louis XVI's eye and win his favor.[2] They sought to make their bons mots as sharp as the swords in their filigreed sheaths that nobles (and only nobles) wore at their waists. Their distinctive red heels clicked on the smooth marble floors. In front of mirrors, the men at Versailles checked their dress suits: dazzling waistcoats embroidered with gold and silver thread, gleaming white lace at collar and cuffs, and elaborate hats worn under the arm (and only under the arm, never atop their powdered wigs).[3] Those hairpieces—obscuring baldness, grayness, and limpness—lent their wearers an aura of vitality. The smell of scented oil, rubbed into the hair before white powder was applied, filled the air with the cloying perfume of flowers, from jasmine to orange blossom.[4] As one French wigmaker put it, wigs were "a matter of imitating beautiful Nature."[5] It took a lot of artifice to make things seem natural—and to mask the pungent smell of sweaty rivalries.[6]

In the French court, and many other places, men worked hard to gain respect, and they lived in fear of losing it.[7] They did not always use that word, but they frequently invoked its opposite: humiliation. To be sure, officials in both France and Britain fretted about threats to imperial power, military might, and economic strength. Still, what they seemed to fear more was the dreadful prospect of losing the respect of the world.

Americans, too, worried about international respect. In the Declaration of Independence, they noted at the outset—even before making their claims to life, liberty, and the pursuit of happiness—that they had "a decent respect to the opinions of mankind." They proclaimed their determination to be a "Free and Independent State," one with the "full Power to levy War, conclude Peace, contract Alliances, establish Commerce, and to all other Acts and Things which Independent States may of right do."

The American desire for respect ran headlong into the centuries-old fight between France and Britain, a conflict that entangled them all. The ability of Americans to broker alliances depended on winning the support—and supplies—of established empires and their diplomats and kings. Americans sought to win friends with their Declaration of Independence in 1776, which one diplomatic historian has termed "a foreign-policy statement."[8] They had to prove their abilities as an "Independent State" to win respect—and arms—from others. As John

Adams recorded decades later, "The Declaration of Independence I always considered as a Theatrical Show," one directed at a world stage.[9]

Nowhere was it clearer that international politics was a "Theatrical Show" than at the court in Versailles. Men in wigs and heels came there to realize their ambitions, showing off for one another. Let's sidle up to a group of them, gliding through those gleaming halls in late 1777, to see how they won respect—and a revolution.

One German soldier was there seeking his next adventure. The glory days had ended in 1763, and rumors about his personal life had propelled him out of the court of a minor German principality. Having spent time at the court of Frederick the Great, he was not especially daunted by the shiny splendor of Versailles. A large medal bearing a red Maltese cross adorned his broad chest; a matching emblem—the same cross beneath the golden crown of the king of Prussia—hung around his neck on a wide red ribbon. The discerning courtiers at Versailles could see that his gorgeous suit—of fine fabric with gilt trim—was French, fashionable, and expensive. What they did not know is that Baron Friedrich Wilhelm von Steuben had bought it on credit and never paid the bill.[10] He was now intent on finding paid employment befitting his station. Still, from time to time, his restless gaze likely lighted upon a handsome face or a well-cut pair of breeches.

Steuben's shrewd glance also took in another foreigner seeking favor, one who described himself as "jolly . . . strong and hearty." Admittedly, this American was not as strong as Steuben, and his plain brown suit was the opposite of stylish. His "thin gray strait hair . . . peep[ed] out" from under his "only coiffure": a simple though "fine Fur Cap." That iconic hat came so far down his forehead that it almost touched his little round spectacles. "Think," Benjamin Franklin wrote to a female friend with flirtatious exuberance, "how this must appear among the powder'd heads of Paris!" He joked that if the French would follow his lead, the money saved on hairdressing could be spent on a trip to England, where, with a retinue of hairdressers, he could fix the heads of ministers there as they were currently "*un peu dérangées*" (a little disturbed).[11]

With impish glee, Franklin sharpened his elbows for the race to

Here is the iconic look of Franklin—in fur hat, round spectacles, and no wig—in Paris in the 1770s.

Louis XVI—and his foreign minister—by flouting convention. His strategy worked. He managed to win the hearts of French men—and women—who saw in him the epitome of "beautiful Nature." More than one French woman recalled the contrast of Franklin—"a well-fed farmer" with his simple dress and straight hair—with the "powdered and perfumed" heads of courtiers, adorned with "gold and sashes."[12]

That season, in Paris, raw insurgence became hot. Crowds chased Franklin wherever he went. One man marveled, "The American insurrection was everywhere applauded, and became, as it were, a fashion."[13] Steuben would have seen sophisticated Frenchmen sporting fur caps, and stylish Frenchwomen with their coiffures arranged *à la Franklin,* mimicking the shape of his distinctive hat. For a few women, there would soon be elaborate wigs in the shapes of victorious warships and even an entire "*habit à l'Insurgente,*" or Rebel's Dress.[14] Men like Steuben had to salute the surprising success of Franklin's sartorial subversion.

After all, the three American commissioners sent to negotiate a treaty with France in late 1776—Franklin, Silas Deane, and Arthur Lee—were an improbable trio for this mission. They didn't speak French particularly well, and they were not much more skilled at diplomacy.[15] They didn't even get along with one another. The older Franklin was well connected and genial but susceptible to flattery (of which he received a great deal). Deane, self-important, was constantly coming up with another scheme, and Lee came off as an insufferable prig. Still, Franklin rode into Paris on a wave of celebrity and goodwill. He had been a "foreign associate" of l'Académie des Sciences since 1772, and he kept up these intellectual contacts throughout his time in France.[16] As one of the few American philosophes, known for his writings and scientific breakthroughs, he had already won many French friends (or at least flatterers).

One Scot—David Murray, Viscount Stormont—watched Franklin at court, expression sour under his wig; he was neither friend nor flatterer. At this point, Stormont, the British ambassador to France, was smarting over what he saw as the ridiculous slurs he had had to read in a letter from the American commissioners about the treatment of rebel prisoners of war. They complained in exaggerated terms about impressment of these men into the British Navy, claiming that Britain forced them either "to fight against their Friends and Relations, a new mode of Barbarity" or shipped them to Africa and Asia. Affronted by the commissioners' audacity, Stormont secretly copied the letter's contents and then carefully resealed it and returned it to the senders with the haughty message: "The Kings Ambassador receives no Letters from Rebels but when they come to implore His Majesty's Mercy." Offended in turn, Franklin annotated the letter: "return'd with Insult."[17] Diplomats were not always that diplomatic.

Watching this drama was a worldly Frenchman in blue-gray velvet: Charles Gravier, the Comte de Vergennes. He had spent most of the last three decades abroad in diplomatic service, notably at the court of Osman III, the Ottoman sultan. Vergennes was a more gifted negotiator than the competent but dour Stormont.[18] He also knew how to dress the part. Indeed, on his arrival to Istanbul, he got into a fierce tussle about his right to appear before the sultan in the fur-trimmed pink gown of a full ambassador to Turkey. He won. His diplomatic (and

This 1770s engraving shows the busy diplomat Vergennes at his desk in his powdered wig and suit with diplomatic sash and medal over his floral waistcoat.

perhaps sartorial) talents had already allowed him to overcome disgrace in France. He had had two children with a widow named Anne Duvivier. In the French court, such was hardly a scandal. Rather, the outrage was that he proceeded to marry her; an ambassador required the king's permission for such an act. This defiance was the official reason for his recall from Turkey in 1768.[19] He had since worked his way back into royal favor, and in 1774, with the accession of Louis XVI, he became le Secrétaire d'État des Affaires Étrangères, or the French foreign minister.[20]

The following year, despite his demanding new role, Vergennes took the time to write some advice for his sons (and only his sons) on how "to play a role in the world" so that they would win "the admiration, the recognition, and the general respect of their country."[21] He had a fair bit to say on this score; he filled one hundred sixty-eight pages with beautifully penned words of guidance. His instructional book—now in a Paris archive, where it rests largely forgotten—showed just how much a man like Vergennes cared about winning respect: for himself, his sons, and his country. He was not alone in this abiding commitment, as the episode between Franklin and Stormont makes clear. Sometimes that respect came from a man wearing a military medal or a fur hat or a pink gown; sometimes it came through insisting on treating prisoners of war in accordance with the conventions of international law. In this particular moment, one of transition from ancient regimes to more modern ones as well as from colonial insurgence to global war, these diverse sources of esteem mattered, especially to men.

In 1776, Americans had imagined that with their Declaration, the French and the Spanish would be willing to help them. They were right—and wrong. Vergennes had noted earlier that year that France and Spain benefited from the war since it distracted Britain and depleted its resources. However, it was not in their interest to join a colonial rebellion against the British. Vergennes was willing to "sustain the courage of the Americans by secret favors and by vague hopes," as he put it in a memo in March 1776.[22] He would provide arms and money to the Americans, but the French would do no more in 1776 (either before or after the Declaration of Independence).

The French dragged their elegant red heels on establishing a full treaty throughout 1776 and most of 1777; as Vergennes framed it, it was in neither the "dignity nor the interest" of the king to do so.[23] As one spy for the British reported in an October 1777 letter labeled "Most Secret," the Americans had three major objectives. The first was to get France and Spain "to an actual War with Great Britain." The second objective was to gain acknowledgment of U.S. independency and at least to win neutrality. The third was to obtain money, supplies, and ships. The secret agent exulted that they had not managed the first two goals, but he lamented that they had had "but too much Success" in the third. In fact, the French and Spanish had set up a fictitious company, Roderigue Hortalez et Compagnie, to funnel arms to the Americans.[24] Still, the French would not (yet) go to war.

The American victory at Saratoga in October 1777 changed the game—or at least furnished a useful pretext for doing so. To many American historians, and in the popular imagination, the victory at Saratoga assured the French that the Americans could win.[25] Others, especially those writing from the British perspective, have argued that Saratoga made it seem more likely that the British would agree to a reconciliation, a possibility the French were eager to thwart.[26] Finally, it may simply be that the news of victory arrived at an opportune moment for a king and a minister who were already willing by late 1777 to join a full alliance.[27] In a 1778 letter to the Spanish king, Carlos III, Louis XVI explained that he had signed a treaty with the United States because he wanted "to weaken England."[28] Vergennes had spent a long time readying France's ships of the line, since they had to go up against Britain's mighty navy. They were ready by late 1777. Whatever the exact reasons, the news of the American victory at Saratoga provided the final push to the French to enter a full treaty with the Americans.

Still, the Franco-American alliance was an improbable one, shot through with ironies. Why would the French—among the more ancient of ancient regimes and Catholic to boot—side with republican upstarts in New England, famous for being filled with the "hotter sort" of Protestant? As one Frenchman later observed, it was surprising to see the enthusiasm with which the American commissioners, "the agents of a people in a state of insurrection against their monarch, were received in France, in the bosom of an ancient monarchy."[29]

Eager to champion a winning cause on the world stage, as he sought to establish himself as a king worthy of his forebears, Louis XVI became a supporter of the Americans, though he would come to regret his own youthful enthusiasm in this matter.[30] Vergennes was not a fan of English-speaking independence either. In that advice book to his sons, Vergennes had counseled them to learn foreign languages—but not English, despite its growing global importance. English writers, Vergennes warned, took "excessive liberty," which led to "theism, Deism, materialism, even atheism." He feared that books in English were perverse, encouraging nothing but vice, "the spirit of independence . . . and contempt for all authority."[31] Vergennes, then, was hardly an obvious candidate for backing an Anglophone Protestant republican insurgency.

For their part, Americans did not find the French likely allies—or saviors—either. "Breaking off such a Nation as this from the English so suddenly, and uniting it so closely with France, is one of the most extraordinary Events that ever happened among Mankind," observed

John Adams in a letter to Vergennes.[32] Anglophone colonists were steeped in Anglo-American patriotism, cultivated in wars of the eighteenth century (and before). They viewed the French as natural foes, prone to ally with Indigenous enemies. Their fierce Protestantism contributed to animosity too. As we have seen, the Quebec Act prompted all kinds of anti-Catholic invective in the lower colonies in 1774–75. The *Pennsylvania Packet* termed Canadian Catholicism an "infection" likely to "spread hither."[33]

American newspaper stories reflected unease with a Franco-American alliance. One satire, like the ad for the broken marriage of Liberty and Loyalty, used a marital analogy to frame relations between John Bull (Britain), Americana, and Nick Frog (France). John Bull and Americana, unhappily married, ended up in a "*divorce* of a very extraordinary nature." Americana would still possess the large estate she had brought to the marriage, and as it was likely that she was going to marry Nick Frog, together they would thus "strip John Bull of his paternal inheritance, and turn him out into the street."[34] Pro-government caricatures also mocked the alliance as one in which King Stork (France) eventually turned against the frogs (Americans), devouring them and making "a meal of his allies." The poem concluded:

> Say, *Yankees,* don't you feel compunction?
> At your unnatural, rash conjunction?
> Can love for you, in him take root,
> Who's Catholic, and absolute![35]

The "unnatural conjunction" of the Franco-American alliance, then, worried both sides; it did not sit quite right. However, if the enemy of one's enemy is one's friend, Britain was a powerful enemy for both.

French ministers denounced England as "the natural enemy of France . . . avaricious, ambitious, unjust, and of bad faith." They considered England's chief desire to be "if not the destruction of France, at the very least its degradation, its humiliation, and its ruin."[36] They smarted from the 1763 peace treaty that had left France in "contempt . . . without credit or influence," stuck in a "sad and humiliating situation."[37] They derided the English "ancient jealousy" that made them bent on attacking France's obvious natural advantages.[38] In seeking to persuade the Spanish to ally with France, the French foreign minister declared that England was "incontestably the rival and natural enemy" of the Bourbon monarchs of both France and Spain.[39] Such claims were more political than economic, as trade between the two countries continued.[40] Nevertheless, this kind of rhetoric was common.

The English returned the favor, seeing in a Franco-American alliance, and an American victory, the prospect of dishonor and degradation. In 1778, Viscount Stormont raged to Parliament that "France and America . . . were indissolubly leagued for our destruction." He continued that Britain's defeat "would render us a petty state of the second class, of no importance, and disgraced in the eyes of all surrounding nations." The Earl of Shelburne concurred that without America, Britain could hardly remain "an independent state; its splendor and glories would be no more, and she would be but a power of the second order."[41] Concerns reached beyond even government. One London debating society in late 1777 asked: "Would not the allowing the Independency of America, expose us to the insults of foreign Nations?" The majority of Londoners in attendance agreed that acknowledging American independence would lead to British humiliation.[42]

Old enemies made new friends. For England, France was an implacable enemy. For France, the alliance with the United States was a way to weaken their old British enemy and to avenge losses from the Seven Years' War. For the United States, France provided the men, supplies, and logistics of a full imperial power of the ancient regime: invaluable for the American cause. In February 1778, the Americans signed a treaty with Louis XVI, ratified by the Continental Congress in May.[43]

Ben Franklin had won the respect and the treaty he sought in Paris, and while there, he continued to field flatterers and office seekers. He received a letter of introduction from an acquaintance recommending Baron de Steuben, who had come to the court to meet him.[44] Aware of Steuben's scandalous past and eager to see him depart, Vergennes recommended him to Franklin with the warmest enthusiasm. Thanks to this intervention, Steuben sailed for North America with a letter of introduction from Franklin to present to George Washington.[45]

Steuben was a man who knew how to make an entrance—at least most of the time. Unfortunately, he entered North America (at Portsmouth, New Hampshire) wearing the brilliant "Scarlet Regimentals" of a British officer, a confusing message for a man intent on supporting the new United States.[46] He soon learned better. He wrote to George Washington to offer "all the Services in my Power, and to deserve the title of a Citizen of America by fighting for the Cause of your Liberty."[47] He headed for Valley Forge, Pennsylvania, where Washington had set up headquarters for the Continental Army. Like a French soldier who also arrived that month, Steuben probably anticipated "an army with uniforms, the glitter of arms, standards . . . military pomp of all sorts . . . [an] imposing spectacle."[48]

It was late February 1778. Valley Forge was cold and damp and bleak. This pathetic rough-hewn camp did not look like the headquarters of an international war. On the less frozen days, snow and rain swirled into the earth, creating conditions that one soldier called "Extriam [extremely] muddy."[49] These skinny, coughing, ragged boys, some shoeless, hardly appeared a force to vanquish the British as they popped their shaggy, lice-ridden heads out of crude huts bleating "no bread, no soldier" (meaning they would not fight without first being fed).[50] When the rains came down hard, as they did in late February, the men also emerged dripping and shivering on account of leaking roofs.[51] There was so little food and clothing that George Washington and others described the army as being in "a starving condition."[52] A surgeon there, missing home, demanded: "Why are we sent here to starve and Freeze?"[53] In a typical diary entry, one colonel, commanding the Rhode Island regiment of Jeremiah Greenman, mourned the loss of several of his men in rapid succession to illness: "what an alarm must this be. . . . to See how we are Struck off . . . one two and three, in the Space of twenty four Hours."[54] Washington and others feared that this dire situation would lead to mutiny, even a "fatal crisis—total want and a dissolution of the Army."[55] Steuben had witnessed plenty of misery, but even he was not fully prepared for what greeted him that February.

Steuben entered Valley Forge on horseback, spine ramrod straight, medals and gilt trim flashing on his broad frame, accompanied by a German servant, two urbane French assistants, and a sprightly Italian greyhound named Azor. He was keen to make a good impression and to win a position fighting for the American cause. With its freezing murk, miserable little cabins, and demoralized soldiers, though, Valley Forge was a far cry from the courtly worlds to which Steuben had become accustomed. Still, Steuben kept any consternation to himself. He may have recalled the advice of his mentor, Frederick the Great: "The dissimulation of the general consists in the important art of hiding his thoughts. He should be constantly on the stage and should appear most tranquil when he is most preoccupied."[56] Projecting serenity, he rolled up his well-tailored sleeves and got to work. He presented his letter of introduction from Benjamin Franklin and met with officers, including General Washington.

Steuben's charm offensive paid off, as soldiers gathered around to see the progress of this unusual bevy and to pet Azor. As John Laurens, aide-de-camp to Washington and son of the president of the Continental Congress, informed his father, Henry: "Baron Steuben has had the fortune to please uncommonly, for a stranger, at first sight."[57] Maybe it helped that Steuben did not speak English, so his aides translated his French into smooth, careful English (though many officers, like John Laurens, could speak French). Officers were impressed by his knowledge of what Laurens termed "the Science of war." Washington himself wrote to Henry Laurens that "He appears to be much of a Gentleman . . . a man of military knowledge and acquainted with the World."[58] Enlisted men were also enthralled. One soldier, then a sixteen-year-old though he would subsequently serve as the president of Princeton and chaplain to Congress, would recall his first slack-jawed view of Steuben: "never before or since, have I had such an impression of the ancient fabled god of war, as when I then looked on the Baron—he seemed . . . the perfect personification of Mars. The trappings of his horse, the enormous holsters of his pistols, his large size, and his strikingly martial aspect, all seemed to favour the idea."[59] Like Franklin, Steuben was in reality a paunchy, balding, middle-aged man. Still, for some dazzled Americans, he registered as large, imposing, and altogether splendid.[60]

While Steuben would likely have enjoyed being seen as the god of war, especially by an admiring young man, he shook his head at the mess at Valley Forge. He had to start as a volunteer, but he was determined to win respect and pay by proving his worth in transforming this straggly group of men into a fighting force ready for a global war. Although there was some confusion (and likely deliberate exaggeration) about his exact rank in the Prussian military, there was no question that he had been trained in a most formidable force, serving Frederick himself, one to outrank in martial discipline and prestige even that of the fearsome Hessians.

Steuben worked hard to get these raw recruits into shape. They did not even know basics like how to march in time, as a Prussian regiment would have done. Strategists of the era believed that a uniform march was critical to strength: "The foundation of training depends on the legs.... Have them march in cadence."[61] To teach the soldiers properly, Steuben demanded that there be no music during the drills, so that the soldiers could learn the steps without distraction. Although he spoke little English, he inspected the troops himself. With his usual brevity, Greenman reported "a new exercise caried on by the prusand general."[62] When soldiers did not perform the new exercise properly, Steuben supposedly cursed at them in German and then French, calling upon his aides to swear at the soldiers in English. Although the enlisted men feared this daunting commander, they found this theatrical sequence of trilingual swearing so ridiculous that they apparently smiled and tried harder until they got it right.[63] He did as Frederick the Great had counseled: "The commander should practice kindness and severity, should appear friendly to the soldiers."[64]

Under Steuben's friendly but watchful eye, the Continental Army improved. Within a month, he became the inspector general.[65] With the help of his loyal aides and translators, Steuben later published the drills in a manual to shape the American forces. In the "Blue Book" they crafted—a popular resource for the American military well into the nineteenth century—they gave instructions about everything, even how a soldier should stand: "straight and firm upon his legs, with the heels two inches apart, the toes a little turned out, the belly drawn in a little without constraint, the breast a little projected, the shoulders square to the front."[66] The manual advised that troops be inspected regularly for health and appearance, to ensure "that their clothes are whole and put on properly; their hands and faces washed clean; their hair combed; their accoutrements properly fixed."[67] It was not easy to achieve all this at Valley Forge, but Steuben pushed them to take more care.

Steuben also worked to raise morale. He had learned from Frederick the Great that "the foundation of an army is the belly."[68] The soldiers needed food, and they needed clothing. In late February, even the privileged John Laurens—Washington's aide-de-camp—was begging his father to send white cloth as he had "but one pair of breeches that are wearable."[69] At the behest of his dauntless aides, Steuben decided to raise spirits by inviting a group of young officers to a dinner party. There was one catch. To be admitted, they had to appear in torn breeches—or in none at all: a sardonic nod to the lack of proper attire at Valley Forge, and perhaps a little more than that. Clubbing their rations together, they managed a jolly meal of "tough beef steaks and potatoes with hickory nuts for our dessert." Lacking wine, they drank moonshine set alight into cocktails they called Salamanders.[70] Occasionally, a revolution is a dinner party.

In the glow cast by those fiery drinks on laughing men in torn breeches, it is possible to spy an alternative culture of intimacies usually in the shadows. That's not the usual textbook image of Valley Forge. Physical relations between men occurred in this era, but it is challenging to find many traces of them in eighteenth-century sources. That particular semi-clad gathering—in conjunction with other evidence culled from a range of sources—allows us to see, however fleetingly, a different view of the dynamics between at least some men in this era.[71] This event provides context for anecdotes such as that told by Steuben's aide, Stephen Du Ponceau, about the conversation between a Frenchman (possibly himself) and an American about different national practices. At the tavern of the Virginia inn where they were staying, the American complained about the "horrid custom" of the French kissing each other at introductions. At this point, the Frenchman headed to bed. The American followed, undressing and readying himself for getting into their shared bed, in the custom of such inns. The Frenchman stopped him, saying: "I shall kiss you as much as you please, but by Jupiter, I'll not sleep with you."[72] The lightness with which Du Ponceau related this story even decades later suggests that there was some tolerance for male intimacies.

In other words, the American Revolutionary War generated not just violence between men, but—at least occasionally—close physical and emotional relations between them. Alexander Hamilton and John Laurens of the torn breeches exchanged letters romantic in tone, with allusions to physical intimacies.[73] Some of the most celebrated soldiers, such as Steuben, also maintained their most significant relationships with other men, including aides-de-camp. Steuben never married or had any long-term relationships with women, and he had had to leave his position at a German court because of rumors of sexual relations with young men.[74] His decision to escape that situation is the reason he ended up at the French court seeking his fortune. In North America, he found it—as well as long-term affections. Steuben later established a family relationship with two men, Benjamin Walker (whom he met at Valley Forge) and William North, adopting them formally and leaving them his estate on his death. These men declared their love for him and for each other.[75]

There were other recorded intimate relationships between military men. There were especially close relations among three men: Major General John Paterson, General Tadeusz Kościuszko, and Agrippa Hull.[76] In a laudatory late-nineteenth-century biography, John Paterson's great-grandson noted the warm relationship that his ancestor had enjoyed with "General Kosciusko, the Polish hero, with whom he formed an especially close and intimate friendship, often, from the necessity of war, sleeping in the same bed. They were spirited, sprightly men"—zesty, one might say. Like Steuben, Kościuszko was a sophisticated European career soldier, also kitted out in a showy uniform topped with a hat bedecked with nodding ostrich plumes. Apparently, the two were known for their saucy games under the blankets, as Paterson's descendant recounted: "Kosciusko was full of life, and sometimes played practical jokes upon General Paterson when in bed, making a trial of strength." In response, Paterson, "who was a great athlete, would take Kosciusko across his knee and hold him till he begged to be released, calling him 'a cruel man.'" These two men "maintained their relationship for many years, both serving throughout the northern campaign, at Saratoga, and later at West Point." There were also close relations between these two men and a talented free Black soldier from Northampton, Massachusetts, Agrippa Hull. Apparently, "his aptness and wit and his readiness in repartee . . . made him a great favorite" of the two leaders. Kościuszko even wanted Hull—who was by then "almost necessary to his comfort"—to come to Poland with him when the war ended. Although "very much attached," Hull ultimately decided not to join him.[77]

Here is a different kind of founding father. A transformed Continental Army, producing major military successes in the American Revolution as well as the drill manual used by the American military through much of the nineteenth century, can be at least partially attributed to what might reasonably be called queer immigrants.[78] This founding moment was so much richer and more unexpected than we usually imagine.

This situation introduces yet another set of ironies. Playing up his background as a sophisticated European, Steuben won the respect and employment he sought in the new United States. While sophisticated Parisians relished the raw American Franklin, republican Americans embraced this courtly Prussian soldier sporting a royal medal around his neck. Even as Friends of Liberty painted Hessian and other German-speaking soldiers as monsters, this German-speaking soldier became an inspiration for the Continental Army. A Polish soldier who had fought against rebels in his own country, Tadeusz Kościuszko, became a soldier for liberty in America, one who came to depend on a Black man, Agrippa Hull, for his "comfort."[79]

It was not all plain sailing. There were strains around American use of foreign officers. In October 1777, Ben Franklin complained about the large number of such soldiers seeking employment. Even as he wished that they could avoid giving any letters of recommendation to these men, in the same letter he noted that Baron de Steuben was carrying papers overseas for him.[80] Although Washington leaned on Steuben in 1778, he also fretted over what he called "military fortune hunters."

Washington felt that too many of these men were either spies or ambitious for personal glory, not true Friends of Liberty. There were also tensions with Steuben himself, as he wanted his own regiment. Alexander Hamilton, another of Washington's aides-de-camp, reported in July 1778 that Steuben was "discontented . . . and almost resolved to quit."[81] Washington concluded his letter, "altho I think the Baron an excellent Officer, I do most devoutly wish that we had not a single Foreigner among us"—with the exception of the Marquis de Lafayette, whom Washington placed in a special category.

To Washington and others, the young, energetic Lafayette personified the best of the Franco-American alliance. He had offered his services—and a ship—to the Americans in 1777, joining the common cause. Once in North America, he and Washington became good friends; Lafayette named one of his sons George Washington Lafayette. He claimed in his memoirs, in a statement often quoted, that "my heart espoused warmly the cause of liberty." He is usually cast as a starry-eyed dreamer enthralled by American freedom. Less often quoted is what he said just before this statement: a realpolitik claim that the war would decide the "destiny of France," in that if Britain kept its American colonies, "all was ended for our West Indies, our possessions in Asia and Africa, our maritime commerce, and consequently our navy and our political existence."[82] Much like Vergennes—no lover of liberty—Lafayette also worried about the ruin and humiliation of France on a world stage.

The French alliance transformed the fundamental nature of the American Revolutionary War. When France entered a formal treaty with the United States, what had been a colonial rebellion became a world war between European imperial powers, much like the Seven Years' War. Britain's chief objective became not defeating the American rebels but vanquishing—or at least containing—the French. One British official conceded: "Tho' attended with many disagreeable, and humiliating Circumstances, There seems no Alternative to abandoning the 13 American Provinces" and instead focusing on the rest of the world, including the West Indies.[83] As the British Board of Admiralty framed it in March 1778, with the treaty, "the contest in America" was reduced to "a secondary consideration" as "our principal object must be distressing France and defending . . . his Majesties possessions."[84]

British victory in 1763 laid a complicated series of trip wires around the globe. British success in the Seven Years' War had enlarged its global empire. Yet 1763's triumph became a source of enduring trouble. Not only were there the challenges of incorporating new kinds of people (Native Americans, French Catholics) into the empire, but the British now had a much larger and more fragile set of holdings to defend. They had also generated a lot of ill will, especially among the French and Spanish, and they had few allies.[85] In the 1770s and 1780s, the British—with few friends and many enemies—came to find one detonation after the other exploding around them. As one commentator put it as early as 1761, it would not be "for the advantage of England to be so overloaded with foreign Possessions" that it would imperil its relationships.[86] He predicted that if the British took Canada, the "North American Colonies" would no longer believe in "their dependance on their Mother Country."[87] He had a point.

The British also confronted the Spanish, who had numerous grievances. They wanted the return of Gibraltar, which the British had taken earlier in the eighteenth century. They were also still smarting from the 1762 British occupation of Havana, the capital of the jewel of Spain's Caribbean crown, Cuba.[88] The Spanish had also tried—and failed—to recapture the Islas Malvinas, or Falkland Islands, in 1770.[89] Relations between the British and the Spanish remained strained in the 1770s.

As a result, the Spanish agreed to join the French, though not officially the United States, in signing the Treaty of Aranjuez in April 1779, in which they promised "to avenge their respective injuries, and to put an end to that tyrannical empire," Great Britain.[90] The Spanish sought the return of East and West Florida, Minorca, and Gibraltar, all of which had been ceded to Britain in 1763. As the Marquis de Lafayette had predicted, from 1778 on, the British faced enemies in West Indies, Asia, and Africa: the French and Spanish, of course, but plenty of others—many Indigenous—too. Indigenous and other leaders wanted respect and autonomy, and they were willing to fight the British to achieve these goals.

The West Indies formed a critical theater of the war, among its most challenging. Both sides were determined to protect their largest and most profitable colonies—Jamaica for the British and Saint-Domingue for the French. Here was another irony: The very aspects that made Jamaica and Saint-Domingue so valuable in peace—their tropical island environments, their sugar monoculture, their considerable population of enslaved laborers—was precisely what made them so vulnerable in war. European authorities knew it, too. Britain sent reinforcements from the mainland under Cornwallis to defend Jamaica in the autumn of 1778, thus seriously weakening British forces on the mainland.[91] The scattered island nature of the Caribbean colonies complicated defensive strategies. Since so much land was given over to sugar, these islands depended on food imports (from places like New England and Ireland), so dangers of famine were, ironically, high for these verdant islands. As early as 1775, the governor of Jamaica worried that it was "deprived of its usual supply of provision from North America."[92] The proliferation of diseases such as yellow fever and malaria in the tropical environment also led to exceptionally high mortality rates for military forces, whom one historian has memorably termed "luckless virus-fodder sent from Europe."[93] Little wonder that such troops possessed an enduring "dread of going to the West Indies."[94]

The American Revolution drove the paranoid fantasies of Jamaican enslavers, as made clear by an alleged slave rebellion plot there in 1776. Jamaican planters believed that their most trusted enslaved men were plotting an insurrection inspired by the American Revolution. In July, one enslaver, blaming the Americans, warned that "there is a most Consummate Rebellion a foot."[95] By early August, magistrates declared themselves "in hourly expectation of a General Rebellion."[96] Enslavers came down extremely hard on this alleged rebellion.[97] When one enslaved witness refused to name others, he was threatened with gibbeting, in which he would have been suspended in an iron suit by a chain, as had been done to insurgents after Tacky's Rebellion in 1761. In 1776, officials tried 135 enslaved individuals, convicting seventy-three of them on the basis of recanted witness testimony and flimsy evidence. Forty-five persons were transported; eleven received "severe corporal punishment"; and seventeen were executed.[98] Many blamed the Jamaican rebellion on "the general Consternation and Allarm spread through this island on the removal of the Regiment."[99] The governor of Jamaica claimed the insurrection started because rebels had known "there were fewer Troops in the Island [as] Great Britain was exerting all her Strength in reducing the Rebellious Colonies of North America."[100]

The British also feared Maroon (free Black and Indigenous) communities in Jamaica and elsewhere. In Jamaica, Maroons, who lived independently in Jamaica's interior, had entered into a fragile alliance with British authorities in 1739. In the 1770s, one admiral noted that the Maroons had "still a strong Inclination to be troublesome."[101] Enslaved witnesses in 1776 implicated the Maroons, averring that they had a plan to "take the Country to themselves, and drive the white people entirely out of it" using "Guns, Powder, and Shot."[102]

Enslaver anxieties about Maroon and Native American communities also emerged in another Caribbean island, St. Vincents. African and Indigenous Kalinago (or Garifuna) people had led a rebellion already, in what came to be called the First Carib War (1769–73). In late 1776, the ever scheming Silas Deane even floated the idea of deliberately inciting rebellions among the Maroons in Jamaica and the Kalinagos in St. Vincents: "Should there arise troubles in these two islands . . . the consequence would be that Great Britain . . . must withdraw a large part to defend her islands."[103]

Even though this plan was not put into action, the defense of Caribbean islands sucked up British energies and troops and supplies. In September 1778, the French took Domenica (lost in 1763); less than a year later, the French captured St. Vincents and Grenada, likely cheered on by Indigenous people in those islands who had endured British rule since 1763.

In South Asia and West Africa, too, Indigenous leaders seeking respect fought the British. One ambitious leader in Southern India, Haidar (or Hyder) Ali, was eager to limit the inroads of the English East India Company. He allied with the French, with one Frenchman praising him to Benjamin Franklin as a "brave Mughal prince."[104] Rising from the ranks of the military, he had become a powerful conqueror. To rouse his generals, he designed a new uniform featuring a white satin vest and pantaloons with yellow facing, a white silk scarf around the waist, a red turban, and yellow velvet boots.[105] In this outfit, Haidar Ali and his generals were ready for war, especially against the English, as "the hatred he conceived against them grew with his power."[106] He apparently rallied other Asian rulers with eloquent speeches in which he denounced the English for having "despoiled the country of its riches, of its inhabitants, of its fertility, of its glory."[107] Although he was not able to prevent the British capture of French trading depots—including, notably, Puducherry (Pondicherry), which was besieged for months—he was working in the late 1770s to build allegiances against the British and "their unjust aggression."[108]

South Asian leaders like Haidar Ali were building strength, convincing the Marathas (local rulers) to enter into an offensive-defensive alliance in February 1780. Ali commanded a military of more than 220,000 soldiers (by comparison, France and Prussia each had militaries of 160,000 men).[109] He later exhorted his son, Tipu Sultan, to protect the empire he had built. He knew it was a vulnerable alliance dependent on the conquests he had made. As he observed: "A sceptre acquired by

This 1762 French engraving shows Haidar Ali (Hyder Ally) well armed "at the head of his army against the English," as the caption notes.

violence is always fragile." Still, he encouraged his son to keep marching in those yellow velvet boots: "The English are to-day all powerful in India. It is necessary to weaken them by war."[110]

Local leaders allied with the French in West Africa also frustrated British ambitions. In 1758, in the area where the Senegal and Gambia rivers met, the British had taken the French forts of St. Louis du Sénégal and Gorée, and they held on to the first in 1763's treaty. There, the British set up their first West African colony: the Province of Senegambia.[111] The Board of Trade tried to create a government similar to "the American Colonies, as far as the difference of Circumstances and Situation will admit."[112] One Englishman predicted that although these locations could be "of infinite use to our Commerce," he conceded that they could also turn out to be "the Grave of our People, and endless source of future quarrels."[113] He was not wrong. African rulers were powerful; half of the colony's budget went toward payments to these leaders as the English recognized that "British Interests... depend... on the good Will and Friendship of the Natives."[114] They complained that such friendship was fragile, as "the French had spirited the Natives up against the English."[115]

The English also managed to "spirit up" local anger when they killed the son of the previously neutral king of Niumi. He sent five hundred soldiers against them in retaliation.[116] English attacks on the nearby Waalo, with a related sharp rise in selling them into the Atlantic slave trade, further imperiled these relations.[117] When an epidemic struck St. Louis in 1778, it fatally weakened the tenuous British hold so that they capitulated immediately to the French arriving there in early 1779. With that, the French took back what they had lost in West Africa in the Seven Years' War.

In other words, British energies and resources were being dissipated around the globe year after bloody year. Steuben, a man praised by Washington as "a man of military knowledge and acquainted with the World," understood this point. He saw the global war for what it was: a chance for American victory—provided the Americans did not squander their advantages. As he assured his old patron, Ben Franklin, in September 1779, "the English will not beat us, if we do not beat ourselves."[118]

The story of the American Revolutionary War, and why the British lost, then, is partly a story of Indigenous power. A desire for respect on the world stage motivated behavior around the globe among all kinds of leaders—and nations. Even if Americans were mostly unaware of it, aid to their cause came from Indigenous fighters around the world: African and Native American communities in the Caribbean, South Asian conquerors, West African kings. The British watched the enlarged empire they had won in 1763 seethe and buckle and turn against them. As we have seen, Haidar Ali knew what the British learned: "A sceptre acquired by violence is always fragile." It was a message some Americans needed to heed as they, too, came up against the force of enduring Indigenous power.

Chapter 9

A Cornfield in the Six Nations

The warriors, shouting in English, descended again, fiery torches in their hands. They seemed to be coming for the three graceful sisters who flitted in the fields—and for anyone else they found, too. The towering cornstalks with their silken tassels burned first, their dry leaves feeding the fire. The other sisters—squash and beans clinging to their beloved corn—followed. The tripod on which life depended disappeared in a puff of smoke.[1] Apple trees were cut and girdled to prevent their ever providing any fruit again. Homes—"framed houses" and "houses of hewed logs" and "bark [long]houses" with multiple fireplaces—were next.[2] The woman heard the soldiers exclaiming over their contents—amazed that these "savages" possessed beautiful leather-bound books—before pilfering all the clothing, blankets, kettles, foods, and dishes they could carry.[3] Whatever they left went up in flames. Things that seemed so permanent turned out to be so fragile. The smoke caught her throat and made her eyes water. It blew and swirled, rising high into the air, sending a message of warning. As the smell reached the quivering noses of bears and wolves far away, they took off. Once the fires flickered out, there was only smoldering ruin, the acrid stench of war and destruction. She trusted the earth to provide, as it always had, but how would she manage now?

The men who found her at harvest time in 1779 called her many things: "a very old Squaw"; a "helpless impotent wretch"; an "antediluvian hag."[4] None of these phrases recognized her as a human being. Only one man recorded a name: "Madam Sacho." Yet we would not know even that much about her if Major General John Sullivan and his men had not stumbled across her. Entering the Land of the Six Nations—the Haudenosaunee Confederacy—in August 1779, Continental Army soldiers expected whooping warriors in loincloths with feathers on their heads, guns and tomahawks raised. What they found instead were houses and towns and farms—and Madam Sacho. Soldiers' diaries recount the astonishment they felt on encountering her, detailing how, through an Oneida interpreter, she conversed with General Sullivan himself. Some wanted to kill her, but, as one soldier recorded, "the common dictates of humanity, a veneration for old age, and a regard for the female world of any age or denomination induced our General to spare her."[5]

This Tuscarora woman surprises still. Most people today imagine in the American Revolution these same fierce fighters, or else they envision tidy lines of redcoats firing against minutemen. That is not how it went here. There were other kinds of battles; here are the fighters in one of them. It may seem an obscure moment: one little old lady against an entire set of Continental Army regiments. Nevertheless, it reveals a great deal. It brings us squarely into the issue at the heart of both the American Revolution and the long war waged over centuries by Indigenous Americans: that of security, and what all kinds of people—from Mohawk mothers to George Washington himself—were willing to do to achieve it.[6] In the Declaration of Independence, the colonists agreed that it was their right, their duty, to overthrow a despotic government after a "long train of abuses and usurpations." In that event, they needed to "provide new Guards for their future security." Abuses, usurpations, and security: such were indeed key challenges of 1779.

Madam Sacho had witnessed war, dislocation, and flight many times before; she may even have been an evacuee in her youth. She identified herself as Tuscarora, the sixth and most recent of the Six Nations, a refugee community welcomed by their "big brothers," the Oneida, following the brutal Tuscarora War with encroaching British settlers in the Carolinas in the 1710s. The Tuscaroras who made it north were the lucky ones, and they knew it. One visitor noted of them, "Always persecuted by wars, they were obliged to go wandering for a long time, until they were received by the Oneidas."[7] Escaping death and enslavement, they had found security in the Land of the Five Nations. The addition of the Tuscaroras, and the strong hands reaching out to them from their brothers and sisters, transformed it into the Land of Six Nations. They thus had reason to love their new homeland south of Lake Ontario, though they regretted having to leave their own.

That northern land was a flourishing one. She and her family would have been invited immediately into a longhouse, shared by several families, hearths down the middle. She would have smelled the steaming corn soup in brass kettles over the fire. Without even thinking about it, even if their harvest had been poor, older women, "hair ty'd behind," would have smiled and filled bowls to warm and nourish them and their family.[8] As they ladled the thick potage, they might have explained through interpreters that the confederacy to which she had arrived mirrored the longhouse itself. The Mohawks—the People of the Flint—were the door keepers to the east; the Senecas—the People of the Great Hill—guarded the entry to the west. In the center were the Onondagas—the People of the Mountain—flanked by the Cayugas and the Oneidas—the People of the Standing Stone—who often looked south to those relations. They might have explained about the three main clans: Wolf, Bear, and Turtle.

These gracious hosts would have pointed out the sachems, leaders of the lineages of those clans, as well as the matrons, the women who had chosen them. Those elite families would have enjoyed prime locations, but no one was above anyone else in those egalitarian longhouses. She needed no explanation of what she already knew from Tuscarora life: "Each of these Nations is an absolute Republick by itself. . . . [Leaders] never execute their Resolutions by Force upon any of their People."[9] If she, a young stranger, had cause to ask a silver-haired sachem for something, he would have given it to her because he knew "A man never refuses when asked."[10] Still, most of her time would have been spent with other women. They planted and tended the fields and gardens, managing crop rotations to make the soil what a visiting European called "the richest and most fertile to be found on our globe."[11] They bore and nursed and raised children. They kept the hearth fires blazing.

In some ways, things were easier for women like her than they had been for their great-grandmothers. Now they had brass kettles to make

This eighteenth-century wampum belt—an item of considerable sacred, diplomatic, political, and economic importance—depicts eight human figures, two dogs, and a cross, demonstrating the syncretic nature of Haudenosaunee representational art and diplomatic aspirations. The linked arms across the horizontal mirror the layout of the longhouse, with dogs guarding the openings at either end.

the jobs of cooking and maple sugaring safer and more efficient. Their husbands, fathers, and brothers could bring home more deer thanks to the guns for which they also traded—though they had to travel farther to find the animals. Trade also furnished them with "stroud" (English woolen blankets), even as it also brought the rum that occasionally made some men sing and shout and fight. A leader could appear at treaty negotiations in "a scarlet coat turned up with lace, and a high gold laced hat," with soft deerskin moccasins on his feet.[12] A prominent wife could wear a calico gown studded with silver brooches that also functioned as currency. A soldier could wear earrings in an ear cut into strips while also toting a European musket.[13] They sang hymns in church, and many were baptized. Yet even as some families moved into smaller log and framed houses, they maintained their identity as the people of the longhouse, treasuring wampum and other markers of their culture. They ate with pewter spoons the soups and stews they cooked communally over hearths even as they also relished tea and coffee sipped from ceramic cups and saucers.[14] They were familiar with the ways of settlers, but their ways were different. They knew their place in the world, and, whether lit with summer sun or covered with winter snows, it was a beautiful one.

However, this lovely land had long been under threat. Along with their guns and kettles, settlers brought with them a desire for this land, to furnish farms for their children and to sell for profit. In 1768, at the negotiations for the Treaty of Fort Stanwix, Indigenous diplomats agreed on the usefulness of a boundary line, but also evinced concern that "we cannot have any great dependance on the white People" when it came to their promises about borders and land.[15] One Oneida leader informed the British Indian agent: "We . . . have been for some time like Giddy People not knowing what to do, where ever we turned about, we saw our Blood." When their young men went hunting in their own land, they "found it covered with [settler] fences."[16] By 1772, Mohawk leaders such as Thayendanegea, also called Joseph Brant, condemned "the ill treatment we have received from several White people, who endeavour to defraud us of our Lands."[17] They feared their very heartland was now under threat. "This fills us with such concern, and is so alarming a nature, that whether we are in our beds, or ranging the woods in quest of game, it . . . deprives us of rest."[18] Men like Thayendanegea had every reason to lose sleep over this problem.

Still, the Six Nations were sovereign nations.[19] This land was theirs. That is why discussions between Britain or the United States and these nations were formal diplomatic events, with welcomes and speeches and feasts and treaties. Even royal officials, such as the Indian agent Sir William Johnson, recognized this fact in the 1760s. When another administrator assumed that Indians, like colonists, were subjects of the king, Johnson corrected him in no uncertain terms: "None of the Six Nations . . . ever declared themselves to be Subjects, or will ever consider themselves in that light." Moreover, he continued, "the very Idea of Subjection would fill them with horror," antithetical as it was to egalitarian Haudenosaunee political values.[20] As another observer had put it earlier in the eighteenth century, "The *Five Nations* have such absolute Notions of Liberty, that they allow of no kind of Superiority of one over another."[21] Johnson pointed out that "the right of Soil always remained" with Indigenous nations.[22] However, this kind of spirited defense became increasingly uncommon. Too many other White men reached with grasping hands, and guns and deeds besides. As a result, the Haudenosaunee sought security—the right to live without threat or subjection of any kind—from their neighbors and sometimes allies.

How could the Six Nations find security in the mid-1770s? There lay the challenge. In addition to the worrisome possibility of trickery and fraud, there were now choices to be made. They did not see this war as theirs. To many members of the Six Nations, the American Revolutionary War looked like simply another conflict between colonizing powers. As Tegoransen, or Little Abraham, a Mohawk leader who tried to remain neutral, noted, it was "not the Business of us Indians to take Part in any Quarrels between the White-People . . . their Affairs do not concern us."[23] Still, despite their best efforts, Tegoransen and everyone else in the Six Nations got dragged into it. Every option had drawbacks. They could actively support the British, but the British had proven untrustworthy in the past. There was still bad blood there. They could support the Americans, but many American settlers were pushing hard for the taking of Indigenous land, which cast doubt on their sweet promises of always being friends. Also, the Americans might lose, and the Indians knew they would be the first to pay the price with vengeful British. They could try to maintain neutrality, but this option was often seen—and punished—as betrayal by both sides, as Pacifist Friends (Quakers) and others found.[24] Individuals of the Six Nations—as elsewhere—often ended up choosing sides after threats, violence, and the breakdown of relations.

The "Yankees," as they were sometimes called by Indigenous people, also sought security.[25] Those who lived near the lands of Six Nations worried that their families, their nursing mothers and babies, were at risk from attacks. They fretted over what they saw as the terrifying ferocity of Haundenosaunee soldiers, faces "dismally painted with red and black," as well as their stunning ability to launch extremely effective attacks—so efficient and deadly that Americans tried to copy their techniques.[26] Distrusting and hating all Indigenous people indiscriminately, many settlers believed security could be found only in their complete eradication—"extirpation," as they termed it. Even in the early eighteenth century, one colonial official, frustrated by the Tuscaroras against whom he was warring, wished that they could "extirpate a savage people with whom no peace can be made."[27] Like this man and also those who perpetrated the Paxton murders during Pontiac's War, many settlers in New York did not distinguish between allied friends and enemy combatants among Indigenous populations. Indian hating was a rich political resource on which Patriots could draw in times of trouble. It rallied men to join the army and fight, and, as we have already seen, it ginned up anger at more conciliatory British policies.

One historian has observed that a war is "an act of communication" with a "'grammar' in which violent acts carry meaning and convey intention."[28] Retaliatory violence provided a useful way to tap into that reserve of Indian hating, even if there were other, more mercenary motives. Settlers knew that the land cultivated by Haudenosaunee women was fruitful; the evidence was right before their eyes. Imagine, men thought to themselves, how much more fertile it could be in the right hands (meaning their own—or their sons'). The late 1770s were an era of what one scholar has termed "a revolution in land policy."[29] Businessmen of the era—often called speculators—eyed these fertile lands and saw lucrative property development.

One of these businessmen was George Washington. His behavior in Indian country does not reveal him at his best.[30] His strategies here reflected two imperatives that ran together in pernicious ways. One was that of an ambitious land surveyor and speculator who recognized the desirable wealth held by Indigenous nations. The other was that of a general who had long been dealing with these nations—whom he knew to be experts in the art of war—and who was beyond frustrated by their enduring power. As a British officer in the Seven Years' War, he had fought them repeatedly and often without success from 1754 on. Like Jeffrey Amherst and others, he and his high command believed Indigenous people to be effective fighters—which they were—but also deserving of treatment not generally to be contemplated for British enemies. Even as early as May 1776, Major General Philip Schuyler suggested that a delegation of Indigenous diplomats should be kidnapped "as a Kind of Hostages, for the peaceable Demeanor of the others." That same month, Washington wrote to Schuyler fretting that "Our Situation respecting the Indians is rather delicate & Embarrassing." He wanted to seize Guy Johnson—William Johnson's nephew and agent since 1774—but worried that in so doing, "there will be Danger of Incurring Resentment."[31]

Their experiences in the Seven Years' War shaped the thinking of both Washington and Schuyler. It also sharpened their frustration about their seeming inability to vanquish Indigenous combatants.[32] As we have seen, one author during that war argued for more rigorous methods in dealing with Indigenous people. He lamented that "We have no Means of making the Indians afraid of us . . . they can always secure their Persons & Families." In his view, the only way to bring them to heel was to use wives and children as leverage, undermining their ability to protect their families. This author outlined plans in which soldiers should move in small parties to "Destroy any Indian Villages they met with . . . & carry off the Women & Children."[33] For too many Americans in the wake of this long war, settler security seemed to lie in Native American terror.

When leaders advance plans for kidnapping women and children as a basic military strategy, it reveals something dark and festering, with deep roots in a longer history of brutality. Indeed, the American Revolutionary War in the Land of the Six Nations had a complicated character, a complex grammar of violence. It was a war of conquest because many Americans had long sought to take over the lands of the Six Nations. Their holdings had already shrunk, keeping those strong Indigenous men awake at night as they worried for the future of themselves and their families. The war itself furnished an opportunity for the Americans to enact the takeover they had long desired. As a borderlands war, the fighting crossed the boundary of separate nations abutting each other: one new confederacy—the United States of America—and one old one: the Haudenosaunee. The birth of the new confederacy fractured the older one, at least temporarily.

The American Revolutionary War became something like a civil war in Haudenosaunee lands, extinguishing the Council Fire shared by all the people of the longhouse. As Tegoransen, or Little Abraham, the Mohawk leader, put it in 1775, "our proper Fire Place [is] where we meet to transact business."[34] Once that fire (literally) went out, each nation was free to determine its own course of action. As one visitor observed, "Their government is known to be democratic."[35] Although brothers hated to fight each other, and tried to avoid it, some ended up on opposite sides. For the most part, Mohawks, Senecas, Cayugas, and Onondagas were pro-British. Among the most compelling voices favoring a British alliance were a Mohawk woman, Konwatsitsiaienni (Molly Brant), and her brother, Thayendanegea (Joseph Brant). These two political leaders were from prominent lineages. Konwatsitsiaienni was a powerful speaker, in the tradition of Haudenosaunee matrons. She was also an effective negotiator with the British, since she was recognized as the wife (and later widow) of Sir William Johnson, the British Indian agent, with whom she had eight surviving children.[36] Thayendanegea visited England in 1776, seeking to represent his people and to negotiate an alliance with the British. While he was there, a leading artist, George Romney, painted his portrait.

On the other side, Oneidas and Tuscaroras tended to support the Patriots. Nia-man-rigounant (or Colonel Joseph Louis Cook) was not an Oneida, but he became the commander of an American regiment of mostly Oneida soldiers. The son of a Black father and an Abenaki mother, he had been taken captive by Mohawks when he was a child, becoming integrated as a member of the Six Nations and baptized as a Catholic. He appeared in the portrait of General Richard Montgomery dying in Québec. At Valley Forge in 1778, stepping out one morning in "American regimentals and two large epaulettes," he astonished Steuben's aide-de-camp by singing fashionable French light opera in "a voice of... extraordinary power," then professing—in French—his affection for the French and their royal family.[37]

In the Land of the Six Nations, individuals like Nia-man-rigounant followed their own inclinations, as it was a cooperative, not a coercive, political structure. As Tenhoghskweaghta, an Onondaga sachem, pointed out to American commissioners in March 1778, "you have some Friends... among the six Nations and you have some Enemies—It is perhaps much with us as it is with you white people." He observed that the Senecas, for instance, had "long since forsaken our Council Fire" in protest. He noted of the Onondagas, "even my Nation are divided in Sentiment."[38] Some supported liberty, others loyalty, some tried to remain neutral—in Indigenous country as in the rest of North America.

Divided sentiments led to tensions. They flared at one conference in which two Mohawks and two Oneidas, all of whom had declared themselves neutral, came to visit Thayendanegea and his people, imploring them to "lay down your Arms" and adopt neutrality. They assured them that "the Rebels will allow you to . . . enjoy your Lands & Villages again in Peace & Security." Tegoransen and others gave speeches, including one "in the Name of the Women, to the Women . . . desiring them to use their Influence over the Warriors." They also presented belts of wampum, including "a white belt with 13 Squares," a nod to the thirteen states of the new nation.

As soon as the pro-British Mohawks opened their mouths to reply, though, the visitors would have known that their efforts were futile. Addressing them with cold precision as "Mohawks & Oneydas," not as "brothers" as was almost always the case in such diplomatic speeches, the hosts rejected these overtures in the strongest and most contemptuous terms: "You Children, you say you come for the Sake of Peace & Quietness, and for the Good of the Six Nations but at the same Time bring a false Heart & a flattering Tongue to breed Confusion amongst us." They warned, too, that American promises could not be trusted: "Rebels . . . have their Hatchet lifted up against you, ready to strike it into your Heads, if you do not act in everything as they would have you." With that, they threw back every single gift of wampum and ended the discussion.[39]

The clatter of pro-American wampum belts hitting the ground was the sound of major fault lines between nations; there were also generational conflicts. Older sachems, favoring peace and neutrality, were measured, plain in appearance and elaborate in speeches. Those who had fought in the Seven Years' War knew the agonies of war firsthand; it made them wary and careful. Young men—kitted out with silver, brass, porcupine quills, and wampum, hair shaved on the sides and faces plucked—were more inclined to pick up the war club.[40] The sachems felt that their authority was no longer respected. As one, Tenhoghskweaghta, complained, "Times are altered with us Indians—Formerly the Warriors were governed by the Wisdom of their Uncles the Sachems but now they take their own Way."[41] An Oneida sachem, the Grasshopper, reported much the same of his people: "Formerly the Sachems were implicitly obeyed by the Warriors, but now the latter have thrown off all Regard to their Council." He warned the young men: "Brother Warriors

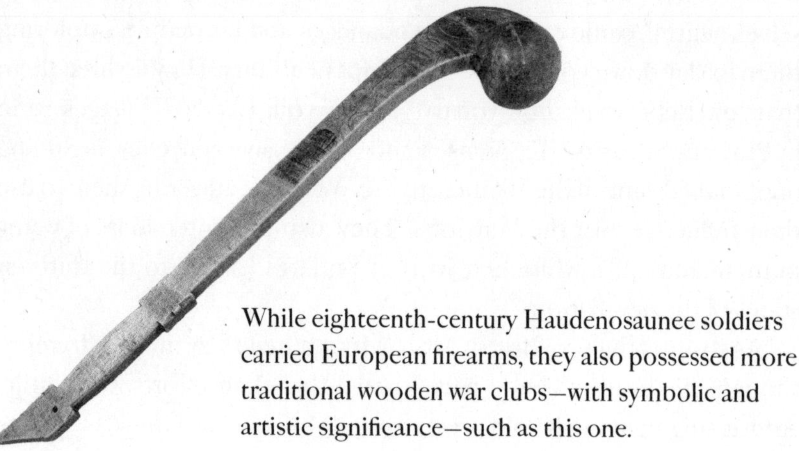

While eighteenth-century Haudenosaunee soldiers carried European firearms, they also possessed more traditional wooden war clubs—with symbolic and artistic significance—such as this one.

reflect for a Moment that at a future Day your Looks will be silvered by Age and then too late will you deplore the Neglect which your Elders now experience from you."[42] Admittedly, older people often lament that the new generation does not respect them as they did their own elders, so such statements need to be interpreted with caution. Still, taken together, they point to a conflict in the Six Nations, especially as the younger men sought to prove themselves through war. Finally, there may have been gendered aspects. Visiting the town of Oquaga in 1776, the Frenchman Hector St. John de Crèvecoeur claimed that the men often retained their "ancient ferocity" while the women were "tractable, docile."[43] One woman later reported that the women of the Six Nations had been "fretting prodigiously, and continually teasing their warriors to make peace."[44]

Many young men—settler and Indigenous—did not wish for peace. Violence flared in the Wyoming Valley in northeastern Pennsylvania in 1778. Exasperated by endless encroachments, Indigenous soldiers sought to remind settlers who had the right of soil in the Land of the Six Nations. That summer, Indigenous and British forces vanquished the Patriots the day before the second anniversary of independence. Newspaper reports in July 1778 bewailed the "horrid cruelty" of these "murderous diabolical emissaries," with claims of Patriot soldiers butchered and women and children locked in a house then set on fire.[45] While men were indeed killed in battle, the rest of the reports were false. There was no civilian massacre. One French settler attested that Native Americans "treated the defenceless ones, the women and children, with . . . humanity."[46] This fact did not stop the reprinting of fake claims across a range of colonial newspapers. Settlers were so alarmed by these reports that many fled, further fracturing Patriot communities. They also continued to narrate the event as a massacre of the innocents, contributing yet more fuel to the flames of Indian hating.

Partly in retaliation for the Wyoming debacle, American officials decided to attack two Haudenosaunee towns: Oquaga and Unidilla. For decades, people had recognized Oquaga, a prosperous farming community located on arable lowlands near two rivers, as a flourishing and diverse community, attractive to migrants. In 1776, Hector St. John de Crèvecoeur described its "neat and warm habitations," with fields "extremely flourishing." He also lauded the "greatly civilized" locals for greeting him "with their usual hospitality."[47] Another visitor praised its "civil and sober" residents (including many women and children) who produced bread, butter, and maple sugar. They lived in longhouses, tended livestock, and grew all kinds of food: "Corn, Beans, Water Melons, Potatoes, Cucumbers, Muskmelons, Cabbage, French Turneps, some Apple Trees, Sallad, Parsnips, & other Plants."[48] Even the Continental Army officer sent to destroy it, William Butler, conceded that it was "the finest Indian Town" he had ever seen. He nonetheless set fire to all the "good houses" and "at least 2000 Bush[e]ls of Corn, a Number of Horses, Cattle, Poultry, their Dogs, household furniture, &c &c." He moved on to Unidilla—a place noted for its gardens and "large and fat" cows in the 1760s—where he burned nearly all the houses and also the sawmill and "the only Grist Mill in that Country."[49] In other words, Butler had curtailed the ability of people from the entire area to grind their grain, whether wheat or corn. He reported with satisfaction that this activity had "secured these Frontiers from any further disturbances from the Savages." For Butler, security lay in destruction or what one global historian has termed "environcide," especially as practiced against Indigenous Americans in wars of conquest.[50]

In fact, as is so often the case, devastation and fake news only inflamed matters. Many in the Six Nations were aware of the false stories of their alleged atrocities in the Wyoming Valley. They knew that in any joint attack with the British, no matter what they actually did, they would be painted as savage devils committing massacres against civilians. As one of the British officers noted, the Patriots "having falsely accused the Indians of Cruelty at Weyomen . . . had much exasperated them."[51]

This background informs what happened at Cherry Valley in November 1778. It was a somewhat bungled attack by the British with their Mohawk and Seneca allies, and it culminated in extreme violence and plundering. Although women and children were not usually killed in such raids (though they were often taken captive), such was not the case at Cherry Valley. Soldiers took some captive but killed others. As some Mohawk leaders informed Patriots in December 1778, they had "Destroyed men, women, and Children" because "you burned our Houses" and those of brother Senecas at Oquaga and Unidilla. In this ominous December 1778 letter to Patriots, they further advised settlers to "Let our brothers live in peace, least you be worst delt with" than those at Cherry Valley. The author, a Mohawk officer, continued that "at present my face is another way, But if you Destroy that place, I will set my face against you."[52] As at Wyoming, stories of atrocities unleashed a new deluge of settler refugees, and they exacerbated Indian-hating. Many settlers set their faces against the Haudenosaunee and others.

1779 witnessed an escalation of tensions. Both Indigenous and Patriot communities shared stories of horrors perpetrated by the other side. Events accelerated Patriot plans, already afoot, for a full-scale attack on the Six Nations. As early as June 1778, the Continental Congress had authorized expenditure for campaigns against enemy Haudenosaunee, especially the Senecas, "in order to chastise that insolent and revengeful nation, and to dispossess the enemy." They argued that such offensive action was vital as a mere "defensive war would . . . prove an inadequate security against the inroads of the Indians."[53] Destroying their towns would "most effectually tend to chastise and terrify the savages."[54] The War Office passed this news on to George Washington, offering him the "Oppertunity . . . to strike the Savages with Terror."[55] However, Washington, now working with the French, was not yet ready to strike.

In early 1779, as Washington became "more and more convinced of the necessity of carrying the War into the Indian Country . . . in order

This 1777 powder horn, made from an ox and holding gunpowder for muskets, belonged to Prince Simbo, a Black soldier in the Continental Army. Its beautiful decorations come from a tradition of artistically carved powder horns in the Connecticut River Valley and what is now upstate New York.

This 1780 watercolor by a European visitor shows a range of Indigenous, Métis, and French women and men in eighteenth-century Canada. It captures the colorful diversity of the inhabitants of places like Detroit and Québec.

This 1764 cartoon mocked those who sought accommodation with Indigenous people in Pennsylvania. Israel Pemberton, a Quaker, turns over tomahawks to Indigenous soldiers while Benjamin Franklin exhorts Indigenous men to fight, saying, "I am content if I can but get the Government"—that is, win the upcoming assembly election.

This 1770 painting shows the Hindu goddess Kali, who represents death, destruction, and rebirth. The Kalighat Temple in Kolkata has existed since at least the fifteenth century, and it remains a place of worship and pilgrimage.

In this 1756 portrait, Ezra Stiles, a young minister and Yale graduate, holds a book and sports a turban and a banyan in golden silk damask, linking him to enlightened intellectuals in Europe and Asia. This was a fashionable look for cosmopolitan American men in the 1750s.

This 1780s image depicts Muhammad Reza Khan, a prominent Bengali leader. In 1765, he became the Naib Diwan of Bengal, appointed by Robert Clive. He recorded his frustrations with the English during the famine in Kolkata in 1770.

This 1774 cartoon shows a grand battle between the forces of empire (including the director of the English East India Company, a devil, and Lord Tryon, former governor of North Carolina and then governor of New York) on the left and the forces of American resistance, garbed as Indigenous Americans, on the right. The drawing appeared in response to the destruction of the tea in Boston Harbor, shown on the left in crates marked with Chinese characters.

This 1775 cartoon ridicules the political organizing and resistance of "Patriotic Ladies" in Edenton, North Carolina, in the tense autumn of 1774. They are working on a petition urging nonimportation while attacking "that Pernicious Custom of Drinking Tea" in the wake of the so-called Intolerable Acts.

This portrait of William Ansah Sessarakoo was painted by Gabriel Mathias in London in 1749. The elite Sessarakoo went to England for his education, sent by his father, the *caboceer,* or commander, of Anomabu castle. On his way there, he was captured and sold into slavery in Barbados, from which his father subsequently redeemed him.

This 1761 rendering of Québec shows Lower Town along the river and Upper Town perched above. It also shows the red-coated British officers who had taken the city over from the French after their triumph at the Battle of the Plains of Abraham in 1759.

The figure of the dying Montgomery, with his dead aide-de-camp at his feet, centers this idealized 1786 painting of the 1775 Battle of Québec. The Oneida leader, Nia-man-rigounant, or Colonel Joseph Louis Cook, is to the left of Montgomery, presenting a vision of American solidarity with the Six Nations.

A Canadian farmer in winter dress is here depicted in a 1778 drawing by a visiting German. His pipe was typical of such French Canadian *habitants.* Despite stereotypes of passive Canadians, many locals supported political resistance in 1775.

This 1784 image shows soldiers of the Land Grenadier Regiment. In keeping with most Hessian regiments, their coats were blue and riding boots tall. Note the drummer boy on the right; many boys under eighteen served with these forces.

In this British cartoon from January 1776, Britannia the mother and America the daughter duke it out, symbolizing a colonial rebellion that many English people still found amusing.

This French fashion plate from 1778—the first year such images were produced—shows a woman in full "Insurgent's Dress," a nod to the popularity in France of the American rebellion. The caption notes that the dress is in an Anglo-American style.

Baron von Steuben in this 1780 portrait wears medals awarded by Frederick the Great of Prussia around his neck as well as on his jacket. The gilt trim on his jacket also indicates the rank and military stature of this Prussian officer who did so much to transform the Continental Army in 1778.

His powdered wig, regal bearing, and gilt-trimmed coat convey the aristocratic and military status of the Marquis de Lafayette, the most beloved of the foreign officers who served the American cause, as evidenced by the many places named after him that dot the USA.

This 1771 map of the Six Nations shows the large extent of their territory at this time, with the Senecas near Lake Erie and the Mohawks near the Catskills. It also shows the boundary line, near Oriska, of the 1768 Treaty of Fort Stanwix.

This image shows the Rock of Gibraltar and the nearby Spanish coast during the opening Spanish attack of 1779. Spanish ships and land forces fire on the British town, protected by fortifications strengthened by the work of William Green and others in the 1760s and 1770s.

This remarkable depiction of the 1780 Battle of Pollilur, designed to appear on the wall of the Tipu Sultan's summer palace, stretches across 32 feet (10 meters). A colorful celebration of the greatest eighteenth-century South Asian victory against the British, it highlights the achievements of both Haidar Ali and Tipu Sultan, who appear here (on the left) on elephants.

The leading British portraitist George Romney painted the diplomat, soldier, and statesman Thayendanegea—in a European shirt but with an Indigenous *gustoweh* (feathered headdress) and breastplate—during Thayendanegea's first London visit in 1775–76. He holds a tomahawk in his right hand, but he also wears a Masonic symbol.

Mariano Salvador Maella, a well-known Spanish portraitist, painted Bernardo de Gálvez in this notable image. He wears the gilt-trimmed coat, waistcoat, and royal medal of the leading officer and statesman he was. A copy of this painting hangs in the U.S. Capitol to indicate his status as an honorary U.S. citizen.

In this line drawing for a lost allegorical painting by Benjamin West, Britannia, flanked by Justice and Religion, welcomes a range of Loyalist refugees: women and men, young and old, Indigenous, Black, and White. Reality rarely matched this ideal.

This unusual 1800 bird's-eye view of Guangzhou shows its many buildings, including several foreign factories in the center (marked by flags). It shows the bustling nature of trade at the inland port city formerly known as Canton, with many sampans (barges) and other boats on the Pearl River.

This 1780 portrait of Pan Zhencheng, the chief trader at Guangzhou, displays both his formal rank and his informal status as the leading international trader in eighteenth-century Guangzhou. The portrait's placement in the Swedish factory at Guangzhou allowed Swedes to demonstrate their close ties with this formidable merchant.

This mother-of-pearl fan depicting foreign ships near Guangzhou was a gift from Chinese officials to the American captain of the *Empress of China* in 1784. The American-flagged ship appears to the left of the other, larger European vessels.

The British flag flies over the small new settlement of Sierra Leone in this 1787 watercolor by a visiting ship's captain, a rare portrayal of the first years of this then-struggling community.

This illustration, showing the inside and outside of termite mounds in the Sierra Leone area, accompanied the text to Henry Smeathman's 1781 treatise "Some Account of the Termites, Which are Found in Africa and Other Hot Climates" for the Royal Society of London. The image, showing Smeathman's local guide, demonstrates the close ties between science, empire, and colonialism in that era.

to give peace and security to our own Frontier," he sought Major General Philip Schuyler's guidance on numbers of troops and methods required.[56] The Continental Congress again gave support for "the chastisement of the savages."[57] Washington planned the attack with close attention to detail.[58] Among the points raised was a reemergence of the plan to take women and children captive. Schuyler suggested: "Should we be so fortunate as to take a considerable number of the women and children of the Indians I conceive that we should then have the means of preventing them hereafter from acting hostily against us."[59] Washington gave his assent, hoping that their "attacks will distract and terrify the Indians." He added, "It is also to be hoped in their confusion, they may neglect in some places to remove the old men women and Children and that these will fall into our hands." Washington argued that American troops would then be able to defeat Indian warriors, or at least the soldiers would "distress... them as much as possible, by destroying their villages, and this year's crop."[60]

Washington gave Major General John Sullivan explicit instructions for total war in the 1779 campaign in the Land of the Six Nations: "The immediate objects are the total distruction and devastation of their settlements and the capture of as many prisoners of every age and sex as possible," since "hostages are the only kind of security to be depended on." Washington also directed the destruction of the crops and houses, ordering that "parties should be detached to lay waste [to] all the settlements around... that the country may not be merely *overrun* but *destroyed*." He stressed the need to achieve "the total ruin of their settlements," since "Our future security will be in their inability to injure us; the distance to which they are driven and in the terror with which the severity of the chastizement they receive will inspire them."[61] In other words, U.S. security lay in terror directed at Native Americans.[62] There were attacks on Onondaga towns in April 1779, as Washington and Schuyler organized for a larger campaign later that year.

On July 4, 1779, George Washington wrote to General Lafayette fretting about "the security of our defences," with the news that General Sullivan was marching with four thousand troops in "an Expedition against the Six Nation's" to "extirpate" them.[63] In fact, Sullivan, delayed, did not begin the expedition until August. He led three regiments up the Susquehanna River while James Clinton and another regiment headed west, meeting in Tioga in late August. News of the impending invasions reached these communities, so that the soldiers came upon empty towns. One soldier noted that the inhabitants had "left the town in Great Haste for they left Kittels [kettles] on the fire."[64] They fled to places like Niagara, under British protection.[65] Continental Army soldiers set about the grim work of destruction, taking their fill and setting fire to the rest. They reached Chenussio, or Genesee Castle, in mid-September, where they torched the biggest Seneca town.

Major General Sullivan later boasted that he had spread desolation, with the destruction of forty towns, 160,000 bushels of corn, and a great deal else.[66] The soldiers—mostly farmers themselves—recognized the land's fruitfulness. One diarist described Madam Sacho's town: "it contained nearly fifty houses... very good.... We found several very fine corn-fields... the greatest plenty of corn, beans, &c."[67] Numerous soldiers stressed the bounty and beauty of the towns and crops they were demolishing. One marveled that "Lands here are exceedingly good and fertile" before expressing misgivings about his task: "there is something so cruel, in destroying the habitations of any people."[68] Another officer wrote home: "I really feel guilty as I applied the torch to huts that were Homes of Contentment until we ravagers came spreading desolation everywhere... carelessly sowing the seeds of Empire."[69]

Sullivan destroyed the fields and houses, but he disregarded Washington's orders to take hostages "of every age and sex." When Sullivan found Madam Sacho, he not only left her alone but also provided her with food and shelter. Several soldiers took exception to his gift of food, when the soldiers themselves did not have much to eat. One man, having already complained of "Hungry bellies and hard Duty," observed with caustic envy: "I suppose she will live in splendour."[70] It was galling to him that an elderly Indigenous woman should receive meat while a Continental Army soldier was stuck with vegetables. Other soldiers, more generous in spirit, celebrated the gallantry of their leader: "General Sullivan gave her a considerable supply of flour and meat, for which, with tears in her savage eyes, she expressed a great deal of thanks."[71]

Stressing Sullivan's personal generosity in this matter (one soldier claimed that she saw him as "her good angel") suggests an uneasy recognition of the "uncivility" of their actions in destroying the harvest.[72]

The soldiers saw a "poor old creature," dependent on Sullivan's "humanity."[73] It was fatally easy for them—and for us—to dismiss the power of the elderly and the long line of connection to the living and the dead they represented among the Six Nations. The assumption has been that her compatriots had abandoned her to her fate on account of her age and infirmity—a disparaging and erroneous conclusion. She likely chose to stay, to sacrifice herself to plant and gather information, which may have helped her countrymen and -women to escape.

In fact, Haudenosaunee people had long celebrated such heroics. Well into the eighteenth century, they still told the story of what had happened in the 1690s. In those days, Algonquian soldiers, allied with the French, had attacked the Land of the Five Nations, burning their houses and fields and sending many fleeing. However, one hundred-year-old Onondaga sachem decided to stay and face his enemies and so "chose this Time to end his Days." Undaunted by age and enemies, he taunted his tormentors before they killed him, calling the French "dogs" and their Indigenous allies mere "dogs of dogs." The tale concluded: "Thus this old Sachem, under all the Weakness of old Age, preserved a Greatness of Soul, and a due Regard for the Honour of his Country, to the last Moment of his breath."[74] Was this Onondaga sachem Madam Sacho's inspiration? She appeared to be merely a nice older lady, but in fact she sacrificed herself and exhibited "a Greatness of Soul." For her part, Sacho reported to the Americans that over the hill there were many women and children, so Sullivan sent four hundred men to find them. They returned without "seeing anything of them."[75] Did she plant misinformation deliberately? She also claimed that the women had not wanted to go to war, which might have meant that they would be treated with leniency if captured.

Although soldiers emphasized Sacho's lonely impotence, she was not in fact alone. When soldiers came back a few weeks later, they found the body of a younger woman who had evidently been helping her. She had been shot, "supposed to be done by some of the soldiers."[76] The killing of this much younger women, a violation of that "regard for the female world" that even several soldiers denounced as the actions of "some inhuman villain," indicates the justified fears of the people of the Six Nations, and why they also might have chosen to leave a very old woman who served as a pitiful figure for the American soldiers.[77] An Onondaga leader later contended that when U.S. soldiers attacked his village, "they put to death all the Women and Children, excepting some of the Young Women, whom they carried away for the [sexual] use of their Soldiers & were afterwards put to death in a more shamefull manner."[78] It is unclear why or how this younger woman was killed, but she was subjected to lethal violence in a way the older woman was not. No one was ever punished for this murder.

In the end, whatever agonized choices they made, most people of the Six Nations ended up in the same dreary place: in a refugee camp, shivering and hungry. Whether they were Mohawks and Senecas who joined with the British or Oneidas who allied with Americans, most were displaced from homelands, facing distress and disease.[79] In October 1779, George Washington wrote to General Gates with pleasure that Sullivan and his men had "fully compleated the destruction of the whole Country of the six Nations," with the likelihood that they would be forced to rely on Canadian charity for food. Moreover, another set of American forces had burned additional Indigenous towns, which "in a great measure compleats the destruction not only of the Country of the Six Nations but of their Allies."[80] It did not destroy the Six Nations. They endure to this day. Nevertheless, it was a terrible set of blows.

"Civilization or death to all American Savages" was the toast drunk by Continental Army warriors on the cusp of Sullivan's Campaign, celebrating the third anniversary of American independence on July 4, 1779, with a round of a dozen toasts. Here was settler colonialism at its bleakest. The rebels did seem to "have their Hatchet lifted up" against Indigenous Americans. For those who led these campaigns, and for at least some participants, security seemed to reside in "extirpation." At that same celebration, the men also toasted General Sullivan and the Western Army, as well as General Lincoln and the Southern Army.[81] Although many soldiers in the Western Army did not exactly relish their duties, those in the Southern Army fared worse. Abuses, usurpations, and security also figure in that grim story.

That Southern Army was looking for security too, but it would prove elusive in 1779–80. The Continental Army in the south came under novel pressures thanks to global transformations. It was not so much that armies marched south, but that navies sailed north from the Caribbean. Considering places such as Georgia and South Carolina as part of the "Greater Caribbean" explains their emergence as places of significant battles in 1779 and 1780. In that period, the war hinged on naval actions and sieges, centered on the Greater Caribbean.

For the first and only time in its history, France's navy was more important than its army.[82] The treaty between France and Spain, signed in the spring of 1779, strengthened France's ability to wage war. In its wake, the French sent sailors and ships into the Caribbean in 1779 to win back colonies and to protect trade, including that between American ports and Caribbean ones.[83] The commander there, Jean-Baptiste Charles Henri Hector, the Comte d'Estaing, who had failed to take Newport, Rhode Island, in 1778, succeeded in taking St. Vincents and Grenada. Flush with victory, he headed north for another Franco-American assault on the mainland. He brought with him the first French free Black military regiment: the Chasseurs-Volontaires de Saint-Domingue, with hundreds of volunteer troops.[84]

French forces arrived near Savannah, Georgia. On spotting them—including apparently twenty-two ships of the line—the British governor immediately impressed enslaved laborers to build defenses for the city.[85] Such contributions were vital to this siege. The bombardment began at midnight on October 3, 1779. Many enslaved people on plantations outside the city took the opportunity to flee, including one "Fanny, that was just delivered" of a baby. She liberated herself and her newborn: a risky enterprise. Other enslaved people were forced to stay with their enslavers in the city under fire. One enslaver, Anthony Stokes, reported that an eighteen-pound cannonball hit his quarters and nearly landed on the head of an enslaved man named Dick. When another shot set his lodging on fire, an enslaved man named George pulled the family's belongings out of the flames.[86]

Despite the bravery of such men, the scene in Savannah was grim, with "women and children ... melting into tears, and lamenting their unhappy fate."[87] Another correspondent wrote to his wife that "The Town was torn to Pieces, and nothing but Shrieks from Women and Children to be heard."[88] One French officer reported in consternation that many women "left the city and presented themselves of their own accord at the French camp. It was necessary for us to take good care of them as they were unwilling to return."[89] Ultimately, though, there was no haven with, or indeed for, the French. The city defenses built by those enslaved workers held, and the siege ended in defeat for the Franco-American alliance. General Casimir Pulaski, a celebrated Polish general leading an American regiment, was killed, and there were hundreds of casualties. The French had to sail off in "terrible and disheartening" circumstances, carrying the wounded with them without even enough linen to dress their injuries.[90]

"Terrible and disheartening" circumstances greeted another Friend of Liberty in the eventful autumn of 1779. Eight months pregnant, Duchess Quamino bore the shock when she learned that her husband, John, had been killed on a privateer ship in the North Atlantic in a skirmish in August 1779. He had had the good luck to win the Newport lottery to pay for his own freedom. However, he had joined up in part to earn the wages to free her and their children, Charles, Cynthia, and Violet. They were still living with their enslavers, the Channings, when they learned that John Quamino's luck—and life—had ended.[91]

Like thousands of their neighbors, the Quaminos had fled Newport in 1776 after the British occupied the town. Soldiers—and even horses—had bunked in its fine houses and churches, and its wharves were broken down for firewood.[92] The Channings and Quaminos sought refuge in Providence. The Quaminos' last child, Katherine Church, was born there in the autumn of 1779. Her father would never gaze down on her sweet face. The Reverend Ezra Stiles baptized baby Katherine in the presence of her mother, siblings, and enslavers in October 1779.[93] Even amid tragedy, the clatter of family life continued. Soon, Duchess Quamino persuaded the Channings to emancipate her and the children, though they maintained ties.[94] How could a woman, widowed and car-ing for several young children, make a living? Duchess Quamino faced a real challenge, made worse by the economy of the nation.

After all, security could also be financial. 1779–80 marked a time of skittering inflation and deep financial uncertainty, as people clutched dollars worth less every day. Careful conserving of cash by worried people proved pointless as that money depreciated at a rapid rate.[95] By late 1779, even a frying pan cost $300.[96] What were ordinary people like Duchess Quamino to do in these hard times? They scrimped and went without. If they could still afford coffee (cheaper than tea), they drank it weak and without sugar.[97] They patched and repatched their homespun. They took extra work where they could find it. They let their empty stomachs rumble so that their children could eat.

The frigid winter of 1779–80—the coldest in living memory—made everything harder. The cost of clothing, firewood, and food kept on escalating. By 1780, this "fiscal chasm," as one scholar has called it, haunted many.[98] As John Adams phrased it, "A depreciating Currency . . . will ruin us."[99] Much of the problem lay in the way the United States financed the war. Starting in June 1775, the Continental Congress issued paper money. This strategy was not new; colonies had done the same in the Seven Years' War. However, unlike the colonies in the earlier era, the congress did not have the power to levy taxes payable in the new currency, thus ensuring its worth. Therefore, Continental dollars—some $200 million by 1779, accounting for some 77 percent of congressional spending—had been losing value.[100] This decline led to what one Virginian later termed "the havoc of paper money."[101] States had also issued their own paper currency, which also depreciated. Authorities started offering military or deprecation certificates, promising payment later. They also simply requisitioned supplies for the military from the population and borrowed from foreign allies, most notably some 11.4 million *livres* from the French.[102] Yet even government loans and bonds started to lose worth as the financial situation grew ever more insecure. One scholar has estimated that the $226,000,000 in currency possessed by the Continental Congress had shrunk to nothing by 1781.[103] Americans needed more security of all kinds.

Amid this financial free fall, war continued. In October 1779, the British evacuated Newport, as soldiers were needed farther south. By early 1780, some of those soldiers headed for Charles Town, South Carolina, where a major clash took place in March 1780. It involved naval battles as well as ground forces, and again the city was besieged, though not as badly as at Savannah.

By May, American forces at Charles Town surrendered, with the entire Southern Army of more than five thousand troops captured by the British. It was the first time the Americans had suffered such a major defeat. The British followed up this victory with another at Waxhaws, also in South Carolina, in a particularly fierce and bloody battle. By June 1780, the British commander, Sir Henry Clinton, was sure that the rebellion in South Carolina was destroyed.

Despite British military superiority for most of 1780, the rebellion in South Carolina was not in fact crushed. The nature of the war there kept animosity at high levels, as did the British alliance with enslaved people. The war took on a protracted and brutal quality. One Loyalist officer, Anthony Allaire, kept a diary of his travels through the Carolinas. In March 1780, he reported that he and the other soldiers were "living on the fat of the land . . . roasting turkeys, fowls, pigs, etc, every night in great plenty."[104] That same month, he entered one town where all but two men—one ill, the other a Loyalist—were away fighting for the American cause, yet he contended that "The women were treated very tenderly, and with the utmost civility, notwithstanding their husbands were out in arms against us."[105]

Such "civility" was breached on some occasions in this brutal period of war. The next month, at Monk's Corner, three women arrived at the British camp "in great distress." They had been "most shockingly abused," one wounded in the hand from a slash by a broadsword and "bruised very much." An officer, a doctor, and a dozen soldiers went to her house to investigate; there they found another woman, likely a survivor of sexual violence, "in the greatest distress imaginable."[106] She and the other women testified against one of the Tory soldiers, who was secured and sent for trial. The news of this horrific assault made locals—including women—even more determined to resist British dominance.

In the autumn, Allaire reported that one area was "Composed of the most violent Rebels I ever saw, particularly the young ladies."[107]

One of those violent "young lady" rebels might have been Eliza Yonge Wilkinson, who wrote about her wartime experiences in South Carolina in an account carefully—not to say ruthlessly—edited by her descendants in the 1830s. In 1780, Wilkinson was a young widow who watched as refugees converged on Charles Town: "It was a melancholy Sight to see such crowds of helpless, distress'd women . . . I pity'd them all greatly." She observed with special sympathy a mother of seven whose youngest was only two weeks old when they had had to flee.[108] These women exchanged information, news, and opinions: "Some said one thing, some another . . . never were greater Politicians than the several knots of Ladies who met together."[109] As she shivered at the approach of the British, she consoled herself with the hope of civility to women with a line from literature: "our weak Sex, incapable of wrong, from either side claims privilege of safety."[110] She was quoting one of the most popular tragedies of the eighteenth century: Nicholas Rowe's *Tamerlane*, a meditation on "War and lawless Rage."[111]

However, women could not always claim the privilege of safety in war, as Wilkinson found firsthand. A group of British soldiers burst into her family's house shouting something like "Where's these rebel bitches?" With that, they pulled off the women's caps to take the pins, and one of them grabbed Wilkinson's arm so hard that he left bruises. With curses and shouts, the men began to gather up what they could plunder, including her clothing. Once they left, she threw herself on her bed, sobbing: "The whole world appeared to me as a theater where nothing was acted but cruelty, bloodshed, and oppression, where neither age nor sex escaped the horrors of injustice and violence . . . and lawless power ranged at large."[112]

Part of what so horrified Wilkinson was what she saw as the unholy alliance of the British and formerly enslaved soldiers. As she put it, "They and their Allies (their Negroes) seem'd to be on a very friendly footing—quite familiar!" They even drank together. She described these soldiers as "very insolent." Elsewhere, she complained that local Black people "were very unruly and doing great mischief." She related moments in which a Black woman served as guide and conductor for a regiment of British soldiers.[113] Patriots like Wilkinson believed only in select liberty.

"Injustice and violence," as Wilkinson framed it, informed life for many, before, during, and after the American Revolution. The lives of enslaved people in South Carolina offer bitter testimony to this fact, as do the lives of Haudenosaunee people. The lines of gender, race, and age etched and molded the experiences of individuals. Just before the line Wilkinson quoted about the privileges of safety—or security—for the "weak sex," one character in the tragedy of *Tamerlane* declaims: "War is the Province of Ambitious Man, / Who tears the miserable World for Empire." Ambition and empire drove a great many actions and individuals in the American Revolution. Yet there was also resistance: in moments of "insolence" and in the survival of newborns in the arms of plucky mothers. Security proved elusive for all kinds of people in a war full of "abuses and usurpations."

Still, as Madam Sacho knew, even fire could not destroy what mattered most. Most of the corn that Sacho's daughters and granddaughters and nieces had planted was burned in 1779. Still, here and there, a few hardy seeds had escaped. Bolstered by their own resilience and nourished by this rich soil, they grew into something green and strong and fruitful. Yet elsewhere in 1780, destruction and barrenness awaited.

Chapter 10

A Rock in Gibraltar

The numbers didn't add up right—literally. In 1780, Captain James Horsbrugh of the 39th Regiment was crunching numbers and fretting. At the start of each year, he compiled the numbers of British troops, in a list entitled "Total Strength of the Garrison." Strength depended on numbers. In January 1780, brow furrowed, he calculated troops as follows:

Artillery 488
Infantry 4635
Artificer Company 120

He totaled the numbers to 5,283 (it's actually 5,243).[1] Just 5,243 British troops to defend the garrison at Gibraltar, a strip of land at the southern tip of Spain. It would never be enough. The chief British military engineer there, William Green, figured at a conservative estimate that it would require eight thousand troops to defend Gibraltar in the face of Spanish determination to take it back. Engineering feats might help remedy deficiencies, but still the number fell far short.

For a place that was so hotly disputed, Gibraltar hardly seemed inviting. Even the Spanish foreign minister dismissed it as a "pile of rocks."[2] New arrivals were mostly struck by its large hulking rock formation. In 1778, Helen Duff wrote her brother: "It is the most uncommon place I ever saw and has a very stricking [*sic*] appearance to a stranger, from the tremendous rock that hangs over it."[3] Another visitor in 1777 wrote in typical dismay: "The shape and face of Gibraltar rock is neither promising nor pleasing, and it is as barren as uncouth."[4] He concluded: "it is exceedingly rocky.... On casting an eye up this barren hill, one would not imagine any living creature could exist upon it."[5]

The importance of Gibraltar did not lie in its landscape or its natural resources; rather, it was its strategic location as an isthmus near the point where Europe meets Africa and where the Bay of Gibraltar meets the Mediterranean Sea. The British had taken the place in 1704, during the War of the Spanish Succession, confirmed by the Treaty of Utrecht in 1713. As one British soldier, John Drinkwater, phrased it, the Spanish "continued to view that garrison with a jealous eye, determined ... to seize" it back.[6] They also sought the return of the Floridas and Minorca. These glaring losses were the chief reason that the Spanish joined the French in that 1779 alliance.

What in the world does Gibraltar have to do with the American Revolution? As it happens, the Franco-Spanish assault on Gibraltar was the largest military action of the American Revolutionary War, involving at least forty thousand soldiers and sailors.[7] Few Americans have any inkling about this siege; even historians of the American Revolution refer to it only in passing. British people may be more aware of it, but few know the details. Why bother about this looming rock, and its ten thousand isolated and frustrated people? In addition to the huge numbers of troops involved, it was also the longest siege ever endured by the British. Beyond these important numbers, there are other reasons to focus on this "pile of rocks." Gibraltar preoccupied British, French, and Spanish attention year after year and affected the course of the global war.

The concern with numbers in Gibraltar also furnishes a surprisingly fruitful entry to larger preoccupations of the age about troops, population, and indeed about life itself, about how to create and sustain it. "Life, liberty, and the pursuit of happiness" mattered. As we have seen in the case of liberty and happiness, these were serious issues, not mere glittering generalities. So was life. Some version of the word appears three times in the Declaration of Independence. The first was that link with liberty and happiness as foundational values. The second was a complaint: the king had destroyed lives and thus forfeited the loyalty of "our people." The final appearance is in the last line, as part of another trio of fundamentals: the pledge to give "our Lives, our Fortunes and our sacred Honor" to win liberty. Here were the greatest gifts people could offer.

In other words, life was a political issue—for signers of the Declaration, for the military officers and apprehensive citizens in Gibraltar, and for countless others. Numbers of troops depended on population size. Population growth (and lack thereof) concerned many in this era. Life had importance both in terms of quantity (population, numbers of troops) and in terms of quality (ensuring the best for families and nations). The American Revolution intersected with other, more intimate kinds of revolutions including those related to family planning. Revolutions took place in beds and homes as well as at sea and in rocky garrisons.

In the event of a prolonged siege, how many mouths would have to be fed? Preparing for Spanish invasion in 1777, the British governor ordered a census of Gibraltar's population to assess both its strength and its needs. There were 3,201 civilians in Gibraltar. The divisions of the census categories convey its diversity; there were Protestants (all British, 506), Catholics (1,832), and Jews (863). Catholics included natives of the town: some Genoese (who had long traded there), Spaniards, Portuguese, Minorcans, and a smattering of French and Irish. Those listed as Jews included Sephardic Jews (from places like Tétouan in Morocco) but also what seemed to be other "Aliens" such as an American-born Black woman named Jane and what were probably her two Gibraltar-born daughters, Nancy (age nine) and Betty (age four), who apparently lived in a Jewish household. Gibraltar was a small but vibrant and cosmopolitan place. Its center in the northwest teemed with mantua makers and oystermen, "Teachers of the Italian," and Sephardic households with two wives.[8] Helen Duff marveled in 1777: "In the Streets . . . you see people of all nations in different dresses and speaking different languages."[9]

Gibraltar's dominant language, though, was English. After all, in the 1770s, the British military population far exceeded the local population of 3,201. Fifteen hundred women and children accompanied the more than five thousand soldiers in five regiments—the 12th, 39th, 56th, 58th, and 72nd—as well as Hanoverian troops and specialists in engineering and artillery. There were more than ten thousand mouths to feed and to defend.

The Spanish were so eager to get this place back that in 1778, they had offered full neutrality to the British in return for Gibraltar alone. The British refused. The Treaty of Aranjuez subsequently confirmed the alliance between Spain and France; France agreed to fight until Gibraltar was secured for the Spanish.[10] The British engineer William Green spent years preparing for the Spanish attack.[11] Although its largest rock was virtually unscalable, from other directions, it was more vulnerable. Green focused his energies on those approaches and on the line of defenses facing the Spanish side, especiallly a fortification called the King's Bastion, which one observer described as "erected lately . . . a very complete piece of fortifications."[12] On June 18, 1779, William's wife, Miriam Green, observed that "The whole Garrison seems . . . uneasy."[13] A week later, as her husband tossed and turned beside her, "restless all Night . . . his Anxiety made him Worse," she woke to the blockade: "it is not to be doubted but the Intention of the Spaniards is to attack this Garrison. I shall therefore from this time call them—*The Enemy*."[14] The assault began in earnest in September 1779.

"*The Enemy*" forced a lot of number crunching. William Green, twitchy, wondered whether his work would hold; he calculated and rebuilt in order to augment defenses. Miriam Green, too, fretted over numbers as the siege continued. Since trade came to a halt, provisions became scarce and costly. Her journal includes long lists of the prices of meat and poultry at the end of 1779. Despite being on the water, she lamented "when ever we got Fish it was beyond all Price."[15]

Inhabitants of Gibraltar watched, wide-eyed, as the price of food ticked up and up and up. The siege diaries all emphasize prices, exchange rates, and shortages. In a typical passage, one soldier complained in September 1779 that "Fresh provisions [were] dear. A duck and small plum-pudding cost seven shillings." A year later, his concerns centered on the prices of salt pork and salt beef, as by then there were few fresh provisions. By 1781, even wood was selling by the pound. Drinkwater moaned, "Provisions of every kind were becoming very scarce and exorbitantly dear." He concluded by noting that "bread, the great essential of life and health, was the article most wanted."[16]

Even the governor of Gibraltar himself—one of those perky, fit, and abstemious sorts (apparently a vegetarian, unusual in 1779)—worked to stretch food to its limits. He "bought up all the hair powder, and eats the puddings made of it," since this hair powder consisted mainly of flour. Soldiers in Gibraltar no longer powdered their hair, though few joined him in eating those puddings. For more than a week, he subsisted on a mere four ounces of rice per day to test how long people could survive on such a small amount of food.[17] His conclusion: eight days.

Calculations of all sorts underpinned this war effort, even beyond Gibraltar. Figuring out the troops available, and where they could be deployed, was a favorite back-of-envelope move in this war, for obscure minor officers like Horsbrugh and for the highest commanders. One 1778 British document exemplifies this fixation on numbers. Its dark imaginings were so frenzied that a later official excused it with an annotation: "These Considerations were wrote . . . at a time when there were not above 8500 Troops in the Kingdom. The reasoning therein contained, seemed to arise from the Situation of the Times." The greatest fear was of an impending "invasion of England or Ireland."[18]

This anonymous author argued that the start of war with France spelled the end of an offensive war with the rebellious colonies. Even if they gave up on those thirteen former colonies, though, North America and its remaining colonies still required troops:

"Our own National Force remaining in America cannot exceed 25,000 Effective Men," the writer calculated. "Of these,

6,000 Must be necessary for the Security of Canada
2,500 For Halifax
1,500 For Florida
4,000 At least sent as a Reinforcement and Security to the West India Islands.

Accordingly, given that total of 14,000, "There will then remain 11,000 to be employed as an Active Army, or brought Home for our Own defence."[19] In other words, giving up the thirteen rebellious colonies was essential.

When France and Spain both allied with the Americans, many other Britons agreed that they should cut their colonial losses. In August 1779, the Pantheon Society in Edinburgh asked, "Is it expedient in the present Crisis, to withdraw our Land Forces from America & employ them against the House of Bourbon?" The speeches lasted nearly two hours, "supported with uncommon Spirit" from the audience of 125 individuals, of whom forty-three were women. Keeping forces in North America only narrowly won.[20]

Anxieties centered around invasion, seemingly a genuine threat in 1778–79 for Ireland and England. The author of the 1778 report envisioned a pincer invasion of Ireland, with the French attacking the south and Americans the north. They assumed that many in Ireland would join the American cause: "These proclaiming Liberty and Licentiousness to the Infatuated Multitude, might occasion much Confusion."[21] The author of the report worried that there were nowhere near enough troops to protect Ireland, especially given what he termed the "worthless disposition of the lower class of the people," so prone to "Domestick Insurrection."[22]

"Domestick Insurrection" was a live possibility in Ireland, especially if combined with invasion. The tensions over centuries of what was called "the injustice of England" reverberated there. In 1779, the College Historical Society of Trinity College, Dublin, unanimously agreed that "America was Justifiable in her Secession from Great Britain."[23] Tensions had been rising in Ireland, with a movement demanding free trade.[24] There was a nonimportation agreement among groups such as the Citizens of Dublin, with parades of Irish people in homespun. Patriotic ribbons—adorned with harp and crown and shamrocks—called for A FREE TRADE for Irish manufactures (especially textiles).[25] In 1779, common Irish toasts were to "a free trade" and "the Irish volunteers."[26] This last toast was a reference to the volunteer movement, mostly but not exclusively Protestant, to defend Ireland in case of invasion and to establish greater control over the island. As one Catholic newspaper

This commemorative pitcher (1778–82) depicts Hibernia, representing Ireland, holding a harp above a stirring statement flanked by volunteer soldiers. The other side depicts the death of General Wolfe in the 1759 Battle of the Plains of Abraham.

put it, "it is now not the cause of religion,—it is the Irishman of every denomination against the injustice of England."[27] Jugs and pitchers were produced celebrating these volunteers, one decorated with images of Hibernia and a harp, along with a poem declaring that "Hibernia's sons will never flee!"[28] Invasion fears filled Irish newspapers, stages, and pulpits in 1779.

Invasion fears racked the English, too, especially when a Franco-Spanish fleet was spied near England's southern coast in the summer of 1779. One soldier in Cornwall reported: "The formidable appearance of this fleet . . . struck such terror" in locals that many had fled while others organized volunteers for defense.[29] Another man in Devon despaired, "Our Empire of the Sea being lost . . . we must be a lost people," dependent on the whims of France and Spain, a situation novel and unwelcome. As in Cornwall, families departed the coast. Although this writer was not a young man, he declared he and his sons would instead join the volunteers, "for 'tis melancholy to sit still and be knocked on the head."[30]

Britain needed more troops in order to avoid being knocked on the head. Recruiting shortages and population disparities preoccupied the British, who had already been augmenting their forces with

German-speaking mercenaries. The fundamental problem was a population one, though. France's much larger population haunted Britons throughout the eighteenth century. In 1776, the population was around 9 million in England, Wales, and Scotland.[31] The population of Spain was only slightly higher (9.3 million or so).[32] At a conservative estimate, in 1776, the population of France was 27 million.[33]

The rapid growth of the Anglophone settler population in the mainland American colonies was also a concern for the British, at a time when many believed their own population was stagnant or declining (although in fact it was rising). In 1776, there were approximately 2.5 million such settlers, but their number was—and was thought to be—increasing fast.[34] This concern had started well before the war. In a publication from 1754, Benjamin Franklin had calculated that the settler population of the North American colonies was doubling every twenty years. He also forecast that the American colonies would soon overtake Britain in population, a point repeated frequently in newspapers and debates. Franklin attributed this colonial growth to prosperity, early marriages, and large families: "When Families can be easily supported, more Persons marry, and earlier in Life."[35] One American preacher boasted in 1772 that "where his Majesty has one soldier . . . America can produce fifty free men."[36] Another—Ezra Stiles—calculated America's rapidly rising population in the 1760s.[37] In 1776, in his *Wealth of Nations,* the Scottish theorist Adam Smith (also, as it happens, the uncle of that anxious engineer William Green in Gibraltar) repeated such claims: "North America is more thriving than England . . . and advancing with much greater rapidity." Smith claimed that it would take Britain five hundred years to double its population, while projecting (like Franklin) that its American colonies would double in a mere twenty years.[38]

Adam Smith and Benjamin Franklin were among the more notable voices in a much larger chorus in the period after 1750. In the late seventeenth century, a new pursuit called "political arithmetick" or the "art of reasoning by figures upon things relating to government" began to engage writers such as William Petty.[39] In a typical claim, Charles Davenant declared: "People are the real strength and riches of a country."[40] In his mid-century *Encyclopédie,* the French *philosophe* Denis Diderot defined "power" in relation to the size of a nation's population: bigger was definitely better.[41] Two Scots, David Hume and Robert Wallace, debated "the populousness of ancient nations" and its causes.

Some of the century's best-known thinkers pondered population growth (or lack thereof); so did some of its lesser lights. Thomas Short—a Scottish physician in England with a multitude of theories about a great many things including water (for instance, the curative power of springs), tea, and milk—offered his own political arithmetic in more than one treatise. He had apparently been partly inspired by a sermon given by Ezra Stiles in 1760 discussing the impressive growth rate of the colonies.[42] In 1767, Short published a tract featuring policy ideas "to make us a strong, respectable, populous Nation." He argued that enacting these measures would mean that "there would be less Occasion, in Time of War, to hire so many foreign Auxiliaries, or to impress Men into the service."[43]

Short presented a program of family values for national strength. He sought to "promote an Offspring of vigorous, lively, healthy Youth," which he saw as critical for international power. He had two main plans to further this goal. First, he wanted to end the use of foundling hospitals (for babies whose parents could not afford to keep them). He asserted that they "tend to encourage promiscuous Whoredom . . . depopulating their Country, and exposing it to the Inroads and Attacks of it's Enemies." He believed that nonmarital sex—whether premarital coupling, prostitution, masturbation, or the catchall category of "excessive Venery"—led to infertility or sickly children—"useless, puny Creatures, begotten in Whoredom."[44] Second, he advocated a tax on men who did not marry. He also suggested that if a man impregnated an unmarried woman, he should either marry her or be transported to the American colonies—not, as it turns out, a popular plan.

While some like Short furnished theoretical considerations on population growth, others offered more hands-on approaches. Short's colleague, another Scottish doctor living in England, Dr. James Graham, was also full of theories, praised by some as fashionable and derided by others as quackery.[45] A "tall handsome man," Graham was an audacious and mesmerizing showman, full of razzle-dazzle. A few years after the war, he apparently demonstrated the "all-cleansing, all-healing, and all-invigorating" properties of a special mud bath by showing up for his lecture in London wearing only a nightshirt, with nothing underneath. As assistants piled up mud around him, he inched the shirt higher, until he pulled it off altogether while the ladies and gentlemen looked on. He then extolled the virtues of mud and its power to enhance genital vigor, while demonstrating this point vividly, in a manner designed "to call up the chaste blushes of the *modest* ladies." As the man recalling these lectures noted in the more restrained era of the early nineteenth century, "It will perhaps hardly be believed that such an exhibition would have been permitted, in what is called an enlightened country." Yet so it apparently was, with the "great encouragement from persons who possessed great influence in the fashionable world."[46]

Although those mud baths lay in his future, Graham in 1780 was having a moment. Crowds of the well-heeled—faces obscured by masks and scarves and hats—flocked to his showrooms in London. An article in a London newspaper (possibly written by Graham himself) reported that Graham's "Temple of Health" was so fashionable that "no lady or gentleman can possibly confess" they had not been there without being seen "as shockingly deficient in taste."[47] Two large and daunting bouncers, sporting "large gold-laced cocked hats" and holding imposing silver staffs, patrolled the entrance. Once people were inside, wonders awaited, including, some whispered, a woman who emerged at least partially nude to represent Vestina, the goddess of health, at a key moment in Graham's lecture.[48]

However, the center of Graham's showrooms was what he called his "CELESTIAL BED." He rented it to barren married couples—or at least couples claiming to be both married and barren—for the night for the exorbitant fee of £50. It was not just any bed. Nine feet by twelve, stuffed with the tail hair of stallions, it rested on glass pillars, which supposedly provided safe conduction for the electricity—or "celestial fire"—with which it throbbed.[49] A dome topped the bed, filled with the heady scent of perfumes "in the style of those in the seraglio of the Grand Turk" (the ultimate potentate, an endless source of fantasy in this era). The sheets were of purple satin, and the bedstead was adorned with

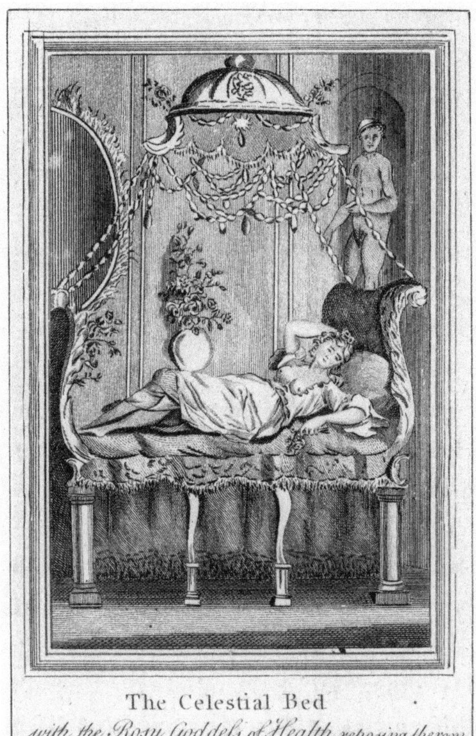

This spicy cartoon, likely from 1780, shows a partially nude woman, representing the goddess of health, reclining on Dr. James Graham's "CELESTIAL BED," which rests on glass columns carrying electrical charges.

naked, cavorting Cupids and the biblical motto "Be fruitful—multiply and replenish the earth!" With customary brio (and hyperbole), Graham claimed that those who tested his miracle bed affirmed its ability to transform the critical *moment* of orgasm into a "critical HOUR!!!" thus making even infertile women and men overflow with pleasure and fruitfulness.[50]

Like many in the eighteenth century, Graham was a man with a vision for the improvement of humanity. Admittedly, that vision involved stimulating the sexual appetite—for women and men—with vibration (those electrical currents), pornography (or at least imagining others copulating), and threesomes. In these ways, Graham could be said to have been ahead of his time. In his condemnation of a married couple regularly sharing a bed as "matrimonial whoredom," his rants against masturbation as "secret pollution," his blaming women for barrenness, and his unremitting emphasis on frequent daily "BATHING... PRIVATE PARTS WITH COLD WATER THOROUGHLY!" (capitalization and punctuation original!), he was perhaps a little less forward-thinking.[51]

International power depended on sexual health, according to Graham. He argued that an emphasis on "domestic enjoyments" rather than war would make "men more happy than they are at present," as they were forced to send "vast sums to America for the destructive purpose of carrying on this war."[52] He also rued the pain of a husband forced to leave his affectionate wife "to pursue with horrid barbarism the destruction of his fellow-creatures; and even to plunge the cold and bloody steel in the hearts of our American brethren."[53] James Graham saw his own mission with clarity: "to restore that manly firmness and vigour, which, from the depravity of human nature, by means of luxury and dissipation, has for more than a century been lost."[54] He cast this work in terms of national strength. In the typical language of political arithmetic, Graham noted that even the king was concerned about domestic happiness, as it underpinned "the security of his throne, [as] the wealth and prosperity of his dominions depends upon the numbers of his subjects."[55] Like Short, Graham imagined that financial incentives might encourage men to turn to their wives for sex when their interest there otherwise flagged. He promoted the idea of a tax on the unmarried, and tax credits for each child born to married couples. Also like Short, Graham suggested that improved fertility would be "sufficient to man our fleets, and increase our armies, as would bid defiance to our most inveterate foes."[56]

Graham had a personal interest in what happened in North America as he had lived there through the early 1770s. In January 1770, he was advertising a public lecture on the eye for "Ladies and Gentlemen" in Annapolis, Maryland.[57] 1770s newspaper notices in Maryland, New York, Pennsylvania, and Virginia touted "DOCTOR GRAHAM, PHYSICIAN and SURGEON, from LONDON," an Edinburgh University–trained expert on eyes and ears. These ads included testimonials from those cured by him. A few of them also highlight his expertise in "FEMALE COMPLAINTS," especially his ability to remove "Disorders to which that delicate Sex" were prone.[58] Such a statement is a possible allusion to abortion, often defined as the removal of an "obstruction" to regular menstruation. It was certainly an unusual addition to advertisement about curing vision and hearing problems. He stayed in no single colony longer than a year or so, moving with restlessness (or perhaps enforced haste?) from one town to another (Annapolis, Baltimore, New York City, Philadelphia, Lancaster, and Williamsburg).

Graham evidently learned about the curative power of electricity in North America. In later years, he mentioned his time in Philadelphia to imply a relationship with that most famous Philadelphian and master of electricity, Ben Franklin—who was actually in London in those same years. Still, there was an American interest in the medical aspects of electricity, especially for purposes of sexual health.[59] Andreas Wiederhold, the Hessian soldier, wrote home in 1782 from New York about "a clever man . . . with an electric machine" in the city hall. Wiederhold detailed

This 1783 print mocks the rivalry between James Graham (left) and his German counterpart, Dr. Katterfelto, over whose inventions were more efficacious and whose "Prime Conductor"—a thinly veiled phallic allusion—was larger. Behind Graham are his two bouncers, nicknamed Gog and Magog, from his Temple of Health and Hymen.

how one elderly man "came to have a certain body part, non-functional by reason of his age, electrified" so that he could enjoy one last act of intercourse.[60] Such experiments seem to have inspired Graham.

Graham returned to Britain in the mid-1770s, where he continued to trade on his medical credentials with lectures and "cures." However, he moved from eyes and ears to other body parts. He undertook a European tour in 1778, at which point he did finally meet Franklin. Before he moved to London, he sojourned in Bristol and Bath, where he spent a good deal of time with Catharine Macaulay, that great republican historian of England, correspondent with Mercy Otis Warren in Massachusetts, and avid supporter of the American cause.[61] So close were the Grahams—both James and his younger brother, William—with Macaulay that scandal erupted. Even as rumors swirled about her relationship with James, she married William. She was forty-six; he was twenty-one. The age difference led people to lament her "fall," tittering that this prominent intellectual had traded the pleasures of Minerva—goddess of wisdom—for those of Venus—the goddess of love and lust.[62] The Graham brothers seemed to promise many of the latter.

Graham's performances resonated in a culture fretful about "excessive Venery" imperiling population growth and national strength. Wallowing in luxury, in their frippery and wigs, modern men seemed to be squandering their "manly firmness" and what Graham called "this balmy—spirituous—vivifying essence" or "exquisitely penetrating seminal liquor" on practices that did not build population.[63] Instead of having fruitful sex with their wives, they were pleasuring themselves or, even worse, paying for the services of other women; a few even indulged in "unnatural" activities with each other. The figures of the macaroni and fop—vain, showy men—haunted Britons in this era.

The connection between martial and sexual prowess appeared in all kinds of places. A ribald Irish ballad, "The Manual Exercise," used the language of military training to offer a risqué account of the sexual induction of an Irish volunteer by a "fair maid" named Kitty. She orders him: "Fall to your exercise without delay. . . . be quick with your motions / present and give fire." Although the volunteer fires three times, Kitty remains unsatisfied, causing him to complain: "my ammunition [is] now fairly spent, / with three rounds dear Kitty you should be content." He concludes: "if that all generals were like unto you, / the volunteers surely would dread a review."[64]

National strength depended on life and its reproduction, what men and women did together. Men talked and wrote and joked and worried about these issues. They made other contributions, too, of course. However, it was women who lived them hard. It was women whose tired, heavy bodies carried pregnancy after pregnancy. It was women who risked death with every birth. It was women, some biological mothers and some other mothers—a number of them enslaved and others paid—who nursed hungry, squalling babies. As Abigail Adams lamented to her sister, frequent childbearing was enough "to wear out an Iron constitution."[65] In other words, it was women's relentless and exhausting reproductive labors that fired demographic growth—and military strength. Much as writers fretted about the sex lives of men, in fact life—population growth and national fitness—very much depended on what women did.

Commentators sometimes noted that certain classes of women—such as sex workers and rich ladies—seemed to have lower birth rates. Short's comments on sex workers are typical. With stomach-churning specificity, he blamed the "Mixture of several genital Liquors" in the wombs of prostitutes for rendering them infertile. He also claimed that "excessive Venery" caused barrenness.[66] While sexually transmitted diseases can cause infertility over time, that cannot explain the situation entirely. At the other end of the spectrum, Adam Smith noted that while country women might have twenty children, a "pampered fine lady" could produce only a couple, if that: "Barrenness, so frequent among women of fashion, is very rare among those of inferior station." He blamed women's own indulgence: "Luxury . . . seems always to weaken . . . the powers of generation."[67] When it came to women's reproductive strategies, even clever men could be remarkably—perhaps willfully—obtuse. These writers rarely considered that these women might have deliberately limited births, taking their lives into their own hands.

If men like Short and Smith and Graham were concerned with increasing the population to augment national strength, at least some women—and men—had other priorities. These strategies are less easily tracked, as they appear not in finger-wagging treatises but instead in whispers between women, quiet exchanges of herbs and astringents, a husband pulling out in the dark, the under-the-counter sale of what were called "English riding coats" and "armour compleat" (condoms of animal skin or intestines).[68] Occasionally, these other priorities surface in printed material, including Benjamin Franklin's contribution to 1753's *American Instructor,* a common textbook. Among its instructions was a way to end what was called "the suppression of the courses," or the stoppage of menstruation—in other words, a way to terminate a pregnancy.[69] Ads for similar remedies appear, if infrequently, in newspapers.[70] There were also very rare legal cases for "taking the trade," as abortion was obliquely called.[71]

Taken together, here was what scholars of reproduction have termed "a different American Revolution," "a fertility revolution," and "a silent revolution, unspeakable."[72] It was a time not only of rising population, but, paradoxically, of rising birth control. The numbers crunched so carefully by modern demographers, using parish registers and other early modern sources, suggest that American and French women led the way in this quiet but monumental transformation. Recent analyses have suggested that there was some birth spacing in England even before the major fertility transition associated with modernity.[73] Still, there was apparently a decline in fertility in the United States and France in the late eighteenth century, ahead of most other places. There were also of course national revolutions in both places around the same time.

Did political revolutions in these two nations broker new ways of thinking? Some scholars have argued that they did, contending that women followed the revolutionary teachings of patriots and began to prioritize the happiness of themselves and their fewer children because these revolutions unleashed a sense that women, too, should be able to pursue life, liberty, and happiness.[74] Yet what if the direction is reversed? What if women of an earlier generation started to cultivate new expectations about life and happiness, ones passed on to sons and daughters who both rose up in rebellion *and* started to practice birth control more? One scholar of birth control has called that transformation "a revolution of rising expectations."[75] In 1766, one British observer carped that "Americans imbibe notions of independence and liberty with their very milk."[76] Maybe they did, getting newfangled ideas from mothers, not just fathers.

One mother who instilled notions of "independence and liberty" with her very milk was Violet Freeman. She had good reason to do so; she and her husband had both been enslaved. She had been serving in the family of Abraham Dearborn in Portsmouth, New Hampshire.[77] Perhaps in church, between 1776 and 1778, she met the young man Newport, from the household of Ezra Stiles. The Stiles household had fled the town of Newport following the British occupation in 1776, and Stiles had taken a position as minister in Portsmouth in 1777 (he left to become president of Yale College in 1778).[78]

In 1778, amid the tumult of war, both Violet and Newport obtained their freedom. Violet was able, apparently, to buy her own liberty. Then, in June 1778, as Ezra Stiles prepared to move to New Haven to take on the presidency of Yale, he noted that he "freed or liberated my Negro Man Newport."[79] This sentence signals so much. Stiles did not call Newport what he was: a slave. Stiles's wording—"freed or liberated"—suggests some uncertainty about this process. This prevarication implies that the momentum for this liberation came from others—most likely Newport himself, who had accompanied Stiles even in his flight from Newport, Rhode Island.

In 1778, then, Newport became a free man—literally. He adopted a new surname: not Stiles, but Freeman. This self-naming also suggests his agency in being "freed or liberated." In November, Newport marked his new status by marrying Violet.[80] At their marriage, she became Violet Freeman, her name indicating her status both as a free person and a legal wife. Yet, despite the name and the marriage, Violet and Newport felt that their family's freedom was fragile. In 1780, likely after the birth of their first son, Jacob, they took him to the town clerk to register all three of them as free people.[81] Whatever hesitancies Stiles had about the process of liberation, the actions of Violet and Newport demonstrate their commitment to a new name—and a new kind of life.

Another woman who shared a commitment to liberty was Esther Reed. In 1780, she and others organized a fundraising campaign for the American soldiers. In aid of that cause, she also published a tract, *Sentiments of an American Woman,* lauding the courage of women from ancient times to the present. She also connected women's reproductive and domestic situation with the war itself. She declared that it was thanks only to the sacrifices of soldiers that "I live happy in the midst of my family . . . and I myself nourish the youngest [child] and press it to my bosom." She also lauded "the most patriotic sacrifices" of Spanish and French women, connecting women across time and space in the shared efforts of patriotism and breaking "the chains of slavery."[82] The women of her association had intended to pay the money raised to soldiers as additional wages. Instead, George Washington asked them to sew shirts which "will be of more service, and do more to preserve [their] health than any other thing."[83] The women agreed to this domestic task—albeit with some reluctance.

Other women also demonstrated commitment to life and liberty even in the period before the American Revolution. In late 1761, in New Hampshire, Robert Hastey warned creditors not to extend loans to his wife, Elizabeth, as she had "Eloped from me without Cause."[84] Elizabeth responded with her own account of what had happened; she was, she said, "now ready to let the World know." She alleged they had lived together for a year, seemingly content. However, apparently to Robert's chagrin, she became pregnant. He wanted her to terminate the pregnancy, as she phrased it "to make me take Poisonous Trade; in order to destroy my Child." Her refusal had allegedly caused him to "beat me unreasonably . . . calling me very hard Names." Big-bellied and heavyhearted, she made her escape. She concluded the counteradvertisement she took out in the newspaper, "I am heartily Sorry that my Husband should be my Enemy, when he ought to be my best Friend, but so it is." This was in some ways an atypical situation (few ads indicate differences over pregnancies). Still, it also accorded with trends of the 1760s: a rising use of newspaper ads even by wives; a strikingly modern understanding of marriage (spouses as best friends); and women's agency in making the choice about their pregnancy and whether or not to "take the trade."[85]

Yet there were further twists to this story of life and reproduction.

Both Elizabeth and Robert already had children from their first marriages, so Robert's anxiety about the pregnancy was likely related to his concerns about supporting this large brood. Despite Elizabeth's reports here, she returned to Robert. They had four children over the next fifteen years.[86] Whether they ended up best friends is impossible to say, but they did remain cohabiting husband and wife. This unusually public story reveals the strong views both women and men held on family planning.

A new world for women, hinging on more restrained fertility, dawned, albeit slowly and unevenly. It peeks through in surprising places. Amid reports of battles and debates, a brief elegy by a thirteen-year-old girl for her grandmother appeared in the *Virginia Gazette* in 1776. This short, sweet poem lauded the grandmother as "the best of woman kind," concluding "She lov'd the Lord, and really she lov'd me."[87] The publisher calculated that this grandmother, Mrs. Barbara Massenburg, died at eighty-one having produced twenty-one children, forty-six grandchildren, and eight great-grandchildren—"in all, 75." The grandmother was born around 1695, the granddaughter—thoughtful and poetic—around 1763. Did the granddaughter seek to follow in her grandmother's footsteps in this exuberant fecundity? It seems unlikely. Unlike the printer, the granddaughter emphasized her grandmother's affection and piety, not her fertility.

Young women increasingly rejected the relentless childbearing of their foremothers. Demographic figures make this clear, and so do individual cases. Another daughter, born in 1777, was the eleventh and last child of a mother who perished shortly after giving birth, as alas all too many women did in this era. This youngest daughter, Charity Bryant, determined never to marry, instead cohabiting for decades with another woman in what people in their town recognized as a long-term same-sex relationship.[88] They had no children. Others also sought to avoid heterosexual marriage, childbearing, and the subordination under which women labored in this era.[89] For all kinds of people, affection rather than fertility characterized the ideal for intimate relationships. For a rising number of women, life was to be carefully managed and nurtured, with an emphasis on quality over quantity. Life was a personal and a political matter.

Still, in 1780, even the most prolific woman could not produce soldiers fast enough to supply all the troops required. Those needs were sufficiently pressing that officials came up with other schemes. Some men, such as Roman Catholics, were ineligible to serve in the British military. The shortage of troops led to the Catholic Relief Act, first proposed in 1778, to offer limited political rights to Catholics. Catholics still could not vote or hold office, but now they could serve in the military, own land, and preach in public. There was no movement for toleration generally; the act was a political expedient to advance Catholic recruitment.[90] The British government apparently had little sense that this would prove a disastrous move.

In the wake of a threatened Franco-Spanish (Catholic) invasion, many British people responded with horror. In 1780, they formed the Protestant Association, with a petition campaign against this act. They obtained more than forty thousand signatures, an unprecedented number at the time. Lord George Gordon, a leading opponent of the bill, headed a huge crowd, wearing blue cockades proclaiming NO POPERY!, to carry this enormous petition to the capital to present it to Parliament on June 2, 1780. The MPs voted overwhelmingly in favor of dismissing it. At that point, disorder erupted.

The Gordon Riots, one of the most incendiary weeks in London's history, commenced on June 2, 1780, with attacks on Catholic chapels. The Irish became targets; several fires were set in Moorfields, where many immigrants lived. On June 6, Ignatius Sancho, a Black Londoner, wrote eloquent letters to a friend describing the events going on outside his windows. He reported that "two thousand liberty boys are swearing and swaggering by with large sticks—thus armed in hopes of meeting with the Irish."[91]

Soon, however, crowds began to strike other sites associated with state power, including prisons holding rioters. Here is Sancho again: "There is about a thousand mad men, armed with clubs, bludgeons, and crows, just now set off for Newgate [prison], to liberate, they say, their honest comrades." The worst destruction came on "Black Wednesday," when the Holborn distillery belonging to a Catholic businessman was ransacked and burned. Gin ran in rivulets in the street, some of it ablaze, lighting up central London. Crowds also destroyed the property of the lord chief justice, Lord Mansfield, one of the supporters of the Relief Act. As Sancho summarized, "The thunder of their vengeance has fallen upon gin and law—the two most inflammatory things in the Christian world." There were also attacks on the Bank of England headquarters. Another observer concluded: "We now come to that period of desolation and destruction, when every man began to tremble, not only for the safety of the city, but for the constitution, for the kingdom, for property, liberty, and life, for every thing that is dear to society, or to Englishmen."[92] Sancho's pithy summation: "anarchy reigns."

At last the military arrived, with orders to shoot without even the customary reading of the Riot Act. Added to the shouts came "the dreadful report of soldiers muskets."[93] Soldiers killed hundreds, and at last an uneasy quiet descended on the smoking city. Eventually, many rioters were convicted; the same issue of the *Morning Chronicle* reporting on James Graham's Temple also included conviction rates for rioters at the Old Bailey prison.[94]

Rumors swirled about who was to blame for this disaster. Sancho hinted darkly: "It is thought by many who discern deeply, that there is more at the bottom of this business than merely the repeal of an act."[95] Those who opposed the Relief Act had long contended that it was a way to oppress their American brethren. As Lord George Gordon phrased it, the Relief Act was for "the diabolical purposes of arming the Papists against the Protestant Colonies in America."[96] Others blamed the Americans, while still others pointed to the French: "The French and American agents are discovered to have been the chief instruments of the present insurrections."[97] The Gordon Riots, energized by anti-Catholicism, formed a kind of pivot in 1780. Although up until then the British had been reasonably successful in their campaign in the southern states, things started to go wrong.

Disasters began to mount for the British in 1780. In April, the governor of Jamaica, with a cockeyed scheme to gain access to the Pacific from the Caribbean, managed to persuade the government to launch an expedition against the Spanish in what is now Nicaragua. Some eighteen hundred British troops trudged through the green and mosquito-infested lands around Lake Nicaragua. Stricken with yellow fever and malaria, they died in droves. By the autumn, only 380 men remained, and most of them were ill. They ended up blowing up the fort of San Juan and evacuating the whole place.[98] They may well have carried disease back to Jamaica, which experienced especially high mortality rates in 1780.

More British soldiers died in Nicaragua than in any other single engagement of the war—for no advantage whatsoever. As if the situation were not dire enough, in October 1780, a series of hurricanes rolled through the Caribbean. The first of these devastated Barbados, killing some four thousand people and destroying more than a million pounds sterling of property.[99] St. Lucia, taken by the British from the French in December 1778, was also hit hard.[100] Tens of thousands died in the Caribbean that autumn, and food shortages affected even more thereafter. Altogether, thousands went to their graves in Latin America and the Caribbean.

In 1780, British troops fell to disease and disaster in the Caribbean; in South Asia, they went down in battle. The military forces of that long-standing enemy of the British, Haidar Ali, "rushed like a prodigious torrent into the Carnatic," culminating in September's Battle of Pollilur.[101] Ali's forces succeeded "in the annihilation of the gallant English army" there.[102] Nearly four thousand British troops were killed or captured. One British major acknowledged that "never was . . . so Dishonourable a retreat made by British Troops."[103]

Haidar Ali's son, Tipu Sultan, later commemorated this monumental victory—the greatest defeat ever inflicted on the English in South Asia—in a huge (32-foot) painting on the wall of his summer palace. This extraordinary work by Indian painters offers in vivid colors a remarkable depiction of eighteenth-century warfare. The British appear in tall hats (a later diplomatic document referred to European soldiers simply as "hat-wearers") and without facial hair, symbolic of their weakness and effeminacy.[104] South Asian soldiers—on foot and horse and camel and elephant—surround them. The wounded British commander, William Baillie, is being carted off in a palanquin, finger to his mouth in a classic gesture of astonishment. In contrast to the soldiers carrying guns, swords, bows and arrows, and cannon, Haidar Ali and Tipu Sultan oversee forces from their majestic elephants, each holding only a flower, symbolizing enlightenment, piety, and power. These serene leaders are surrounded by decapitated heads, bodies spurting blood, men engaged in fierce hand-to-hand combat, other men falling, and cannons being lit and fired.[105]

The drama of Pollilur enhanced diplomatic ties between these leaders and the French. Tipu Sultan assured the French that "I want to expel them [the English] from India. I want to be the friend of the French all my life."[106] He subsequently launched diplomatic missions to the French, sending letters on silk, embroidered with flowers, as well as coins and guns of excellent quality.[107] Admittedly, neither the Indians nor the French entirely trusted each other. Yet they could both agree on what South Asian officials called the "oppression and tyranny" of the English.[108] In late 1780, the British were on the defensive in at least some parts of South Asia.

Without some sense of this global panorama, it is impossible to understand the trajectory of American mainland campaigns in the southern states. By 1780, of the hundred thousand British troops available worldwide, fewer than 30 percent were deployed in North America.[109] John Adams pointed out "what a great Number of Posts they [the British] have to sustain."[110] British successes in Charleston and Savannah soon gave way to a much more challenging situation. They still managed some victories, including one at Camden, South Carolina, in August 1780. However, they also experienced a series of reversals and challenges.

Cornwallis had a numbers problem on the southern mainland in 1780. He counted too much on local loyalties, and he did not take account of mosquitoes and malaria. Both problems meant that he lacked men. Cornwallis and others overestimated support in the Carolinas; the assumption—as one British officer, Charles O'Hara, phrased it—was "that Thousands . . . would Flock to the King's Standard."[111] The British generally assumed that the settlers in South Carolina—with its verdant climate, large population of enslaved people, and staple crop economy—would behave like those in the Caribbean islands. Cornwallis was constantly surprised when they did not. In August 1780, he complained: "the Severity of the Rebel Government has so terrified & totally subdued the Minds of the People that it is very difficult to rouze them." By early 1781, he rued "the distresses and dangers of marching some hundreds of miles" in a "hostile" country.[112] As O'Hara put it in 1781, they had received "repeated Assurances . . . that a great Majority of the People of the Carolina's . . . were waiting with the utmost impatience, for the arrival of our Troops." As he concluded, though, the British had been "grossly deceived. Fatal infatuation!"[113]

An even more fatal miscalculation was sending unseasoned British troops to fight in "the torrid zones" in the summer, a lesson they should have learned in the Caribbean. By August 1780, Cornwallis reported, "Our sickness is . . . truly alarming." A month later, he conceded he was forced to stay in the area because of "the great sickness of the Army, the intense heat, and the necessity of totally subduing the Rebel Country."[114]

High levels of illness hastened the loss of morale and help to explain why there were several British defeats in South Carolina, including at King's Mountain in October 1780 and at Cowpens in January 1781. After this last, one American Patriot reported on the "very grave faces" of the British and Loyalists then in Charlestown, South Carolina. Even the British victory in March 1781 at Guilford Courthouse was of dubious value, as British losses there were considerable.[115] The remainder of the British forces, as O'Hara complained, were "very Shatter'd, exausted [*sic*], ragged," so that "the Spirit of our little Army has evaporated a good deal."[116] As Sir Henry Clinton later framed it, the battle of King's Mountain was "the first link in a chain of evils that . . . ended in the total loss of America."[117]

The British were losing ground in the north, too. They had already evacuated Newport, Rhode Island, in 1779. Americans had moved in over the bitter winter of 1779–80, when a few men froze to death at their guard posts. In July 1780, French troops landed there. The residents of Newport watched from their windows, "sad and depressed," as yet another invading force made themselves at home among them.[118] Still, under orders, the residents illuminated the town that night with candles.[119] Six thousand French soldiers made Newport their home for nearly a year, starting in July 1780. At least one soldier in a French regiment was impressed by Newport. He recorded that it was "adorned with a very beautiful Town Hall as well as a beautiful church tower."[120] Still, there were so many homesick Frenchmen there that they even started publishing a French-language newspaper, *La Gazette Françoise,* in November 1780, with several issues in 1780–81. Its articles came from both French and American papers, keeping the local forces informed.

In late 1780, *La Gazette Françoise* reported on rising tensions between the British and the Dutch.[121] Trading with the French and Americans, the Dutch had long vexed the British. Many of the arms to Americans went through the free trade port of the Dutch Caribbean island of St. Eustatius. French influence in Holland increased in the 1770s, so Dutch "neutrality" was arguably pro-French.[122] The British also resented that the Dutch were supplying the Spanish in Gibraltar. Henry Laurens, the former president of the Continental Congress, went to Holland to negotiate a treaty with the Dutch in 1779. On his return voyage, the British intercepted his ship, discovering a draft treaty between the United States and Holland. On this basis, they arrested Laurens on a charge of treason, whereupon he became the only American ever held in the Tower of London.[123]

On the basis of this and other episodes, the British declared war on the Dutch in December 1780. By early 1781, prospects were looking bad for the British. As one English vicar marveled, it was "an incredible Thing" that Britain held out for so long against a "most formidable & unprovoked Confederacy . . . viz, France, Spain, the united Provinces of the Netherlands, & the 13 revolted Colonies of North-America."[124]

Against all odds, British soldiers tried to maintain their posts. Flung to rocks in Gibraltar, lakes in Nicaragua, and rice fields in Tamil Nadu and South Carolina, these sons, brothers, fathers, and husbands held on, clutching their hats. Even one British officer noted that his soldiers, who had marched across the Carolinas and its large rivers, "deserve the highest praise, under every possible disadvantage, contending against a powerfull [*sic*] current . . . under a very heavy Fire."[125] In these grim conditions, many ended up dead or disabled in the service of the global commitments of the British government.

By the spring of 1781, the British were facing a range of challenges around the globe, as Captain Horsbrugh in Gibraltar could attest. Troop numbers became a point of fixation, there and elsewhere. This manifestation of national strength appeared to rest on intimate choices by women and men. Population concerns drove politics to a large extent in this era, in locations as diverse as American bedrooms, showrooms in London, and defenses in Gibraltar.

In the spring of 1781, Horsbrugh recorded another round of attacks by the Spanish on Gibraltar. One night, the Spanish (whom Horsbrugh, like Miriam Green, termed simply "the Enemy") "fired a good deal" into the British garrison. In the morning, British soldiers went out in gunboats to return the favor. There was heavy fire on both sides. The town was "set on fire in several places," with some houses "totally consumed." Ever attentive to numbers, Horsbrugh recorded "1 killed, 11 wounded, 1 Drummer wounded." Then came another blast: "A shell came thro' my house, the Explosion of which threw me down and hurt me."[126] Spanish shelling would alarm and hurt many more British soldiers in the rough spring of 1781.

Chapter 11

A Cabaña in Havana

HONOR

The storms had cleared at last. The time had come for revenge.[1] In February 1781, the early morning sky shifted from black to pink to blue as the Spanish flotilla made its way out of Havana's harbor, heading for Pensacola in British West Florida.[2] When Antonio de Soledad had departed this harbor in 1763, the imposing fort known as Fortaleza de San Carlos de la Cabaña (or La Cabaña, as locals called it) had not been there. In 1781, when he sailed out again, it was impossible to miss it even in the half-light of dawn. A mason by training, Soledad knew how much effort went into raising such a thick stone and brick edifice. When La Cabaña was completed in 1774, it joined other fortifications including the iconic El Morro at the entrance of the harbor with its twelve guns and fifty-two cannons.[3] This construction confirmed that this already well-fortified city was now likely the best-protected one in the Americas.[4]

Soledad's level head and skilled hands had not only helped build the walls of Havana, they had defended them, too.[5] When Soledad had left Havana on that 1763 trip, it marked a bright personal triumph in a time of otherwise dim national humiliation. Then, he was heading to Madrid in celebration of his valiant service during Havana's occupation by the British during the Seven Years' War. During that event, British forces had grouped in the area where La Cabaña was built: Never again would Cuban authorities permit such a mortifying gathering.[6] As one official framed it, "Since that unfortunate event the defenses of the fortification had been augmented, and today it appears to be impregnable."[7] Spanish officials did much else to thwart the British in the 1770s and 1780s.

The heavy walls of the fort known as La Cabaña, shown here in a late-nineteenth-century photograph, were built between 1763 and 1774. El Morro (with its lighthouse) is visible in the distance, to the right of the masts.

Strange as it may seem, the line to Yorktown, Virginia—and the loss of the thirteen colonies that that engagement engendered—runs through Havana and Pensacola. Spanish involvement in the American Revolution made a significant difference. The Spanish were looking to restore their honor by taking back lost lands. Honor was a code of behavior so fundamental in many early modern societies that it is now almost invisible to contemporary audiences.[8] Yet it flared in moments mundane (a street encounter) and exalted (the victory of an army). The last line of the Declaration of Independence pledged the signatories to support independence with "our sacred Honor." The adjective, unusual in this document, made honor a quasireligious ideal, a national imperative that depended on personal commitment.

Honor—an ancient concept associated with nobility—was repurposed in this period to serve the needs of a changing political landscape.[9] It resonated in Spain and its empire as well as in the new United States.[10] A Spanish dictionary of the 1780s offered definitions associating the "fame" of honor with "virtue and good reputation."[11] To have honor, a man needed courage and credit; he had to be a man of his word.[12] Although elites had long dominated honor culture, other kinds of people—including workingmen and -women—also claimed honor within their communities, occasionally in unexpected ways.[13] One Massachusetts woman who donned a soldier's uniform, serving in the Continental Army for more than a year, was said to have achieved "honor [because] she has served in the character of a soldier . . . displayed herself with activity, alertness, chastity and valor."[14]

Personal honor was supposed to support the larger national project, as in the case of that Massachusetts soldier. When these values harmonized, a person could pursue individual ambitions, bringing glory on family, community, and nation—as Antonio de Soledad had done. However, the two aspects did not always work together in these ways. Sometimes they clashed, especially in a period in which honor cultures were changing. The global politics of 1781 revealed flashes of honor—and dishonor—at levels both personal and national.

In 1762–63, Antonio de Soledad had won honor for himself and his regiment. As captain of the Batallón de morenos libres de la Habana (Free Black Battalion of Havana), Soledad and his regiment had shown "care and dedication" to the Spanish crown.[15] As a result, he and his lieutenant Ignacio Albarado had been invited to the court in Madrid, to perform a display of arms for Carlos III himself to celebrate Christmas 1763. In recognition of "the honor of having kissed His Royal Hand," they both received a gold medal bearing a likeness of the king.[16]

When he sailed from Havana to Pensacola in 1781, Soledad likely recalled 1763's voyage to Madrid; it had made him a minor celebrity. This trip was different, though. His proud visit to Madrid was almost twenty years ago. In 1781, he was in his sixties, hair grayer and sparser, not quite as fast on the draw. Nevertheless, his gun was cleaned and ready. Every Sunday, he served his king by joining his regiment as well as thousands of other soldiers to drill in case of attack.[17]

However, Soledad worried for the future. Havana was becoming tougher, less and less the kind of place to celebrate a Black man who could execute a perfect display of arms for the king of Spain. The port had been opened to trade with the new United States. More and more enslaved Africans arrived in Havana in ships—some of them flying the new U.S. flag—to work on sugar plantations; the times were changing.[18]

Soledad's Cuba was in the process of what one historian has called a "cascading set of changes"; so was Spain's empire.[19] In 1763, when the Seven Years' War ended, the Spanish managed to claw back two major imperial holdings: Cuba as well as Manila in the Philippines (which the British had also occupied). The French ceded Louisiana to the Spanish; however, the Spanish had to give up the island of Menorca, as well as the Floridas, East and West, to the British. They did not forget these losses, which still rankled.

No one was more determined to recover the Floridas and to achieve honor for himself and his king than the dynamic new governor of Spanish Louisiana, Bernardo de Gálvez, a thirty-four-year-old member of a family recently risen in Spanish society. His father was a distinguished general who had become the president of Guatemala. His uncle was the minister of the Indies who instituted major reforms. He had joined the military young, at age sixteen, and he had made a reputation in Mexican wars against the Apaches and other nations. Wounded repeatedly, he had pushed on. Even when he was a teenager, his tenacity was notable.

Gálvez was determined to succeed—for himself and his country. He was educated at the Royal Military Academy of Ávila. There he became part of a group of young officers committed to innovation, including scientific reorganization of the military and promotions for merit. These *barbilampiños,* or "beardless ones," stood in opposition to the *mozos viejos,* or "old boys," who believed that promotion should come through the time-honored routes of seniority or battle courage.[20] The impetus for restructuring gained momentum from 1763's losses.

By the 1770s, vigorous reformers—including Carlos III, the Bourbon king—were busy reorganizing empire. They instituted stronger American defensive measures including new fixed corps of local soldiers and fortifications like La Cabaña, completed in 1774.[21] Gálvez spent three years in France working with a Franco-Spanish regiment in the early 1770s. In 1775, the Spanish, seeking to show off their new prowess, undertook an Algerian invasion, the court newspaper declaring with hyperbole that "His Majesty will not put down the sword" until he had proved "the honor of Spanish arms."[22] The invasion was not a success, and Gálvez was again wounded. Still, it contributed to the continued impetus for reform.

Bernardo de Gálvez arrived in New Orleans in May 1776 to become the first colonel of the Louisiana Fixed Infantry Regiment, whose motto was "Honor and Faithfulness." The American Revolutionary War offered an excellent opportunity for Gálvez to win one and to demonstrate the other. At thirty, he became Louisiana's governor. He wanted to make a good impression to win the French over. Marrying a rich young French Creole widow helped, as did his fluency in French.[23] He reported to his uncle with delight that Spanish-style dresses and *mantillas* (shawls) now adorned the fashionable women of New Orleans.[24]

Yet Gálvez wanted more: the Floridas. He first provided secret support to the Americans in a 1778 raid against the British in West Florida, led by James Willing. Spain had not yet entered the war, so Gálvez was taking a calculated risk. Willing and his forces traveled along the Mississippi River, attacking various British plantations.[25] It was a start. Once the Treaty of Aranjuez was signed in 1779, though, Gálvez began figuring out how best to regain the Floridas. The military leaders of Havana scoffed at his ambitions. They wanted only to protect that city, since it was worth more than "fifty Mobiles and Pensacolas," as one naval officer sneered.[26] Gálvez was more ambitious—and tenacious.

Despite having paltry supplies, Gálvez led a successful siege of Mobile in March 1780. Although Spanish forces were limited (about thirteen hundred), British defenders were far fewer: around two hundred.[27] Unsurprisingly, the Spanish managed to take the fort there. Gálvez remained dismayed, though, by the continued lack of support from Havana. He complained to his uncle that if only a fleet had arrived from Cuba to help, it could have been another stunning defeat of the British as in Saratoga.[28]

After the Spanish victory at Mobile in the spring of 1780, Gálvez turned his attention to a more significant prize: Pensacola. To take West Florida's capital required support and matériel to be found only in Havana. Gálvez headed back there to win approval—as well as troops, ships, and supplies—for a new expedition. Gálvez argued that Cuba's safety depended on preventing the British from launching attacks from the north. It was not easy convincing senior commanders, but by the middle of October 1780, he was ready. Under the command of José Solano, some four thousand soldiers and officers (possibly including Soledad) left Havana for Pensacola.

This fleet ran smack into a hurricane, on the third of October.[29] As one Spanish officer observed while sailing elsewhere in the Caribbean, no ships were to be seen, but only the floating remnants of "masts, planks, chicken coops ... a big piece of keel, a part of a side of ship ... and other fragments of vessels," the result of "the great hurricane that had spread ruin through those seas."[30] Many ships were destroyed, others "returned laboriously to Havana," with "one 36-gun frigate ... dashed to pieces on the coast of Yucatán."[31] The expedition was called off.

Yet even hurricanes couldn't defeat the dauntless Gálvez. He spent the winter regrouping with the help of an old friend of similar age and outlook: Francisco Saavedra de Sangronis. Saavedra possessed a genius both for organizing and for charming Havana's naval "old boys," who viewed the expedition with skepticism. Saavedra wooed the commanders, promising each that Pensacola's conquest would further his "personal glory." Gálvez also received help from his uncle, the minister of the Indies, who endorsed the plan. Gálvez was given carte blanche to command as he saw fit, "since [His Majesty] trusts that you will have no other aim but the glory and honor of the Royal Army, and the good and prosperity of the nation."[32]

The honor of the nation required not just battlefield courage; it also depended on hardtack biscuits. To achieve success, they needed supplies, not always easy to find. First, there was a lack of flour. Before the war, most flour in Havana came from Spain and France, a line of supply now cut off by British ships. Cubans turned to Robert Morris, a leading merchant and financier in Philadelphia. He sent the first ships carrying flour to Havana from Baltimore and Philadelphia; the import of American flour skyrocketed from 1780 on, bringing much-needed silver pesos into U.S. coffers.[33] Even once they had flour, though, they still did not have biscuits. A tiny guild of bakers, who owned all the ovens, controlled production of all bread and biscuits in Havana. Saavedra had to get more ovens built—an unexpected undertaking, but one he accomplished. By February, the army intendant provided him with "enough food for 4,000 men for a period of three months," the planned duration of the expedition.[34] At last, they had the supplies. Cuban soldiers like Soledad would be munching on hardtack made with flour from Pennsylvania farms and baked in Havana as they attempted to conquer British Pensacola.

Still, when Saavedra strolled with Gálvez in Havana's narrow streets in 1781, both men knew that although they now had enough food, they did not have enough men, even assuming reinforcements from Louisiana and Mobile. However, they were both uneasily aware that "in the subtropics of America a campaign season begins in November and ends in May, when the season of rains, storms, and illnesses begins."[35] It was already February. Gálvez, impatient for action, feared that requesting more soldiers would lead to delay. He could not afford to wait. He forged ahead.[36] Saavedra promised his friend that he would do everything in his power to raise more troops. In the meantime, five warships, twenty-seven smaller vessels, and more than fifteen hundred soldiers—including those from the Free Black Battalion under Captain Antonio de Soledad—departed for Florida.[37]

By the middle of March 1781, the ships had reached the narrow inlet that led to Pensacola. They made camp on Santa Rosa Island near Pensacola Bay, and soon the men were "marching in column formations by the sea."[38] The British and their Indigenous allies—more than eighteen hundred men in a set of fortifications—fired on them day after day.[39] Spanish forces captured a boat, taking its passengers prisoner and learning that Jamaican reinforcements were on their way: not good news for the Spanish.[40]

Gálvez pushed on. By March 17, 1781, he had brought land and sea forces together, his own ship entering "the harbor without the least harm" despite enemy attacks. His men sent up "continuous cheers" out of their "delight and loyalty to him"—at least according to Gálvez's own

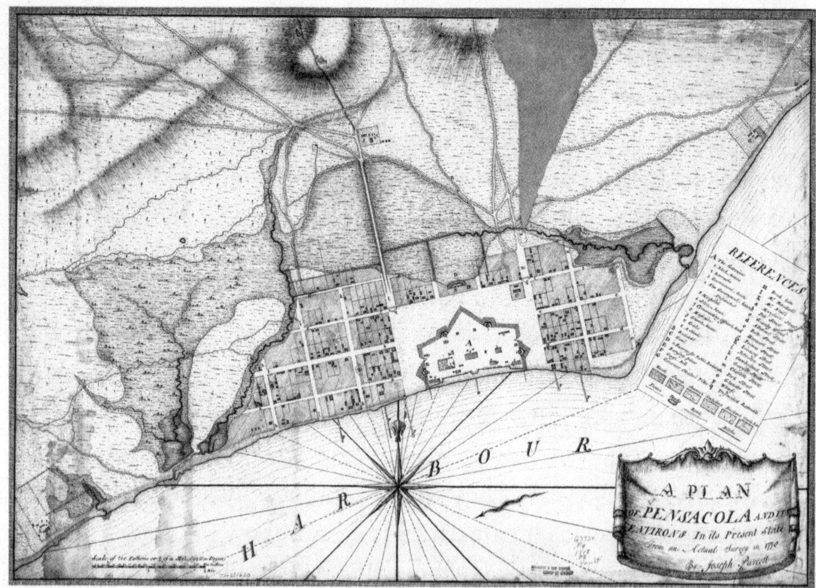

This plan of Pensacola shows the town just before the 1781 Spanish siege, with the distinctive star fort recently built by the British.

account.[41] Aware of Soledad's reputation, he gave Soledad's regiment the honor of firing the first shots.[42] Thus the siege began, with daily exchanges of fire. Gálvez was aware that the odds were against him.

On March 23, 1781, Spanish forces were relieved when ships appeared from New Orleans and Mobile, carrying arms, supplies, and sixteen hundred men, including New Orleans's "white and colored Militia."[43] The free Black militia of New Orleans included "famous marksmen," so their arrival was especially welcome.[44] In the meantime, Gálvez worked to broker agreements of neutrality with the leaders of the Talapuz nation, who were willing to supply the camp with fresh meat.[45] Although bolstered by the arrival of these convoys, Gálvez knew the challenges of besieging a city with limited troops, especially while his forces were being attacked by Indigenous soldiers. Indeed, one of them fired directly at him, sending a bullet through one finger and into his abdomen.[46]

As Gálvez recovered, he fretted over the prospects for success. He almost choked when he heard reports of a fleet in the distance, assuming it to be British reinforcements from Jamaica. In fact, the ships were from Havana, carrying his old friend Saavedra—true to his word—who had managed to bring sixteen hundred soldiers, fourteen hundred sailors, and seven hundred additional French troops.[47] It is little wonder that "Gálvez received us with a vivid display of joy."[48] He was also happy to learn that his father, the president of Guatemala, "had dislodged the English from the Castle of Nicaragua," firing a triple salute in celebration.[49]

Still, time—and munitions—were running out. Gálvez now had enough men, but not enough cannonballs. They had only two days' worth left. He had to pay his men to collect those fired by the English for reuse.[50] Meanwhile, the sultry humidity was building, reminding the general with each swipe of his sweaty brow that the season for conquest was passing. Soon they would face withering heat, mosquitoes, and illnesses, including what the Spanish called *el vómito negro,* or black vomit (yellow fever). In May 1781, one official in Havana wrote to another that he hoped to hear news of the surrender of Pensacola, which he recognized would be "such an important victory" for them.[51]

At one o'clock in the morning on May 6, a "furious storm broke" over the Spanish camp. A strong wind, what Saavedra described as a "tornado," ripped up their tents; one officer lamented, "There was not a single bed that was not made into soup because all the tents were rotten." The trenches they had dug were flooded up to the waist; the general gave those stuck there an extra grog ration. Presumably, it helped them choke down the damp hardtack. There was nothing to do but shake off their misery and keep going.[52]

Meanwhile, the British were trying their best to withstand the assault, although their leaders—Governor Peter Chester and General John Campbell—did not inspire the loyalty that Gálvez did. Chester had arrived in Pensacola as governor in 1770; things did not go well. After a 1772 dispute over election procedures, he dissolved the assembly for several years.[53] After concluding that Chester lacked "military talents . . . by any means sufficient," General Howe sent Campbell to West Florida to take command.[54]

General Campbell arrived to find a dispirited crew at Pensacola. In 1771, Chester had already warned that "We are . . . environ'd on all sides by the Spaniards . . . Three or four Ships . . . from the Havanna would . . .

make a most easy Conquest of us."[55] Even in 1776, West Florida had only eight hundred troops, most of them untrained and unhappy, and its forts were crumbling in the humidity.[56] Soldiers posted there hated it. One who arrived from Jamaica in 1779 rued the change: "I am now in the worst part of the world... it is so damn'd Hot Fish stinks before it can be boil'd." He concluded with sardonic greetings to his friends: "tell them not to come to Pensacola."[57] Even General Campbell begged for a transfer: "I shall be very unhappy and discontented as long as I remain in this province. You cannot therefore bestow a greater favour upon me, than to recall me from West Florida."[58] His pleas went unanswered.

In no case was the lack of enthusiasm in leaders more palpable—or problematic—than in terms of British relations with their neighbors, the Muscogees (Creeks), Choctaws, Chickasaws, and other nations of this area.[59] The British had taken over the nominal government of West Florida in 1763, and they had been fumbling these relations ever since. In 1771, Chester acknowledged that connections with Indigenous nations—"on which our Security so much depends"—were deteriorating, foundering on the usual tangles of disputes over trade, resources, alcohol, and diplomatic failures.[60] Chester did hold conferences with Muscogee leaders, but such meetings proved ineffective. Muscogee leaders were not inclined to ally themselves to Chester when he shrugged with empty hands: "I wish I had it in my power to be more Liberal... but... it is not in my power to Supply" gifts.[61] Chester bumbled, while General John Campbell was actively contemptuous of Indigenous people. The Indian superintendent complained: "He does not understand anything of Indians or their affairs. He thinks they are to be used like slaves or a people void of natural sense."[62]

With characteristic insight, Saavedra recognized these dismal dynamics. Given the "cruel and continual war" waged by settlers against them, he was unsurprised that "all these nations regard whites with irreconcilable hatred, especially Anglo-Americans, whose vexatious proximity, usurping their lands every day, is reducing them to deeper poverty."[63] In the end, only a couple hundred allied Indigenous soldiers showed up to help the British under siege.[64] Spanish and French forces outnumbered them all considerably.

Meanwhile, the siege continued, with the hapless men still at it on

May 7, 1781, the day after the storm. Laying out their soaked tents and clothing to dry, the damp Spanish brigades continued firing on Pensacola into the morning of May 8, when they suddenly heard "a great explosion" with "a terrifying noise" from the town; they soon spied "a great column of smoke rising toward the cloud." By chance, their howitzers had fired a grenade that hit the fort's magazine, blowing it up and killing more than a hundred soldiers. Saavedra termed this hit a "remarkable event," and it effectively ended the siege.[65] That afternoon, the Spanish saw the sight for which they had longed: the white flag of surrender. Campbell soon agreed to a full capitulation. In a hastily consecrated warehouse in Pensacola, on May 11, 1781, Spanish forces sang a Te Deum of thanksgiving for the reconquest of Florida.[66] Those sweet notes of praise floated over the Gulf of Mexico along with Saavedra, who landed in Havana on May 26 with the news that "caused universal joy" and led to a more formal but equally jubilant Te Deum in Havana's cathedral.[67]

This French engraving, likely from 1784, depicts the moment that Spanish artillery hit the English magazine, causing the massive explosion that effectively ended the siege of Pensacola.

Cubans, including Soledad, had reason to raise their voice in song for the victory and the impressive leadership that lay behind it. Thanks to canny organization and strategy, they had avenged the taking of Havana. Gálvez and Saavedra—the military leader and the organizational one—were both forces of nature: strategic, energetic, and above all determined. Both brought immense positive energy to their mission in the face of repeated setbacks. They were at the vanguard of what came to be called the Bourbon reforms, in which Spanish monarchs of the House of Bourbon instituted systematic reorganization throughout Spain's considerable empire. Although neither man was American by birth, both brought a kind of cockeyed American optimism in the face of hurricanes, recalcitrant naval commanders, war wounds, and the many forces, human and natural, arrayed against them.[68]

In no case were these reforms more successful than in the military reorganization capitalizing on the considerable talents of men of color like Antonio de Soledad. In the 1760s, the prominence of local militias grew, as did the deployment of such men. These militia units received more pay and benefits than regular troops. They also had the right to bear arms and to wear uniforms, thus distinguishing them from enslaved people. Their fierce loyalty to their own communities and to their own honor as free men made them powerfully effective soldiers.[69] Two veterans of the siege of Havana, Josef Uribe and Pedro Oporto, were so keen to fight for Florida that they even sold their own possessions in order to finance a company to join Gálvez's forces.[70]

British and especially U.S. Americans were more hesitant about arming Black men. They did it—as shown by Dunmore's proclamation—but slowly and reluctantly.[71] On the U.S. side, there were a few bold experiments including the First Rhode Island Regiment, which enlisted Black and Indigenous soldiers, offering freedom to enslaved men from 1777 on; of its two hundred and twenty-five men, one hundred forty were "negro, mulatto, or mustee." Jeremiah Greenman, whom we have met before, served as one of its lieutenants from 1780 to 1783. At least one man, Caesar Updike, achieved an "Honorary Badge of Distinction," after five years' brave service.[72] Yet these distinctions were rarer. Spanish authorities like Gálvez were more welcoming, offering major honors to notable militiamen. Soledad's trip to Madrid and his medal from the king show how much the Spanish crown valued their services. In his time in Louisiana, Gálvez had recommended many Black men for citations, which may partially explain why these men became "famous marksmen."[73] In the late 1780s, veterans from the free Black battalion still celebrated their time in Gálvez's service, praising him as an inspirational leader.[74]

Spanish military and financial leadership proved essential to the Patriot cause in the summer of 1781. Spanish, French, and U.S. forces were working together to try to defeat the British. A Frenchman, the Comte de Grasse, hatched a plan "of taking possession of Chesapeake Bay . . . in order to . . . prevent the reinforcement of the army of Lord Cornwallis." Then other forces, under Washington, Lafayette, and the Comte de Rochambeau, "would encircle him on all sides with their respective troops and . . . oblige him to surrender."[75] This move depended on troops and supplies from the French and Spanish Caribbean islands. Washington and Rochambeau were to march south to the Chesapeake while de Grasse sailed north with troops and supplies from the Caribbean.

This bold plan for a Chesapeake attack held promise, but it required money and matériel—much of it furnished by the Spanish. The new United States was deficient in silver, and it could not pay for goods. Much discontent flowed from poor provisions in the army. Alexander Hamilton observed that "The providing of supplies is the pivot of every thing else." He fretted that the army was "now a mob, rather than an army, without cloathing, without pay." Continental currency had lost considerable value. By May 1781, a New York newspaper with British sympathies reported on a Philadelphia street protest in which participants allegedly tarred and "feathered" a dog with congressional paper dollars in place of the feathers to demonstrate how worthless the currency had become.[76] It was impossible to finance the war in these circumstances. Yet, as George Washington had observed in 1780, "In modern Wars the longest purse must chiefly determine the event."[77]

The Continental Congress finally took action to address this financial crisis. They looked for someone with a head for numbers, an array of assets, a network of global connections, and a willingness to do whatever it took. In Robert Morris—who had begun shipping flour to Havana in exchange for silver and enslaved laborers—they found just the man, even though some—like Joseph Reed (a leading Pennsylvania official)—derided him as "a pecuniary dictator."[78] Thanks to business savvy and political commitment, he had already become effectively the underwriter of the American Revolution.[79] In February 1781, the Continental Congress offered him the position of superintendent of finance. Alexander Hamilton, then Washington's aide-de-camp, exhorted him to accept the challenging position "by which you may render America and the world no less a service than the establishment of American independence!" Hamilton argued that such a move would make Morris a hero: "Tis by introducing order into our finances—by restoreing public credit—not by gaining battles, that we are finally to gain our object."[80] Morris reluctantly started in June 1781.

Morris's commitment to improving the economy—in the interest of both personal and national success—started to bear fruit, especially with the help of a Polish immigrant, Haym Salomon, who, like Morris, put his own credit on the line in order to help the situation (though Morris had insultingly called him the "Jew Broker" in earlier correspondence).[81] In the first year of his tenure, Morris obtained loans from France worth $1,000,000—more than the total of all French loans up to that point.[82] This money helped to provide that necessary "Subsistence." Rising U.S. trade with Cuba—that American flour sold to Havana—also provided silver for the United States treasury. As one observer noted, "a very beneficial trade to the Havana has poured a great quantity of specie into the country."[83]

Havana was the source of even more direct funding to the new nation. In July 1781, Saavedra accompanied de Grasse to Saint-Domingue, where they sought financial backing without success. De Grasse fretted that he was about to lose the opportunity to attack in concert with American forces, as "the lack of money was making it impossible for him to launch the expedition."[84] Saavedra suggested that they head to Havana. They arrived shortly after the silver fleet had just departed for Spain. The treasury was empty. More silver was expected soon, but no one knew when. Havana's empty coffers were a blow, but Saavedra was hardly one to crumble, despite "all this difficulty." With customary brio, he suggested that they turn directly to the populace there, with a promise that loans would receive 2 percent interest. Since everyone knew that silver ships were expected soon, giving to the cause was both a patriotic and a prudent act. "Two French officers went to collect the funds, and in six hours the requisite amount was gathered." That same afternoon, Gálvez arrived in Havana to "joyous celebration," and the silver collected went off that evening with his delighted approval.[85] Since Saavedra had also promised to put Spanish sailors on patrol in Cap-François, all of de Grasse's considerable forces could sail out from Havana to the Chesapeake.[86]

Meanwhile, under orders from General Clinton, Lord Cornwallis stationed his forces at a base near the York River estuary on the Chesapeake Bay. He had already endured one sweaty, mosquito-ridden summer of campaigning in the south, and now he got another. By June, one Hessian soldier complained that "the heat was so terrific that it was hardly endurable." In their heavy uniforms, men died of heatstroke.[87] The Hessian officer Johann Ewald reported on heat and "the torment of several billions of insects."[88] Thousands of formerly enslaved people, seeking freedom with the British, labored to build fortifications.

Supplies started to run dangerously low. By October, things had grown so desperate that Cornwallis ordered the mass slaughter of the baggage horses so as not to have to feed them. Their carcasses were dragged into the river. They soon returned, reeking, to the shore with the tide "as if they wanted to cry out against their murder."[89] Next, Cornwallis expelled the malnourished Black laborers who had joined them, returning them to their enslavers and in some cases to disease and death.[90]

At the end of September 1781, American and French troops gathered to besiege the British forces, firing on encampments and houses nearby. One soldier in a French regiment, Georg Daniel Flohr, recorded his experience at Yorktown, where "General Kornwallis of the English had dug in with 12,000 men, ravaging the country very badly."[91] French and American forces kept firing on the redoubts. Between the noise and the fear of being blown up, British and German soldiers hardly slept.[92] Flohr was horrified by the devastation, seeing "people flying into the air with outstretched arms" and hearing the screams of the dying.[93]

By mid-October, the catastrophe for the British had worsened, Flohr observing that "The whole redoubt was so full of dead and wounded that one had to walk on top of them." Cornwallis took refuge in a bunker as the carnage continued.[94] By the time the American and French forces made it into the British camp, they stared in shock at a "veritable scene of destruction" and hundreds of unburied corpses "the majority . . . blacks."[95] The British offered capitulation (Cornwallis, claiming illness, remained in his bunker). After all the cannons and the cries and shouts, a "solemn stillness prevaild" on a clear, starry night. The next morning a Scottish regiment played a mournful bagpipe, answered by the band of Flohr's French regiment.[96] Such were the sounds of the British capitulation at Yorktown.

Amid the stars of surrender, Johann Ewald searched still for honor. He did not find it. He concluded in dismay that "all hearts had turned to stone." He condemned the shameful behavior of the British high command. He was horrified that they had turned over "our black friends" to their enslavers, in what he termed "a cruel happening."[97] He pitied the "poor sick and wounded" who were obliged to endure their pain with neither medicine nor provisions, their "amputated arms and legs . . . eaten by the dogs." Cornwallis stormed about, grim-faced, unwilling to help anyone.

Ewald reflected on the demands of honor: "When a man chooses a calling, he must do everything that can be done in that calling, so that he can never suffer reproach for having done only half of his duty." He reminded himself of the wisdom of the seventeenth-century French poet Nicolas Boileau:

> Honor is like an island,
> Steep and without shore:
> They who once leave,
> Can never return.[98]

The Hessian soldier Andreas Wiederhold, too, prayed: "If we were only out of this affair with honor!"[99]

Even if Cornwallis inevitably lost national honor in the surrender, he could have retained personal honor. In this instance, he did not. The dishonor lay not in surrender but in failing to "do everything that [could] be done" to protect allies and to relieve suffering.

Although people commonly assume that the surrender at Yorktown in 1781 ended the American Revolutionary War, in fact, fighting dragged on for more than a year around the world. However, the "thirteen colonies" were not where most of that conflict took place. Ewald observed, correctly, that "This disaster, the capture of the army under Lord Cornwallis, will give the Opposition Party in England enough impetus to carry through its plan to give up the dominions in North America."[100] The British government, tired of war and its costs, gave up on retaining the thirteen former colonies.

However, the global war launched in 1778 continued in South Asia, in the Caribbean, and in the Mediterranean. The British kept fighting Hyder Ali and then his son, Tipu Sultan, in the Second Anglo-Mysore War, which ended in a stalemate in 1784.[101] In 1782, the British experienced further losses in Menorca (reconquered by the Spanish); in the Caribbean at St. Kitts, Montserrat, and Nevis; and in the Bahamas in May.

The British did achieve some triumphs. They managed successfully to defend vital Caribbean sites, most notably Jamaica. Despite endless Franco-Spanish plots, the island was never invaded. De Grasse and his forces attempted to conquer it in April 1782, but they were repulsed by Admiral George Rodney and his forces at the Battle of the Saintes. This naval battle represented a monumental victory for the British, since Jamaica was their most valuable colony.

The British also retained Gibraltar despite a massive Franco-Spanish siege in September 1782 of thirty-five thousand troops and advanced floating batteries.[102] At the time of this enormous assault, there were only some seventy-five hundred British troops on Gibraltar (four hundred of whom were in the hospital following an influenza epidemic); it is remarkable that the British were able to hold on. Yet they did. The siege finally ended in February 1783; the British welcomed "this return of tranquillity, this prospect of plenty and relief."[103]

By late 1782, negotiations for peace had already begun, with treaties signed in 1783 and 1784. Given the number of participants and the complicated and novel nature of this war, it is hardly surprising that these negotiations—which began when fighting was still taking place around the world—took several months.[104] Ultimately, three treaties were signed in Paris and Versailles in 1783, with a fourth signed with the Dutch in 1784.[105]

The Treaties of Paris of 1783 formally ended the American Revolutionary War, though not quite the Nine Years' War, which continued into 1784. Still, American newspapers reported congressional approval of the formal peace on January 14, 1784.[106] These treaties recognized the United States of America as a free and sovereign nation, adjudicating its boundaries. The treaty between the United States and Britain was short but contained several critical points, including that Loyalists were given one year to seek restitution for losses and the British promised to release prisoners of war and not to remove any enslaved people.[107] There were a number of omissions (such as the exact borders of the United States), which would subsequently cause conflict.

The most striking silence—about Indigenous peoples—was a thunderbolt to those allies. As Thayendanegea (Joseph Brant) informed the British in 1786, "we were struck with astonishment at hearing we were forgot in the treaty . . . we could not believe it possible such firm friends and allies could be so neglected by a nation remarkable for its honor and glory."[108] So many allies of the British—from the Haudenosaunee in the north to the Muscogees in the south—had had to seek refuge elsewhere, as their towns were destroyed. In some cases, they could return and rebuild, but not always. Konwatsitsiaienni (Molly Brant) put two daughters in boarding school in Montréal and settled in Carleton Island in New York, remaining a leader in exile. At the end of the war, she moved to Cataraqui (Kingston, Ontario), where General Haldimand rewarded her with the largest pension given to a Native American ally.[109]

Still, most Indigenous people received no compensation at all, and no support from their supposed allies.

The diverse range of Loyalists in 1783 appears in a strikingly inclusive painting by Benjamin West. It depicts government officials and Indigenous soldiers adorned with wampum, mothers clutching babies and Black men with arms aloft. Presenting their cases to British judges, all are sheltered in Britannia's embrace, flanked by Justice and Religion. As a symbol, it's notable. Still, it was an idealized vision, far from the realities faced by allies and Loyalists.

Loyalists—who had "abandoned everything for their king, picked up weapons in the defense of his honor and justice [and] willingly shed their blood," as Andreas Wiederhold put it—faced a challenging future in 1783.[110] All kinds of people, including Anglican ministers, Scottish merchants, and pacifist Quakers, had fled the new states. Relying on family and community networks, they had made their uncertain way out: to Britain, but also to other parts of the world.[111] Some sixty thousand Loyalists, along with fifteen thousand enslaved people they took with them, left the new nation: about 1 in 40 of the population.[112]

Decent treatment of the exiled Loyalists would have been a way for Britain to demonstrate what historians have called the "moral responsibility" and "moral capital" of the nation.[113] The most egregious aspect of the Treaty of Paris, declaimed one MP in February 1783, was that "it strikes at the very honour and honesty of the nation, in deserting and abandoning your best friends, those who have sacrificed every thing."[114] Lord North declared "we should, at least, have protected them, to have preserved our own honour.... Never was the honour of a nation so grossly abused as in the desertion" of the Loyalists.[115]

In response, the British government set up the Loyalist Claims Commission in 1783 to hear the cases of those who had lost their livelihoods in the war. Such an organized governmental commission for compensation was virtually unprecedented, certainly on the scale at which it was undertaken.[116] In order to win approval of their claims, Loyalists generally had to present their cases in person, with a paper trail of character references and documentation of losses. More than five thousand people submitted paperwork. Overall, Loyalists sought compensation for more than £7 million in property and £2 million in unpaid debts—an amount equivalent to nearly £1 billion today.[117] The government paid out only in the hundreds of thousands, finding every reason to limit payments. It was much easier for government officials, ministers, and merchants to make a successful case. Although some five hundred White women and Black men made appeals, they tended to receive far less.[118]

Even many elite Loyalists did not recover anything like what they had forfeited, as some of them fumed. Joseph Galloway, a Pennsylvania politician who had fled in 1778, gained a reasonably generous pension of £500 per annum, but he remained distraught. He was the kind of man who turned distress into printed words (he wrote thirteen treatises between 1775 and 1788). His tracts appealed to "national honour and national justice," which could, in his telling, be achieved only through generous reparations.[119] Galloway sought to mitigate his personal damages. When he went to England in 1778 with his daughter Betsy, he left his wife, Grace, in Philadelphia, in hopes she would be able to preserve their property. Grace rued "this cruel seperation [*sic*]."[120]

Grace Galloway fought hard to keep her family's property. Despite her reduced circumstances, she reassured friends that although she had been "stripped & Turn'd out of Doors yet I was still ye same." She reminded herself in her diary "that it was Not in their [the soldiers'] power to humble Me for I shou'd be Grace Growdon Galloway to ye last." She concluded that she would survive, "safe ashore," even though she was being "tost by Tempestuous billows."[121] Despite her brave words to herself, the raging billows eventually pulled her under. She could not hold on to the property, and she became ill. She died in Philadelphia in 1782, never reunited with her husband or beloved daughter.

Wives and children often suffered for choices made by husbands and fathers. Law in this era assumed that if the husband was a Tory, the wife was one too.[122] Catherine Crooke Dudley was a Newport native, born in 1750. Her father, Robert Crooke, had been a major instigator of protest during the Stamp Act crisis. However, in 1769, his daughter had married Charles Dudley, a British customs commissioner. Her own political sentiments are unclear. By the autumn of 1775, Charles, having already been attacked and beaten once, had taken refuge on board a British ship in Newport Harbor before fleeing for England. During the war, she followed him to England and they had two children there. When peace came, it was still uncertain what would happen to the four of them. The Loyalist Claims Commission was reluctant to make up for lost salaries as opposed to property losses. In the early 1780s, the Dudleys continued to press for restitution, eking out a living in England even as they endured what one Loyalist called "the strange misfortunes of the family."[123]

Richard Weaver, a Black man from Philadelphia who had arrived in London in 1779, was another candidate for Loyalist compensation in 1783. He sought transportation costs for himself and his family to move to Nova Scotia, Canada, where the government was offering land to refugees. Although he presented character references, they were deemed insufficient. In 1784, the Commission declared that Weaver, whom they assumed had been enslaved, "proves no Loyalty." They sniffed: "we are apt to imagine that besides losing nothing he has gained his Liberty by the War . . . nothing ought to be given to this Man."[124]

In the wake of transformative revolution, so much *might* have changed. In many cases, little did. In London, men like Richard Weaver did their best, without much success, to surmount the forces arrayed against them in the 1780s. Economic realities and prejudice made postwar life challenging for many. In New England, Newport and Violet Freeman experienced knocks too. Prospects had looked bright for them in 1778, when, both free, they had married. Like Grace Galloway, Newport Freeman stated his name as an assertion of his status. The name of Freeman also connected him to his wife and son in kinship. Yet by October 1781, Newport and Violet Freeman indentured themselves back to Ezra Stiles for seven years for £20: a step backward.[125] Not enslaved, they were also not free.

Even more surprisingly, after they moved into the Stiles household in New Haven, Connecticut, the Freemans indentured their two-year-old son, Jacob, to Stiles for twenty-two years.[126] As Violet and Newport watched their son toddling across the floors of the Stiles household, they had to imagine him staying there, whether he wanted to or not, until he turned twenty-four, effectively repeating his father's enslavement from childhood. Their prospects must have been dim indeed for them to make this arrangement. Without equality and prosperity, liberty was an uncertain thing even for those who valued it as highly as the Freemans.

In Havana, too, Antonio de Soledad, Ignacio Albarado, and others in their regiment confronted the bleak forces of prejudice. Economic changes wrought by the war advanced the sugar industry and the slave trade, tightening the screws on the Black population of the city. The information that these men fired the first shots at Pensacola comes from their legal case against a commander who had flogged to death a comrade, a decorated veteran of the 1762 siege of Havana and the 1781 conquest of Pensacola. His regiment pressed the crown for punishment for this killing, citing this dead man's—and their—gallant service and noting that Gálvez had granted them "the glory of being the first to open fire against the enemy," which they did out of their willingness "to sacrifice their lives for the honor of arms." These soldiers protested that the brutal commander had treated their comrade "like a slave," or even "worse than slaves," acting "as if the life of a man, even if Black, had not cost Jesus Christ the same as that of a white man." They complained that these days, in Havana, "they are called dogs, and they are treated as such, even if they wear the uniform that Your Majesty has given them." Valiant service and occupational success had long afforded them rank and reputation in Havana, which were now in jeopardy.[127]

Wearing the uniform of the Spanish military, these men had made a vital difference in Pensacola, ensuring that Britain lost a colony that was not even rebelling.[128] They had won honor for themselves, their nation, their king. Spanish support for the American Revolution had made a vital difference, in terms of victories such as Pensacola and in terms of finance and support at critical moments such as the battle of Yorktown. By contrast, men like Cornwallis had lost honor for himself, his nation, and his empire. Even compensation for Loyalists could not recoup that lost honor.

Connections between Cuba and the new United States remained important in the 1780s and beyond. Flour and provisions went from the United States to Cuba in exchange for enslaved people and Spanish silver, a much sought-after global commodity in the 1780s. Some of that

Spanish silver traveled far indeed. Spanish American silver paid for tea and silk and porcelain in Pacific port cities.[129] Some 500 million silver pesos entered China in the eighteenth century, with 200 million going through Manila in the Philippines.[130] "Tost by Tempestuous billows," those tarnished silver coins, stamped CAROLUS III, made their way into the coffers of merchants first in Manila—and then in Guangzhou.[131]

Chapter 12

A Mansion in Guangzhou

Fortunes

Watching the Americans trying to eat with chopsticks at his home was amusing, but Pan Zhencheng (潘振承) did not smile.[1] By 1784, he was used to the spectacle of foreigners in Guangzhou trying to master his ways, usually without much success. The guests had paid for the food and wine with their Spanish silver—and his talented chefs never squandered the finest ingredients on foreigners anyway—so let them drop mushrooms in their laps if they could not manage them better.[2] His own chopsticks moved with ease and efficiency in a wrinkled hand emerging from his thick silk robe.

The *Empress of China*—the first ship under the U.S. flag to reach China—arrived at Guangzhou in August 1784, carrying American ginseng and Spanish silver. Its officers were eager to get into Pan Zhencheng's good graces, and they were delighted to accept his invitation to a banquet at his family compound. In 1784, Americans desired more than life and liberty; they also wanted fortunes and the elegant porcelain, reviving tea, and soft silk that went along with them. Liberated from the restrictive policies of British imperialism, Americans could finally negotiate for themselves. As an officer for the *Empress of China* put it, "To every lover of his country . . . it must be a pleasing reflexion, that a communication is thus happily opened between us and the eastern extreme of the globe."[3]

The men who signed the Declaration of Independence pledged to devote "our Lives, our Fortunes, and our sacred Honor" to the furtherance of national interests. Wealthy men, they gave this bold pledge on credit. Many others had to make it good with hard specie—their own lives, limbs, families, and subsistence. People sought fortune—a word implying both luck and prosperity—in novel ways in the tough years of the 1780s. A few intrepid individuals explored and exploited new trade links—with Asia, Latin America, the West Indies, the Mediterranean, and Europe—as well as land speculation in the homelands of many Indigenous nations. Some fortunes depended on misfortunes.

The mid-1780s were an age of hustle. Historians, frequently passing over this era quickly, recount the few critical years after the Treaty of Paris in 1783 as if Americans living then could see the U.S. Constitution and a reconfigured national government at the end of the road, as if they were all just galloping toward the Constitutional Convention of 1787. Such a narrative arc emphasizes that the U.S. economy and government were utterly hopeless, verging on anarchy, and that everyone knew it. This storyline is inherited from the men who crafted the Constitution and sold it to the American people. It captures certain aspects of what happened, but it misses others. The economy did pose challenges, but on the whole, Americans rose to meet them.

By starting in China, at a moment of high hopes and building excitement, we can correct this tendency to look back from 1787 to assume the worst of the 1780s. Beginning in Guangzhou reveals some of the same flashing signals (economic problems, worries about U.S. standing in the world). However, it also allows us to follow the lively steps and quick turns and fresh hopes of a great many people whose attentions were otherwise engaged. It was a time of austerity yet also one of new connections and adventures. After all, no one told Americans in 1784 that they needed to put their aspirations on hold until they got a new government; they just got on with it.

In fact, the 1780s were a period of remarkable ambition and optimism, even amid economic uncertainty and rising inequalities. In the aftermath of the war, many Americans jostled and pushed their way to fortunes. That hustle had its costs, though.

Like an increasing number of Americans, Pan Zhencheng had secured his fortune through global trade connections. He had followed his father into the overseas trade. In his youth, he left his home in Fujian to pursue business in Manila, which was awash with Spanish silver. While there, he learned Spanish, converted to Catholicism, and established lifelong connections with the merchant community there. Those resentful of Pan Zhencheng's success claimed that he had been baptized only in order to enjoy a lower tax rate and greater commercial prospects.[4] Once back in Guangzhou, he started selling tea, silk, and porcelain to the English East India Company, building up dangerously high levels of debt to outperform his rivals. It worked, and he managed—sometimes very narrowly—to avoid firm-destroying loss. By the 1770s, he had repaid those debts. By 1781, even EIC officials acknowledged: "the Superiority of PuanKhequa is so great, that the other merchants dare not deviate from the rules he lays down."[5]

A diversified range of international links in an increasingly globalized economy allowed Pan Zhencheng to achieve domination, taking risks others could not manage—or survive. His trading partners hailed from China, Southeast Asia, Spain, France, Britain, and Sweden. Swedish traders even put his portrait—showing a man at the top of his game—on display in their headquarters. With his *chaozhu,* or necklace, and his blue-black silk court dress with its dragons and crane (symbolizing longevity and denoting rank), he now appeared as the high-level official he had become (having bought the office).[6] Court regulations determined the details of that outfit with minute oversight. Sartorial rules, including specifying the color of the silk worn, indicated Pan Zhencheng's place in these rankings. The Qianlong emperor, at the top of the hierarchy in imperial yellow and red, had ascended to the throne in the 1730s, just as Pan Zhencheng established himself in Guangzhou.[7] The Qianlong emperor presided over the eighteenth-century expansion and centralization of the Qing empire, as well as the growth of the lucrative canton trade system in Guangzhou. Both Pan Zhencheng and the Qianlong emperor enjoyed fortunes to the end of their days—and of that century.[8] Here, in lustrous silk, shone prosperity and global power. And Americans wanted a piece of the action.

The glittering financial possibilities of Guangzhou drew ambitious men from all over the world—other parts of China, Southeast Asia, the Philippines, India, Pacific islands including the Hawai'ian islands, Africa, the Middle East, Europe, and, from 1784 on, the United States.[9] It was a place where a man could make—or lose—a fortune. Interest rates in Guangzhou were high, attracting foreign capital.[10] Unlike most ports in this era, it was open for trade without restriction on nation, race, or religion. Those who arrived there could see from afar ancient pagodas and groves of fruit trees. They heard the hum of deals as wooden beads on abacuses whirled and clicked. Porters and sailors loaded and unloaded sampans—or barges—with tea, ceramics, pepper, cinnamon, silk, cotton, blue-and-white gingham, and other desirable delights.[11]

Since Guangzhou was a free port, Americans had the right to trade there, but it was not free in financial terms. To conduct business, they had to hire a *fiador*—security merchant—and a *comprador*—who furnished provisions at set prices—and a linguist to serve as translator.[12] The linguists also tutored foreigners on the protocol of meeting the *hoppo*—the administrator of canton customs appointed by the emperor himself. They had to learn to bow and to offer greetings. Linguists usually negotiated deals in advance, since the *hoppo* didn't want to waste time on meetings that did not result in deals. Americans reported with exasperation that these officials were tough negotiators.[13] Americans, like other foreigners, were confined to the "factories," or cantons, "on a narrow strip of land on the river's bank."[14]

Despite struggles with chopsticks, Americans wanted a place at Pan Zhencheng's table—even if they had to pay for it. The Americans hoped

This gilded punch bowl depicts the foreign factories including the Swedish and the British at Guangzhou in the 1780s.

the next step would be their own factory on the river, stars and stripes aloft, like the European flags already there. One of the sailors on the *Empress* wrote home: "the Chinese had never heard of us, but we introduced ourselves as a new Nation." The Americans explained about their revolution, making clear their desire for trade. Their hosts appeared "perfectly to understand" and to wish for the same.[15]

The Americans were also pleased when the magistrate of Guangzhou presented the captain of the *Empress* with two lengths of silk and a mother-of-pearl fan that depicted the *Empress* in the harbor along with European vessels. The American ship was a little less impressive than the others, and it rode shallower waters. The agent for the owners of the ship recounted on their 1785 return that "The Chinese were very indulgent towards us. They stiled us the new people." The Americans got out a map to show off their nation (so much bigger than Britain!), and they bragged about its growing settler population (rising so much faster than Britain's!). After this display, the Chinese were apparently "highly pleased at the prospect of so considerable a market."[16]

The Chinese in Guangzhou were "indulgent," but the fan—portraying that more diminutive American vessel—also made a political point. In fact, this new people did not even make it into official Qing records until several years later.[17] Swift noted ruefully that in the future they should send ships of 700 tons, as "our's is much too small" to make a good impression.[18] The American ship (between 400 and 500 tons) was less commanding than most European vessels, including those of the East India Company. Some even thought that the American vessel was merely heralding the arrival of the imposing EIC ships (700–800 tons), especially given similarities between the flags of the EIC and the USA.[19]

Such was not the grand entry to international trade the Americans had sought. In their ships and their maps and their deals, Americans imagined their country as great and mighty. Many in the rest of the world, though, dismissed them as minor players. Columbia seemed like nothing so much as the irritating kid sister of Britannia, a little twerp. Americans had to work hard to build a global brand.

With independence, U.S. involvement in global trade changed. The new nation lost its protected trading relationship with Britain. While most welcomed this autonomy, it was also perilous. Americans had long sent products and provisions to the British Caribbean, but now the British closed those ports to them. However, British and French and Dutch merchants could send goods through free American ports, unbalancing trade.[20]

In the 1780s, the American national economy also posed challenges. To fight its war, the United States had relied on overseas capital—mostly from the French. It also leaned on the goodwill of Americans, especially men and women who served on the front lines, often badly undersupplied and not paid for months. Some—even those disabled in service—received little to nothing by way of wages.[21] European governments and creditors also went unpaid. A lot of people were owed a lot of money. As happens so often at a war's end, the U.S. domestic economy sagged and softened, with trade in the doldrums.

Economic challenges arose on all sides. There were so many demobilized soldiers and sailors. Lean and hungry, they were now also unemployed. Some had families to support: wives, children, aging parents. That put a spring in their step. Some of them were willing to seek their fortune wherever they could find it—in the west, in the Mediterranean, even farther afield.[22]

A small subset of globally minded Americans in the 1780s looked to Asia, risky but lucrative. Even before the Treaty of Paris was signed in 1783, one Baltimore merchant was floating plans for "a good Voyage . . . to China," but he calculated that it would require more than a million French *livres*.[23] That same year, John Ledyard—a visionary American hustler who had accompanied Captain Cook on his last Pacific voyage in the 1770s—persuaded Robert Morris, the superintendent of finance, to provide backing for a trading trip to China. However, the project did not come to pass, and Ledyard melted away to pursue European ventures.[24]

Still, the idea of an American trading journey to China lingered. By August 1783, a newspaper reported on a ship being prepared in Boston for "this first venture from the new world to the old."[25] Robert Morris, along with Parker & Co. in New York, backed the voyage. Morris had already made a fortune and helped the nation. In the *Empress of China,* he again saw the possibility for personal and national advancement. As he wrote in November 1783, "I am sending some ships to China, in order to encourage others in the adventurous pursuits of commerce."[26]

The officers on the *Empress*—all veterans—were up for those "adventurous pursuits of commerce." Morris chose John Green—an imposingly large Irish-born Continental Navy veteran—as captain. One man who crossed paths with Green in 1777 described him as "the most Violent American I ever met with—His daily toast is Success to Washington & downfall of the British."[27] Green was twice captured by the British. The second time, he ended up in England's Mill Prison, held with hundreds of other American POWs there.[28] He corresponded with Henry Laurens, negotiating for their release. Green fretted that the sailors might write directly to Laurens to obtain missing wages. He advised Laurens not to reply as "there would be no end to it" due to so many unpaid wages.[29] After his 1782 release, Morris commissioned Green to captain a ship in 1783. Green carried flour and beef to exchange for Spanish silver at Havana. On his way home, his ship confronted a British squadron nearby. Shots exchanged in this minor skirmish mark the last American involvement in naval warfare during the American Revolutionary War.[30]

The supercargo—or business representative—of the *Empress* was also a veteran seeking his fortune. Shaw had enlisted in 1775 on his twenty-first birthday. He had imagined that this move would help make him—and the nation—independent. However, in 1776, he was begging his father for money, as he had not been paid for two months.[31] He served in several campaigns, becoming Major General Henry Knox's aide-de-camp. By 1781, he was due a full year's back pay.[32] In 1782, he was still lamenting, "We have experienced for years together the most oppressive treatment that ever an army endured."[33] In 1783, he wondered whether America was ready for peace: "What system has she, adequate to the government and prosperity of her rising empire? No money, no funds, and . . . the death of public credit."[34] The ship's purser, John Swift, was also struggling. He had joined that ill-fated Québec campaign in December 1775, in which he was wounded. Another veteran on the *Empress* was the surgeon, Dr. Robert Johnson, who had served as a medic in the Continental Army. He had begun working for the *Empress* before the ship even set sail, as he was commissioned to procure ginseng.

In 1784, ginseng was the key commodity to be sold to the Chinese. Valued for its medicinal and tonic properties, ginseng was among the few American products in which the Chinese had any interest. It grew well in the Appalachians, which were thriving Indigenous homelands now under severe threat due to the presence of this desirable global commodity. In late 1783, Robert Johnson headed west to source the ginseng. He managed to get the promise of a consignment of ginseng, but he needed $5,000—cash in hand. He begged the backers of the voyage for more cash, fretting that he would lose good deals without it, and they ponied up. Thanks to this money, he was finally able to obtain 57,000 pounds of "Ginseng of ye 1 st quality." With ginseng and Spanish silver, the *Empress* and its crew of veterans and fortune seekers departed for China in early 1784.

In order to make international deals, Americans needed cash, credit, and goods. In the 1780s, all were hard to come by. Elite men like Robert Morris and Alexander Hamilton fretted that Americans lacked "credit abroad." In order to ensure "national strength and wealth," Hamilton had proposed "the institution of a National Bank" in order "to increase public and private credit."[35] Morris had founded the Bank of North America, the first U.S. commercial bank, in January 1782. Its main purpose was to make short-term loans to the national government.[36] There were very few banks in the 1780s, with only two more started before 1787.[37]

In other words, the United States lacked the financial infrastructure of more established nations. There were a few attempts at founding insurance and other companies, but they did not even attempt to obtain formal charters until the 1790s.[38] There was a 1786 proposal, backed by John Adams, to set up an American East India Company. Those who floated this plan imagined that Americans needed a strong, centralized trading authority to compete successfully against the might of the English East India Company. Congress rejected the plan, arguing that Asian trade "would be more prosperous if left unfettered in the hands of private adventurers, than if regulated by any system of a national complexion."[39]

If a few "private adventurers" like Morris envisioned prosperity ahead, many others were still enduring hard times. Shipping slowed, almost grinding to a halt in some previously hectic ports. Before the Revolution, some 125 ships left Massachusetts annually. In 1784, only forty-five sailed, and in the ensuing three years, only fifteen to twenty annually left the state.[40] While some shipping may have moved to other ports (the *Empress of China* sailed from New York), there was an overall slowdown in shipping through the 1780s.

Figures for the international slave trade from West Africa also show a considerable drop in American (and British) numbers during the American Revolution. Americans launched hardly any slave trading voyages during the years of the American Revolution. Even later in the 1780s, there were very few American slave trading ventures. American and British slave trading did not reach prewar levels until 1792. While other European powers stepped in to take over some of this trade, overall, fewer ships left West Africa carrying enslaved people between 1777 and 1783.[41] The effects of this slowdown have yet to receive the full attention of scholars.[42] However, the kinds of voyages that had made port towns like Newport and Charleston so prosperous had effectively disappeared, at least temporarily, on account of the American Revolution.

By every measure, the American economy remained stagnant through the 1780s.[43] People lamented that they could not afford to pay their taxes.[44] Many blamed the situation on the lack of paper money. Workingmen, one newspaper reported, believed that "cash was never so scarce before." Others thought the problem lay in the balance of trade. As another article in that same issue contended, "the life of our trade is panting for existence . . . we have a load of public debt, and an empty treasury." It concluded "that a general dissatisfaction pervades the whole State."[45] Yet many remained hopeful about prospects for the long term.

After hard days, many Americans dreamed of easy living. As Phillis Wheatley Peters (now married) phrased it in 1784, capturing her times: "So Freedom comes array'd with Charms divine, / And in her

Train Commerce and Plenty shine."[46] Working hard for commerce and plenty, people had choices to make. They made some good ones—and some very bad ones. For many families, this period, as much as the Revolution itself, determined their trajectories for decades. Let's follow the fortunes of a cluster of people as they navigated the obstacles of the 1780s.

Financial challenges fractured some families, especially Loyalist ones. As we have seen, Catherine Dudley and her husband, Charles, the customs commissioner, had fled Newport, Rhode Island, during the war. By 1784, they were living in England with their two children. Catherine was used to the good life; she had grown up in a grand house full of fine furniture. Charles was determined to recover his fortunes to support her and their children. In 1784, likely for financial reasons, Catherine, pregnant, took the two children back to Newport, while Charles stayed in London pressing his case. After her difficult transatlantic journey, Catherine suffered a stillbirth. Emphasizing her misery, she begged Charles to return. For years, though, he refused, rejecting the "pitiable station" of living off her family. Instead he worked for a "respectable Situation . . . better for us and our Children." In 1788, Charles finally obtained a more generous compensation package. At last he could return to Newport with his head held high. By then, though, his health was deteriorating. He passed away in London in 1789, never reunited with his wife, son, and daughter.[47] Catherine Dudley did not remarry.

In the 1780s, another Newport widow, Duchess Quamino, managed to "bake her way" not just to freedom but even to a kind of limited fortune.[48] It was not an easy road. As we have seen, her husband, John Quamino, had been killed in 1779. By the early 1780s, Duchess was apparently still living with her former enslavers, the Channings, and raising her children without their father. William Channing, who had grown up in the same house, reported that "the dignity of her aspect and manner bespoke an uncommon woman."[49] After war's tragedies, she seems to have found solace in mixing flour, sugar, and spices. She also found a living. She started "an establishment of her own," becoming "the most celebrated cake-maker in Rhode Island." Life was still hard; she lost her son, Charles, and her youngest daughter, little Katherine, and she never remarried. Still, she had achieved a great deal. For Duchess

Quamino, liberty and fortune smelled like Asian cinnamon and looked like a neat row of frosted plum cakes, including those she baked when Rhode Island celebrated "Washington's birth-night ball."[50]

One man who might also have celebrated Washington's birth-night was Jeremiah Greenman, the soldier who had joined up in Newport in 1775, fighting in Québec and elsewhere. He had become an officer in the Continental Army, developing skills in managing accounts, words, and men. In December 1783, he recorded that British officers had shared the news that "the Definitive Treaty" of Paris had arrived at New York. Still, he and his soldiers remained stuck "in Garrison waiting anxiously" for the order that they could leave. Having endured shoeless privation himself, he now worried about them: "our men in a Miserable Condition," some had "not a Shoe or a Stocking to their feet" despite the cold.[51] Finally, in early 1784, they got word that they were free to go.

Greenman was now twenty-five; he had spent his entire adult life as a soldier in the American Revolutionary War. In 1784, he decided to move to Providence, an up-and-coming town, with his widowed mother. He started a shop with another veteran, Joseph Masury. As the laconic Greenman phrased it, with more emotion than usual, he and Masury "put our small Interest togeth[er], which we had been fighting, bleeding, and all most dying for,—for the Space of 8 long years in the Army." The "small Interest" was the five years of pay officers received from the Continental Congress (instead of half-pay for life, the original promise).[52] They bought dry goods and started a shop.

Jeremiah Greenman had great expectations of independence and fortune. We do not know exactly what Greenman and Masury sold, but similar shops in that era in Providence offered "choice Jamaica and New-England Rum, Sugar, Melasses, Coffee, Madeira and Teneriffe Wine, Bar-Iron, Philadelphia Flour, Broadcloths, Bearskins . . . Irish Linens, Italian Flowers."[53] They likely also sold Asian tea, porcelain, and spices. After years of deprivation, it might have been a small, quiet pleasure for this young man to survey shelves full of bottles and boxes, to run his hands over soft fabrics, to smell the rich aroma of coffee beans as he measured them out.

It was a period of bright promise. He met and courted a young woman; the *Providence Gazette* reported the marriage of Lt. Jeremiah

Greenman and Miss Polly Eddy in October 1784.[54] However, that same autumn, because business had "grow'd very dull" with Masury, Greenman set up shop on his own. He spent another year straightening goods on the shelves and fretting over the account books, until he finally conceded that the retail life was not for him. Maybe domestic life was also less appealing than he had anticipated. His officer's pay was long gone. He decided to go to sea, entering "the Nautical line of business to gain a lively hood."[55] His travels took him to West Africa, the Caribbean, and Europe; he eventually became a captain. He did not work an Asian route, but his ships passed those that did.

Some of those ships may have been commissioned by Robert Morris, who also hustled in the 1780s. He had left his post as superintendent of finance in the mid-1780s, but his business interests continued apace. He continued to trade in Guangzhou and Havana. In 1785, he also became the American agent for tobacco sold to France. The French, fond of snuff, favored American tobacco, frequently smuggling it to circumvent the British.[56] The prospect of trading directly with American tobacco planters had been a powerful incentive for French support of

This image appearing on the corner of a 1751 map of Virginia depicts semi-clad enslaved laborers preparing tobacco for transatlantic shipping and carrying drinks to Virginia tobacco merchants (one of whom sports a fashionable Indian banyan).

the Revolution.[57] In 1785, Morris brokered a deal to supply the French with tobacco in the largest single French trade contract undertaken prior to the French Revolution, with a signing bonus to him of one million *livres* (about $200,000).[58]

Morris's million *livres* depended on the hard labor of enslaved men and women. They planted, cultivated, and dried tobacco leaves. Many fortunes of the eighteenth-century Chesapeake in places like Virginia and Maryland—where enslaved people constituted something like 40 percent of the population—came from tobacco. A 1751 map includes an image of enslaved laborers—one carrying a goblet, others rolling or sealing hogsheads of tobacco—as planters and merchants negotiate over the crop.

Another Virginia planter also hustled in the 1780s. Having received the thanks of the nation, George Washington had resigned his position as commander in chief of the Continental Army at the end of 1783. His properties were in disarray after his long absence.[59] In early 1784, when a relative asked to borrow money, Washington declined, noting that he was in no "condition to advance money." He continued with frustration: "I made no money from my Estate during the nine years I was absent, and brought none home with me."[60] To recoup his fortunes, he looked to his land holdings in the west, near the Kanawha and Ohio rivers.

Washington went west himself to check the lands and to ensure that they generated income. He was pleased to visit various spots including "a tract of mine . . . which . . . must be very valuable."[61] However, farther west, he found aggressive squatters not paying rent and also aggrieved Indigenous people. Both worried Washington. The trip strengthened his conviction that the country needed a strong central government to manage these challenges.[62] Robert Morris also looked to the west, soon becoming one of the greatest land speculators in the country.[63]

Personal hustle like Washington's radiated outward into national treaties with Indigenous nations. Americans sought to displace Canadians as the principal brokers of the lucrative fur trade in the interior.[64] There was another Treaty of Fort Stanwix in 1784 (to supplement the 1768 one). These negotiations were supposed to make up for the exclusion of the Six Nations—and all other Indigenous nations—from the Treaty of Paris. They did not go well. Internal divisions emerged between different Haudenosaunee nations, and between federal authorities and those representing New York and Pennsylvania. Under pressure, Haudenosaunee delegates gave away land; however, when they returned home, the Council of the Six Nations refused to ratify the treaty, arguing that the delegates were not empowered to cede this land. That did not stop many settlers from setting themselves up on it.[65]

Many of the Six Nations were horrified by the 1784 Fort Stanwix treaty. Seneca leaders including Cornplanter later complained, "our Nation was surprized to hear, how great a Country you had compelled them to give up" without any payment. "We asked each other what we had done to deserve such severe chastisement."[66] In protest, Thayendanegea (Joseph Brant) organized a confederation. He also complained to the British home secretary, Lord Sydney, that peace was still not "settled with us, which causes great uneasiness through all the Indian nations."[67] He noted that they had already waited three years and yet "we have had no answer, and remain in a state of great suspense and uneasiness of mind." He added that "Our trouble and distress is greatly increased by many things the Americans have said."[68] It took three months even to get a vague reply from Sydney, making it clear that the British were not going to help. At the same time, Americans like John Jay fretted that "Uneasiness prevails through the Country and may . . . produce untoward Events." He anticipated further "Trouble" with Indigenous people.[69] Americans were suspicious that the British in Canada would encourage Indigenous people to go to war.[70]

In the meantime, much of the land of the Six Nations ended up prey to settlers, squatters, and speculators. George Washington bought land in Mohawk Valley; James Madison and James Monroe bought 900 acres in what had been Oneida country.[71] The Oneidas had allied with the United States; nevertheless, most of their farms had been seized or destroyed. The following year, one Cherokee leader, Utsi'dsata (Old Corn Tassle), observed with dismay that borders agreed upon in treaties, supposedly meant to "stand as long as the Sun shined or water

Run," were often "forgot" by settlers. He continued: "you have Taken almost all our Country from us without our consent." Yet, he marveled, Americans remained unsatisfied, still talking "of fire and sword."[72]

Indigenous people continued to seek security. In 1790, Seneca leaders informed President George Washington that they sought "that security in the possession of our lands which your commissioners... promised us." They concluded their letter: "We know that you are strong and we have heard that you are wise; and we wait to hear your answer... that we may know that you are just."[73] In the meantime, though, more settlers moved west, sanctioned eventually by the 1787 Northwest Ordinance, one of the last acts of the government under the Articles of Confederation. The Americans claimed ownership of huge parts of western territory, and they still wielded fire and sword. Conflicts with Indigenous nations in the Ohio Valley continued with brutal intensity through much of the 1790s.[74]

The American hustle for fortune was costly. It made Indigenous people justifiably "uneasy." In the wake of victory, state and federal governments viewed Indigenous homelands as a means to solve their financial problems.[75] They thought they could sell off this land to speculators and settlers to pay off their war debts. Displaced Indigenous people paid the price. Enslaved people did too, on tobacco and other plantations.

The promise of fortune dazzled many Americans in the 1780s, even as they endured uncertainties at home. In 1785, John Adams touted American activity in Asia: "There is no better Advice to be given to the Merchants of the United States, than to push their Commerce to the East Indies as fast and as far as it will go." He hoped that if Americans acted in China with "irreproachable Integrity, Humanity and Civility... they may easily become the most favoured nation," outflanking—and outselling—their European rivals in deals with people like Pan Zhencheng.[76] Ezra Stiles also envisioned American success around the world. "This great american revolution," Stiles argued, should be "contemplated by all nations."[77] Stiles anticipated that "Navigation will carry the American flag around the globe itself; and display the thirteen stripes and new constellations at *bengal* and *canton*, on the *indus* and *ganges*, on the *whang-ho* and the *yang-tse-kiang*."[78]

Newspapers, too, celebrated the arrival of Asian goods—and people. In fact, the first published report of a Chinese national in the United States was a 1785 reference to Chinese sailors in Baltimore. The *Maryland Journal* reported on the return of a ship from Guangzhou with "a most valuable Cargo, consisting of an extensive Variety of Teas, China, Silks, Satins" and boasted of the multinational composition of the ship's crew: "Chinese, Malays, Japanese, and Moors, with a few Europeans, all . . . employed together as Brethren." The article continued: "it is thus Commerce binds and unites all the Nations of the Globe with a golden Chain."[79]

In the 1780s, Americans worked to establish their new nation as a serious contender on the world stage. They hustled around the world, in all kinds of places and at all kinds of costs. Invocations of the "golden Chain" of global commerce rendered bright and lustrous what was often dark and dismal, depending as it did on iron, not golden, chains. It generated fortunes for some, and misery for others.

"We are become a great people," declared one Pennsylvania woman when she heard about the arrival of a ship "from Canton in the East Indies—with a full cargo."[80] Despite the tough times, there was optimism in the 1780s—perhaps more than there should have been. Their ships were still small, their political economy still precarious, there was plenty of "Trouble" with Indigenous people. One group of Americans—eager to avoid further problems—decided to seek their fortune in West Africa, hoping also to become "a great people."

Chapter 13

A Settlement in Sierra Leone

Equality

It was a brave experiment. In a world plagued by oppression and despotism, a group of courageous people banded together to try something audacious. They rejected tyranny and slavery, dreaming of a more egalitarian world for themselves and their children. Pushed and pummeled by imperial ambitions, profit-mindedness, and indifference to human suffering, these individuals had the courage to risk everything for liberty and equality. Amid threats and empires, they staked out an innovative government. It was an age of revolution, and they were on the cutting edge. They were the founders of the Sierra Leone settlement.

At this historic moment, Susane Smith sought just one thing: soap. She wanted to wash her family's clothes. A refugee from the American Revolution, she and her family had crossed the Atlantic to West Africa. They came to join a free Black settlement. She had been ill on arrival, as had many. She explained in a letter to the governor: "I want to git Some Sope verry much . . . we are not fit to be Seen for dirt."[1] Given the dramatic transformations of her life and times, her hopes seem surprising in their modesty and specificity. Was she like the mother in detergent ads who holds up her family's stained clothing with an exasperated eyeroll, fretting about getting them *really white*? It's possible. Still, it's more likely that this mundane request reveals something important about Smith's situation and the challenges of her era, as we shall see.

Global shocks propelled novel schemes for colonial experimentation in the 1780s. Loyalists migrated to diverse destinations around the globe including Sierra Leone. As one British official put it, "The Burden of near a Ten Years War, the dismemberment of the Empire, its present poverty & alarming Emigrations" all caused problems, requiring "an Asylum of Rest."[2] A variety of people made cases for new colonies. Among the suggestions: an island in the Gambia River in West Africa; Nicaragua and Honduras in Central America; and South Africa (one officer's wife asserted that a colony there "could compensate Britain for the loss of her American colonies").[3] One Loyalist, James Matra, begged the British government to set up a haven for "those unfortunate American Loyalists" in New South Wales in what became Australia, a place he had visited with Captain Cook in the 1770s.

British officials liked the idea of a colony in New South Wales, but they had a different population in mind: convicts. Here was the seamy underbelly of eighteenth-century empire. Over the course of the eighteenth century, fifty thousand convicted felons whose sentences had been commuted from death to transportation had been sent to the American colonies, especially those in the mid-Atlantic.[4] With independence, Americans stopped accepting them. This refusal jammed the system. In 1785, an official wrote to the Home Secretary to complain of "the present alarming state" of London jails, overcrowded with convicts awaiting transportation.[5] The British tried to start a West African convict colony. It was a disaster.[6] New South Wales was the next place they tried, leading to the origins of modern Australia. Among other locations envisioned as Loyalist asylums were Nova Scotia and Sierra Leone.

The transformations—and devastating losses—generated by the American Revolution were the crucible for creative ventures on the part of people and governments. A few of these schemes carved out an unusual new space linking freedom and equality. Brilliant historians have narrated the radicalism and dashed hopes of the Sierra Leone settlers, but they have not so often considered them in parallel to American political projects of the era.[7] Doing so illuminates both Sierra Leone and the United States—and the ways in which hopes and schemes for liberty and equality could never carve out a space large enough to escape the pernicious intrusions of slavery, colonialism, and inequality.

Equality was a principle enshrined in the Declaration of Independence: "all men are created equal." There was also a claim that the new nation deserved "a separate and equal station." These are two distinct points: one having to do with the equality of human beings, the other with that of nations in the world. Both had radical potential. Thomas Paine's *Common Sense* had argued for equality of birth and against monarchy, aristocracy, and "hereditary succession": "For all men being originally equals, no *one* by *birth* could have a right to set up his own family in perpetual preference to all others for ever."[8] This overt rejection of monarchy and aristocracy distinguished the United States even as racial and other inequalities endured in the new nation.

Equality was—and is—a thorny issue. How far was it supposed to go? Did it conflict with liberty?[9] Did equality mean people should have equal resources, or at least equal access to resources? Some in the 1780s agreed that they should, while others used that very notion of equality to condemn what they saw as fiscally and socially irresponsible plans for the leveling of society.

These tensions played out in the new United States—and in the new settlement in Sierra Leone. Those who founded that settlement imagined a promised land of prosperity where distinctions of race, class, and gender would not matter (much). Every woman and man could pursue happiness in freedom and without threat. This vision rested on a form of government with origins in the ancient past yet advancing modern values of democracy and equality. It was bold, startling, original—and doomed.

Against all odds, Susane Smith and others found themselves in Sierra Leone on what was called the "Grain Coast" of West Africa. The greenish-brown hills overlooked a bay formed by the confluence of rivers, including the one then called the Sierra Leone River. The location was beautiful and striking. As one settler later recalled, the mountains rising up behind it "appeared like a cloud to us."[10] Sierra Leone's gorgeous views and verdancy made it seem like the promised land. New arrivals soon learned otherwise.

Henry Smeathman, the brainchild behind this venture, was an ingenious idealist. A scientist, he had a multitude of plans and schemes.[11] He shared his designs for one of them—a hot air balloon—with Ben Franklin in Paris in 1784. The ever genial Franklin, constantly besieged by men with plans and schemes, "launched half a sheet of paper obliquely in the air . . . evident proof of the propriety of my doctrines," while assuring Smeathman that Bostonians would really love his idea. Even Smeathman recognized that this vague endorsement was not going to sell his hot air balloon to anyone.[12]

Smeathman's main interests, though, were termites and ants. Parisians called him Monsieur Termites.[13] Armed with pins, nets, boxes, and cabinets, he had arrived at the mouth of the Sierra Leone River in 1771.[14] There were plenty of others like him in this era, traipsing about with their nets to catch pretty new species for science and empire. Some of them—like Smeathman—were opposed in principle to slavery, though they worked with slave traders. In his four years in Sierra Leone, he observed wildlife, ran experiments, planted a garden, and married the daughters of local rulers (taking two wives in the "custom of the country").[15]

In 1786, although Smeathman had earlier testified about the dangers of sending British convicts to Sierra Leone, he convinced a group of philanthropists that it would be the perfect place for Black refugees.[16] Smeathman made many promises to the people who funded the Sierra Leone venture and to those who risked their lives to join it. He promised that a man with an ax, a hoe, a knife, and a change of clothing would soon achieve "an easy and comfortable situation."[17] He promised that the climate was mild and fertile. He promised that the locals were welcoming. He promised that formerly enslaved settlers would enjoy "perfect freedom."

Why did people accept Smeathman's half-baked promises? They were desperate to solve problems of war, peace, poverty, and inequality. Some three thousand Black refugees had evacuated New York City with the British in 1783, recorded in a ledger called the Book of Negroes. Some ended up in London, others in Nova Scotia. We have already seen how little compensation they received from the Loyalist Claims Commission. In the economic doldrums of the 1780s, free but lacking resources, hunger haunted them.

London was exciting but expensive. It was also cold and damp, full of demobilized soldiers and sailors competing for limited employment.

Granville Sharp, an abolitionist and chief backer of the Sierra Leone scheme, worried that many were "starving about the streets."[18] Charities provided them with bread, but a long-term solution was needed.[19]

Nova Scotia was cold, literally and metaphorically, a difficult place for Black refugees, clustered in Birchtown, to scratch a living. They arrived with little, and they received less land than other refugees.[20] Even when they managed to obtain a small patch of less desirable land, they still did not have the right to vote. They were both politically and economically disenfranchised. Boston King, who later went to Sierra Leone, recalled "a dreadful famine" in which people had to sell clothing for flour. They also sold their labor for years to come.[21] A carpenter, he was himself "pinched with hunger and cold," fainting in the streets, dragging wooden furniture he had crafted to sell in order to feed himself and his wife, Violet. Such were the heavy burdens of being a refugee in the wake of the American Revolution.

The London Committee for the Relief of the Black Poor, and Granville Sharp in particular, believed that a colonization scheme offered a solution. There was an aspect of benevolence and antislavery here; Sierra Leone was to be a free settlement. Yet there was also self-interest on the part of do-gooders. They wanted to clear London's streets of the "Black Poor." They sought to enhance British colonial presence in West Africa, developing trade links. They were eager to recoup "moral capital" on the world stage, demonstrating Britain's benevolence in the wake of the loss of colonies.[22] As one London newspaper put it in 1786, Black refugees had "hazarded their lives, and even . . . spilt their blood" in Britain's service. In order to preserve Britain's "honour inviolate," it was necessary to provide for "these poor humble assertors of her rights."[23] This small and uncertain settlement represented sizable imperial ambitions.

With his knowledge of the area, Smeathman was to lead the venture, provided that the government furnished the supplies (including hoes, axes, and knives), arms, and clothing (for men, two jackets, two pairs of trousers, two pairs of shoes, and four shirts, with "Cloathing for the women in proportion"—a list clearly written by a man).[24] Smeathman advised a jacket with wide sleeves, as "our shirts are very troublesome licking up the dirt." He also noted that shoes and stockings would hide "the dust & dirt."[25] Susane Smith was not the only one to worry about dirt.

Sharp, Smeathman, and others managed to convince hundreds of Black families in London to resettle. Some were understandably skeptical. Others had already refused charity, seeking instead to return to their American homes.[26] As Boston King—who had been beaten by enslavers for much of his youth—observed: "I had suffered greatly from the cruelty and injustice of the Whites, which induced me to look upon them, in general, as our enemies."[27] There was little reason for trust, but many refugees like King and Smith—buffeted on the waves of oceans and fate—longed for a capacious African solidarity. There was a hunger here for more than bread. Having cast their lot for liberty, these refugees dreamed big, envisioning equality and prosperity for themselves and their children.

No one could ever follow up with Smeathman about all his promises, though. No sooner had he persuaded officials to launch this expedition than he died—of the malaria he had contracted there. It was not an auspicious start. Still, in the autumn of 1786, the settlers decided to forge ahead. None of them had much knowledge of this area, and Smeathman's deputy and now the leader—Joseph Irwin—had never even been to Africa.

These migrants went on board ships anchored in the Thames by November 1786. Fifty people died from disease before they even left London.[28] Floating next to these hulks were ships full of convicts ready to leave for Botany Bay in the Pacific. Their presence, and the delay, seemed so ominous that those on board feared that they were being kidnapped for the convict colony.[29] At the time, many people, among them officials, saw connections between the ventures in Sierra Leone and Australia.[30]

A central choice of the era was liberty or death. Many settlers in Sierra Leone got both. In May 1787, after months of delay, the emigrants finally arrived, just as the rainy season was starting. A nearby ship's captain recorded storms so violent that he called them "tornadoes."[31] They hit the 377 surviving settlers, sending rivulets down faces and soaking clothing and tents. They washed out the English seeds the settlers planted. They caused provisions to rot and fester. They formed stagnant pools where mosquitoes carrying malaria and other diseases could breed. The new arrivals soon began suffering from "fevers, fluxes & bilious complaints," which "carried off a great number" including the director, Joseph Irwin.[32]

Smeathman's interest in insects had led him to direct settlers to an area with numerous large mounds of them: appealing for Monsieur Termites, less so for young families living in tents. He never mentioned the hungry leopards and snakes, but they were there too.[33] Also on the prowl for the vulnerable were slave traders, seeking more individuals for the transatlantic market.[34] People living there—already on the defensive against European incursions—were not keen on having a settlement imposed on them.

By the autumn of 1788, the settlers were lamenting "the many miseries . . . since our landing."[35] The settlement at Granville Town started to resemble a sinking ship. The rats made their escape, joining the slave traders. As Granville Sharp phrased it, a few—mostly White—entered this "detestable service . . . some even on board the slave-ships."[36] The defection of one in particular—whom Sharp had helped to release from bondage—made even the usually mild leader fume over the perfidy of this "dealer in Slaves!"[37] He fulminated: "the practices of *slave-dealing* and *slave-holding* are inimical to the *whole species of man* by subverting charity, equity, and every social and virtuous principle."[38] Equity was a virtue to be treasured.

Relations with locals also soured fast. The leader of the settlers, Richard Weaver, the refugee from Philadelphia whom we earlier met being denied compensation by the Loyalist Claims Commission, brokered an agreement with King Naimbanna. Weaver and the settlers received what they thought was perpetual ownership of land in exchange for a set of gifts (including "a crimson satin embroidered waistcoat . . . two pairs of pistols, one telescope . . . and two cheeses weighing twenty-eight pounds.")[39] However, treaties here usually provided for usage, not perpetual ownership. Moreover, this leader lacked the authority to sign away the land, so the treaty was null. Soon, the settlers also complained that although they had been told there would be oyster shells to mix with limestone to build houses, there were none to be had, as "the Natives are so very crafty" that they would never let the settlers near their oysters.[40]

As tensions escalated, those in Granville Town feared being "massacred" by neighbors "swarming round thousands thick." After a violent confrontation with British slave traders in late 1789, one local leader retaliated by burning Granville Town to the ground. With only sixty-four settlers remaining, the venture was on the verge of collapse.[41] To prevent that, the founders recruited twelve hundred settlers from Nova Scotia. They arrived in 1792, also suffering fevers as they settled in. Among their number was Susane Smith.

From these dismal origins, this obscure woman rose with her hopes for soap, ready to clean up a dirty and disheartening world. Washing clothes for a loved one can be a declaration of affection. It can also be a tedious, exhausting chore embedded in power dynamics and domestic, often gendered, obligations. Here it had further meanings. Keeping her family clean was a way of asserting order amid what other settlers called "anorky."[42] Smith's desire for soap also indicated her hope for hygiene in a tense and terrifying moment when "putrid fevers" were carrying off neighbors and friends. Smith maintained high standards of respectability in the face of catastrophe. She wanted her children clean, deserving of respect.[43] She also had the courage to demand better from the government she evidently trusted, as shown by her letter.

The government of Sierra Leone was reasonably responsive (though we don't know whether Smith got her soap). It was also egalitarian. Of course there was to be no slavery. "As soon as a slave shall set his foot within the bounds of the new settlement," Sharp advised, "he shall be deemed a *free man*."[44] Settlers were going to live on land only with "the consent . . . of the *native inhabitants*."[45] It was a "free settlement," not, apparently, a colony. The model harked back to the ancient Saxon system of frank-pledge and the theocracy of the ancient Israelites.

For all that its founders looked to the past, though, Sierra Leone developed one of the most progressive governments in the world at that time. Every head of household got a vote; groups of households elected

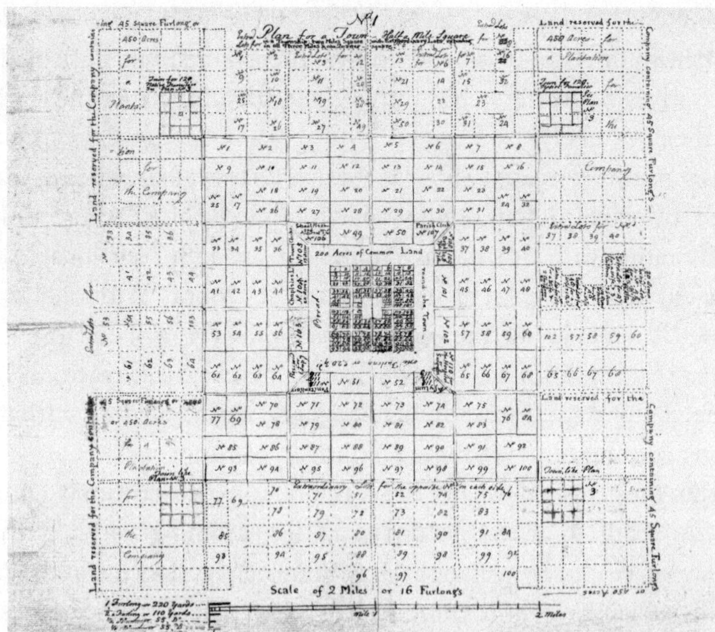

This 1791 plan of Freetown, the second capital of Sierra Leone (after Granville Town was burned down), shows the egalitarian and orderly parcels of land to be distributed to settlers, with 200 acres of "common land" at the center.

higher officials. Since by 1792 one-third of households were headed by women, this provision meant that women voted.[46] Men aged sixteen to sixty defended the settlement.[47]

There was also economic egalitarianism, as "the meanest cottager" received "a due share of the land," a farm and a one-acre lot, whether man or woman. There were also public lots for the poor.[48] An early plan for Freetown—the settlement's principal town, replacing the earlier burned-down Granville Town—showed even rectangles imposed on the undulating green: individual farms, in neat parcels for each household. A bell rang the schedule for all: a workday that started at the end of prayers at 6:00 a.m., and ended at 4:00 p.m., with a two-hour siesta. In a world, including Britain, where the routine workday lasted twelve hours, here was an eight-hour workday.[49] Everyone paid sixty-two workdays of labor as taxes, and those who refused to work had to pay additional taxes.[50]

In Sierra Leone, no one proclaimed that "all men are created equal." Instead, they lived that principle. Women and men of all ranks had access to property. For the first several years of the settlement's existence, according to economic historians, Sierra Leone settlers maintained a "highly egalitarian" system of land distribution, compared with either North America or other African settlements.[51]

Even decades later, visitors were shocked at the egalitarianism of Sierra Leone. One elite visitor, Mary Church, interviewing for a house servant, was aghast when "an elderly black woman with a muslin gown and apron on, a coloured handkerchief tied round her head" entered the room and insisted on shaking her hand and making herself at home on the sofa. "She seemed not to consider herself at all inferior," grumbled a dismayed Church, as "gradations of society . . . do not seem very well understood here."[52] Gradations based on race and rank were in fact well understood. They were also rejected.

Yet the egalitarian space that settlers in Sierra Leone managed to scratch out—free, they thought, from slavery and inequality—was such a tiny one in a terrifying and tumultuous world. For all their dreams and hopes, they remained tied by the pernicious threads of global trade to the system of slavery they deplored. Their economy depended on slave-trading neighbors and slave-trading ventures in their harbor. Their distribution of land hinged on claiming property belonging to Indigenous people and on colonial assumptions of superiority. The same might be said for the United States, facing the troubling 1780s, victorious but uncertain.

Equality became a lightning rod for political controversies in the United States, as some began to use it as a club to beat down forces of agitation for debt relief and more inclusive economic policies. In the cauldron of anxieties of the later 1780s, equality took on fiercely contested meanings. Even as some argued for greater equality—in political terms, but also in racial and economic ones—others used the notion to cast their enemies as suspect "levelers." Just as threats of slave rebellion, Native American war, and Hessian incivilities had generated anxieties in the

1770s, so did the specter of economic and racial equality—and dangerous men prepared to use force to achieve it—become the bogeymen of the 1780s.

Equality mattered for several reasons. First, Americans had taken radical steps that unnerved many. In a world dominated by monarchies and aristocracies, they had rejected them in favor of equality. They also curtailed the traditional system of primogeniture (inheritance concentrated on the firstborn son).[53] These moves were not uncontroversial, though. Stepping into a new era of republican equality was a disconcerting move for many. At least some still longed for the old certainties of hierarchy and deference, the gradations of humankind, that had long shaped their laws, traditions, and societies.

Second, some Americans imagined that monarchy and aristocracy furnished a kind of structural support to counterbalance the institutional power of merchants or the excesses of democracy. In fierce debates over whether Pennsylvania should institute a state bank in 1786, one of its opponents argued that the bank would monopolize power, undermining the state. In his view, the new states lacked the traditional structures of monarchy, aristocracy, laws of primogeniture, and "wealthy companies of merchants incorporated" to counterbalance an institution with so much political and economic clout.[54]

Third, equality took on particular significance in a period of rising economic disparities. States as diverse as Pennsylvania—one of the oldest—and Kentucky—one of the youngest—furnish useful examples. Even before 1776, wealth inequalities were rising in Pennsylvania, making equality *the* "keyword in Pennsylvania's Revolution," according to one historian.[55] In the hard times of the 1780s, there were thousands of foreclosures; firms went out of business at the rate of one a month. Money moved out of the hands of ordinary people into the bulging pockets of the few well-placed oligarchs—like Robert Morris—able to buy up property at this tough time. In Philadelphia in 1780, the top 10 percent held 44 percent of the city's wealth. By 1789, they held 67 percent—a number that continued to rise into the 1790s.[56] In Kentucky, by the end of the 1780s, the top 1 percent (just over a hundred men) controlled one-third of Kentucky's lands. Meanwhile, 75 percent of the White men in what was supposed to be a good poor man's country had no land at all.[57] Such men felt dispossessed from the promise of the Revolution by what one historian has called "structural inequality and limited opportunity."[58]

In such circumstances, what did equality mean, exactly? Workers from Kentucky's saltworks to Rhode Island's ports wondered. Rhode Island denizens—like Pennsylvanians, inclined to protest inequalities—also fretted over their inability to repay debts. Rhode Island had already frustrated many in 1781. A national attempt to raise a much-needed import duty of 5 percent foundered on the refusal of Rhode Island to sanction this tax. Since the structure of the Articles of Confederation required every single state to approve new measures, Rhode Island's rejection meant that it failed.[59]

In 1786, still plotting its own maverick course, Rhode Island took the controversial decision to issue its own currency. As in 1781, other states did not approve. One critic complained that this move was only done "to cheat all creditors—and to produce a new system of public difficulties." They started to call it "Rogue-Island." One mocking newspaper article claimed that the Rhode Island Assembly had passed "*An ACT for the more equal Distribution of political Happiness*" declaring that all debts would be abolished, all property would be equally distributed, and men would be punished with lashes and prison time if they tried actually to repay their creditors.[60] Rhode Island had of course done no such thing.

"Equality" became a dangerous word. The author of this satire caricatured both kinds of equality in the Declaration: that between persons and that between nations. This article begins with a mock Declaration of Independence: "WHEREAS the God of nature made all men equal . . . whereas the great objects of the late war were the rights of equality, then violated by the rapacities of British power." Yet, the article goes on, some individuals had made more money than others in the late war, thus casting doubts on equality as a political virtue. Second, "all nations should be equal," so although "France, Spain and Holland, make demands for money lent," Rhode Islanders refused to pay them back, to ensure equality of nonpayment. This article made equality into a joke, a virtue only for those who could not—or would not—pay their bills.[61]

Similar tensions erupted more violently elsewhere—including in neighboring Massachusetts. The underlying issues were much the same: rising inequality and economic hardship. Many middling folk, including many Revolutionary veterans, continued to lack the means to pay taxes in Massachusetts. As one of their opponents, Henry Knox, wrote, "they feel . . . their own poverty, compared with the opulent."[62] Many ended up being sued for debt in court, in an era when being a debtor could result in prison time and public humiliation.[63]

In 1786, these Massachusetts debtors started to block courts from meeting so that foreclosures could not take place. "We seem to be in danger of Anarchy," fretted one observer.[64] As in the Rhode Island satire, Knox lambasted these men for their supposed desire "to annihilate all debts" and their absurd ideals of "equity and justice." He also saw this problem as a larger one of too much variability between different states: "Our political machine constituted of thirteen independent sovereignties, have been constantly operating against each other, and against the federal head." He also worried that disaffected individuals would join forces with suspect groups on the borders—Indigenous nations and Canada—to overthrow the new government.[65]

George Washington agreed with Knox's analysis of impending anarchy, warning, "There are combustibles in every State, which a spark may set fire to." He saw the potential for violent rebellion lurking in every state's fight over paper money and debt, as he confided to Knox in late 1786. He imagined dark British machinations behind this "disorder." After all, Great Britain was even now "sowing the Seeds of jealousy and discontent among the various tribes of Indians." The British, he assured Knox, were also working to "foment the spirit of turbulence within the bowels of the United States."[66]

American tumult drove challenges on the international stage. As John Jay phrased it in a letter to Thomas Jefferson, "To be respectable abroad it is necessary to be so at Home, and that will not be the Case until our public Faith acquires more Confidence, and our Government more Strength." Jay argued that domestic "uneasiness" made diplomatic negotiations and trade deals impossible. He pointed to all kinds of "Difficulties," from "the present State of our Indian Affairs" to complications with the British and other Europeans, including the Dutch, who seem to "regret our having found the Way to China." These problems, he concluded, "give me much Concern."[67]

It was no surprise to Jay, Washington, or Knox when the Massachusetts commotions resulted in a confrontation later called "Shays's Rebellion." Aggrieved western Massachusetts debtors organized behind a respected veteran, Daniel Shays. They called themselves Regulators, a nod to the moral probity of Herman Husband and the North Carolina resisters of state tyranny some twenty years earlier. The governor sent thousands of volunteers—paid for by creditors—to suppress the resistance. Shays and his followers tried to seize the arsenal in Springfield, Massachusetts. They did not succeed, and a few men were killed and others wounded. They quickly dispersed.

Still, this confrontation provided men like Washington and Knox with what they saw as proof positive of the likelihood that the United States would soon fall to its "lowest state of humiliation & contempt," as Washington put it.[68] Alexander Hamilton lamented "the dark catalogue of our public misfortunes" that put the fledging republic at "almost the last stage of national humiliation."[69] One Massachusetts magazine announced, "The view of our situation is indeed truly alarming; we are upon the brink of a precipice."[70] Something had to be done, such men agreed.

That something was the Constitutional Convention. Although not especially eager to participate, George Washington joined fifty-four other well-heeled men in Philadelphia in May 1787. Every state was represented except Rhode Island, still going its own way with paper money. Nearly half of the delegates were enslavers; others were lawyers and merchants. Whatever debt load they may in fact have been carrying, these men—smoothing their silk waistcoats in the wilting heat—basked in their status as creditors. They prioritized property and security over equality.

These men viewed American developments through the eyes of the British. Edmund Randolph wanted to avoid "the fulfillment of the prophecies of the American downfall." He did not need to add whose prophecies those were. Although the problems of the Articles of Confederation were considerable, he continued, he did not blame their authors, since back then "no rebellion [like Shays's] had appeared... —foreign debts had not become urgent—the havoc of paper money had not been foreseen."[71] A newspaper puff piece agreed. After lauding the heroic men at the Philadelphia convention, the author maintained that only through their deliberations could "America... yet enjoy peace, safety, liberty, and glory." Otherwise, the author warned, the nation would dissolve into "anarchy, poverty, infamy, and SLAVERY."[72]

Emphasizing the threat of anarchy was a powerful way to scare people into supporting a new plan, one designed to "secure the Blessings of Liberty"—or at least of property and "domestic Tranquility." In the economically straitened 1780s, in the aftermath of a devastating war, few still had the stomach to fight for radical equality. At the Constitutional Convention, as in the Constitution itself, the word "equal" appeared more often in its mathematical definition (meaning the same amount) than in terms of shared humanity. In the convention, debates over equality were confined to whether states should be represented equally or by size of population. Smaller states worried that they would lose out to larger ones. Convention delegates argued over James Madison's Virginia Plan—favoring larger states and allowing the composition of both the Senate and the House of Representatives to be determined by population size. The New Jersey Plan offered an alternative for smaller states, giving the same number of representatives to each state regardless of size. Delegates reached a compromise, with the senators apportioned equally by state (two each) and representation in the House determined by population. Figuring out the size of the population—and whether to count enslaved people for the purposes of representation—led to the Constitution's most notorious clause: counting an enslaved person as three-fifths of a person.

Yet the words "slave" or "slavery" did not appear in the Constitution; neither did "equality" or "paper money." Its most contentious issues thrummed behind the words that did appear. This circumlocution, what one historian has called "silence, compromise, and artful design," reveals the points of greatest controversy, as well as the attempts to underplay them for the wider audience whose ratification was still needed.[73] In addition to issues of representation, there was also a heated controversy over whether—or when—to end U.S. involvement in the international slave trade. Again, this conflict resulted in a compromise, that the "importation of such Persons . . . shall not be prohibited by the Congress" before 1808. The cost was another two hundred thousand Africans forced into American slavery in the interim.[74] In addition, free states agreed to return enslaved people who had made their escape from slave states. In other words, free states remained complicit in the regime of slavery they wanted to avoid. All these concessions to enslavers highlight that the Constitution prioritized security and property over equality.

The same emphasis on security and property underlay other debates, including those on issuing currency. The Constitution prohibited states (including Rhode Island) from issuing bills of credit or from making anything legal tender other than hard specie (gold or silver). No one had expected the transformation of monetary powers—now controlled by the federal government—that the Constitution had wrought. One economic historian has described it as "nothing short of revolutionary."[75] In terms of equality, neither an individual state nor the United States was allowed to "grant any Title of Nobility." This stipulation had been part of the Articles of Confederation, and its inclusion attracted little debate. The convention concluded in September 1787.

The Constitution then went to the states for ratification. Those in its favor—the Federalists—launched a public relations campaign to sell it to the voting public, leading to a series of essays (later called the Federalist Papers) by James Madison, Alexander Hamilton, and John Jay, published in 1787 and 1788. Unlike the Articles of Confederation, the Constitution did not require unanimous ratification by all the states (only a majority of nine of thirteen). Some states held out. A Rhode Island referendum resulted in a refusal to ratify by an overwhelming majority. July 4, 1788, brought one aggressively Anti-Federalist celebration in Rhode Island including toasts not to the new constitution but to the "old Confederation" and state sovereignty.[76] The Anti-Federalists argued that the Constitution privileged federal over state powers and property over liberty. They were especially concerned about the lack of safeguards on individual and state liberties. To ameliorate these concerns, lawmakers added the first ten amendments, which many people now see as the most critical safeguards of rights. Even so, it took until 1790 for all the states—including that last hold-out, Rhode Island—to ratify.

By July 4, 1788, however, the nine states required for ratification had voted in favor of the new Constitution, which gave celebrations that year a particular éclat. Ezra Stiles, now the president of Yale, oversaw "public literary exhibitions" in New Haven, Connecticut, to celebrate "the day which gave birth to the American Empire."[77] First there was a parade celebrating the Constitution. Then there were speeches and readings. Then there was a dinner. Toasts followed, including those to "The Federal Constitution, the illustrious characters who formed it, and the States who have adopted it." There were a few other politically pointed toasts: "May the reign of anarchy never revive," and "A perpetual quietus to paper money, tender laws, and African slavery."[78] Were Newport and Violet—presumably still laboring in Stiles's household but close to finishing their seven years of service for him—present to hear these toasts? If their son, Jacob, was still alive, he would have been eight, with another sixteen years of labor owed to Stiles.

In other words, African slavery was far from quiet or dead even in New England's "free" states. No matter what kinds of spaces for freedom formerly enslaved people tried to carve out, the pernicious tentacles of slavery reached them wherever they went. Connecticut had passed a gradual abolition law that allowed all currently enslaved persons to remain enslaved while outlawing the enslavement of those born after March 1, 1784—but only after they turned twenty-five. In other words, as one legal scholar has put it, "the law freed no slaves." The ending of slavery in Connecticut was protracted for enslaved people and was not in fact fully complete until 1848.[79]

Admittedly, some enslaved people voted for liberty with their feet, and there was less will to return them to enslavers.[80] Few people still lived in slavery in New England by 1820. Still, Jacob Freeman's indenture to age twenty-four would in fact have been a lifetime of servitude had his mother still been enslaved when he was born in 1780. Even Rhode Island's abolition laws would not have freed someone born there before March 1, 1784. Jacob Freeman's children, if he had any, would not have lived in slavery, but he himself would have. In other words, gradual abolition was just that: gradual. In autumn 1786, George Washington hoped, in language that registers as slightly dreamy and delusional, that "slavery in this Country may be abolished by slow, sure, & imperceptable degrees."[81]

Slavery did not wither away, as Washington and others hoped. Enslaved people pushed hard for freedom and "equity," but it was a struggle. A group of them sent their list of toasts to the *United States Chronicle* after their Fourth of July gathering in Providence, Rhode Island. They celebrated the Constitution for allowing the possibility of ending American involvement in the international slave trade—although they had to wait twenty years for that happy event. Another toast was that Africans should "enjoy their natural Privileges unmolested" and their hope that "Freedom" be restored to all enslaved Africans "in different Parts of the World." They also drank to the "Restoration of Equity and Peace."[82]

These toasts demonstrate the global solidarity, resilience, and hope of Black citizens in Rhode Island. They comprehended the limitations of reform all too well. It would be another two decades before the United States would pull out of the international slave trade. Their children might be kidnapped and sold into slavery in the south, a specter that haunted parents aware of the thriving domestic slave trade.[83] A relative or a friend who had fled southern slavery could be forcibly returned. Farms, workshops, and factories near them helped to produce grains, textiles, and other goods sold to enslavers in the south.[84]

In other words, slavery "stained" the Constitution and the new nation, as the British reformer Granville Sharp wrote in dismay to Benjamin Franklin. He warned that "the crimes of *slave-dealing* and *slave-holding* become *crying sins*" likely to spell the end of "the political existence of any state."[85] The Reverend Samuel Hopkins of Newport, Rhode Island—whom we met earlier sponsoring missionaries to go to West Africa—agreed. In his view, both Newport and the United States were headed for "inevitable ruin" because they had "flourished in times past, at the expense of the blood, the liberty, and happiness of the poor Africans." Slavery, he warned, had "become a national sin." U.S. complicity in slavery explained why the British threatened its global trade prospects, why Indigenous nations planned war on it, and why Algerian pirates attacked American vessels. Hopkins concluded that the United States was "disappointed in our expectations of peace, prosperity, and happiness. . . . Instead of rising to honor, dignity, and respect among the nations, we have suddenly sunk into disgrace and contempt."[86]

In this atmosphere, Sierra Leone twinkled as a beacon for those who recognized the limitations of reform in the new United States. Granville Sharp wrote to John Jay, former diplomat, president of the New York Manumission Society, and soon to be first chief justice of the United States. Sharp noted that he had heard that there were many Black people "at New York, and other parts of America, who wish to find a comfortable settlement on the coast of Africa." They saw in Sierra Leone what seemed a new kind of community, one predicated on equality. Sharp noted that he had long imagined that "the Province of Freedom" would become a "happy asylum" for free Black people from the United States, the West Indies, and Britain.[87]

West Africa shaped thinking in the new American republic. Samuel Hopkins furnishes an excellent example. As we have seen, he had long dreamed of sending Africans to Africa, but his perception of the best way to do this shifted over the course of the American Revolution. Prior to the Revolution, he had been involved in the plan to send John Quamino and Bristol Yamma to preach the gospel in West Africa. The missionaries left their families in Rhode Island, and they expected to return home to them. In the 1780s, such schemes took on a decidedly different character—thanks, in part, to Sierra Leone.

Sierra Leone seemed to offer an equality impossible to achieve in the United States. In January 1789, Hopkins contacted Granville Sharp about his hopes of relocating Black New Englanders to Sierra Leone. He related his own history of seeking to end the slave trade and his delight in discovering Sharp's shared commitment. He observed that even in Rhode Island, "the circumstances of the Freed Blacks are . . .

unhappy" because their neighbors were "disposed to treat them as underlings," denying them education, jobs, and opportunities. These grim circumstances had prompted many formerly enslaved people "to desire to return to Africa, and settle there among their equals and brethren."[88] Hopkins envisioned Sierra Leone as a place of equality and solidarity. Sharp replied that the settlement had faced many challenges, including the fact that White settlers had "been wicked enough to go into the service of the Slave Trade." Still, he encouraged Hopkins to consider sending new migrants—and the money and supplies for them to succeed.[89]

Hopkins started to favor Sharp's idea of permanent relocation of African American families to West Africa. After the Revolution, he imagined that an African settlement "might be greatly beneficial to the commercial interest both of this nation and of those in Africa." Moreover, he contended, "there are a considerable number of free blacks" in the United States who were industrious, pious, and "desirous to remove to Africa." He argued that since White people treated Black people "as an inferior class of beings," it was impossible that they could ever "be raised to an equality with the whites, and enjoy all the liberty and rights to which they have a just claim." He asserted that only by moving permanently to Africa could African Americans "enjoy . . . equality and liberty."[90]

Increasingly, for some American abolitionists, Sierra Leone furnished a way for them to imagine racial equality—as long as it was outside the United States. As with the constitutional compromises, they sought to avoid confronting the structural inequalities underpinning the new nation. Assuming the impossibility of radically reforming race relations, Hopkins tried to displace the problem of inequality that would continue to plague the nation. Even if American involvement in the international slave trade was ended (as it would be in 1808), even if the northern states abolished slavery altogether (albeit in a slow and protracted way), there was no way to escape the pernicious inequalities wrought by centuries of slavery and its continued existence in many states.

A transformation took place—in Hopkins's thinking and in the larger republic. In the 1770s, Hopkins regarded African Americans as part of a global Christian community. By the later 1780s, he felt African Americans were likeliest to thrive outside the United States. Others came to agree, promoting an ideal of colonization for free Black and Indigenous people in what one historian has termed a "founding principle": the idea that races should be "separate but equal."[91]

In other words, slavery was unavoidable even in spaces of theoretical freedom and potential equality in the late 1780s, whether in Freetown or Newport or Philadelphia. No matter how innovative new schemes were, slavery's reach was too long, its tentacles too strong. Slavery, the domestic slave trade, and racial inequalities still marred even new "free" states and territories. The cost was the blood, liberty, and happiness of Black Americans.

The Age of Revolution sparkled with novel visions for the reordering of society and government. Both Sierra Leone and the United States offered original examples of innovative governments. Yet the prioritizing of security and property over liberty and equality in both places meant that their brightest points were dulled. The U.S. Constitution, especially before the first ten amendments were added, marked a new set of U.S. priorities, ones designed to foster security and property rather than equality and liberty. Even the most optimistic of visions foundered on the threats of imagined anarchy. The politics of fear made "equality" a dirty word in postrevolutionary politics. As Susane Smith well knew, no matter how hard a mother scrubbed, she could never get things clean enough in this fallen world.

Conclusion

The American Revolution was an extraordinary event of both American and global history with beautiful yet destructive powers. A global perspective brings larger processes and events into view to trace out how the United States was embedded in them. Such a view also highlights how the United States took its own distinctive path based on factors of locality, particularity, and contingency. In other words, this perspective illuminates both the global and the local better.

In the later eighteenth century, a revolutionary spirit was alive across the British Empire. There was rising anger across many locations about being treated (especially by British authorities) "like a slave." A rejection of slavery—and its implied limits of autonomy, mobility, and consent—motivated many different people: Pontiac and his compatriots in Detroit; rioters in the Caribbean; angry, hungry people in Kolkata; traders and refugees in Anomabu; farmers (and lawyers) in Pennsylvania. In the British North American colonies, the end of the Seven Years' War sharpened expectations for prosperity and peace even as it also brought a more heavy-handed imperial authority. Around the world, 1763's peace, so favorable to Britain, provoked resentment, as did slightly bungling attempts by the British to reorganize and renovate their empire.

Yet only half of the British colonies in North America rebelled. The questions, then, become more interesting (though also more challenging): not just why and how the traditional thirteen colonies rebelled (hard enough to answer), but why and how the other thirteen did not. This book has built on rich scholarship on these other colonies to gesture toward some answers, but much more remains to be done. Why didn't the West Indian or Canadian colonies join in the Revolution? In 1765, there appeared to be solidarity across all these colonies. What happened?

Caribbean enslavers rejected being treated "like slaves," yet local protests in places like St. Kitts did not translate into formal resistance. Why not? Specific features of the West Indies and the mainland colonies help to answer this question. In the Caribbean, as opposed to most of the mainland colonies, there was greater per capita wealth among landowners, who sometimes resided in Britain. The island situation, and the very large population of enslaved people, led to planters' enduring fears that a combination of large-scale slave rebellion and invasions by the French and Spanish would wreck their society. There was also a challenging disease environment that precluded stable demographic growth, creating a population filled with newcomers, less liable to join up in rebellion. There were also stronger cultural and educational ties to Britain. At the same time, one of the major forces knitting together settlers in the mainland colonies—a shared history of attempted conquest of Indigenous nations—was less salient in the Caribbean, where elites and working people did not join together in protest in the same ways as they did in mainland colonies. Conflict with Indigenous nations, then, influenced this famous course of events. American rebels gained from appeals to being "freeborn Englishmen" in a land shared by plenty of people who were not. These claims became critical aspects of this Revolution, helping to knit together disparate people in enduring ways.

Canada looked even more likely to join the common cause, an assumption animating many in Québec, Nova Scotia, and the thirteen rebelling colonies including members of the Continental Congress in the 1770s. Yet, as we have seen, the disaster at Québec and the lack of supplies, credit, and good behavior on the part of rebels spelled the end of such hopes, though the United States, with typical optimism, still left the door open in the Articles of Confederation for Canadians to join. However, the outcome of attempted conquest, the continued presence and power of French and Indigenous Canadians who rejected U.S. overtures, and the migration to Nova Scotia of many aggrieved

Loyalists—Black and White—further shaped Canada's distinctive character, ensuring quite a different trajectory.

Placing the American Revolutionary War in a global context also alters how we understand the nature of revolutionary wars, the crisscrossing of many different strands of civil war, imperial war, settler war, and global war. What happened at Yorktown furnishes a fine example. By 1781, the British—fighting in the Caribbean, Central America, South Asia, and elsewhere—were far less concerned with the thirteen colonies than Americans were. At the same time, in all kinds of ways—supplies, arms, money, soldiers, strategies—French and Spanish contributions were critical. Yet even beyond the involvement of France and Spain (of which historians have long been aware), fighters like Haidar Ali and Antonio de Soledad also aided, sometimes inadvertently, the American cause by diluting British resources and energies in a lot of places beyond the thirteen colonies, in far-away India and in nearby Florida.

The global background helps to explain the course of the war, including the famous surrender at Yorktown. The continued loyalties of those in the British Caribbean shaped Cornwallis's expectation that the Carolinas would be as full of British supporters as the West Indian islands were. They were not. Cornwallis also did not take enough account of environmental factors such as heat and mosquitoes, malaria and dysentery—though the history of the Caribbean in war should have taught him that. Yet the global milieu interacted with local features. Cornwallis opted for a riverside base, which made foraging impossible: not a good choice. That decision, and the contingencies of the battle itself, influenced what happened. Taking account of this global panorama, then, allows us to see more clearly the interplay of the global and the local at Yorktown.

This wider perspective also helps to correct an unsustainable and outmoded American exceptionalism too often plaguing this history. Women stepped out and demanded happiness and new kinds of lives in Edinburgh as well as Edenton; the American Revolution did not cause this shift. Rather, other transformations—in rising levels of education, expectations, and enlightened ideals—affected these trajectories. Correlation should not be confused with causality. The desire for respect and honor motivated a good deal of behavior, not only for men like Thomas Jefferson and Alexander Hamilton but also for Baron de Steuben and the king of Niumi. Sierra Leone and the United States both founded extraordinary new governments promising equality even amid grim realities of slavery. The "American paradox" was not unique to the United States of America.

Yet the keywords here, partly because of their prominence in the Declaration of Independence, also took on specifically American valences. In no case is this more apparent than in the case of freedom. The enshrinement of liberty in the Declaration of Independence meant that it became a foundational U.S. value. Soldiers (and their powder horns) and debaters proclaimed "Liberty or Death!" It became a war cry. When enslaved women embroidered the word on the shirts of their Virginia enslavers, liberty took on specific, and ironic, meanings, which start to look more distinctive. Freedom became in some cases "a freedom to dominate," a rallying cry for rebels and revolutionaries, but also for pro-slavery Confederates in the nineteenth century, segregationists in the twentieth, and insurrectionists in the twenty-first.[1] Liberty has taken on force among people who shout it the loudest, giving it complex resonances in the U.S. context. Yet it also means freedom of expression, of solidarity, of the press, of assembly, of worship, of peaceful protest: critical democratic and civic values. As Franklin Delano Roosevelt argued in 1941, it can even mean freedom from want and fear.[2] The concept's flexibility helps in part to explain its endurance.

Liberty had many meanings for Prince Simbo, too, as he plodded through the murk of Valley Forge and beyond in 1778 and 1779. For him, it was likely a personal dream as well as a national ambition. His labors in the Continental Army may have helped secure both. Simbo continued in active service until December 1779, when he was injured. At that point, he was transferred to the Invalid Corps, where he helped with training. When the war ended, he came home to Connecticut. Like so many veterans, Prince Simbo endured lifelong disability. Still, he had a wife, named Phebe, and they had children. He died in December 1810, in a nation still practicing slavery. By this time, his family was probably free, though we don't know for sure. In later years, did he—like the formerly enslaved Christmas Hunt who had served with the Rhode Island First Regiment—brush out his "old uniform" taking "great pride appearing on parade days" for veterans?[3] The fact that Simbo's powder horn remains in such good condition suggests that he and his family treasured it. They commemorated the sacrifices he had made for liberty and this new nation.

Thanks to his descendants, and the federal government, Prince Simbo's remarkable powder horn survives. Its googly-eyed sun still shines. Its stag continues to stand at attention. The all-seeing eye yet gazes out and judges. The urgent work of revolution continues. LIBERTY, reads that banner held by a bird soaring above a big, wide world. Complicated, elusive freedom still beckons and flutters above us all.

Acknowledgments

"I . . . beg you would accept my thankful acknowledgements," wrote Benjamin Franklin to Don Gabriel Antonio de Bourbon in late 1775, as both watched "the first efforts of a rising State."[1] Like Franklin, I offer my thankful acknowledgments to extraordinary institutions, colleagues, and friends in many places.

I am beyond grateful for a yearlong grant, what turns out to have been the last round of the original National Endowment for the Humanities Public Scholars Program, although any views, findings, conclusions, or recommendations expressed in this book do not necessarily reflect those of the National Endowment for the Humanities. The NEH and its commendable staff have understood that telling the American story to a wide audience with rigor and attention to all is a patriotic act. The British Library has also been generous. I thank Polly Russell and the Eccles Institute for an early research fellowship as well as for creating and providing me with a Distinguished Visiting Fellowship in the American Revolution.

At Johns Hopkins, I thank Deans Chris Celenza and Christopher Cannon and History Department Chair Tobie Meyer-Fong, who let me use that NEH grant to extend one semester of leave into three. That made all the difference. I also appreciate the research assistance funding provided by the Hopkins International Studies Program. I received early support from the Mellon Fund for American History and the Mellon Professor of American History, Gary Gerstle, and the Faculty of History at Cambridge and its Chair, Alexandra Walsham.

This book would never have been written without my amazing students at Cambridge and Johns Hopkins. It has been my privilege to teach them and to learn from them. Field trips to *Hamilton* in London as well as to the

Washington Monument in Baltimore proved especially memorable. The labors of research assistants at Johns Hopkins—Ellie Palazzolo, Josephine Sayre Burwell, Elyjah Bassford, and especially the incomparable Hilary Gallito—helped bring it home.

Staff at numerous archives and libraries have provided sources, references, and general support, even during COVID lockdowns and malware attacks. The Cambridge University Library, the British Library, and the National Archives at Kew, as well as archives in Sheffield, Glasgow, Suffolk, and elsewhere, provided material, as did archivists in multiple locations of the Bibliothèque National de France in Paris. The Library of Congress, the Library and Archives of Canada, the New York Public Library, the Connecticut State Library, the Beinecke Rare Book & Manuscript Library at Yale, and the Princeton University Library, among others, also provided illuminating documents. Getting library books delivered to my office remains a thrill, for which I thank the Johns Hopkins University Libraries and the Borrow Direct Program.

Many thanks to University of North Carolina Press for permission to publish (in Chapter 9) parts of an essay, "Recentering Indian Women in the American Revolution," originally published in *Why You Can't Teach United States History Without American Indians* edited by Susan Sleeper-Smith, Juliana Barr, Jean M. O'Brien, Nancy Shoemaker, and Scott Manning Stevens (UNC Press, 2015).

I thank lecture audiences for their probing questions at the University of Virginia, the Colonial Society of Massachusetts, the Autry Museum, the Clements Center for Southwest Studies at Southern Methodist University, the University of Southern California / Huntington Library, and the Bavarian American Academy / University of Bayreuth, Münich. A timely lecture at Northwestern University, my old stomping grounds, was a special treat. Thank you, Amy Stanley, Director of the Chabraja Center for Historical Studies, for the invitation, and Kate Masur, Peter Carroll, Caitlin Fitz, Susan Pearson, Melissa Macaulay, Deborah Cohen, and others for insights and kindnesses. I am grateful for the critical and encouraging feedback from the Triangle Early American History Seminar and the Working Group in Feminism and History, University of North Carolina (and to Kathleen DuVal, who hosted); the Global History Seminar, Yale University (and to Lauren Benton and Mark Peterson who hosted, and to Wulfstan Scouller, my former undergraduate student, for comments); the Early American Seminar, Columbia University (and to Hannah Farber who hosted, as well as the cheering crew of NYC-based faculty who showed up); and to the Atlantic Seminar and the Geminar at Johns Hopkins. Elena Schneider provided research notes and counsel at a critical juncture. My outstanding former Ph.D. student Meg Roberts shared her insights on caregiving. Adrian Langan provided encouragement from Ireland, even if we never managed that Guinness.

This book had its origins in the Cambridge History Faculty. I have had many stimulating and enjoyable conversations about this project (and much else) with Andrew Arsan, Melissa Calaresu, Ben Griffin, Mary Laven, Peter Mandler, Renaud Morieux, Helen Pfeifer, Ulinka Rublack, Magnus Ryan, and Ruth Watson, among others. Robinson College and its staff, students, fellows (especially Amy Erickson and David Woodman), and Warden have not only tolerated having me back repeatedly but welcomed me warmly.

Thanks to colleagues at Johns Hopkins, especially those who provided advice and references: Sharon Achinstein, Tarak Barkawi, Angus Burgin, Nathan Connolly, Mary Fissell, Didier Gondola, Jean Hébrard, Louis Hyman, Jessica Marie Johnson, Martha S. Jones, Anne Lester, Julian Lim, Jennifer Luff, Laura Mason, Erin Rowe, and Sasha Turner. I am particularly grateful to Michael Kwass, Tobie Meyer-Fong, and Mohsin Noor for intelligent feedback on individual chapters. Thanks, too, for impressive administrative support from Rachel LaBozetta, Katilin Manik, and Megan Zeller.

I remain grateful for what I have learned—indeed, what I am still learning—from encouraging and wonderful scholars of this era who have, alas, passed away: Trevor Burnard, Sylvia Frey, Edward G. Gray, Ronald Hoffman, Jan Lewis, Leonard Sadosky, Hamish Scott, Betty Wood, and Alfred F. Young.

Warmest thanks, too, to fantastic colleagues—Brian DeLay, Kathleen DuVal, François Furstenberg, Ari Kelman, and Matthew Mulcahy—as well as to my long-suffering graduate students—Eric Eisner, Hilary Gallito, Alexandra Langer, and Nicholas McKenna—for reading an entire draft of the manuscript and providing insightful critiques. They much improved it; the mistakes remaining are entirely my own.

James Pullen at the Wylie Agency has been a wonder from start to finish; thank you so much. I appreciate the work of many others at Wylie including Alena Cashdan, Lina Infante, Lily Middlemass, Thomas Wee, and more. I am thrilled to have ended up at Doubleday with the lovely Kristine Puopolo, who showed welcome enthusiasm for this project from the beginning. William J. Thomas has also provided timely and sage advice. Faith Griffiths offered help and answered my queries. Emily Mahon designed a beautiful and fitting jacket. At Picador, Ravi Mirchandani asked good questions early on, and Alpana Sajip has taken up the baton with panache. Lewis Russell has kindly seen it through. At Rowohlt Berlin, Sandra Schnädelbach and Felix Stern have shepherded the manuscript with care, and Andreas Wirthensohn has undertaken the work of translating.

My fellow (former) Cambridge Americanists Andrew Preston and Gary Gerstle offered encouragement early on in critical ways; my fellow Hopkins Americanist François Furstenberg has done so at later stages. Chris Clark and I have been talking about revolutions for years; I'm so grateful for his genius. Joya Chatterji has been an inspiration throughout. Jane Kamensky has been generous and generative about this project and much else. Thanks, too, to Mark Johnson, who provided excellent company through the lockdown. John Rogers and Andrea Walkden shared the delights of Toronto. A timely invitation brought a magical week of reconnection with the hospitable Therese Frierichs as well as Kirsten Leong, Helen Otterson, Jennifer Peyton, and Megan Clowse. Mary Fissell, Melissa and Matthew Green, Priscilla Morales and Joe Pabón, Jeff Martin, Tamar Mendelson, and Rena Hoisington and Jim Gibbons, among others, supplied a warm welcome to Baltimore.

Many thanks to Anthony Pearsall for accommodating both his demanding sister and the caustic Wiederhold, and to Pauline Pearsall for her lively and engaged comments on a draft. Cornelia Pearsall has offered support, solidarity, and ice cream as needed. Emma Griffin and David Milne provided the warmest hospitality and kindness throughout. Amy Gambrill makes everything better, and her father, James Gambrill, provided useful comments at late stages, for which I am grateful. I thank Kevin Mullaney (and my lucky stars) for coffee, fireworks, and delicious soup. Edward Kail makes me proud and happy every day, for which I could not be more grateful. He and his generation give me hope that the principles outlined here can thrive. Over to you, kids!

A Note on Sources

I have built this story from the words of participants, following the guiding lights of generations of previous historians. Since some of the individuals covered here could not leave firsthand accounts, I also looked to the stuff of daily life such as petticoats and powder horns. I visited collections where I could, though the COVID pandemic, alas, put paid to some of my wilder ambitions. Many primary sources, both textual and otherwise, can now be found in some version online, thanks to genealogists, librarians, and archivists; leaders of local and state historical societies; recordkeepers for Indigenous nations; federal employees at the Smithsonian Institution and the National Park Service; and others. These labors have made my account possible. I urge you to engage with such sources also.

I have spelled out puzzling abbreviations, but I have otherwise kept intact original spellings, diction, italics, and capitalization. My aims here are both to be faithful to the original sources and to remind readers of the distance between their world and ours.

In the endnotes for each chapter, I have indicated the secondary sources on which I most relied. Taken together, they provide a guide to further reading. I have tried where my abilities permitted to use both primary and secondary sources in their original language, translating silently. However, I have had to rely on some translations, for which I thank the translators. Such dependence is the cost of a global framework, but one I consider worth paying. *Viva la revolución.*

Notes

Dedication/Preface

1. George Washington to "Fellow Citizens of the Senate, and of House of Representatives," Dec. 7, 1796, *Founders Online*, National Archives, https://founders.archives.gov.

Introduction

1. "Powder Horn Carved with the Name of Revolutionary War Soldier Prince Simbo," Collection of the Smithsonian National Museum of African American History and Culture, https://www.si.edu/.
2. William H. Guthman, *Drums A'beating, Trumpets Sounding: Artistically Carved Powder Horns in the Provincial Manner, 1746–1781* (Hartford: Connecticut Historical Society, 1993), 20–21, 24, 52.
3. Philip Zea, "Engraved Powder Horns from the French & Indian War," *Historic Deerfield Magazine* (2008): 20–27, and Alex Palmer, "The Revolutionary War Patriot Who Carried This Horn Was Fighting for Freedom—Just Not His Own," *Smithsonian Magazine* (June 2016): 1–8.
4. Zea, "Engraved Powder Horns," 26, and Jennifer Y. Chuong and Kailani Polzak, "Contact, and Contact Again: Reflections on an Eighteenth-Century Powder Horn," in "When and Where Does Colonial America End?" Colloquium, *Panorama: Journal of the Association of Historians of American Art* 7, no. 2 (Fall 2021): 1–6: 4.
5. Guthman, *Drums A'beating*, 53–56; Chuong and Polzak, "Contact, and Contact Again," 1–3.
6. Robert Baird powder horn, Zea, "Engraved Powder Horns," 26; Amasa Yale horn, Guthman, *Drums A'beating*, 111.
7. Philip D. Morgan and Andrew Jackson O'Shaughnessy, "Arming Slaves in the American Revolution," in Christopher Leslie Brown and Philip D. Mor-

gan, eds., *Arming Slaves: From Classical Times to the Modern Age* (New Haven, CT: Yale University Press, 2006), 180–208, especially 183–84.

8. Guthman, *Drums A'beating,* 172–203.
9. Howland/Rowland horn, Oct. 1775; Jonathan Gardner horn, Guthman, *Drums A'beating,* 199–203.
10. "State of Connecticut to Select Men of Glastenbury: Collo Wyllys Receipts April 21st 1778," in Palmer, "Revolutionary War Patriot," 5.
11. Shuja-ud-Din Muhammad Khan (Shujauddin Khan) to Khan Durran, cited in India Office, Bengal Public Consultations, June 18, 1753, quoted in Michael H. Fisher, ed., *The Politics of the British Annexation of India, 1757–1857, Oxford in India Readings: Themes in Indian History,* series ed. Basudev Chatterji, Neeladri Bhattacharya, and C. A. Bayly (Delhi: Oxford University Press, 1993), 88.
12. "From the Antigua Gazette," *Boston Evening-Post,* July 22, 1754.
13. Eunice Davis advertisement, *New-Hampshire Gazette,* Aug. 6, 1762. Thanks to Kirsten Sword and her *Wives Not Slaves: Patriarchy and Modernity in the Age of Revolutions* (Chicago: University of Chicago Press, 2021).
14. [Robert Navarre,] *Journal of Pontiac's Conspiracy 1763,* ed. M. Agnes Burton, trans. Richard Clyde Ford (Detroit: Clarence Monroe Burton / Michigan Society of the Colonial Wars, 1912), 120, online at American Journeys: Wisconsin Historical Society.
15. *Massachusetts Gazette (Boston News-Letter),* Nov. 21, 1765.
16. Wilfred B. Kerr, "The Stamp Act in the Floridas, 1765–1766," *Mississippi Valley Historical Review* 21:4 (1935): 463–70: 466, and Affidavit of Robert Collins, 1766, quoted in Kerr, "Stamp Act," 468.
17. Richard Brew to William Devaynes, Castle Brew, May 2, 1770, T 70/1531, National Archives, Kew (hereafter NA), 94.
18. Petition of William Allen, April 29, 1771, in *The Annual register, or a view of the history, politics, and literature, for the year 1771* (London: J. Dodsley, 1772): 196–99: 199.
19. Phillis Wheatley, "To the Right Honourable William, Earl of Dartmouth," in Vincent Carretta, ed., *The Writings of Phillis Wheatley* (Oxford: Oxford University Press, 2019), 81–82: 81.
20. Mercy Otis Warren to Catharine Macaulay, Dec. 29, 1774, Gilder Lehrman Collection, Gilder Lehrman Institute of American History, https://www.gilderlehrman.org/.
21. Toasts of Society of Free Citizens in Dublin, "Dublin, July 19," *Virginia Gazette (Dixon & Hunter),* Oct. 28, 1775.
22. [Thomas Paine,] *Common Sense; Addressed to the Inhabitants of America,* 2nd ed. (Philadelphia: W. & T. Bradford, 1776), online at Project Gutenberg, paragraph 107.

23. Quoted in H. V. Bowen, "British Conceptions of Global Empire, 1756–83," *Journal of Imperial and Commonwealth History* 26:3 (1998): 1–27: 5.
24. Michael A. McDonnell, "War Stories: Remembering and Forgetting the American Revolution," in Patrick Spero and Michael Zuckerman, eds., *The American Revolution Reborn* (Philadelphia: University of Pennsylvania Press, 2016): 11–29: 12–13; Alan Taylor, "Introduction: Expand or Die: The Revolution's New Empire," *William and Mary Quarterly* 74:4 (2017): 619–32: 631; and Jefferson Cowie, *Freedom's Dominion: A Saga of White Resistance to Federal Power* (New York: Basic Books, 2022).
25. Vincent Brown, *Tacky's Revolt: The Story of an Atlantic Slave War* (Cambridge, MA: Harvard University Press, 2020); Marjoleine Kars, *Blood on the River: A Chronicle of Mutiny and Freedom on the Wild Coast* (New York: New Press, 2021); Christopher Taylor, *The Black Carib Wars: Freedom, Survival, and the Making of the Garifuna* (Jackson: University of Mississippi Press, 2012); and Tessa Murphy, *The Creole Archipelago: Race and Borders in the Colonial Caribbean* (Philadelphia: University of Pennsylvania Press, 2021), 161–69.
26. Colin G. Calloway, *The Indian World of George Washington: The First President, the First Americans, and the Birth of the Nation* (Oxford: Oxford University Press, 2018), 177.
27. Kathleen DuVal, *Independence Lost: Lives on the Edge of the American Revolution* (New York: Random House, 2015), xv.
28. François Furstenberg, "The Significance of the Trans-Appalachian Frontier in Atlantic History," *American Historical Review* 113:3 (June 2008): 647–77, at 650, 663, 677, and Calloway, *Indian World of George Washington*, 14.
29. *The History of Hyder Shah, alias Hyder Ali Khan Bahadur and of his son Tippoo Sultan*, revised and corrected by Prince Gholam Mohammed [Tipu's son] (London: W. Thacker & Co., 1855), 262, and American Battlefield Trust, Yorktown, https://www.battlefields.org/.
30. Elizabeth A. Fenn, *Pox Americana: The Great Smallpox Epidemic of 1775–1782* (New York: Hill and Wang, 2001); J. R. McNeill, *Mosquito Empires: Ecology and War in the Greater Caribbean, 1640–1914* (Cambridge: Cambridge University Press, 2010); and Andrew Wehrman, *The Contagion of Liberty: The Politics of Smallpox in the American Revolution* (Baltimore: Johns Hopkins University Press, 2022).
31. Fenn, *Pox Americana*, 211–15, 219, 50.
32. Matthew Mulcahy, *Hurricanes and Society in the British Greater Caribbean, 1624–1783* (Baltimore: Johns Hopkins University Press, 2006), especially 77–82, 115; Stuart B. Schwartz, *Sea of Storms: A History of Hurricanes in the Greater Caribbean from Columbus to Katrina* (Princeton, NJ: Princeton University Press, 2015), 93; Stuart B. Schwartz and Matthew Mulcahy, "Natural Disasters in the Caribbean to 1850," in Philip D. Morgan, J. R. McNeill, Mat-

thew Mulcahy, and Stuart B. Schwartz, eds., *Sea and Land: An Environmental History of the Caribbean* (Oxford: Oxford University Press, 2022), 187–252: 203; and American Battlefield Trust, American Revolution FAQs, "How Many Soldiers Served in the War?" https://www.battlefields.org/.

33. Vaughn Scribner, *Under Alien Skies: Environment, Suffering, and the Defeat of the British Military in Revolutionary America* (Chapel Hill: University of North Carolina Press, 2024). There is also forthcoming work by David Hsiung and Blake McGready.

34. David Armitage and Sanjay Subrahmanyam, *The Age of Revolutions in Global Context, c. 1760–1840* (Basingstoke: Palgrave Macmillan, 2010); Rosemarie Zagarri, "The Significance of the 'Global Turn' for the Early American Republic: Globalization in the Age of Nation-Building," *Journal of the Early Republic* 31 (Spring 2011): 1–37; Suzanne Desan, Lynn Hunt, and William Max Nelson, eds., *The French Revolution in Global Perspective* (Ithaca, NY: Cornell University Press, 2013); and David A. Bell, "Questioning the Global Turn: The Case of the French Revolution," *French Historical Studies* 37, no. 1 (Winter 2014): 1–24.

35. Pauline Maier, *American Scripture: Making the Declaration of Independence* (New York: Knopf, 1997); David Armitage, *The Declaration of Independence: A Global History* (Cambridge, MA: Harvard University Press, 2007); Eliga H. Gould, *Among the Powers of the Earth: The American Revolution and the Making of a New World Empire* (Cambridge, MA: Harvard University Press, 2012); Danielle Allen, *Our Declaration: A Reading of the Declaration of Independence in Defense of Equality* (New York: Liveright/Norton, 2014); Steve Pincus, *The Heart of the Declaration: The Founders' Case for an Activist Government* (New Haven, CT: Yale University Press, 2016); and Steven Sarson, *The Course of Human Events: The Declaration of Independence and the Historical Origins of the United States* (Charlottesville: University of Virginia Press, 2025).

36. Piers Mackesy, *The War for America, 1775–1783* (London: Longmans, 1964); R. Ernest Dupuy, Gay Hammerman, and Grace P. Hayes, *The American Revolution: A Global War* (New York: David McKay, 1977); Jonathan Dull, *A Diplomatic History of the American Revolution* (New Haven, CT: Yale University Press, 1985); Barbara W. Tuchman, *The First Salute: A View of the American Revolution* (New York: Random House, 1988); Stephen Conway, *The War of American Independence, 1775–1783* (London: Edward Arnold, 1995); and David K. Allison and Larrie D. Ferreiro, eds., *The American Revolution: A World War* (Washington, DC: Smithsonian, 2018). There are also global aspects in Alan Taylor, *American Revolutions: A Continental History, 1750–1804* (New York: Norton, 2016); Woody Holton, *Liberty Is Sweet: The Hidden History of the American Revolution* (New York: Simon & Schuster, 2021);

and Rick Atkinson, *The Fate of the Day: The War for America, Fort Ticonderoga to Charleston, 1777–1780* (New York: Crown, 2025).

37. H. M. Scott, *British Foreign Policy in the Age of the American Revolution* (Oxford: Clarendon Press, 1990); H. T. Dickinson, ed., *Britain and the American Revolution* (Abingdon, UK: Routledge, 1998); Stephen Conway, *The British Isles and the War of American Independence* (Oxford: Oxford University Press, 2000); Eliga H. Gould, *The Persistence of Empire: British Political Culture in the Age of the American Revolution* (Chapel Hill: Omohundro Institute of Early History and Culture / University of North Carolina Press, 2000); P. J. Marshall, *The Making and Unmaking of Empires: Britain, India, and America, c. 1750–1783* (Oxford: Oxford University Press, 2005); Troy Bickham, *Making Headlines: The American Revolution as Seen Through the British Press* (DeKalb, IL: Northern Illinois University Press, 2009); Andrew Jackson O'Shaughnessy, *The Men Who Lost America: British Leadership, the American Revolution, and the Fate of the Empire* (New Haven, CT: Yale University Press, 2013); Larrie D. Ferreiro, *Brothers at Arms: American Independence and the Men of France and Spain Who Saved It* (New York: Knopf, 2016); and Trevor Burnard and Andrew Jackson O'Shaughnessy, *Empire and Republic: Crisis, Revolution, and America's Early Independence* (New Haven, CT: Yale University Press, 2025).

38. Lester D. Langley, *The Americas in the Age of Revolution, 1750–1850* (New Haven, CT: Yale University Press, 1998); Wim Klooster, *Revolutions in the Atlantic World: A Comparative History* (New York: New York University Press, 2009); Maya Jasanoff, *Liberty's Exiles: American Loyalists in the Revolutionary World* (New York: Knopf, 2011); Jane Kamensky, *A Revolution in Color: The World of John Singleton Copley* (New York: Norton, 2016); François Furstenberg, *When the United States Spoke French: Five Refugees Who Shaped the Nation* (New York: Penguin, 2015); Caitlin Fitz, *Our Sister Republics: The United States in an Age of American Revolutions* (New York: Norton, 2016); Jonathan Israel, *The Expanding Blaze: How the American Revolution Ignited the World, 1775–1848* (Princeton, NJ: Princeton University Press, 2017); Matthew Lockwood, *To Begin the World Over Again: How the American Revolution Devastated the Globe* (New Haven, CT: Yale University Press, 2019); Eliga Gould and Rosemarie Zagarri, eds., Forum: "Situating the United States in Vast Early America," *William and Mary Quarterly* 78, no. 2 (April 2021): 187–312; Nathan Perl-Rosenthal, *The Age of Revolutions and the Generations Who Made It* (New York: Basic Books, 2024); John Ferling, *Shots Heard Round the World: America, Britain, and Europe in the Revolutionary War* (New York: Bloomsbury, 2025); and Richard Bell, *The American Revolution and the Fate of the World* (New York: Riverhead Books, 2025).

39. DuVal, *Independence Lost;* Patrick Griffin, *American Leviathan: Empire, Nation,*

and Revolutionary Frontier (New York: Farrar, Straus and Giroux, 2007); Michael McDonnell, *Masters of Empire: Great Lakes Indians and the Making of America* (New York: Macmillan, 2015); Patrick Spero, *Frontier Rebels: The Fight for Independence in the American West, 1765–1776* (Philadelphia: University of Pennsylvania Press, 2018); Jeffers Lennox, *North of America: Loyalists, Indigenous Nations, and the Borders of the Long American Revolution* (New Haven, CT: Yale University Press, 2022); Ned Blackhawk, *The Rediscovery of America: Native Peoples and the Unmaking of U.S. History* (New Haven, CT: Yale University Press, 2023), chs. 5 and 6; Robert G. Parkinson, *The Heart of American Darkness: Bewilderment and Horror on the Early Frontier* (New York: Norton, 2024); and Johann Neem and Andrew Shankman, eds., "The Revolution at 250: A Special Issue," *Journal of the Early Republic* 24:4 (Winter 2024): 511–625, especially T. H. Breen, Kathleen DuVal, Leslie M. Harris, Michael D. Hattem, and Serena Zabin, "The Revolution at 250: A Conversation," 513–79.

40. Kathleen DuVal, *Native Nations: A Millennium in North America* (New York: Random House, 2024), and Elizabeth Ellis, *The Great Power of Small Nations: Indigenous Diplomacy in the Gulf South* (Philadelphia: University of Pennsylvania Press, 2023). On the terminology used, see Brooke Bauer and Elizabeth Ellis, "Indigenous, Native American, or American Indian? The Limitations of Broad Terms," *Journal of the Early Republic* 43:1 (Spring 2023): 61–74.
41. Bowen, "British Conceptions of Global Empire," 11.
42. Benjamin H. Irvin, *Clothed in Robes of Sovereignty: The Continental Congress and the People Out of Doors* (Oxford: Oxford University Press, 2014).
43. Mia Bay, Farah J. Griffin, Martha S. Jones, and Barbara D. Savage, eds., *Toward an Intellectual History of Black Women*, John Hope Franklin Series in African American History, Waldo E. Martin, Jr., and Patricia Sullivan, series eds. (Chapel Hill: University of North Carolina Press, 2015); Laurent Dubois, "An Enslaved Enlightenment: Rethinking the Intellectual History of the French Atlantic," *Social History* 31:1 (February 2006): 1–14; and Bianca Premo, *The Enlightenment on Trial: Ordinary Litigants and Colonialism in the Spanish Empire* (Oxford: Oxford University Press, 2017).
44. [Alexander Hamilton,] *The Farmer Refuted* (New York: James Rivington, 1775), 38.
45. "An Oration Delivered by a Citizen of the United States, on the 4th of July," in *American Mercury* (Hartford, CT), July 10, 1800.
46. Frederick Douglass, *Oration, Delivered in Corinthian Hall Rochester, July 5, 1852* (Rochester, NY: Lee, Mann, & Co., 1852), 38, https://archive.org/.
47. Martin Luther King, Jr., Speech in Memphis, April 3, 1968, CNN, https://www.cnn.com/.

Chapter 1: A Gallows in Bkejwanong

1. The single best account of Pontiac's War is Gregory Dowd, *War Under Heaven: Pontiac, the Indian Nations, and the British Empire* (Baltimore: Johns Hopkins University Press, 2002). See also David Dixon, *Never Come to Peace Again: Pontiac's Uprising and the Fate of the British Empire in North America* (Norman: University of Oklahoma Press, 2005); Fred Anderson, *Crucible of War: The Seven Years' War and the Fate of Empire in British North America, 1754–1766* (New York: Knopf, 2000), chs. 54–56, 63–65; Tiya Miles, *The Dawn of Detroit: A Chronicle of Slavery and Freedom in the City of the Straits* (New York: New Press, 2017); McDonnell, *Masters of Empire;* Brett Rushforth, *Bonds of Alliance: Indigenous and Atlantic Slaveries in New France* (Chapel Hill: Omohundro Institute of Early American History and Culture / University of North Carolina Press, 2013); Richard White, *The Middle Ground: Indians, Empires and Republics in the Great Lakes Region, 1650–1815*, 2nd ed. (Cambridge: Cambridge University Press, 2012); and Susan Sleeper-Smith, *Indian Women and French Men: Rethinking Cultural Encounter in the Western Great Lakes* (Amherst: University of Massachusetts Press, 2001).
2. William Johnson, *The Papers of Sir William Johnson*, 14 vols. (Albany: University of the State of New York, 1925) (hereafter *WJP*), vol. 4: 98.
3. *WJP,* vol. 10: 520–21.
4. Thomas Mante, *History of the Late War in North-America, and the islands of the West Indies* (London: W. Strahan and T. Cadell, 1772), 481.
5. Captain Henri-Louis Deschamps de Boishébert, "Plan of the Villages of the Odawa Savages at Détroit Erié 1732," Bibliothèque nationale de France, Paris, Département des Estampes, vol. 20b, and Brian Leigh Dunnigan, *Frontier Metropolis: Picturing Early Detroit, 1701–1838* (Detroit: Wayne State University Press, 2001).
6. Susan Sleeper-Smith, *Indigenous Prosperity and American Conquest: Indian Women of the Ohio River Valley, 1690–1792* (Chapel Hill: Omohundro Institute of Early American History and Culture / University of North Carolina Press, 2018), especially 13–16 and 27–66.
7. "Account of the voyage on the Beautiful river made in 1749," Reuben Gold Thwaites, ed., *The Jesuit Relations and Allied Documents*, 71 vols. (Cleveland, 1899) (hereafter *JR*), vol. 69: 191.
8. Dowd, *War Under Heaven*, 60.
9. Brehm to Amherst, Feb. 23, 1761, PRO WO 34/49, 21–24ff., quoted in Dunnigan, *Frontier Metropolis*, 48; Mante, *History of the Late War*, 524.
10. [Navarre,] *Journal of Pontiac's Conspiracy 1763*, 16.
11. "Chief Sachem and Warriors of Stockbridge, dated Stockbridge March 12 1764," in *WJP,* 1199.

12. Susan Sleeper-Smith, ed., *Rethinking the Fur Trade: Cultures of Exchange in an Atlantic World* (Lincoln: University of Nebraska Press, 2009); Anne Hyde, *Born of Lakes and Plains: Mixed-Descent People and the Making of the American West* (New York: Norton, 2022), ch. 1; and Sarah M. S. Pearsall, *Polygamy: An Early American History* (New Haven, CT: Yale University Press, 2019), ch. 2.
13. Tracy Neal Leavelle, *The Catholic Calumet: Colonial Conversions in French and Indian North America* (Philadelphia: University of Pennsylvania Press, 2011).
14. Louis-Antoine de Bougainville, *Adventure in the Wilderness: The American Journals of Louis Antoine de Bougainville,* ed. and trans. Edward P. Hamilton (Norman: University of Oklahoma Press, 1990), 8.
15. "Among the Illinois this 8th of June 1750," *JR*, vol. 69: 147.
16. George Croghan, *A Selection of George Croghan's Letters and Journals relating to Tours into the Western Country, November 16, 1750–November, 1765*, 2:118, 120.
17. Alexander Henry, *Travels and Adventures in Canada and the Indian Territories, between the years 1760 and 1776,* ed. James Bain (New York: Burt Franklin 1969 [1901]), 107.
18. Rushforth, *Bonds of Alliance,* and Christian Ayne Crouch, *Nobility Lost: French and Canadian Martial Cultures, Indians, and the End of New France* (Ithaca, NY: Cornell University Press, 2014).
19. Miles, *Dawn of Detroit,* ch. 1.
20. "Among the Illinois this 8th of June 1750," *JR*, vol. 69: 145.
21. *WJP*, vol. 11: 353.
22. Charles Moore, ed., "The Gladwin Manuscripts," in *Historical Collections: Collections and Researches made by the Michigan Pioneer and Historical Society* (Lansing, MI: Robert Smith Printing, 1897), vol. 27: 605–80: 644.
23. Henry Gladwin to Jeffrey Amherst, April 20, 1763, in *WJP*, vol. 4: 95–96.
24. [Navarre,] *Journal of Pontiac's Conspiracy,* 120.
25. Mante, *History of the Late War*, 481.
26. Jeffery Amherst, *The Journal of Jeffery Amherst, 1757–1763* (East Lansing: Michigan State University Press, 2015), 198.
27. Moore, "Gladwin Manuscripts," vol. 27: 674, and Henry Gladwin to Jeffrey Amherst, April 20, 1763, in *WJP*, vol. 4: 95–96.
28. Rushforth, *Bonds of Alliance,* 254, 258.
29. Gloria Whiting, *Belonging: An Intimate History of Slavery and Family in Early New England* (Philadelphia: University of Pennsylvania Press, 2024), 157, 176–79.
30. [Navarre,] *Journal of Pontiac's Conspiracy,* 143–45.
31. [Navarre,] *Journal of Pontiac's Conspiracy,* 16, 20–21.
32. Nicole Eustace, *Covered with Night: A Story of Murder and Indigenous Justice in Early America* (New York: Liveright, 2021).
33. Bougainville, *Adventure in the Wilderness,* 117.

34. Bougainville, *Adventure in the Wilderness*, 105.
35. [Navarre,] *Journal of Pontiac's Conspiracy*, 26.
36. [Navarre,] *Journal of Pontiac's Conspiracy*, 28, 30.
37. McDonnell, *Masters of Empire*, 216.
38. [Navarre,] *Journal of Pontiac's Conspiracy*, 234, 236.
39. Andrew Keith Sturtevant, *Jealous Neighbors: Rivalry and Alliance Among the Native Communities of Detroit, 1701–1776*, Ph.D. diss., College of William and Mary, 2011, especially ch. 5.
40. "Mrs. Meloch's Account," and "Mr. Pettier's Account," in "Conspiracy of Pontiac," *Collections of the Pioneer Society of the State of Michigan*, 2nd ed. (Lansing, MI: Wynkoop, Hallenbeck Crawford Co., 1907): vol. 8: 340–63: 341, 359–60. "A Conference with Foreign Nations," Aug. 9–11, 1764, *WJP*, vol. 4: 476, and Sturtevant, *Jealous Neighbors*, 265.
41. Lisa Brooks, *Our Beloved Kin* (New Haven, CT: Yale University Press, 2018).
42. "Mr. Charles Gouin's Account," in "Conspiracy of Pontiac," vol. 8: 344–51: 345.
43. Mante, *History of the Late War*, 486.
44. "An Indian Conference, Johnson Hall, Feb. 1–4, 1764," *WJP*, vol. 11: 353.
45. Henry, *Travels and Adventures*, 76–96.
46. Amherst Papers, WO 34/102, NA.
47. William Trent, "William Trent's Journal at Fort Pitt, 1763," ed. A. T. Volwiler, *Journal of American History* 11:3 (1924): 390–413: 395, 400. Elizabeth A. Fenn, "Biological Warfare in Eighteenth-Century North America: Beyond Jeffery Amherst," *Journal of American History* 86:4 (2000): 1552–80: 1574.
48. Henry Barclay to Sir Wm Johnson, Oct. 5, 1763, *WJP*, vol. 13: 300.
49. "A Narrative of the Late Massacres, [30 January? 1764]," *Founders Online*, National Archives, Franklin documents, https://founders.archives.gov.
50. *Newport Mercury*, Nov. 4, 1765.
51. Daniel Richter, "Native Americans, the Plan of 1764, and a British Empire That Never Was," in *Cultures and Identities in Colonial British America*, ed. Robert Olwell and Alan Tully (Baltimore: Johns Hopkins University Press, 2006), 269–92: 269.
52. Mante, *History of the Late War*, 480.
53. *A Declaration and Remonstrance of the distressed and bleeding Frontier Inhabitants of the Province of Pennsylvania* (Philadelphia, 1764), 12.
54. Declaration of Independence, National Archives, America's Founding Documents, https:// archives.gov/.

Chapter 2: A Tavern in St. Kitts

1. William Tuckett to George Thomas, Dec. 5, 1765, and Thomas to Henry Seymour Conway, Dec. 21, 1765, CO/152/47, NA.

2. The best accounts of the Stamp Act disturbances remain Edmund S. Morgan and Helen M. Morgan, *The Stamp Act Crisis: Prologue to Revolution* (Chapel Hill: Institute of Early American History and Culture / University of North Carolina Press, 1953) and Edmund S. Morgan, *Prologue to Revolution: Sources and Documents on the Stamp Act Crisis, 1764–1766* (Chapel Hill: Institute of Early American History and Culture / University of North Carolina Press, 1959). See also Fred Anderson, *Crucible of War: The Seven Years' War and the Fate of Empire in British North America, 1754–1766* (New York: Knopf, 2000), chs. 66–74. On the Caribbean and St. Kitts in this era, see Andrew Jackson O'Shaughnessy, *An Empire Divided: The American Revolution and the British Caribbean* (Philadelphia: University of Pennsylvania Press, 2000), and Natalie Zacek, *Settler Society in the English Leeward Islands, 1670–1776* (Cambridge: Cambridge University Press, 2010).
3. *Public Advertiser,* Jan. 28, 1766; *St. James's Chronicle, or British Evening Post,* Jan. 25–28, 1766; *Lloyd's Evening Post,* Jan. 27–29, 1766.
4. William Smith, *A Natural History of Nevis, and the Rest of the English Leeward Charibee Islands in America* (Cambridge: Cambridge University Press, 2014), 233.
5. Tuckett to Thomas, Dec. 5, 1765, CO/152/47, NA; *Public Advertiser,* Jan. 28, 1766; *St. James's Chronicle, or British Evening Post,* Jan. 25–28, 1766; *Lloyd's Evening Post,* Jan. 27–29, 1766.
6. Bryan Edwards, *The History, Civil and Commercial of the British Colonies in the West Indies,* 2 vols. (Dublin: Luke White, 1793), vol. 1: 427.
7. Thomas to Conway, Antigua, Dec. 21, 1765, NA.
8. *Public Advertiser,* Jan. 28, 1766.
9. Stephen Hopkins, *The Grievances of the American Colonies Candidly Examined* (London: J. Almon, 1766), 7.
10. Zacek, *Settler Society,* 18–19.
11. Samuel Martin, *An Essay upon Plantership,* 4th ed. (Antigua: Samuel Clapham, 1765), 15.
12. Andrew J. O'Shaughnessy, "The Stamp Act Crisis in the British Caribbean," *William and Mary Quarterly* 51:2 (1994): 203–26: 216.
13. Vincent Brown, *The Reaper's Garden: Death and Power in the World of Atlantic Slavery* (Cambridge, MA: Harvard University Press, 2008), introduction.
14. Zacek, *Settler Society,* 242.
15. "Excavating Slavery," St Kitts-Nevis Digital Archaeology, National Museums Liverpool, Archaeology of Slavery / Excavating Slavery, https://www.liverpoolmuseums.org.uk/.
16. Janet Schaw, *Journal of a Lady of Quality: Being the Narrative of a Journey from Scotland to the West Indies, North Carolina, and Portugal, in the years 1774 to 1776,* ed. Evangeline Walker Andrews with Charles McLean Andrews, introduc-

tion by Stephen Carl Arch (Lincoln: University of Nebraska Press, 2005), 121, 127, 128, and Smith, *Natural History of Nevis,* 232.

17. Trevor Burnard, "'Prodigious Riches': The Wealth of Jamaica Before the American Revolution," *Economic History Review* 54:3 (2001): 506–24: 521.
18. Smith, *Natural History of Nevis,* 243.
19. Stuart B. Schwartz and Matthew Mulcahy, "Natural Disasters in the Caribbean to 1850," and J. R. McNeill, "Disease Environments in the Caribbean to 1850," both in Philip D. Morgan et al., *Sea and Land,* 187–252: 187–88 and 130–86: 166–68.
20. Brown, *Tacky's Revolt.*
21. Minutes of St. Kitts Council and Assembly, Jan. 4, Feb. 20, and July 29, 1760, CO 241/8, NA, quoted in Zacek, *Settler Society,* 211.
22. Sharon V. Salinger, *Taverns and Drinking in Early America* (Baltimore: Johns Hopkins University Press, 2004), 221–23, 236; and Peter Thompson, *Rum Punch and Revolution: Taverngoing and Public Life in Eighteenth-Century Philadelphia* (Philadelphia: University of Pennsylvania Press, 1999), 75.
23. Susan E. Klepp and Karin Wulf, eds., *The Diary of Hannah Callender Sansom: Sense and Sensibility in the Age of the American Revolution* (Ithaca, NY: Cornell University Press, 2010), 90, 105.
24. Thompson, *Rum Punch and Revolution,* 151.
25. Sarah Hand Meacham, *Every Home a Distillery: Alcohol, Gender, and Technology in the Colonial Chesapeake* (Baltimore: Johns Hopkins University Press, 2009), 67.
26. Peter Clark, *The English Alehouse: A Social History, 1200–1830* (London: Longman, 1983), and Charles Luddington, *The Politics of Wine in Britain: A New Cultural History* (Basingstoke, UK: Palgrave Macmillan, 2013).
27. Morgan and Morgan, *Stamp Act Crisis,* 209.
28. Benjamin Franklin, "Fragments of a Pamphlet on the Stamp Act [Jan. 1766]," *Founders Online,* National Archives, https://founders.archives.gov.
29. Thomas Pitt, Jr., quoted in "Grenville, George (1712–1770), of Wotton, Bucks," in *The History of Parliament: The House of Commons 1754–1790,* ed. L. Namier and J. Brooke (London, 1964), https://historyofparliament online.org/.
30. James Otis, *Considerations on Behalf of the Colonists. In a Letter to a Noble Lord* (London: J. Almon, 1765), 249, Liberty Fund online, https://oll.libertyfund .org/.
31. O'Shaughnessy, *Empire Divided,* 65.
32. Franklin, "Fragments."
33. C. A. Weslager, *The Stamp Act Congress with an Exact Copy of the Complete Journal* (Newark, DE: University of Delaware Press, 1976), 39.

34. Justin DuRivage, *Revolution Against Empire: Taxes, Politics, and the Origins of American Independence* (New Haven, CT: Yale University Press, 2017), 108.
35. George Johnstone to John Pownal, April 1, 1766, quoted in Wilfred B. Kerr, "The Stamp Act in the Floridas, 1765–1766," *Mississippi Valley Historical Review* 21:4 (March 1935): 463–70: 469.
36. Hopkins, *Grievances,* 31.
37. John Pendleton Kennedy, ed., *Journals of the House of Burgesses of Virginia, 1761–1765* (Richmond: The Colonial Press, 1907), lv, 302, 360, and Anonymous, "Journal of a French Traveller in the Colonies 1765," *American Historical Review* 26:4 (1921): 726–47: 745–46.
38. DuRivage, *Revolution Against Empire,* 127.
39. *Connecticut Courant,* Aug. 26, 1765.
40. *Newport Mercury,* Sept. 2, 1765.
41. *Newport Mercury,* Sept. 2 and 9, 1765; Thomas Hutchinson to Richard Jackson, Aug. 30, 1765, in Morgan, *Prologue,* 108–9; James Gordon to William Martin, "Boston Sepr. 10 1765," *Proceedings of the Massachusetts Historical Society* 13 (1899–1900), "January Meeting," 379–424: 393–94.
42. *Massachusetts Gazette (Boston News-Letter),* Nov. 21, 1765.
43. Johnstone to Pownal, February 26, 1766, in Kerr, "Stamp Act in the Floridas," 467–68.
44. Kerr, "Stamp Act in the Floridas," 466, 468.
45. W. B. Kerr, "The Stamp Act in Quebec," *English Historical Review* 47:188 (1932): 648–51: 648, and Philip Lawson, *The Imperial Challenge: Quebec and Britain in the Age of the American Revolution* (Montreal: McGill-Queen's University Press, 1989), 92.
46. *Quebec Gazette,* May 29, 1766, Thomas Fisher Rare Book Library, University of Toronto, https://digitalcollections.mcmaster.ca.
47. *Massachusetts Gazette (Boston News-Letter),* Nov. 21, 1765.
48. *Newport Mercury,* Nov. 11, 1765.
49. *Newport Mercury,* Nov. 11, 1765, and *Massachusetts Gazette (Boston News-Letter),* Nov. 21, 1765. See also Wilfred B. Kerr, "The Stamp Act in Nova Scotia," *New England Quarterly* 6:3 (1933): 552–66: 556.
50. *Newport Mercury,* Nov. 4, 1765; "Pennsylvania Resolves," Sept. 21, 1765, from *Pennsylvania Archives,* 8th series, 7 (1935): 5779–80; *Archives of Maryland* 59 (1942), 30–32; C. J. Hoadley, ed., *Public Records of the Colony of Connecticut* (Hartford, 1850–90), vol. 12, 421–25, in Edmund Morgan, *Prologue,* 51, 53, 55; Hopkins, *Grievances* (London: J. Almon, 1766), 6.
51. David Ramsay, *The History of the Revolution of South-Carolina,* 2 vols. (Trenton, NJ: Isaac Collins, 1785), vol. 1:13.
52. *Boston Evening Post,* Oct. 7, 1765, and Karen Severund Cook, "Benjamin

Franklin and the Snake That Would Not Die," *British Library Journal*, 22:1 (Spring 1996): 88–111: 99–100.

53. "Excerpts from William Samuel Johnson's Diary," in C. A. Weslager, *The Stamp Act Congress with an Exact Copy of the Complete Journal* (Newark, DE: University of Delaware Press, 1976), 256–60: 257.
54. Shelburne to Grant, Oct. 25, 1766, quoted in Kerr, "Stamp Act in the Floridas," 464.
55. *Boston Post Boy*, Dec. 30, 1765; Henry Seymour Conway to Govr George Thomas St. James, March 13, 1766, and April 1766, 120–25, CO/152/47, and John Howell to Secretary of State, Spanish Town, May 31, 1766, CO/137/62, NA.
56. John Howell to Secretary of State, Spanish Town, May 31, 1766, CO/137/62; George Walker to the Barbados Committee of Correspondence, Nov. 19, 1765, Minutes of the Council of Barbados, CO/31/33; Pinfold to the Board of Trade, Feb. 21, 1766, CO/28/32, NA.
57. O'Shaughnessy, *Empire Divided*, 81.
58. John Dickinson, *An Address to the Committee of Correspondence in Barbados* (Philadelphia: William Bradford, 1766), i, 2, 7.
59. *Boston Gazette*, Dec. 16, 1765, and John Adams, *Diary*, vol. 1, Jan. 2, 1766, Adams Papers, https://www.masshist.org/.
60. Adams, *Diary*, Jan. 2, 1766, and Humphrey Ploughjogger (John Adams), *Boston Gazette*, Oct. 14, 1765.
61. *Boston Gazette*, Dec. 23, 1765, and *Barbados Mercury*, Feb. 1, 1766.
62. *Boston News-Letter, or Massachusetts Gazette*, March 27, 1766.
63. Edwin Wolf 2d, "Benjamin Franklin's Stamp Act Cartoon," *Proceedings of the American Philosophical Society* 99:6 (December 1955): 388–96: 390, 392, and DuRivage, *Revolution Against Empire*, 137.
64. *Virginia Gazette (Purdie & Dixon)*, June 20, 1766.
65. *Providence Gazette*, March 12, 1766.
66. *Virginia Gazette (Purdie & Dixon)*, June 20, 1766.
67. Letter VII, *Letters from a Farmer in Pennsylvania, in Empire and Nation: Letters from a Farmer in Pennsylvania (John Dickinson)*, ed. Forrest McDonald (Indianapolis: Liberty Fund, 1999), https://oll.libertyfund.org/; Craig Yirush, *Settlers, Liberty, and Empire: The Roots of Early American Political Theory, 1675–1775* (Cambridge: Cambridge University Press, 2011), 236; and Silas Downer, *A discourse, delivered in Providence, in the colony of Rhode-Island upon the 25th day of July 1768* (Providence, RI: John Waterman, 1768), 4.
68. *New-London Gazette*, April 15, 1768, and Laurel Thatcher Ulrich, "Political Protest and the World of Goods," *Oxford Handbook of the American Revolution* (Oxford: Oxford University Press, 2012): 64–84: 75–76.

69. *Boston Evening Post,* May 29, 1769; "To the FAIR-SEX in North-America," *Newport Mercury,* May 8, 1769; Mary Beth Norton, *Liberty's Daughters: The Revolutionary Experience of American Women, 1750–1800* (Boston: Little, Brown and Co., 1980), 164–69; Laurel Thatcher Ulrich, *The Age of Homespun: Objects and Stories in the Creation of an American Myth* (New York: Knopf, 2001), 176, 178; Ezra Stiles, *The Literary Diary of Ezra Stiles,* 3 vols., ed. Franklin Bowditch Dexter (New York: Charles Scribner's Sons, 1901), vol. 1: 53; *Boston Evening Post,* May 29, 1769, 1; *Virginia Gazette (Purdie & Dixon),* Dec. 14, 1769; and Thomas Anburey, *Travels through the interior parts of America* (London: W. Lane, 1789), vol. 2: 246.
70. *New Hampshire Gazette,* Aug. 25, 1769.
71. O'Shaughnessy, *Empire Divided,* 32.
72. *Bath Chronicle and Weekly Gazette,* July 30, 1772, and William Tuckett to Charles James Fox, Bridgewater, April 21, 1782, in *Public Advertiser,* April 30, 1782.
73. Advertisement for Catherine from Thomas Bridgwater, *St. Christopher's Gazette,* Sept. 4, 1765.
74. "Just imported from Liverpool," *St. Christopher's Gazette,* Sept. 4, 1765.
75. Tirthankar Roy, *The East India Company: The World's Most Powerful Corporation* (Haryana: Penguin Random House India, 2012).

Chapter 3: A Street in Kolkata

1. "Account of the late famine in India," *Gentleman's Magazine and Historical Chronicle,* vol. 41 (London: D. Henry, Sept. 1771), 402.
2. William Wilson Hunter, *The Annals of Rural Bengal* (London, 1868), 26; David Kinsley, *Tantric Visions of the Divine Feminine: The Ten Mahāvidyās* (Berkeley: University of California Press, 1997), 7; and Ranjit Sen, *A Stagnating City: Calcutta in the Eighteenth Century* (Calcutta: Institute of Historical Studies, 2000), 73–85.
3. Muhammad Reza Khan, May 15, 1770, in *Calendar of Persian Correspondence,* vol. 3, 1770–1772 (Calcutta: Superintendent Government Printing, India, 1919), 64–65; "Complaint of Rajah Purtub Sing Zemindar of the Purgunnah Durrumpoor in the District of Tyrhoot," Proceedings of the Committee of Circuit, February 2–9, 1773, *Famine and Dearth in India and Britain, 1550–1800,* West Bengal State Archives, https://famineanddearth.exeter.ac.uk/; Seid Gholam Hossein Khan, *The Sëir Mutaquerin, or, View of Modern Times, being an history of India, from the year 1118 to the year 1194 of the Hedjrah . . .* (Calcutta: Printed for the Translator, 1789), vol. 2: 411, https://archive.org/.
4. Shujauddin Khan to Khan Durran, no date, cited in India Office, Bengal Public Consultations, June 18, 1753, quoted in Fisher, ed., *Politics of the British Annexation,* 88.

5. Eliga H. Gould, "Zones of Law, Zones of Violence: The Legal Geography of the British Atlantic, circa 1772," *William and Mary Quarterly* 60: 3 (2003): 471–510, and Lauren Benton, *They Called It Peace: Worlds of Imperial Violence* (Princeton, NJ: Princeton University Press, 2024).
6. Edmund S. Morgan, *The Gentle Puritan: A Life of Ezra Stiles, 1727–1795* (New Haven, CT: Institute of Early American History and Culture / Yale University Press, 1962), 121.
7. Jonathan Eacott, *Selling Empire: India in the Making of Britain and America, 1600–1830* (Chapel Hill: Omohundro Institute of Early American History and Culture/University of North Carolina Press, 2016), chs. 3 and 4; H. V. Bowen, "Perceptions from the Periphery: Colonial American Views of Britain's Asiatic Empire, 1756–1783," in Christine Daniels and Michael V. Kennedy, eds., *Negotiated Empires: Centers and Peripheries in the Americas, 1500–1820* (Oxford: Taylor & Francis Group, 2002), 283–300: 289; Henry Pattullo, *An Essay upon the Cultivation of the Lands, and Improvements of the Revenues, of Bengal* (London: T. Becket and P. A. DeHondt, 1772), 25.
8. On the tea and its context, see Alfred F. Young, *The Shoemaker and the Tea Party: Memory and the American Revolution* (Boston: Beacon Press, 1999); Benjamin Woods Labaree, *The Boston Tea Party* (Oxford: Oxford University Press, 1964); Benjamin L. Carp, *Defiance of the Patriots: The Boston Tea Party and the Making of America* (New Haven, CT: Yale University Press, 2010); and Jane T. Merritt, *The Trouble with Tea: The Politics of Consumption in the Eighteenth-Century Global Economy* (Baltimore: Johns Hopkins University Press, 2017).
9. Richard M. Eaton, *India in the Persianate Age, 1000–1765* (London: Penguin, 2019), 353; Robert Clive to William Pitt, Calcutta, Jan. 7, 1759, quoted in Fisher, ed., *Politics of the British Annexation*, 60; William Watts, *Memoirs of the Revolution in Bengal* (London: A. Millar, 1760), 1; Alexander Dow, "An Enquiry into the State of Bengal," in Alexander Dow, *A History of Hindostan, From the Death of Akbar to the Complete Settlement of the Empire Under Aurungzebe* (London: T. Becket and P. A. DeHondt, 1772), lxxviii, lxxii; Sauda, quoted in Ralph Russell and Khurshidul Islam, *Three Mughal Poets: Mir, Sauda, Mir Hasan* (Cambridge, MA: Harvard University Press, 1968), 67–68.
10. P. J. Marshall, *East Indian Fortunes: The British in Bengal in the Eighteenth Century* (Oxford: Oxford University Press, 1976); John McLane, *Land and Local Kingship in Eighteenth-Century Bengal* (Cambridge: Cambridge University Press, 1993), especially 195; Robert Travers, *Ideology and Empire in Eighteenth-Century India: The British in Bengal* (Cambridge: Cambridge University Press, 2007); Tillman W. Nechtman, *Nabobs: Empire and Identity in Eighteenth-Century Britain* (Cambridge: Cambridge University Press, 2010); Roy, *East India Company*, 171; William Dalrymple, *The Anarchy: The East India Company, Corporate Violence, and the Pillage of an Empire* (Lon-

don: Bloomsbury, 2019); and Fisher, ed., *Politics of the British Annexation*, 11–12.

11. Sen, *Stagnating City*, 45, and Rajat Kanta Ray, "Indian Society and the Establishment of British Supremacy, 1765–1818," in P. J. Marshall and Alaine Low, eds., *The Oxford History of the British Empire*, vol. 2: *The Eighteenth Century* (Oxford: Oxford University Press, 1998): 508–29.
12. Jemima Kindersley, *Letters from the Island of Teneriffe, Brazil, the Cape of Good Hope, and the East Indies* (London: J. Nourse, 1777), 274, 292, 278, https://archive.org/.
13. Henry Prinsep, *3 Generations in India*, India Office Records, Mss Eur C/97/1, 8–9, British Library (hereafter BL); Travers, 34; Vansittart to Richard Becher, Midnapore, Dec. 21, 1767, MSS Eur. F331/1, 8, BL.
14. Vansittart to Lt. Rooke Midnapore, May 31, 1768, MSS Eur. F331/1, 76–77, BL; Kindersley, *Letters from the Island of Teneriffe*, 180–81.
15. Sept. 30, 1769, and Nov. 23, 1769, in Narenda Krishna Sinha, ed., *Fort William–India House Correspondence*, vol. 5: 1767–69 (Calcutta: National Archives of India / Sri Lal Chand Roy at Gossain & Co., 1949), 603, 605; May 15 and June 2, 1770, from Muhammad Reza Khan in *Calendar of Persian Correspondence*, vol. 3: 1770–1772 (Calcutta: Superintendent Government Printing, India, 1919), 64–65, 71.
16. On the political uses of famine, see David Arnold, "Hunger in the Garden of Plenty: The Bengal Famine of 1770," in Alessa Johns, ed., *Dreadful Visitations: Confronting Natural Catastrophe in the Age of Enlightenment* (New York: Routledge, 1999), 81–112; Joya Chatterji, *Shadows at Noon: The South Asian Twentieth Century* (London: Bodley Head, 2023), 14; "Memoir by [Sir] George Campbell on the Famines which Affected Bengal in the Last Century," J. C. Geddes, *Administrative Experience in Former Famines* (Calcutta: Bengal Secretariat Press, 1874), 408–22: 411; "A poem on the Famine of 1176," from *Itibas Ashrito Bangla Kobita (1751–1855)*, ed. Suprakash Bandopadhyay (Calcutta: M. C. Sarkar & Sons, 1954); *Famine and Dearth in India and Britain, 1550–1800;* Gholam Hossein Khan, *The Sëir Mutaqherin*, 404; "Account of the late famine in India," 402; Vansittart to Richard Becher Dinagepore, Aug. 6, 1770, OIOC, MSS Eur. F331/2, 111, BL.
17. Dow, *History of Hindostan*, xcvi, xcvii. xciv.
18. Dow, *History of Hindostan*, 84; *Pennsylvania Journal, or, Weekly Advertiser*, May 23, 1771; *Connecticut Journal and New-Haven Post-Boy*, May 31, 1771; *Pennsylvania Gazette*, June 13, 1771; *New-York Journal*, June 6, 1771; and *Boston News-Letter*, June 13, 1771. See also *Essex Gazette*, Sept. 24, 1771; *Boston News-Letter*, Sept. 26, 1771; *Massachusetts Spy*, Sept. 26, 1771; *Connecticut Gazette*, Sept. 27, 1771; *Boston Post-Boy*, Sept. 30, 1771; *Connecticut Journal*,

Oct. 4, 1771; *Providence Gazette,* Oct. 5, 1771; *New-York Journal,* Oct. 10, 1771; *Boston Post-Boy,* June 28, 1773; *New-York Gazette,* June 28, 1773; *Virginia Gazette,* July 1, 1773; *Pennsylvania Journal,* July 18, 1773; *New-York Gazette,* Aug. 2, 1773; and "To John Prinsep," March 4, 1771, Mss Eur C/97/1, xii, BL.

19. "A Narrative of the Riot in St. George's Fields, Southwark on the 10th of May, 1768," in *The Tyburn Chronicle,* 4 vols. (London: J. Cooke, 1768), vol. 4: 282, 284–85; Petition of William Allen, April 29, 1771, in *The Annual Register... 1771* (London: J. Dodsley, 1772), 196–99, at 199.
20. Eric Hinderaker, *Boston's Massacre* (Cambridge, MA: Harvard University Press, 2017); Serena Zabin, *The Boston Massacre: A Family History* (New York: Houghton, Mifflin Harcourt, 2020); and Christopher F. Minty, *Unfriendly to Liberty: Loyalist Networks and the Coming of the American Revolution in New York City* (Ithaca, NY: Cornell University Press, 2023).
21. John Gilbert McCurdy, *Quarters: The Accommodation of the British Army and the Coming of the American Revolution* (Ithaca, NY: Cornell University Press, 2019), 193–97; *New-York Gazette, or Weekly Post-Boy,* Feb. 5, 1770.
22. Jesse Lemisch, "Jack Tar in the Streets: Merchant Seamen in the Politics of Revolutionary America," *William and Mary Quarterly* 25:3 (1968): 371–407; Peter Linebaugh and Marcus Rediker, *The Many-Headed Hydra: Sailors, Slaves, Commoners, and the Hidden History of the Revolutionary Atlantic* (Boston: Beacon Press, 2003); Paul Gilje, *Liberty on the Waterfront: American Maritime Culture in the Age of Revolution* (Philadelphia: University of Pennsylvania, 2003); Nathan Perl-Rosenthal, *Citizen Sailors: Becoming American in the Age of Revolution* (Cambridge, MA: Harvard University Press, 2015); Christopher P. Magra, *Poseidon's Curse: British Naval Impressment and the Atlantic Origins of the American Revolution* (Cambridge: Cambridge University Press, 2016); and *New-York Gazette, or Weekly Post-Boy,* Feb. 5, 1770.
23. *Boston Gazette,* Feb. 26, 1770; Phillis Wheatley, "On the Death of Mr Snider Murder'd by Richardson," in Robert C. Kuncio, "Some Unpublished Poems of Phillis Wheatley," *New England Quarterly* 43:2 (June 1970), 287–98: 297.
24. Diary of John Rowe, March 8, 1770, vol. 7 (Aug. 5, 1769–Aug. 31, 1770): 1078, Massachusetts Historical Society, https://www.masshist.org; Antonio T. Bly, "Wheatley's on the Affray in King Street," *The Explicator* 56:4 (1998): 177–80; David Waldstreicher, *The Odyssey of Phillis Wheatley: A Poet's Journey Through American Slavery and Independence* (New York: Farrar, Straus and Giroux, 2023), 103–4; and Betsy Erkkila, "Provocation: Phillis Wheatley on the Streets of Revolutionary Boston and in the Atlantic World," *Early American Literature* 56:2 (2021): 351–72: 360; Mark Peterson, *The City-State of Boston: The Rise and Fall of an Atlantic Power, 1630–1865* (Princeton, NJ: Princeton University Press, 2019), 294–325; *Boston Gazette,* March 12, 1770.
25. Marjoleine Kars, *Breaking Loose Together: The Regulator Rebellion in Pre-*

Revolutionary North Carolina (Chapel Hill: Omohundro Institute of Early American History and Culture / University of North Carolina Press, 2002); Catherine W. Bishir, *North Carolina Architecture* (Chapel Hill: Historic Preservation Foundation of North Carolina / University of North Carolina Press, 1990), 45; and John Whiting to Ezra Stiles, April 8, 1767, quoted in Alonso Thomas Dill, *Governor Tryon and His Palace* (Chapel Hill: University of North Carolina Press, 1955), 114, 118, 267, 269.

26. "PETITION TO THE HOUSE OF REPRESENTATIVES: TO THE WORSHIPFUL HOUSE OF REPRESENTATIVES OF NORTH CAROLINA," Oct. 7, 1768, in *North Carolina Historical Review* 8:3 (July, 1931), 342–44: 343; Stuart Marshall, "Facing East from Tryon Mountain: New Vantages on the 'Great Wolf,' Rogues, and Regulators," *North Carolina Historical Review* 99:1 (January 2022): 1–35.
27. Tryon to Colonel James Sampson, Newbern, Dec. 22, 1770; William Tryon to Colonel Edmund Fanning, Newbern, December 26, 1770; Bethabara Diary in William S. Powell, James K. Huhta, and Thomas J. Farnham, *The Regulators in North Carolina: A Documentary History, 1759–1776* (Raleigh: North Carolina State Department of Archives and History, 1971), 296, 298, 30; "Copy of his Excellency Gov Tryon's Letter to the Commanding Officers of several Regiments of Militia," Newbern, March 19, 1771, *Colonial Records of North Carolina,* 8:540; Kars, *Breaking Loose Together,* 188, 199; "Petition of Orange County, 1771" to Governor William Tryon, *North Carolina Digital Collections,* Documents, https:// digital.ncdcr.gov/.
28. *Boston Gazette and Country Journal,* June 17, 1771; Stiles, *Diary,* vol. 1: 111–12.
29. Captain William Smith to Governor Francis Fauquier, April 3, 1766, in Francis Fauquier, "Letters of Governor Francis Fauquier," April 5, 1766, *William and Mary Quarterly* 21:3 (1913): 163–171: 167; Benjamin H. Irvin, "Tar, Feathers, and the Enemies of American Liberties, 1768–1776," *New England Quarterly* 76:2 (2003): 197–238.
30. William R. Staples, ed., *The Documentary History of the Destruction of the Gaspee* (Providence, RI: Knowles, Vose, and Anthony, 1845), 17, 13.
31. [Richard Allen], *An Oration upon the Beauties of Liberty, Delivered on the Annual Thanksgiving, December 3rd, 1772* (Boston: D. Kneeland and N. Davis, 1773), 27.
32. George van Cleve, "'Somerset's Case' and Its Antecedents in Imperial Perspective," *Law and History Review* 24:3 (Fall 2006): 601–645: 602.
33. [Allen], *Oration,* 19, ix, 20, 22, xiii, ix, 28.
34. Wheatley, "To the Right Honourable William, Earl of Dartmouth," *Writings of Phillis Wheatley,* 80–81.
35. *Virginia Gazette (Purdie & Dixon),* March 14, 1770, and April 5, 1770. *Maryland Gazette,* May 13, 1773.
36. Karen Cook Bell, *Running from Bondage: Enslaved Women and Their Remark-*

able Fight for Freedom in Revolutionary America (Cambridge: Cambridge University Press, 2021), 18–19, 43–46, 51, 54–62, 65–66.

37. Travers, *Ideology and Empire,* 39.
38. *Boston Evening Post,* Oct. 25, 1773; L. F. S. Upton, "Proceedings of Ye Body Respecting the Tea," *William and Mary Quarterly* 22:2 (1965): 287–300: 299, 298.
39. Hampden, "The Alarm II," New York, Oct. 9, 1773, 2; "The Alarm V," New York, Oct. 27, 1773, 4, 3.
40. "A Mechanic," *To the tradesmen, Mechanics, &c, of the Province of Pennsylvania* (Philadelphia: no publisher, 1773), Evans Early American Imprints Online, New York Public Library; *Boston Post-Boy,* Dec. 6–13, 1773; Mercy Otis Warren to Catharine Macaulay, Dec. 29, 1774, Gilder Lehrman Collection, Gilder Lehrman Institute of American History, https://www.gilderlehrman.org/.
41. John Dickinson, "Two Letters on the Tea Tax," Nov. 1773, in Jane Calvert, ed., *Complete Works of John Dickinson* (Newark, DE: University of Delaware Press, 2020), 459–60.
42. Dickinson, "Two Letters," 460.
43. Merritt, *Trouble with Tea,* 90.
44. George Robert Twelves Hewes, quoted in Alfred Young, *The Shoemaker and the Tea Party* (Boston: Beacon Press, 1999), 44.
45. Philip Deloria, *Playing Indian* (New Haven, CT: Yale University Press, 1998), 5.
46. Young, *Shoemaker,* 85–131; *St. James's Chronicle, or British Evening-Post,* Jan. 22, 1774; Diary of John Rowe, December 16/17 , 1773, vol. 10, 1727; *Boston Evening Post,* Feb. 7, 1774.
47. B. B. Thacher, *Traits of the Tea Party; Being a Memoir of George R.T. Hewes* (New York: Harper & Brothers, 1835), 182–83.
48. Vansittart to Richard Becher, Midnapore, Dec. 21, 1767, MSS Eur. F331/1, 8, BL.
49. Eacott, *Selling Empire,* 193–94; Adams *Diary,* Feb. 14, 1771, vol. 16 (January 10, 1771–Nov. 28, 1772), Massachusetts Historical Society, Digital Adams Archive, https://www.masshist.org/; Arthur Meier Schlesinger, "The Uprising Against the East India Company," *Political Science Quarterly* 32:1 (Mar. 1917): 60–79: 64–65; Thomas Jefferson to Thomas Adams, June 1, 1771, *Founders Online,* National Archives, https://founders.archives.gov/.
50. *Providence Gazette,* Dec. 14, 1771; *Essex Gazette for 1771,* Dec. 10, 1771; *Connecticut Courant,* Jan. 7, 1772.

Chapter 4: A Society in Edinburgh

1. Pantheon Society Minutes 1773–1779, MS Gen 1283, Special Collections, Glasgow University Library (hereafter Pantheon Minutes). On 1774, see

Mary Beth Norton, *1774: The Long Year of Revolution* (New York: Knopf, 2020); and T. H. Breen, *American Insurgents, American Patriots: The Revolution of the People* (New York: Farrar, Straus and Giroux, 2010); and *The Will of the People: The Revolutionary Birth of America* (Cambridge: Harvard University Press, 2019).

2. Rufus Choate (1856), quoted in Carli Conklin, *The Pursuit of Happiness in the Founding Era: An Intellectual History* (Columbia: University of Missouri Press, 2019), 4; John Locke, *An Essay Concerning Human Understanding in Focus,* ed. Gary Fuller, Robert Stecker, and John P. Wright (London: Routledge, 2000), 94.
3. Peter Clark, *British Clubs and Societies, 1580–1800: The Origins of an Associational World* (Oxford: Oxford University Press, 2000), 2; Ross Hinds and Declan Budd, *The Hist and Edmund Burke's Club* (Dublin: Lilliput Press, 1997); and Patrick M. Geoghegan, *Trinity College Dublin: The College Historical Society Oratory and Debate, 1770–2020* (Dublin: Lilliput Press, 2020).
4. David Hume, "The Sceptic," in *Essays Moral, Political, and Literary* (hereafter *EMPL*), ed. Eugene F. Miller, rev. ed. (Indianapolis: Liberty Fund, 1987), 159–80: 167.
5. "Act of COUNCIL regulating the Time for emptying and laying down Ashes, foul Water and other Nastiness," Edinburgh, July 12, 1749, National Library of Scotland, Broadsides from the Crawford Collection, https://digital.nls.uk/.
6. David Hume, "Of Refinement in the Arts," RA 2, Mil 269, Hume Texts Online, https://davidhume.org/; Lord Kames, Henry Home, *Essays on the Principles of Morality and Natural Religion* (Liberty Fund, 1779), ch. 8.
7. William Alexander, *The History of Women, from the Earliest Antiquity, to the Present Time*, 2 vols. (London: W. Strahan and T. Cadell, 1779), vol. 1: 103.
8. April 28, July 6, and December 15, 1774; Jan. 3, 1775; and June 20, 1776, Pantheon Minutes.
9. Hume, *EMPL,* 166, and James A. Harris, "Hume's Four Essays on Happiness and their Place in the Move from Morals to Politics," *Rivista di Storia della Filosofia* 62:3 (*Supplemento*: New Essays on David Hume, 2007), 223–35.
10. James Boswell, *Life of Johnson,* 6 vols., ed. George Birkbeck Hill and L. F. Powell (Oxford: Oxford University Press, 1934), vol. 2 (1766–1776): 9.
11. W. L. Calver, "A Loaded Cane from a Revolutionary Fort," *New-York Historical Society Quarterly Bulletin,* 14:3 (October 1930): 100–101.
12. Two accounts, one from *The Massachusetts Spy,* sympathetic with the protest, appeared in the *Essex Gazette,* Feb. 1, 1774; Young, *Shoemaker,* 46–51.
13. *Essex Gazette,* Feb. 1, 1774.
14. *Essex Gazette,* Feb. 1, 1774; Ann Hulton, *Letters of a Loyalist Lady: Being the*

Letters of Ann Hulton . . . 1767–1776, Jan. 31, 1774 (Cambridge, MA: Harvard University Press, 1927): 69–72.

15. Pantheon Minutes, Aug. 11, 1774; Mr. Sawbridge, Lord North, Mr. Pownall, March 14, 1774, in R. C. Simmons and P.D.G. Thomas, eds., *Proceedings and Debates of the British Parliaments Respecting North America, 1754–1783*, 5 vols. (White Plains, NY: Kraus International Publications, 1985), vol. 4 (Jan.–May 1774): 80, 59, 77.
16. Mr. Fuller, March 21, 1774, Mr. Rushout, March 14, 1774, in Simmons, and Thomas, *Proceedings and Debates*, vol. 4: 86, 64.
17. Norton, *1774: The Long Year of Revolution*, passim, and *Morning Post*, March 17, 1774.
18. *An Act for the better regulating the Government of the Province of the Massachusetts-Bay in New England*, 14 Geo. III, c. 45, 20 May 1774, https://avalon.law.yale.edu/.
19. Circular Letter of the Boston Committee of Correspondence (May 13, 1774), Avalon Project in Law, History and Diplomacy, https://avalon.law.yale.edu/.
20. Ollivier Hubert and François Furstenberg, *Entangling the Quebec Act: Transnational Contexts, Meanings, and Legacies in North America and the British Empire* (Montreal and Kingston: McGill-Queen's University Press, 2020); Mark Anderson, *Battle for Fourteenth Colony: America's War of Liberation in Canada, 1774–1776* (Hanover, NH: University Press of New England, 2013), 39; Guy Carleton to the Earl of Dartmouth, Quebec, Sept. 23, 1774, in *Documents relating to the Constitutional History of Canada, 1759–1791*, ed. Adam Shortt and Arthur G. Doughty, 2nd ed., part 2, vol. 1 (Ottawa: J. et L. Taché, 1918), vol. 1: 583.
21. *Pennsylvania Packet*, Aug. 29, 1774; *Newport Mercury*, Nov. 14, 1774; Stiles, *Diary*, Aug. 23, 1774, vol. 1: 455.
22. Cook, "Benjamin Franklin," 102–6.
23. Jonas Clarke Minot to Arnold Welles, Quebec, Sept. 9, 1774, and [Unsigned], Boston, Oct. 10, 1774, to Minot, *MHS, Collections of the MHS*, series 4 (Boston: Little, Brown, 1858), 4:70-71; Letter from Charleston, S.C, June 20, 1774; Frederick County (MD) Resolutions, June 20, 1774; and John Dickinson to Josiah Quincy, Fair Hill, June 20, 1774, all in Peter Force, ed., *American Archives, 4th series; containing a documentary history of the English colonies in North America*, 6 vols. (Washington, DC: M. St. Clair Clarke and P. Force, 1837), vol. 1: 28; Adams, *Diary*, Aug. 31, 1774, MHS, https://www.masshist.org/.
24. Charles C. Tansill, ed., *Documents Illustrative of the Formation of the Union of the American States* (Washington, DC: Government Printing Office, 1927), House Document No. 398, https://avalon.law.yale.edu/.

25. Abigail Adams to John Adams, Braintree, Aug. 19, 1774; John Adams to Abigail Adams, Prince Town, New Jersey, Aug. 28th, 1774; John Adams to Abigail Adams, Sept. 25, 1774; John Adams to Abigail Adams, Phyladelphia, Oct. 9, 1774, Adams Family Papers, MHS, https://www.masshist.org/.
26. Worthington Chauncey Ford, ed., *Journals of the Continental Congress, 1774–1789*, 34 vols. (Washington, DC: Government Printing Office, 1904), 1 (1774): 35 (Sept. 17, 1774), and Tansill, *Documents Illustrative of the Formation of the Union of the American States.*
27. Force, *American Archives*, vol. 2: 309–12.
28. Force, *American Archives*, vol. 2: 35–36; Janet Schaw, *Journal of a Lady of Quality*, 154, 181; Nicholas Cresswell, *The Journal of Nicholas Cresswell* (New York: Dial Press, 1924), 46.
29. *Virginia Gazette (Purdie & Dixon)*, March 3, 1774.
30. Letter from Carlisle, Pennsylvania, *Pennsylvania Gazette*, July 13, 1774, in Reuben Gold Thwaites and Louise Phelps Kellogg, eds., *Documentary History of Dunmore's War, 1774* (Madison: Wisconsin Historical Society, 1905), 57, and Eric Hinderaker and Peter C. Mancall, *At the Edge of Empire: The Backcountry in British North America* (Baltimore: Johns Hopkins University Press, 2003).
31. Circular letter of Col. William Preston, Smithfield, July 20, 1774, Isaac Shelby to John Shelby, Oct. 16, 1774, in Thwaites and Kellogg, *Documentary History*, 92, 273; James Madison to William Bradford, Virginia, Nov. 26, 1774, *Founders Online*, National Archives, https://founders.archives.gov/.
32. Madison to Bradford, Nov. 26, 1774.
33. Madison to Bradford, Nov. 26, 1774; *Essex Journal and Merimack Packet*, Oct. 19, 1774.
34. *Essex Journal and Merimack Packet*, Oct. 19, 1774.
35. *Essex Journal*, Jan. 19, 1774.
36. *Connecticut Courant*, Aug. 13 and Aug. 27, 1771.
37. Cynthia Kierner, "The Edenton Ladies: Women, Tea, and Politics in Revolutionary North Carolina," in Michele Gillespie and Sally G. McMillen, eds., *North Carolina Women* (Athens: University of Georgia Press, 2014), 12–33.
38. *Virginia Gazette (Purdie & Dixon)*, Nov. 3, 1774; *The Middlesex Journal, and Evening Advertiser*, Jan. 17, 1775; and *The Morning Chronicle, and London Advertiser*, Jan. 16, 1775. Information about tea from Richard Dillard, *The Historic Tea-Party of Edenton, North Carolina* (Edenton, NC: no publisher, 1898).
39. Arthur Iredell to James Iredell, "London, Queen Square, Jan. 31st, 1775," in Griffith J. McRee, ed., *Life and Correspondence of James Iredell*, 2 vols. (New York: D. Appleton and Co., 1857), vol. 1: 230–32.
40. Kierner, "Edenton Ladies," 24–30.

41. Ad for ROAD by Josiah Hall, *Virgina Gazette* (Pinckney), Williamsburg, June 15, 1775.
42. *Essex Journal and Merimack Packet,* Feb. 16, 1774.
43. "On the Death of the Rev. Dr. Sewell, 1769"; "On the Death of Rev. Mr. George Whitefield, 1770"; "On the Death of a Young Lady of Five Years Old," "To S. M. a Young African Painter, on Seeing his Works," and "To the Right Honourable WILLIAM, Earl of DARTMOUTH, His Majesty's Principal Secretary of State for North-America," in Wheatley, *Writings of Phillis Wheatley,* 57–60, 100, 81–82.

Chapter 5: A Castle in Anomabu

1. Paul Erdmann Isert, "Revolt on a Danish Slaving Voyage," *The Ghana Reader: History, Culture, Politics,* ed. Kwasi Konadu and Clifford C. Campbell (Durham, NC: Duke University Press, 2016): 131–38: 131; Ottobah Cugoano, "Narrative of the Enslavement of Ottobah Cugoano" (London: Hatchard and Co. and J. and A. Arch, 1825), 124, https://docsouth.unc.edu/; Rebecca Shumway, *The Fante and the Transatlantic Slave Trade* in *Rochester Studies in African History and Diaspora,* ed. Toyin Falola (Rochester, NY: University of Rochester Press, 2011), 9; Randy J. Sparks, *Where the Negroes Are Masters: An African Port in the Era of the Slave Trade* (Cambridge, MA: Harvard University Press, 2014); Trevor R. Getz, "Mechanisms of Acquisition and Exchange in Late Eighteenth Century Anomabu: Reconsidering a Cross-Section of the Atlantic Slave Trade," *African Economic History* 31 (2003): 75–89; *Itineraries,* vol. 1:76, in Ezra Stiles Papers [microfilm], Redwood Library and Athenaeum cited in Sam Dinnie, "The Labor Behind the Learned: A Reexamination of Ezra Stiles," Newport Historical Society, Sept. 8, 2023, https://newporthistory.org/.
2. Ruth Fisher, ed., "Extracts from the Records of the African Companies [Part 4]," *Journal of Negro History* 13:3 (1928): 367–94: 372, and Sparks, *Where the Negroes Are Masters,* 77.
3. On a Barbados-bound ship, Sessarakoo was illegally sold. Corrantee managed to redeem him, and Sessarakoo continued to London as a foreign dignitary. Sparks, *Where the Negroes Are Masters,* 45.
4. Edmund S. Morgan, *American Slavery, American Freedom* (New York: Norton, 1975) as well as David Brion Davis, *The Problem of Slavery in the Age of Revolution, 1770–1823* (Ithaca, NY: Cornell University Press, 1975); Sparks, *Where the Negroes Are Masters,* 120; Richard Brew to William Devaynes, Castle Brew, May 2, 1770, T 70/1531, 94, NA; "log," *Oxford English Dictionary Online.*
5. Shumway, *Fante,* 4, 2; Sparks, *Where the Negroes Are Masters,* 127; John Thornton, *Warfare in Africa, 1500–1800* (London: UCL Press, 1999).
6. Lila O'Leary Chambers, "Alcohol Diplomacy, Gender and Power in the

Late Seventeenth-Century Gold Coast Slaving Complex," *Past & Present* 264:1 (2024): 48–83.

7. Shumway, *Fante,* 108, 2, 133, and Sparks, *Where the Negroes Are Masters,* ch. 1; "Cape Coast Castle, Aug. 11, 1772, Oct. 10, 1781 [Company of Merchants trading to Africa: Acts of Council (Cape Coast Castle)], T 70/152, NA; John Bell to John Fletcher, Cape Coast Roade, Dec. 15, 1776, in Elizabeth Donnan, *Documents Illustrative of the History of the Slave Trade to America,* 4 vols. (Washington, DC: Carnegie Institute, 1930–35 [1932]), vol. 3: 323.
8. On slavery and freedom in the American Revolution, Benjamin Quarles, *The Negro in the American Revolution,* reissued edition, introduction by Gary B. Nash (Chapel Hill: Omohundro Institute of Early American History and Culture/University of North Carolina Press, 1996 [1961]); Sylvia Frey, *Water from the Rock: Black Resistance in a Revolutionary Age* (Princeton, NJ: Princeton University Press, 1991); Gary B. Nash, *The Forgotten Fifth: African Americans in the Age of Revolution* (Cambridge, MA: Harvard University Press, 2006); Annette Gordon-Reed, *The Hemingses of Monticello: An American Family* (New York: Norton, 2008); Douglas Egerton, *Death or Liberty: African Americans and Revolutionary America* (New York: Oxford University Press, 2009); Catherine Adams and Elizabeth H. Pleck, *Love of Freedom: Black Women in Colonial and Revolutionary New England* (Oxford: Oxford University Press, 2010); Alan Gilbert, *Black Patriots and Loyalists: Fighting for Emancipation in the War for Independence* (Chicago: University of Chicago Press, 2012) as well as work on Sierra Leone (see ch. 13); *Connecticut Gazette,* March 11, 1774.
9. Neil Roberts, *Freedom as Marronage* (Chicago: University of Chicago Press, 2015).
10. Voyage of the *Venus,* Voyage ID 36207, Captain William Pinnegar, 1757 from Anomabu to Kingston, Jamaica, Slave Voyages Trans-Atlantic Slave Trade Database, https://www.slavevoyages.org/; Henry Smeathman to Dru Drury, July 10, 1773, Uppsala University Library, Ms. D. 26–28, quoted in Starr Douglas, "The Making of Scientific Knowledge in an Age of Slavery: Henry Smeathman, Sierra Leone, and Natural History," *Journal of Colonialism and Colonial History* 9:3 (2008); Sparks, *Where the Negroes Are Masters,* 17–18.
11. Morgan, *Gentle Puritan,* 36.
12. Jay Coughtry, *The Notorious Triangle: Rhode Island and the African Slave Trade, 1700–1807* (Philadelphia: Temple University Press, 1981), 25; Jonathan D. Sassi, "'This whole country have their hands full of Blood this day': Transcription and Introduction of an Antislavery Sermon Manuscript Attributed to the Reverend Samuel Hopkins," *Proceedings of the American Antiquarian Society* (2004): 29–92: 50.
13. David S. Lovejoy, "Samuel Hopkins: Religion, Slavery, and the Revolution," *New England Quarterly* 40:2 (1967): 227–43, and Morgan, *Gentle Puritan.*

14. Cherry Fletcher Bamberg, "Bristol Yamma and John Quamine in Rhode Island," *Rhode Island History* 73:1 (2015): 4–31: 9–10.
15. Catherine A. Brekus, *Sarah Osborn's World: The Rise of Evangelical Christianity in Early America* (New Haven, CT: Yale University Press, 2013), 252–53.
16. "William Ellery Channing letter," in Wilkins Updike, *Memoirs of the Rhode-Island Bar* (Boston: Thomas H. Webb & Co., 1842), 100.
17. Bamberg, "Bristol Yamma," 10, 9.
18. Waldstreicher, *Odyssey of Phillis Wheatley*, 112–14, and Tara Bynum, "Phillis Wheatley on Friendship," *Legacy* 31:1 (2014): 42–51.
19. Bob Harris, *Gambling in Britain in the Long Eighteenth Century* (Cambridge: Cambridge University Press, 2022), especially 126–222, and John Wood Sweet, *Bodies Politic: Negotiating Race in the American North, 1730–1830* (Baltimore: Johns Hopkins University Press, 2003), 78.
20. Bamberg, "Bristol Yamma," 14–15.
21. Stiles, *Diary*, vol. 1: 503.
22. Henry Laurens to Richard Oswald, C[harles]T[own], Jan. 4, 1775, and John Laurens to Henry Laurens, London, Jan. 20, 1775, in David R. Chesnutt, ed., *The Papers of Henry Laurens* (hereafter *PHL*), 16 vols. (Columbia: South Carolina Historical Society / University of South Carolina Press, 1985), vol. 5: 22, vol. 10: 37.
23. *Rivington's New York Gazette*, Feb. 2, 1775.
24. Henry to Thomas Denham, C[harles]T[own], Feb. 7, 1775, *PHL*, vol. 10: 63.
25. Abigail Adams to Mercy Otis Warren, Feb. 3, 1775, *Founders Online*, National Archives, https://founders.archives.gov/; Brian DeLay, "The Arms Trade and American Revolutions," *American Historical Review* 128:3 (Sept. 2023): 1144–81; Henry Laurens to John Laurens, CharlesTown, Jan. 22, 1775, Henry Laurens to John Delagaye, CharlesTown, Jan. 25, 1775, and Henry Laurens to Thomas Denham, C[harles]T[own], Feb. 7, 1775, *PHL* 10: 45, 50, 63; Stiles, *Diary*, vol. 1: 514.
26. "To the King's Most Excellent Majesty in Council: The humble Petition and Memorial of the Assembly of Jamaica, Voted in Assembly the 28th of December, 1774," Force, *American Archives*, vol. 1:1073.
27. "To the King's Most Excellent Majesty in Council: The humble Petition and Memorial of the Assembly of Jamaica, Voted in Assembly the 28th of December, 1774," Force, *American Archives*, vol 1:1073; O'Shaughnessy, *Empire Divided*, 138–42; Stiles, *Diary*, vol. 1: 519.
28. Stiles, *Diary*, vol. 1: 519, 521.
29. Stiles, "Sermons on Thanksgivings," Nov. 20, 1760, in Morgan, *Gentle Puritan*, 213; Sarah Osborn quoted in Peterson, *The City-State of Boston*, 306.
30. Stiles, *Diary*, vol. 1: 527.
31. Force, *American Archives*, vol. 2: 318–19.

32. "London," *St James Chronicle,* April 6–8, 1775.
33. Stiles, *Diary,* vol. 1: 530.
34. Deposition of Elijah Sanderson, Lexington, April 25, 1775, Force, *American Archives,* vol. 2: 489.
35. Force, *American Archives,* vol. 2: 363.
36. Stephen Conway, *A Short History of the American Revolution* (London: Bloomsbury, 2023), 55–56.
37. Force, *American Archives,* vol. 2: 488.
38. *New-England Chronicle, or, the Essex Gazette,* May 12, 1775, 2.
39. Anonymous to Rogers, April 23, 1775, WWM/R150-2, Papers of 2nd Marquis of Rockingham, Sheffield City Archives.
40. *New-England Chronicle,* May 12, 1775, 2.
41. Stiles, *Diary,* vol. 1: 537.
42. Psalm 79:2–3, King James Version.
43. Stiles, *Diary,* April 23, 1775, vol. 1: 538.
44. Stephen Conway, *A Short History of the American Revolutionary War* (London: I.B. Tauris, 2013), 57.
45. Stiles, *Diary,* May 17, 1775, vol. 1: 553.
46. Stiles, *Diary,* June 20, 1775, vol. 1: 574–75.
47. Captain Solomon Uhhaunauwaunmut Speech, April 11, 1775, Force, *American Archives,* vol. 2:315.
48. Watertown, June 8, 1775, Force, *American Archives,* vol. 2: 937.
49. [Le Congrès Général de l'Amérique Septentrionale], *Lettre Adressée aux Habitans de la Province de Québec* (Philadelphie: Fleury Mesplet, 1774), and James H. Hutson, *A Decent Respect to the Opinions of Mankind: Congressional State Papers, 1774–1776* (Washington, DC: Library of Congress, 1975).
50. Victor Coffin, *The Province of Quebec and the Early American Revolution,* Bulletin of University of Wisconsin History series (Madison: University of Wisconsin Press, 1896), 485.
51. Henry Livingston and Gaillard Hunt, "Journal of Major Henry Livingston, of the Third New York Continental Line, August to December 1775," ed. Gaillard Hunt, *Pennsylvania Magazine of History and Biography* 22:1 (1898), 9–33: 29, and *Connecticut Gazette,* June 16, 1775.
52. "To the Oppressed Inhabitants of Canada, Pennsylvania Journal, June 14, 1775," Hutson, *A Decent Respect,* 85–86; Jean-Paul de Lagrave, *Voltaire's Man in America,* trans. Arnold Bennett (Montreal: Robert Davies Multimedia Publishing, 1997), 45.
53. George Washington to Richard Henry Lee, Cambridge, Nov. 27, 1775, in W. W. Abbot, ed., *The Papers of George Washington, Revolutionary War Series* (Charlottesville: University of Virginia Press, 1987), 32 vols., vol. 2 (Sept. 16, 1775–Dec. 31, 1775): 436.

54. Force, *American Archives,* vol. 3: 482, 483, 486, 494, 488.
55. "An Address of the Twelve United Colonies of North-America by their Representatives in Congress to the People of Ireland" (Philadelphia: William and Thomas Bradford, 1775), Hutson, *A Decent Respect,* 114–16.
56. *Virginia Gazette (Dixon & Hunter),* Oct. 28, 1775.
57. *Pennsylvania Gazette,* March 1, 1775, in Hutson, *A Decent Respect,* 135–37.
58. Fenn, *Pox Americana,* 13-15.
59. George Washington to Martha Washington, June 18, 1775, *Founders Online,* National Archives, https://founders.archives.gov.
60. Hutson, *A Decent Respect,* 91.
61. Kennedy, ed., *Journals of the House of Burgesses,* vol. 13: 256.
62. Hutson, *A Decent Respect,* 130.
63. "End of July 1775," Creswell, *Journal,* 99–100.
64. Henry Laurens to John Laurens, Charles Town, June 7, 1775, *PHL,* vol. 10: 162–63.
65. Henry [Laurens] to John Laurens, C[harles]T[own], Aug. 20, 1775, *PHL,* vol. 10: 321.
66. J. William Harris, *The Hanging of Thomas Jeremiah: A Free Black Man's Encounter with Liberty* (New Haven, CT: Yale University Press, 2009).
67. Petition of James Arbuckle, June 9, 1775, in John Pendleton Kennedy, ed., *Journal of the House of Burgesses of Virginia,* vol. 13 (1773–1776): 208.
68. Enclosure, William Campbell to John Coram, *PHL,* vol. 10: 334.
69. John Laurens to Henry [Laurens], London, Oct. 4, 1775, *PHL,* vol. 10: 450.
70. *Pennsylvania Journal, or Weekly Advertiser,* Dec. 6, 1775.
71. Thanks to Dr. Erin Rowe for guidance on this point.
72. George Washington to Richard Henry Lee, Cambridge, Nov. 27, 1775, in the *Papers of George Washington Digital Edition, Revolutionary War Series,* vol. 2 (Sept. 16, 1775–Dec. 1775): 436.
73. Levi Hart, *Liberty Described and Recommended . . .* (Hartford, CT: Eben Watson, 1774).
74. Hart, *Liberty Described,* 9.
75. Hart, *Liberty Described,* 16.
76. Hart, *Liberty Described,* 18.
77. Hart, *Liberty Described,* 20.
78. "To the SONS of LIBERTY in CONNECTICUT," *Providence Gazette and Country Journal,* Oct. 22, 1774, 2.
79. Samuel Hopkins, *A Dialogue Concerning the Slavery of the Africans* (Norwich, CT: Judah P. Spooner, 1776), 28, and Sassi, "'This whole country,'" 91–92.
80. Samuel Hopkins to Thomas Cushing, Newport, Dec. 29, 1775, *Founders Online,* National Archives, https://founders.archives.gov/.
81. Zara Anishanslin, *The Painter's Fire: A Forgotten History of the Artists Who*

Championed the American Revolution (Cambridge, MA: Harvard University Press, 2025), 148–57.

82. *Connecticut Gazette,* March 11, 1774; Mark Peterson, *The City-State of Boston* (Princeton, NJ: Princeton University Press, 2019): 294–325.
83. Barbara DeWolfe, ed., *Discoveries of America: Personal Accounts of British Emigrants to North America During the Revolutionary Era* (Cambridge: Cambridge University Press, 1997), 210–12.
84. Margaret Livingston to [Catharine Livingston], Oct. 20, 1776, Ridley Papers, MHS, quoted in Linda K. Kerber, *Women of the Republic: Intellect and Ideology in Revolutionary America* (New York: Norton, 1980), 35.
85. Undated poem by Grace Growden Galloway, Joseph Galloway Family Papers, Manuscripts Division, Library of Congress; Norton, *Liberty's Daughters,* 45.
86. Stiles, *Diary,* vol. 1: 351.
87. *Virginia Gazette (Dixon & Hunter),* Dec. 16, 1775.
88. Samuel Hopkins to Thomas Cushing, Newport, Dec. 29, 1775.
89. Bamberg, "Bristol Yamma," 21.

Chapter 6: A Wall in Québec

1. *Journal of the Most Remarkable Events which happened in Canada between the months of July 1775 and June 1776* (hereafter *Journal*), Library and Archives of Canada, MG23 B7, 32–33. Useful accounts of Canadian relations include George M. Wrong, *Canada and the American Revolution: The Disruption of the First British Empire* (New York: Macmillan, 1935); Gustave Lanctôt, *Canada and the American Revolution, 1774–1783,* trans. Margaret M. Cameron (Toronto: Clarke, Irwin, & Company, 1967); Mark R. Anderson, *The Battle for the Fourteenth Colony: America's War of Liberation in Canada, 1774–1776* (Hanover, NH: University Press of New England, 2013); Gavin K. Watt, *Poisoned by Lies and Hypocrisy: America's First Attempt to Bring Liberty to Canada, 1775–1776* (Toronto: Dundurn, 2014); Amy Noel Ellison, "Montgomery's Misfortune: American Defeat at Quebec and the March Toward Independence, 1775–1776," *Early American Studies* 15:3 (2017): 591–616; and Lennox, *North of America.*
2. Robert C. Bray and Paul E. Bushnell, *Diary of a Common Soldier in the American Revolution, 1775–1783: An Annotated Edition of the Military Journal of Jeremiah Greenman* (hereafter *Greenman*) (DeKalb: Northern Illinois University Press, 1978), 23 (Dec. 30–31, 1775).
3. *Greenman,* Dec. 30 and 31, 1775, 23.
4. Caleb Haskell, Dec. 15, 1775, in Kenneth Roberts, ed., *March to Quebec: Journals of the Members of Arnold's Expedition* (New York: Doubleday, Doran & Co., 1940), 484.

5. *Journal,* 35.
6. *Journal,* 43.
7. *Greenman,* xiv.
8. *Greenman,* "Obituary," 306.
9. Richard Henry Lee to Catharine Macaulay, Philadelphia, Nov. 29, 1775, *Letters of Delegates to Congress, 1774–1789,* 15 vols., ed. Paul H. Smith (Washington, DC: Library of Congress, 1977): vol. 2 (Sept.–Dec. 1775): 404–7: 405.
10. François Baby, Gabriel Taschereau, and Jenkin Williams, *Quebec During the American Invasion, 1775–1776: The Journal of François Baby, Gabriel Taschereau, and Jenkin Williams,* ed. Michael P. Gabriel, trans. S. Pascale Dewey (East Lansing: Michigan State University Press, 2005), 15.
11. Benedict Arnold to the Continental Congress, "Crown Point June 13 1775," in Force, *American Archives,* vol. 2: 976.
12. Jacob Bayley to New-York Congress, Newbury, June 29, 1775, in Force, *American Archives,* vol. 2: 1134.
13. George Washington to John Hancock, Camp at Cambridge, Sept. 21, 1775, *Founders Online,* National Archives, https://founders.archives.gov/.
14. Stiles, *Diary,* Sept. 15, 1775, vol. 1: 615.
15. *Pennsylvania Packet,* Jan. 22, 1776.
16. Valentin Jautard, quoted in Jean-Paul de Lagrave, *Voltaire's Man in America,* 61.
17. Anderson, *Battle for the Fourteenth Colony,* 17; Gratien Allaire and Celine Cooper, "Province of Quebec, 1763–1791," *The Canadian Encyclopedia,* https://www.thecanadianencyclopedia.ca/.
18. *Journal,* 32–33.
19. John Hancock to Richard Montgomery, Nov. 30, 1775, *Letters of Delegates to Congress,* vol. 2, September 1775–December 1775, Library of Congress, item 76002592, online at https://www.loc.gov/.
20. Livingston, "Journal of Major Henry Livingston," 22.
21. *Boston Gazette, or, Country Journal,* January 15, 1776.
22. George Washington to John Hancock, Camp at Cambridge, Sept. 21, 1775, National Archives, *Founders Online,* https://founders.archives.gov/.
23. Aaron Burr quoted in Thomas A. Desjardin, *Through a Howling Wilderness: Benedict Arnold's March to Quebec, 1775* (New York: St. Martin's Griffin, 2006), 54.
24. Haskell, in Kenneth Roberts, *March to Quebec,* 481.
25. Richard Montgomery to Janet Montgomery, Montreal, Nov. 24, [1775], in Louise Livingston Hunt, *Biographical Notes Concerning General Richard Montgomery, together with hitherto unpublished letters* (Poughkeepsie, NY: "News" Book and Job Printing House, 1876), 15.
26. Haskell, in Roberts, *March to Quebec,* 482.

27. Haskell, in Roberts, *March to Quebec,* 478.
28. *Greenman,* 7, 14–18, especially 14, 18.
29. John Joseph Henry, "Journal," in *March to Quebec,* 326.
30. George Washington to John Hancock, Camp at Cambridge, Sept. 21, 1775, National Archives, *Founders Online,* https://founders.archives.gov/.
31. *Greenman,* Dec. 23, 1775, 23.
32. *Journal,* Dec. 26, 1775, 35.
33. Haskell, in Roberts, *March to Quebec,* 486.
34. *Greenman,* Dec. 23, 1775, 23.
35. Haskell, in Roberts, *March to Quebec,* 486.
36. Ellison, "Montgomery's Misfortune," 603.
37. Haskell, in Roberts, *March to Quebec,* 489.
38. *Journal,* Jan. 1, 1776, 44.
39. *Journal,* Jan. 1, 1776, 45.
40. *Greenman,* Dec. 31, 1775–Jan. 2, 1776, 23–24.
41. *Journal,* Jan. 1, 1776, 47.
42. Haskell, in Roberts, *March to Quebec,* 488.
43. *Pennsylvania Packet,* Jan. 22, 1776.
44. Guy Carleton to Earl of Dartmouth, Quebec, Nov. 11, 1774, and Guy Carleton to Earl of Dartmouth, "Montreal 7 June 1775," in *Documents Relating to the Constitutional History of Canada, 1759–1791,* ed. Adam Shortt and Arthur G. Doughty, 2nd ed., part 2 (Ottawa: J. de l. Taché, 1918), vol. 2: 588, 665.
45. Baby et al., *Quebec During the American Invasion,* 60.
46. Lennox, *North of America,* 43.
47. *Quebec Gazette,* Oct. 5, 1775, reprinted in Historical Section of the General Staff, eds., *A History of the Organization, Development and Services of the Military and Naval Forces of Canada from the Peace of Paris in 1763 to the Present Time,* 2 vols. (Ottawa: Department of Militia and Defence of Canada, 1919), vol. 1: 87–89.
48. *Journal,* 23.
49. *Journal,* 113.
50. Lennox, *North of America,* 20, and Baby et al., *Quebec During the American Invasion,* xv.
51. *Journal,* 24.
52. *Journal,* 20.
53. *Greenman,* Dec. 10, 1775, 22.
54. "Copy of a Note from Major [Andrew] Skene to Fitz Maurice, in May Fair [London], 28 Jan. 1776, Co5, 1107, p 335, LAC," quoted in Anderson, *Battle for the Fourteenth Colony,* 220.
55. Commissioners to Canada to [John Hancock], Montreal, May 6, 1776, *Founders Online,* National Archives, https://founders.archives.gov/.

56. Major General Philip Schuyler to General George Washington, Fort George, April 27, 1776, *Founders Online*, National Archives, https://founders.archives.gov/.
57. Commissioners to Canada to [John Hancock], Montreal, May 8, 1776, *Founders Online*, National Archives, https://founders.archives.gov/.
58. Baby et al., *Quebec During the American Invasion*, 23.
59. Mark R. Anderson, ed., *The Invasion of Canada by the Americans, 1775–1776, as told Through Jean-Baptiste Badeaux's Three Rivers Journals and New York Captain William Gosforth's Letters*, trans. Teresa L. Meadows (Albany: State University of New York Press, 2016), 109, and Appendix I ("The Accounts of the Three Rivers Ursuline Nuns") 171–83, especially 183, footnote 42.
60. Guy Johnson to Lord Dartmouth, Montreal, Oct. 12, 1775, in *Historical Section of the General Staff*, in *Documents Illustrative of the Canadian Constitution* (Toronto: Carswell, 1891), 95–96.
61. "Speech of Captain Brant to Lord George Germain"/"The Speech of Thayendenegeh a Chief, accompanied by Oteroughyanento a Warrior, both of the Six Nations, March 14, 1776," E. B. O'Callahan and John Romeyn Brodhead, eds., *Documents Relative to the Colonial History of the State of New-York: Procured in Holland, England, and France*, 15 vols. (Albany, NY: Weeds, Parsons, and Company, 1857), vol. 8: 670–71.
62. "The letter to the Inhabitants of the Province of Canada," Jan. 24, 1776, in *Journals of the Continental Congress, 1774–1789*, vol. 4 (Jan. 1–June 4, 1776): 85–86.
63. Alan Taylor, *Divided Ground;* Lennox, *North of America*, 43.
64. Brantz Mayer, ed., *Journal of Charles Carroll of Carrollton during his Visit to Canada in 1776* (Baltimore: Maryland Historical Society/J. Murphy, 1845), 80 (May 23, 1776).
65. Commissioners to Canada to [John Hancock], Montreal, May 8, 1776, *Founders Online*, National Archives, https://founders.archives.gov/.
66. Moses Hazen to Philip J. Schuyler, April 1, 1776, George Washington Papers, Series 4, General Correspondence, https://loc.getarchive.net/.
67. Stiles, *Diary*, Jan. 20, 1776, vol. 1: 658.
68. General George Washington to Brigadier General Benedict Arnold, Cambridge, Jan. 27, 1776, *Founders Online*, National Archives, https://founders.archives.gov/.
69. "Short History of my Conduct in America," Thomas Paine to Henry Laurens, Jan. 14, 1779, *The Writings of Thomas Paine*, 4 vols., ed. Moncure Daniel Conway (New York: G. P. Putnam's Sons, 1896), vol. 4: 430, https://oll.libertyfund.org/.
70. [Thomas Paine], *Common Sense; Addressed to the Inhabitants of America*, 2nd ed. (Philadelphia: W. & T. Bradford, 1776), online at Project Gutenberg,

paragraphs 163, 139, 96, 125, 140, 141, 160, 86. See also Sophia Rosenfeld, *Common Sense: A Political History* (Cambridge, MA: Harvard University Press, 2011), 136–80.

71. William Smith, *An Oration in Memory of General Montgomery, and of the Officers and Soldiers, who fell with him, December 31, 1775, before Quebec* (Philadelphia: John Dunlap, 1776), 29, and "Proposed Alterations in William Smith's Oration on General Montgomery, [before 6 March 1776]," *Founders Online,* National Archives, Franklin Documents, https://founders.archives.gov/.
72. Basil Keith to George Germain, March 27 1776, CO/137/71, 98, NA.
73. Creswell, *Journal,* Jan. 26, 1776, 136.
74. Baron de Kalb to Duc de Choiseul, Nouvelle York, Feb. 28, 1768, NAF 9435, BnF Richelieu, Paris.
75. Stephen Moylan to Joseph Reed, Jan. 2, 1776, 4, New-York Historical Society, item 129835, https://digitalcollections.nyhistory.org/.
76. William Smith, *An Oration in Memory of General Montgomery* (Philadelphia: John Dunlap, 1776), 25.
77. Smith, *Oration,* 34, and Ann Eliza Bleecker, "Elegy on the death of Gen. Montgomery," in *The Posthumous Works of Ann Eliza Bleecker* (New York: T. and J. Swords, 1793), 226.
78. *Maryland Journal,* March 20, 1776.
79. Smith, *Oration,* 38.
80. [Thomas Paine], *A Dialogue between the Ghost of General Montgomery just arrived from the Elysian Fields; and an American delegate* (Philadelphia: R. Bell, 1776), 16.
81. Paine, *Dialogue,* 5, 13.
82. Charles Lee to President of Congress, Williamsburg, April 6, 1776, Force, *American Archives,* vol. 5: 800.
83. Robert R. Livingston to Thomas Lynch, January 1776, *Letters of Delegates to Congress,* Library of Congress, 26 vols., vol. 3, https://www.loc.gov/collections/ (hereafter *LDC*). On the general situation, see John Adams, "Notes on Foreign Alliances," March 1, 1776, *LDC,* vol 3.
84. Samuel Adams to Samuel Cooper, April 3, 1776, *LDC,* vol. 3.
85. James and Mercy Otis Warren to John Adams, Nov. 14, 1775, *Founders Online,* National Archives, https://founders.archives.gov/.
86. *New-York Gazette, and Weekly Mercury,* April 8, 1776.
87. "Candidus," Philadelphia, March 6, 1776, Force, *American Archives,* vol. 5: 88.
88. "An American," March 15, 1776, Force, *American Archives,* vol. 5: 227.
89. "Salus Populi," Force, *American Archives,* vol. 5: 98.
90. "To the Inhabitants of New York," New York, April 11, 1776, Force, *American Archives,* vol. 5: 856.

91. "A Lover of Order," Philadelphia, March 9, 1776, Force, *American Archives,* vol. 5: 146.
92. Maier, *American Scripture,* 47–97.
93. Brad Jones, *Resisting Independence: Popular Loyalism in the Revolutionary British Atlantic* (Ithaca, NY: Cornell University Press, 2021), 149, and Holger Hoock, *Scars of Independence: America's Violent Birth* (New York: Crown, 2017).
94. George Washington to Benedict Arnold, Jan. 27, 1776, *Founders Online,* National Archives, https://founders.archives.gov/.
95. Robert Morris to Horatio Gates, Apr. 6, 1776, *LDC,* vol. 4.
96. Caesar Rodney to Thomas Rodney, Philadelphia, May 29, 1776, *LDC,* vol. 4.
97. Major General Philip Schuyler to General George Washington, April 27, 1776, *Founders Online,* National Archives, https://founders.archives.gov/.
98. Lee Resolution (1776), National Archives, Milestone Documents, https://www.archives.gov/.
99. Richard Henry Lee to Landon Carter, Philadelphia, June 2, 1776, Gilder Lehrman Institute of American History, Gilder Lehrman Collection, #GLC03421, https://www.gilderlehrman.org/.
100. John H. Powell, ed., "Notes and Documents: Speech of John Dickinson Opposing the Declaration of Independence, July 1, 1776," *Pennsylvania Magazine of History and Biography* 65 (Oct. 1941): 458–81: 471, 478, 475.
101. "candid," Oxford English Dictionary, http:/www.oed.com/, and Samuel Johnson, *Dictionary,* 4th ed. (1773), https://johnsonsdictionaryonline.com/.
102. Allen, *Our Declaration,* 76.
103. Dull, *Diplomatic History,* 52, and Leonard J. Sadosky, *Revolutionary Negotiations: Indians, Empires, and Diplomats in the Founding of America* (Charlottesville: University of Virginia Press, 2009), 84.
104. "A Treaty of Alliance and Friendship Entered into and concluded by, and between the Governors of the State of Massachusetts Bay, and the Delegates of the St. Johns, and Micmack Tribes of Indians," July 19, 1776, Guy Johnson Papers, Series III, Gen Mss 494, Box 2, folder 38, Beinecke Library, Yale University, object 230211, archives.yale.edu/.
105. John Dickinson et al., Articles of Confederation & perpetual Union … Draft, June 17–July 1, 1776, *LDC,* vol. 4.
106. *Journals of the Continental Congress,* vol. 9 (Oct. 3–Dec. 31, 1777): 981.
107. *Greenman,* 27, 29, 31, 33.
108. DuVal, *Independence Lost,* xxi.
109. DuVal, *Independence Lost,* xxi, 351.
110. *Boston Gazette and Country Journal,* July 29, 1776, and Sassi, "'This whole country,'" 60–61.
111. *Newport Mercury,* June 10, 1776.

Chapter 7: A Village in Hessen-Kassel

1. "King of the Golden Mountain," in Jacke Zipes, trans. and ed., *The Complete First Edition of the Original Folk and Fairy Tales of the Brothers Grimm* (Princeton, NJ: Princeton University Press, 2014), vol. 2, story 6, 301–7.
2. Peter K. Taylor, *Indentured to Liberty: Peasant Life and the Hessian Military State, 1688–1815* (Ithaca, NY: Cornell University Press, 1994), 240–41.
3. Samuel Adams to John Adams, Baltimore, Jan. 9, 1777, *LDC*, vol. 6 (Jan. 1 1770–April 30 1777): 64.
4. William Hooper to Robert Livingstone, Sept. 25, 1776, *LDC*, vol. 5 (Aug. 16, 1776–Dec. 31, 1776): 238.
5. Josiah Bartlett to John Langdon, Philadelphia, May 19, 1776, *LDC*, vol. 4 (May 1776–Aug. 1776): 39.
6. On violence in the Revolutionary War, see Sharon Block, "Rape Without Women: Print Culture and the Politicization of Rape, 1765–1815," *Journal of American History* 89: 3 (2002); Sharon Block, "Rape in the American Revolution: Process, Reaction, and Public Re-Creation," in *Sexual Violence in Conflict Zones: From the Ancient World to the Era of Human Rights*, ed. Elizabeth D. Heineman (Philadelphia: University of Pennsylvania Press, 2011), 25–38, 262–64; Hoock, *Scars of Independence;* Ned Blackhawk, *The Rediscovery of America: Native Peoples and the Unmaking of U.S. History* (New Haven, CT: Yale University Press, 2023), chs. 5–6.
7. Wayne E. Lee, *Barbarians and Brothers: Anglo-American Warfare, 1500–1865* (Oxford: Oxford University Press, 2011).
8. Jakob Piel in Bruce E. Burgoyne, ed. and trans., *Defeat, Disaster, and Dedication: The Diaries of the Hessian Officers Jakob Piel and Andreas Wiederhold* (Westminster, MD: Heritage Books, 1997), 23.
9. Reginald Savory, *His Britannic Majesty's Army in Germany During the Seven Years' War* (Oxford: Clarendon Press, 1966), 126, 134.
10. Friederike Baer, *Hessians: German Soldiers in the American Revolutionary War* (Oxford: Oxford University Press, 2022), 45. Baer's is the best account of the Hessians.
11. Andreas Wiederhold to Georg Ernst von und zu Gilsa, Weddewarden in Frisia, April 1, 1776, in *Krieg in Amerika und Aufklärung in Hessen: die Privatbriefe (1772–1784) an George Ernst von und zu Gilsa* (Marburg: Hessisches Landesamt für geschichtliche Landeskunde, 2010), 81–83. All Wiederhold letter translations by Anthony Pearsall unless otherwise noted.
12. Suffolk to Faucitt, St. James, Nov. 14, 1775, SP 81/181, NA.
13. Baer, *Hessians,* 31.
14. Baer, *Hessians,* 16.
15. Frederick the Great of Prussia to Voltaire, a Potsdam, le 18 juin 1776, Vol-

taire, *Oeuvres Complètes de Voltaire,* 13 vols. (Paris: Th. Desoer, 1817), vol. 12 (*Correspondance Particulière*): 629.

16. *The Connecticut Courant,* July 1, 1776.
17. Peter Taylor, *Indentured to Liberty,* 209.
18. Johann Ewald, *Diary of the American War: A Hessian Journal,* trans. and ed. Joseph P. Tustin (New Haven, CT: Yale University Press, 1979), xix, and Baer, *Hessians,* 2.
19. Baer, *Hessians,* 39, 41–42.
20. Baer, *Hessians,* 40.
21. Charles Rainsford, "Commissary Rainsford's Journal of Transactions, etc, 1776–1778," New-York Historical Society, Publication Fund, vol. 12, *Collections of the NYHS for the year 1879* (New York: New-York Historical Society, 1879): 313–543: 406.
22. General Riedesel to Baroness von Riedesel, Leifert, Feb. 22, 1776, in Frederika Charlotte Louise [von Massow] von Riedesel, *Baroness von Riedesel and the American Revolution: Journal and Correspondence of a Tour of Duty, 1776–1783,* trans. and ed., Marvin L. Brown, Jr., with the assistance of Marta Huth (Chapel Hill: Institute of Early American History and Culture for the University of North Carolina, 1965), especially chs. 3–4. Since the original was destroyed in World War II, this translation uses a nineteenth-century published version.
23. Riedesel, *Baroness von Riedesel,* 3–4, 5, 13.
24. Andrew Jackson O'Shaughnessy, *The Men Who Lost America: British Leadership, the American Revolution, and the Fate of the Empire* (New Haven, CT: Yale University Press, 2013), 88.
25. Ambrose Serle, *The American Journal of Ambrose Serle, Secretary to Lord Howe, 1776–1778,* ed. Edward H. Tatum, Jr. (San Marino: The Huntington Library, 1940), May 26–29, 1776, 9.
26. O'Shaughnessy, *Men Who Lost America,* 90.
27. Earl of Sandwich to Earl of Suffolk, Hindingbrook, Dec. 23, 1775, SP 81/181, NA.
28. O'Shaughnessy, *Men Who Lost America,* 92.
29. Wiederhold was born in 1732. Andreas Wiederhold to Georg Ernst von und zu Gilsa, Long Island, Aug. 29–31, 1776, German History Intersections, document 37, https://germanhistory-intersections.org/.
30. Diary of Colonel Johann August von Loos, in Valentine C. Harris, *Hessian Journals: Unpublished Documents of the American Revolution* (Columbia, SC: Camden House, 1981), 11–61: 61.
31. Andreas Wiederhold to Georg Ernst von und zu Gilsa, Sandy Hook Bay, New York, Aug. 14, 1776, https://friederikebaer.com/.
32. Serle, *American Journal,* Aug. 27, 1776, 77–79.

33. Margaret Livingston to [Catharine Livingston], Oct. 20, 1776, Ridley Papers, MHS, quoted in Kerber, *Women of the Republic*, 47.
34. George Washington to John Hancock, Aug. 31, 1776, *Founders Online*, National Archives, https://founders.archives.gov/.
35. Ira D. Gruber, *The Howe Brothers and the American Revolution* (New York: Institute of Early American History and Culture / Atheneum, 1972), 106, 110; O'Shaughnessy, *Men Who Lost America*, 93–95.
36. Andreas Wiederhold to Georg Ernst von und zu Gilsa, "In the Long Island camp near New York, August 31, 1776," German History Intersections, document 37, https://germanhistory-intersections.org/.
37. Wiederhold to Gilsa, August 31, 1776.
38. George Washington to Samuel Chase, Morris Town, Feb. 5, 1777, *Founders Online*, National Archives, https://founders.archives.gov/.
39. Serle, *American Journal*, 47.
40. Serle, *American Journal*, 72, 40, 46.
41. Sept. 1, 1776, Serle, *American Journal*, 77, 142–43, 86–87.
42. Ezra Tilden, manuscript diary, *America, 1492–1945*, Gilder Lehrman Institute of American History, 35, https://www.gilderlehrman.org/.
43. Holly Mayer, *Belonging to the Army: Camp Followers and Community During the American Revolution* (Columbia: University of South Carolina Press, 1996), 46, 140–42, and Kathleen M. Brown, *Foul Bodies: Cleanliness in Early America* (New Haven, CT: Yale University Press, 2009), 111–12, 178.
44. Tilden, manuscript diary, 9–10.
45. Tilden, manuscript diary, 31, 29, 5.
46. Tilden, manuscript diary, 36, 64, 19.
47. Tilden, manuscript diary, 132.
48. Thomas Nelson to Thomas Jefferson, Baltimore, Jan. 2, 1777, *LDC*, vol. 6 (Jan. 1, 1770–April 30, 1777), 25.
49. "Trial of John Dunn and John Lusty, 7 Sept. 1776," WO 71/82, 405–6, 412–25, NA. Block, "Rape in the American Revolution" and Holger Hoock, "*Jus in bello:* Rape and the British Army in the American Revolutionary War," *Journal of Military Ethics* 14:1 (2015): 74–97: 81, 88.
50. "Trial of John Dunn and John Lusty," 416.
51. "Trial of John Dunn and John Lusty," 414.
52. "Trial of John Dunn and John Lusty," 420.
53. "Trial of John Dunn and John Lusty," 424.
54. Sharon Block, *Rape and Sexual Power in Early America* (Chapel Hill: Omohundro Institute of Early American History and Culture / University of North Carolina Press, 2006), 126–238.
55. "Trial of John Dunn and John Lusty," 424.
56. Neither Block nor Hoock mentions this change of verdict. On these

challenges: Sharon Block, "Rewriting the Rape of Rachel: Historical Methods, Historical Justice," *William and Mary Quarterly* 80:4 (2023): 649–76.

57. Trial of William Fenton, William Hodgetts, James Croker, and John Bitsworth, WO 71/149, 1, NA.
58. [William Howe], *The Narrative of Lt. Gen. Sir William Howe, in the Committee of the House of Commons, on the 29th of April, 1779, relative to his Conduct during His Late Command of the King's Troops in North America* (London: H. Baldwin et al., 1780), 58.
59. Sezor (Cesar) Phelps to Charles Phelps, Sept. 30, 1776, Porter-Phelps-Huntington Family Papers, box 4, folder 12, UMass Special Collections and University Archives, https://www.ats.amherst.edu/.
60. George Washington to John Hancock, December 20, 1776, *Founders Online,* National Archives, https://founders.archives.gov/.
61. George Washington to Jonathan Trumbull, Sr., December 21, 1776, *Founders Online,* National Archives, https://founders.archives.gov/.
62. George Washington to Robert Morris, December 22, 1776, *Founders Online,* National Archives, https://founders.archives.gov/.
63. George Washington to John Hancock, December 16, 1776, *Founders Online,* National Archives, https://founders.archives.gov/.
64. Benjamin Franklin to Silas Deane, Dec. 7, 1776, *Founders Online,* National Archives, https://founders.archives.gov/.
65. George Washington to Robert Morris, December 22, 1776, *Founders Online,* National Archives, https://founders.archives.gov/.
66. George Washington to John Hancock, December 16, 1776, *Founders Online,* National Archives, https://founders.archives.gov/.
67. James M. Deitch, "Johann Gottlieb Rall: Tactical Negligence or Personal Negligence at Trenton?," *Journal of the American Revolution*, Feb. 7, 2023.
68. George Washington to John Hancock, December 20, 1776, *Founders Online,* National Archives, https://founders.archives.gov/.
69. George Washington to Colonel John Cadwalader, December 24, 1776, *Founders Online,* National Archives, https://founders.archives.gov/.
70. George Washington to John Hancock, December 27, 1776, *Founders Online,* National Archives, https://founders.archives.gov/.
71. George Washington to Robert Morris, December 30, 1776, *Founders Online,* National Archives, https://founders.archives.gov/.
72. Piel, in Burgoyne, *Defeat, Disaster, and Dedication,* 20.
73. George Washington to John Hancock, December 27, 1776, *Founders Online,* National Archives, https://founders.archives.gov/.
74. George Washington to Major General John Sullivan, January 28, 1777, *Founders Online,* National Archives, https://founders.archives.gov/.

75. George Washington from Robert Morris, January 1, 1777, *Founders Online*, National Archives, https://founders.archives.gov/.
76. Ewald, *Diary*, 44, 55.
77. Wiederhold, in Burgoyne, *Defeat, Disaster, and Dedication*, 79, 83.
78. Ewald, *Diary*, 91.
79. Wiederhold, in Burgoyne, *Defeat, Disaster, and Dedication*, 82.
80. Ewald, *Diary*, 69.
81. Ewald, *Diary*, 69, 143, 140; Scribner, *Under Alien Skies*, 35–110.
82. Wiederhold to Gilsa, "August 31, 1776."
83. Wiederhold, in Burgoyne, *Defeat, Disaster, and Dedication*, 90, 107.
84. Johann Friedrich Specht, *The Specht Journal: A Military Journal of the Burgoyne Campaign*, trans. Helga Doblin and ed. Mary C. Lynn and Donald M. Londahl-Smidt (Westport, CT: Greenwood Press, 1995), 106 (Oct. 25, 1777).
85. Carl Leopold Bauermeister, *Revolution in America: Confidential Letters and Journals 1776–1784 of Adjutant General Major Bauermeister of the Hessian Forces*, ed. and trans. Bernhard A. Uhlendorf (New Brunswick, NJ: Rutgers University Press, 1957), 150.
86. Ewald, *Diary*, 122.
87. Specht, *Specht Journal*, 106.
88. Wiederhold, in Burgoyne, *Defeat, Disaster, and Dedication*, 95.
89. Wiederhold, in Burgoyne, *Defeat, Disaster, and Dedication*, 96–97.
90. Blake Grindon, "Hilliard d'Auberteuil's *Mis Mac Rea:* A Story of the American Revolution in the French Atlantic," *William and Mary Quarterly* 79: 4 (October 2022): 563–94.
91. Tah-won-ne-ahs or Chainbreaker [Governor Blacksnake], *Chainbreaker: The Revolutionary War Memoirs of Governor Blacksnake, as told to Benjamin Williams*, ed. Thomas S. Abler (Lincoln: University of Nebraska Press, 1989), 128.
92. Aaron Sullivan, *The Disaffected: Britain's Occupation of Philadelphia During the American Revolution* (Philadelphia: University of Pennsylvania Press, 2019), and Donald F. Johnson, *Occupied: British Military Rule and the Experience of Revolution* (Philadelphia: University of Pennsylvania Press, 2020).
93. Riedesel, *Baroness von Riedesel*, 48.
94. "Saratoga: Freeman's Farm / Bemis Heights," American Battlefield Trust, https:// www.battlefields.org/.
95. Gary B. Nash and Graham Russell Gao Hodges, *Friends of Liberty: Thomas Jefferson, Tadeusz Kościuszko, and Agrippa Hull: A Tale of Three Patriots, Two Revolutions, and a Tragic Betrayal of Freedom in the New Nation* (New York: Basic Books, 2008), 22.

96. Riedesel, *Baroness von Riedesel,* 63, 64.
97. Riedesel, *Baroness von Riedesel,* 65.
98. Riedesel, *Baroness von Riedesel,* 65, 49.
99. Riedesel, *Baroness von Riedesel,* 40.
100. Ewald, *Diary,* xx.
101. Ewald, *Diary,* 219.
102. Tah-won-ne-ahs or Chainbreaker, *Chainbreaker,* 131.
103. Ewald, *Diary,* 361.
104. Wiederhold to Gilsa, Bremerlehe, April 20, 1784, *Krieg in Amerika,* 400–401.
105. American Commissioners to [the Comte de Vergennes], Dec. 4, 1777, *Founders Online,* National Archives, https://founders.archives.gov/.
106. Peter M. Ascoli, "The French Press and the American Revolution: The Battle of Saratoga," *Proceedings of the Fifth Annual Meeting of the Western Society for French History,* ed. Joyce Duncan Falk (Santa Barbara, CA, 1978): 46–54.

Chapter 8: A Hall in Versailles

1. Colin Jones, *Versailles* (New York: Basic Books, 2018), 4–5; Emmanuel de Waresquiel, *Sept. Jours: 17–23 juin 1789 La France entre en revolution* (Paris: Éditions Tallandier, 2020), 23.
2. Jones, *Versailles,* 92.
3. Kimberly Chrisman-Campbell, *Fashion Victims: Dress at the Court of Louis XVI and Marie-Antoinette* (New Haven, CT: Yale University Press, 2015): 111–112, and Michael Kwass, "Big Hair: A Wig History of Consumption in Eighteenth-Century France," *American Historical Review* 111:3 (2006): 631–59: 643.
4. Monsieur François de Garsault, *The Art of the Wigmaker* (1767), trans. and ed. J. Stevens Cox (London: Hairdressers' Registration Council, 1961), 8, and William Moore, *The Art of Hair-Dressing, and Making it Grow Fast* (Bath, England: J. Salmon, 1780?), 14.
5. Garsault, *Art of the Wigmaker,* 9.
6. Also stale urine in corridors. Jones, *Versailles,* 66–67.
7. Piers Macksey, *The War for America, 1775–1783* (Lincoln: University of Nebraska Press, 1993 [1964]; Jonathan R. Dull, *A Diplomatic History of the American Revolution* (New Haven, CT: Yale University Press, 1985); Larrie D. Ferreiro, *Brothers at Arms: American Independence and the Men of France and Spain Who Saved It* (New York: Knopf, 2016); and Stacy Schiff, *A Great Improvisation: Franklin, France, and the Birth of America* (New York: Henry Holt, 2005). On Baron de Steuben, Philander Dean Chase, "Baron von Steuben in the War of Independence," Ph.D. diss., Duke University, Department of History, 1972.

8. Dull, *Diplomatic History,* 52.
9. John Adams to Benjamin Rush, Quincy, June 21, 1811, *Founders Online,* National Archives, https://founders.archives.gov/.
10. Steuben had had the suit made for him in eastern France, on his way from the German court to Paris. In 1783, the tailors wrote to Franklin for help in getting payment. Louis Frederic Stromeyer and Straub to Benjamin Franklin, Strasbourg, June 28, 1783, *Franklin Papers,* https://franklinpapers.org/. It was not uncommon for nobles to take years to pay such bills. Natacha Coquery, *Tenir Boutique à Paris aux XVIII siècle: luxe et demi-luxe* (Paris: Editions du comité des travaux historiques et scientifiques, 2011), 203–9.
11. Benjamin Franklin to Emma Thompson, February 8, 1777, *Founders Online,* National Archives, https://founders.archives.gov/.
12. Elisabeth Vigée Le Brun, *Souvenirs,* 2 vols., ed. Claudine Herrmann (Paris: Edition des Femmes, 1983), vol. 2: 255–56, and Jean Chalon, ed., *Mémoires de Madame Campan, Première Femme de Chambre de Marie-Antoinette,* notes par Carlos de Angulo, 2 vols. (Paris: Mercure de France, 1988), vol. 1:152.
13. Count Ségur, *Memoirs and Recollections of Count Segur, Ambassador from France to the Courts of Russia and Prussia* (Boston: Wells and Lilly, 1825), 61.
14. Chrisman-Campbell, *Fashion Victims,* 162–63.
15. Schiff, *A Great Improvisation,* 9–10 and 188–89.
16. Gilbert Chinard, "The Apotheosis of Benjamin Franklin, Paris, 1790–1791," *Proceedings of the American Philosophical* Society 99:6 (1955): 440–73: 448.
17. Benjamin Franklin and Silas Deane to Viscount Stormont, Paris April 2, 1777, and the American Commissioners to Lord Stormont, Paris April 3, [1777], *Founders Online,* National Archives, https://founders.archives.gov/.
18. Scott, *British Foreign Policy,* 295, and H. M. Scott, "Entry: David Murray, Seventh Viscount Stormont and Second Earl of Mansfield," *Oxford Dictionary of National Biography* online, 2008, https://www.oxforddnb.com.
19. J. F. Labourdette, *Vergennes: Ministre Principal to Louis XVI* (Paris: Editions Desjonquéres, 1990), 48.
20. Labourdette, *Vergennes,* 67.
21. Charles Gravier, comte de Vergennes, *Recueil d'observations, de conseils et de maximes, adressé aux fils de M. le comte de Vergennes, ministre et secrétaire d'État au département des Affaires étrangères, pour servir à leur éducation. 1775,* Ms-2328, BNF Arsenale, 1, 126.
22. Henri Doniol, *Histoire de la Participation de la France à l'établissement des États Unis d'Amérique,* 6 vols. (Paris: Imprimerie Nationale, 1886–99), vol. 1: 273–78, quotation at 276.
23. Doniol, *Histoire,* vol. 1: 277.

24. Brian N. Morton, "'Roderigue Hortalez' to the Secret Committee: An Unpublished French Policy Statement of 1777," *The French Review* 50:6 (May 1977): 875–90.
25. Hoock, *Scars of Independence,* 203–4.
26. Brendan Simms, *Three Victories and a Defeat: The Rise and Fall of the First British Empire, 1714–1783* (New York: Basic Books, 2007), 611–12, and Holton, *Liberty Is Sweet,* 350–51.
27. Dull, *Diplomatic History,* 95; Ferreiro, *Brothers at Arms,* 95–96; Conway, *A Short History,* 85–86; Taylor, *American Revolutions,* 187–88.
28. Louis XVI à Vergennes, 9 Mars 1778, John Hardman and Munro Price, eds., *Louis XVI and the Comte de Vergennes: Correspondence, 1774–1787* (Oxford: Voltaire Foundation, 1998), 260.
29. Ségur, *Memoirs and Recollections,* 81.
30. In the early 1790s, when asked to help with an Indian insurrection, Louis XVI declined as it reminded him of the American war which he never considered without regret. Hardman and Price, *Louis XVI,* xiii, 43.
31. Vergennes, *Recueil d'observations,* 12.
32. John Adams to Vergennes, Paris, July 13, 1780, *Founders Online,* National Archives, https:// founders.archives.gov/.
33. *Pennsylvania Packet,* Aug. 29, 1774.
34. *Connecticut Courant,* June 2, 1778.
35. *Rivington's Royal Gazette,* New York, Dec. 5, 1778.
36. Doniol, *Histoire,* vol. 1: 243–49: 244.
37. Doniol, *Histoire,* vol. 1: 2–3.
38. Doniol, *Histoire,* vol. 1: 567–77: 568.
39. Doniol, *Histoire,* vol. 2: 460–69: 461.
40. John Shovlin, *Trading with the Enemy: Britain, France, and the Eighteenth-Century Quest for a Peaceful World Order* (New Haven, CT: Yale University Press, 2021).
41. Cobbett, *Parliamentary History, Volume XX: comprising the period from the seventh of December 1778, to the tenth of Feb. 1780,* Bodleian Digital B 762 Eng Gallery, Col. 28, 30.
42. "London Debates: 1777," in *London Debating Societies: 1776–1799,* Dec. 19, 1777, ed. Donna T. Andrew (London, 1994), British History Online, https:// www.british-history.ac.uk/.
43. Ferreiro, *Brothers at Arms,* 99–101.
44. Peter P. Burdett to Benjamin Franklin, Carlsehue [before] June 10, 1777, *Founders Online,* National Archives, https://founders.archives.gov/.
45. Benjamin Franklin to George Washington, Passy, near Paris, Sept. 4, 1777, *Founders Online,* National Archives, https://founders.archives.gov/.

46. Peter Stephen Du Ponceau, "The Autobiography of Peter Stephen Du Ponceau," ed. James L. Whitehead, *Pennsylvania Magazine of History and Biography* 63:2 (April 1939): 189–277: 199.
47. Baron de Steuben to George Washington, Portsmouth [N.H., December 6, 1777], *Founders Online,* National Archives, https://founders.archives.gov/.
48. Chevalier de Pontgibaud, "A French Volunteer in the War of Independence," in Hugh F. Rankin, ed., *Narratives of the American Revolution, as told by a young sailor, a home-sick surgeon, a French volunteer, and a German general's wife* (Chicago: Lakeside Press / R. R. Donnelley & Sons, 1976), 207–86: 224.
49. "The Israel Angell Diary, 1 October 1777–28 February 1778," ed. Joseph Lee Boyle, *Rhode Island History* 58:4 (2000): 103–38: Feb. 2, 1778, 127.
50. *Greenman,* 109.
51. "Israel Angell Diary," Feb. 27, 1778, 130.
52. George Washington to Major General Israel Putnam, Feb. 6 1778, Head Quarters [Valley Forge] 6th Feby 1778, and Gouverneur Morris to John Jay, Camp Valley Forge, Feb. 1, 1778, *Founders Online,* National Archives, https://founders.archives.gov/.
53. Albigence Waldo, "A Surgeon at Valley Forge, 1777–78," in Rankin, ed., *Narratives of the American Revolution,* 165–206: 181.
54. "Israel Angell Diary," Jan. 25, 1778, 126.
55. George Washington to William Buchanan, Head Quarters Valley Forge 7th Feby 1778, and George Washington to Major General Nathanael Greene, Valley Forge, Feb. 12 1778, *Founders Online,* National Archives, https://founders.archives.gov/.
56. Frederick the Great, "The Secret Instructions of Frederick the Great," Thomas R. Philips, ed., *Roots of Strategy: The Five Greatest Military Classics of All Time* (Harrisburg, PA: Stackpole Books, 1985), 301–400: 346.
57. John Laurens to Henry Laurens, Head Quarters, 9th March 1778, in John Laurens, *The Army Correspondence of Colonel John Laurens, in the Years 1777–8, Now First Printed from Original Letters Addressed to His Father, Henry Laurens, President of Congress, with a Memoir* (New York: The Bradford Club, 1896), William Gilmore Simms Digital Edition, University of South Carolina, 131, https:// digital.tcl.sc.edu/.
58. George Washington to Henry Laurens, "Valley Forge Feby the 27th 1778," *Founders Online,* National Archives, https://founders.archives.gov/.
59. Ashbel Green, *The Life of Ashbel Green, V. D. M., begun to be written by himself in his eighty-second year and continued to his eighty-fourth* (New York: R. Carter & Bros, 1849), 109.
60. Chase, "Baron von Steuben," 25.

61. Marshal Maurice de Saxe, "My Reveries Upon the Art of War," in Thomas R. Philips, ed., *Roots of Strategy: The Five Greatest Military Classics of All Time* (Harrisburg, PA: Stackpole Books, 1985), 177–300: 201–3.
62. *Greenman,* 119.
63. Du Ponceau, "Autobiography," 219.
64. Frederick the Great, "Secret Instructions," 348.
65. General Orders, March 28, 1778, *Founders Online,* National Archives, https://founders.archives.gov/.
66. Frederick William, Baron von Steuben, *Baron von Steuben's Revolutionary War Drill Manual: A Facsimile Reprint of the 1794 Edition* (New York: Dover Publications, 1985), 23.
67. Baron von Steuben, *Drill Manual,* 87.
68. Frederick the Great, "Secret Instructions," 323.
69. John Laurens to Henry Laurens, Head Quarters, Feb. 24, 1778, *Army Correspondence of John Laurens.*
70. Du Ponceau, "Autobiography," 208.
71. John Gilbert McCurdy, *Vicious and Immoral: Homosexuality, the American Revolution, and the Trials of Robert Newburgh* (Baltimore: Johns Hopkins University, 2024).
72. Du Ponceau, "Autobiography," 203–4.
73. Richard Godbeer, *The Overflowing of Friendship: Love Between Men and the Creation of the American Republic* (Baltimore: Johns Hopkins University Press, 2009), 124–38.
74. John McAuley Palmer, *General von Steuben* (New Haven, CT: Yale University Press, 1937), 92.
75. Godbeer, *Overflowing of Friendship,* 137–42.
76. Nash and Hodges, *Friends of Liberty.*
77. Thomas Egleston, *The Life of John Paterson, Major-General in the Revolutionary Army, by his Great-Grandson, Thomas Egleston,* 2nd ed. (New York: G. P. Putnam's Sons, 1898), 308–10.
78. Josh Trujillo and Levi Hastings, *Washington's Gay General: The Legends and Loves of Baron von Steuben* (New York: Abrams ComicArts Surely, 2023), 128, and Ferreiro, *Brothers at Arms,* 158.
79. Nash and Hodges, *Friends of Liberty,* 59.
80. Benjamin Franklin to James Lovell, Passy, near Paris, Oct. 7, 1777, *Founders Online,* National Archives, https://founders.archives.gov/.
81. Alexander Hamilton to Elias Boudinot, Head Quarters [White Plains, NY], July 26, 1778, and George Washington to Henry Laurens, White Plains [NY], July 26, 1778, *Founders Online,* National Archives, https://founders.archives.gov/.
82. Gilbert du Motier, Marquis de Lafayette, *Memoirs, Correspondence and Manu-*

scripts of General Lafayette, 3 vols. (New York: Saunders and Otley, 1837), vol. 1: 6.

83. Add. MS 33118, Pelham papers, f., 32:2–3, BL.
84. Admiralty Board to Lord Richard Howe, March 22, 1778, quoted in Piers Mackesy, *The War for America: 1775–1783* (Lincoln: University of Nebraska Press, 1993 [1964]), 186.
85. Mackesy, *War for America,* 1.
86. Duke of Bedford to Duke of Newcastle, Woburn Abbey, May 9, 1761, Add. MSS 32922, Newcastle papers, f. 449–52, BL.
87. Duke of Bedford to Duke of Newcastle, Woburn Abbey, May 9, 1761, Add. MSS 32922, Newcastle papers, f. 449–52, BL.
88. Elena Schneider, *The Occupation of Havana: War, Trade, and Slavery in the Atlantic World* (Chapel Hill: Omohundro Institute of Early American History and Culture / University of North Carolina Press, 2018).
89. McCurdy, *Quarters,* 208–9, and Simms, *Three Victories and a Defeat,* 560–63.
90. Treaty of Aranjuez, quoted in Simms, *Three Victories and a Defeat,* 618.
91. Mackesy, *War for America,* 275, and O'Shaughnessy, *Men Who Lost America,* 341.
92. Keith to Dartmouth, Nov. 6, 1775, CO/137/71, 19, NA, and Matthew Mulcahy, "'Miserably Scorched': Drought in the Plantation Colonies of the British Greater Caribbean," *Atlantic Environments and the American South,* ed. Thomas Blake Earle and D. Andrew Johnson (Athens: University of Georgia Press, 2020): 65–89: 79.
93. McNeill, *Mosquito Empires,* 143.
94. Vincent Brown, *The Reaper's Garden: Death and Power in the World of Atlantic Slavery* (Cambridge, MA: Harvard University Press, 2008), 18.
95. James Williams, July 20, 1776, CO/137/71, 249, NA.
96. Keith to Germain, Aug. 6, 1776, CO/137/71, 227–33, NA.
97. Sarah M. S. Pearsall, "1776 in Jamaica," in *Cambridge History of the American Revolution,* ed. Marjoleine Kars, Michael A. McDonnell, and Andrew M. Schocket, 3 vols. (Cambridge: Cambridge University Press, 2026), vol. 2: 251–65.
98. Keith to Germain, Aug. 6, 1776, CO/137/71, NA.
99. Keith to Germain, June 6, 1776, CO/137/71, 152–55, NA.
100. Keith to Germain, Aug. 6, 1776, CO/137/71, 227–31, NA.
101. Admiral George Rodney, quoted in O'Shaughnessy, *Empire Divided,* 147.
102. Examination of Pontack, July 28, 1776, CO/137/71, 276–79, NA.
103. Silas Deane to the Committee of Secret Correspondence, Paris, Oct. 8, 1776, and Deane to John May, Paris, Dec. 3, 1776, in Francis Wharton, ed., *Revolutionary Diplomatic Correspondence of the United States,* 6 vols. (Washington, DC: Government Printing Office, 1889), vol. 2: 167, 213.

104. Comte de Tressan to Benjamin Franklin, Paris, June 24, 1777, *Founders Online*, National Archives, https://founders.archives.gov/.
105. M.M.D.L.T., *The History of Hyder Shah, alias Hyder Ali Khan Bahadur and of his son Tippoo Sultaun*, revised and corrected by Prince Gholam Mohammed (London: W. Thacker & Co., 1855), 16.
106. *Michaud's History of Mysore under Haidar Ali and Tipu Sultan*, trans. V. K. Raman Menon (New Delhi: Asian Educational Services, 1985), 24–25.
107. *Michaud's History*, 25.
108. Prince Golam Mohammed, *History of Hyder Shah*, 139.
109. Kaushik Roy, *War, Culture and Society in Early Modern South Asia, 1740–1849*, ed. Peter Lorge (London: Routledge, 2011), 79; Mackesy, *War for America*, 380; and Richard Sambasivam, "British Global Ambitions and Indian Identity," in David K. Allison and Larrie D. Ferreiro, *The American Revolution: A World War* (Washington, DC; Smithsonian Books, 2018), 92–107, 98.
110. *Michaud's History*, 47–48.
111. Christopher Leslie Brown, "Empire Without America: British Plans for Africa in the Era of the American Revolution," in *Abolitionism and Imperialism in Britain, Africa, and the Atlantic*, ed. Derek R. Peterson, Harri Englund, and Christopher Warnes (Athens: Ohio University Press, 2010), 84–100, and Joshua D. Newton, "Naval Power and the Province of Senegambia, 1758–1779," *Journal for Maritime Research* 15:2 (2013): 129–47.
112. Board of Trade to George III, Feb. 21, 1765, CO 389/31, NA.
113. Bedford to Newcastle, May 9, 1761, Add. MSS 32922, f. 451, BL.
114. Lords of Trade to William Pitt, Jan. 23, 1758, CO 267/6, NA.
115. Newton, "Naval Power," 137.
116. Newton, "Naval Power," 136–37.
117. Newton, "Naval Power," 139–40.
118. Baron von Steuben to Benjamin Franklin, Head Quarters, West Point, Sept. 28. 1779, *Franklin Papers*, https://franklinpapers.org/.

Chapter 9: A Cornfield in the Six Nations

1. Erminnie A. Smith, "The Myths of the Iroquois" (Washington, DC: Smithsonian Institution, Bureau of Ethnology, 1883), 53.
2. "Account of Losses Sustained by the Oneidas & Tuscaroras in Consequence of their Attachment to the United States in the Late War," 1794, Timothy Pickering Papers, vol. 62: 157–66 (Letters and Papers of Pickering's Mission to the Indians, 1792–1797), MHS.
3. "Diary and accounts [manuscript] 1779 June 9–Sept. 16" for Lt. Daniel Clapp, VAULT Ayer N.A. 162, Newberry Library.
4. Lieutenant Samuel Shute and Major Jeremiah Fogg in Frederick Cook, ed., *Journals of the Military Expedition of Major General John Sullivan against the*

Six Nations of Indians in 1779 (Auburn, NY, 1887), 267–74: 271; 92–101: 97, 100. It is distinctly possible that some of the diaries from this expedition were copied after the fact in order to prove service for pension applications, so they need to be read with care. Nevertheless, enough witnesses support the encounter between Sacho and Sullivan.

5. Fogg, in Cook, ed., *Journals,* 92–101: 100.
6. The best accounts of the Haudenosaunee and the American Revolution include Colin G. Calloway, *The American Revolution in Indian Country: Crisis and Diversity in Native American Communities,* in Frederick E. Hoxie and Neal Salisbury, series eds., *Cambridge Studies in North American Indian History* (Cambridge: Cambridge University Press, 1995), and Calloway's *The Indian World of George Washington* (Oxford: Oxford University Press, 2018); Alan Taylor, *The Divided Ground: Indians, Settlers, and the Northern Borderland of the American Revolution* (New York: Knopf, 2006); Daniel K. Richter, *The Ordeal of the Longhouse: The Peoples of the Iroquois League in the Era of European Colonization* (Chapel Hill: University of North Carolina Press, 1992); Karim M. Tiro, *The People of the Standing Stone: The Oneida Nation from the Revolution Through the Era of Removal* (Amherst: University of Massachusetts Press, 2011); Joseph T. Glatthaar and James Kirby Martin, *Forgotten Allies: The Oneida Indians and the American Revolution* (New York: Hill and Wang, 2006); Barbara Graymont, *The Iroquois in the American Revolution* (Syracuse, NY: Syracuse University Press, 1972); Max M. Mintz, *Seeds of Empire: The American Revolutionary Conquest of the Iroquois* (New York: New York University Press, 1999); Joseph R. Fischer, *A Well-Executed Failure: The Sullivan Campaign Against the Iroquois, July–September 1779* (Columbia: University of South Carolina Press, 1997); and Barbara Alice Mann, *George Washington's War on Native America* (Lincoln: University of Nebraska Press, 2008).
7. Cesare Marino and Karim M. Tiro, eds. and trans., *Along the Hudson and Mohawk: The 1790 Journey of Count Paolo Andreani* (Philadelphia: University of Pennsylvania Press, 2006), 64.
8. "[Sat. May 16, 1767]," Francis Grant, "Journal from New York to Canada, 1767," *New York History* 53 (April 1932): 181–96: 187. Observations of hospitality: Marino and Tiro, *Along the Hudson and Mohawk,* 63; Cadwallader Colden, *The History of the Five Indian Nations Depending on the Province of New-York in America: A Critical Edition,* with essays by John M. Dixon and Karim M. Tiro (Ithaca, NY: Cornell University Press, 2017), 206; DuVal, *Native Nations,* 155–57.
9. Colden, *History of the Five Indian Nations,* 200.
10. William N. Fenton, "This Island, the World on the Turtle's Back," *Journal of American Folklore* 75 (1962): 283–300: 298.
11. Marino and Tiro, *Along the Hudson and Mohawk,* 55.

12. David McClure, *Diary of David McClure, Doctor of Divinity, 1748–1800,* ed. Franklin B. Dexter, Aug. 18 [1772] (New York: Knickerbocker Press / privately printed, 1899), 42.
13. Marino and Tiro, *Along the Hudson and Mohawk,* 57. See also the 1796 portrait of *Gayëtwahgeh (The Cornplanter)* by Frederick Bartoli, New-York Historical Society, http://www.nyhistory.org/.
14. "Account of Losses," Timothy Pickering Papers; Richard Smith, *A Tour of Four Great Rivers: The Hudson, Mohawk, Susquehanna and Delaware in 1769,* ed. Francis W. Halsey (New York: Charles Scribner's Sons, 1906), 68–69, 84; and Maeve Kane, *Shirts Powdered Red: Haudenosaunee Gender, Trade, and Exchange across Three Centuries* (Ithaca, NY: Cornell University Press, 2023).
15. Council leaders, Oct. 28, 1768, E. B. O'Callaghan, ed., *Documents Relative to the Colonial History of the State of New-York,* 15 vols. (Albany: Weed, Parsons and Co., 1857), vol. 8: 120.
16. Speech of "Conoghquiesor Chief of Oneida," March 4, 1768, in O'Callaghan, *Documents,* vol. 8: 40.
17. Speech by Joseph, Mohawk, July 28, 1772, O'Callaghan, *Documents,* vol. 8: 304.
18. Speech by Joseph, Mohawk, July 28, 1772, O'Callaghan, *Documents,* vol. 8: 304.
19. Amanda J. Cobb, "Understanding Tribal Sovereignty: Definitions, Conceptualizations, and Interpretations," *American Studies* 46: 3/4 (2005), 115–32: 125.
20. Sir William Johnson to Thomas Gage, Oct. 31, 1764, *WJP,* vol. 11: 395.
21. Colden, *History of the Five Indian Nations,* 208.
22. Sir William Johnson to John Tambor Kempe, Sept. 7, 1765, *WJP,* vol. 11: 925, and to Thomas Gage, Oct. 31, 1764, *WJP,* vol. 11: 364.
23. Speech of Little Abraham at council on Feb. 17, 1780, "A Copy of Proceedings with four Rebel Indians . . . ," "Niagara Feby 12, 1780," Add. MS 21,779, Haldimand Papers, f. 73–78: 75, BL.
24. See, among others, Richard Godbeer, *World of Trouble: A Philadelphia Quaker Family's Journey Through the American Revolution* (New Haven, CT: Yale University Press, 2019), and Travis Glasson, *Nobody Men: Neutrality, Loyalties, and Family in the American Revolution* (New Haven, CT: Yale University Press, 2025).
25. Luke Swetland, *A Very Remarkable Narrative of Luke Swetland* (Hartford, CT: Luke Swetland, 1780[?]), 6.
26. Swetland, *Very Remarkable Narrative,* 13, and Calloway, *Indian World of George Washington,* 216.
27. Charles Craven to the House, Aug. 6, 1712, *South Carolina Commons House Journal,* quoted in David La Vere, *The Tuscarora War: Indians, Settlers, and*

the Fight for the Carolina Colonies (Chapel Hill: University of North Carolina Press, 2013), 153.

28. Lee, *Barbarians and Brothers,* 2.
29. Michael Blaakman, *Speculation Nation: Land Mania in the Revolutionary American Republic* (Philadelphia: University of Pennsylvania Press, 2023), especially chs. 1 and 2, quotation 61.
30. Calloway, *Indian World of George Washington.*
31. Philip Schuyler to George Washington and George Washington to Philip Schuyler, May 22, 1776, Revolutionary War Series, vol. 4 (April 1–June 15, 1776), vol. 4: 388, 373, *The Papers of George Washington,* digital edition (Charlottesville: University of Virginia Press, Rotunda, 2008).
32. Jane T. Merritt, *At the Crossroads: Indians and Empires on a Mid-Atlantic Frontier, 1700–1763* (Chapel Hill: Omohundro Institute of Early American History and Culture / University of North Carolina Press, 2003).
33. Anonymous manual on war, Amherst Papers, WO 34/102, 191–92, NA.
34. Speech of Abraham Chief of the Mohawks, "Answer of the Mohawks . . . May 25 1775," Guy Johnson Papers, Series III, Gen MSS 494 Box 1, Folder 35, Beinecke Library, Yale University.
35. Smith, *Tour of Four Great Rivers,* 84, 85.
36. David McClure, *Diary of David McClure, Doctor of Divinity, 1748–1800,* ed. Franklin B. Dexter (New York: Knickerbocker Press, 1899), 10, and Tench Tilghman, *Memoir of Lt. Col. Tench Tilghman* (Albany, NY: J. Munsell, 1876), 83.
37. Du Ponceau, "Autobiography," 222–23.
38. "Speech of Tenhoghskweaghta an Onondaga Chief at the Johnstone Conference," March 10, 1778, Philip Schuyler Papers, Indian Papers, New York Public Library Digital Collections (Manuscripts and Archives Division), image ID 56998659.
39. "A Copy of Proceedings with four Rebel Indians . . . ," "Niagara Feby 12, 1780," Add. MS 21,779, Haldimand Papers, f. 73–78, BL.
40. Francis Grant, "Journal from New York to Canada, 1767," ["Sat May 16 1767,"] *New York History* 53 (April 1932): 181–96: 187.
41. Speech of Tenhoghskweaghta, March 10, 1778, *Philip Schuyler Papers,* image ID 56998660-56998661.
42. "The Grasshopper an Oneida Sachem," March 10, 1778, Philip Schuyler Papers, image ID 56998663.
43. Hector St. John de Crèvecoeur, "Crevecoeur on the Susquehanna, 1774–76," ed. H. L. Bourdin and S. T. Williams, *Yale Review,* vol. 14 (1924–25): 552–84: 582.
44. Lt. Col. Adam Hubley, in Cook, ed, *Journals,* 145–67: 163.
45. *Connecticut Courant,* July 21 and 28, 1778.

46. Hector St. John de Crèvecoeur, *Sketches of Eighteenth Century America: More "Letters from an American Farmer,"* ed. Henri L. Bourdin, Ralph H. Gabriel, and Stanley T. Williams (New Haven, CT: Yale University Press, 1925), 192–206: 201.
47. Crèvecoeur, "Crevecoeur on the Susquehanna," 581.
48. Smith, *Tour of Four Great Rivers,* 64–72, 87, 67.
49. Smith, *Tour of Four Great Rivers,* 64.
50. "William Butler's Successful Expedition," in Hugh Hastings, ed., *Public Papers of George Clinton, First Governor of New York, 1777–1795, 1801–1804...,* 9 vols. (Albany, NY: James B. Lyon, 1900), vol. 4: 222–32: 225, 226, 223; Emmanuel Kreike, *Scorched Earth: Environmental Warfare as a Crime Against Humanity and Nature* (Princeton, NJ: Princeton University Press, 2021), introduction, 59–96, 138–72, 245, 251–52, 279–317 (he does not address the Sullivan campaign).
51. Walter Butler to Frederick Haldimand, "Nov. 17 1778," Haldimand Papers, Add. Mss. No. 21,760, f. 77–80, as transcribed by Judy Longley, https://montgomery.nygenweb.net/.
52. William Johnson, et al., "Decemb'r 13th 1778," in Hastings, ed. *Public Papers of George Clinton,* vol. 4: 364.
53. *Journals of the Continental Congress,* vol. 11 (May 2–Sept. 1, 1778): 587–90, 589, 588.
54. *Journals of the Continental Congress,* vol. 11: 720–22: 721.
55. Richard Peters, War Office, to George Washington, July 27, 1778, *Papers of George Washington,* Revolutionary War Series, vol. 16: 182.
56. George Washington to Philip Schuyler, "Head Quarters, Philadelphia, January 25, 1779" in *Papers of George Washington,* Revolutionary War Series, vol. 19: 72–74.
57. *Journals of the Continental Congress,* vol. 13 (Jan. 1–April 22, 1779): 251–53; quotation 252.
58. Calloway, *Indian World of George Washington,* 247.
59. Philip Schuyler to George Washington, Feb 4, 1779, *Founders Online,* National Archives, https://founders.archives.gov/.
60. George Washington to Philip Schuyler, "Head Quarters, Middle Brooks, March 25, 1779," *Papers of George Washington,* Revolutionary War Series, vol. 19: 610–13. Mintz, *Seeds of Empire,* 82, and Calloway, *American Revolution in Indian Country,* 51.
61. George Washington, "Instructions to Major General John Sullivan," "Head Quarters, Middle Brook, May 31, 1779," *Papers of George Washington,* Revolutionary War Series, vol. 20: 716–20.
62. Andrew Preston, *Total Defense: The New Deal and the Invention of National Security* (Cambridge, MA: Harvard University Press, 2025), 16–17.

63. George Washington to General Lafayette, "New Windsor July 4 1779," *Papers of George Washington,* Revolutionary War Series, vol. 21:349–50.
64. Lt. Rudolphus Van Hovenburgh in Cook, ed., *Journals,* 279.
65. Taylor, *Divided Ground,* 99.
66. *Maryland Journal and Baltimore Advertiser,* Oct. 19, 1779, in Cook, ed., *Journals,* 303.
67. Lt. Col. Adam Hubley, in Cook, ed., *Journals,* 145–67: 158.
68. Dr. Jabez Campfield, in Cook, ed., *Journals,* 53, 54.
69. Mintz, *Seeds of Empire,* 186.
70. Lt. Erkuries Beatty in Cook, ed., *Journals,* 15–37: 33, 35.
71. Lt. Col. Adam Hubley, in Cook, ed., *Journals,* 145–67: 164.
72. Samuel Shute in Cook, ed., *Journals,* 267–74: 271.
73. Majors Jeremiah Foggin and John Burrowes, in Cook, ed., *Journals,* 92–101: 96, 100, 45.
74. Colden, *History of the Five Indian Nations,* 182.
75. Beatty, in Cook, ed., *Journals,* 15–37, 28.
76. Burrowes, in Cook, ed., *Journals,* 42–51: 49.
77. Hubley, in Cook, ed., *Journals,* 145–67: 164.
78. As quoted in Calloway, *American Revolution in Indian Country,* 53.
79. Calloway, *Indian World of George Washington,* 258.
80. George Washington to Major General Horatio Gates, West Point, October 16, 1779, *Founders Online,* National Archives, https://founders.archives.gov/.
81. Lt. Col. Henry Dearborn, Cook, ed., *Journals,* 64.
82. Olivier Chaline and Jean-Marie Kowalski, "French Naval Operations," in Allison and Ferreiro, *American Revolution,* 52–66: 52.
83. Chaline and Kowalski, "French Naval Operations," 59.
84. Ferreiro, *Brothers at Arms,* 200, 202.
85. Anthony Stokes in Frank Moore, ed., *Diary of the American Revolution from Newspapers and Original Documents,* 2 vols. (New York: Charles T. Evans, 1863), vol. 2: 223.
86. Stokes, in Moore, *Diary,* vol. 2: 223.
87. Stokes, in Moore, *Diary,* vol. 2: 226.
88. *Royal Rivington's Gazette,* Dec. 29, 1779, in Franklin B. Hough, ed., *The Siege of Savannah by the Combined American and French Forces*... (Albany, NY: J. Munsell, 1866), 84.
89. French officer in Charles Jones, ed., *The Siege of Savannah in 1779, Described in Two Contemporaneous Journals*... (Albany, NY: John Munsell, 1874), 64.
90. Jones, ed., *Siege of Savannah,* 67.
91. Cherry Fletcher Bamberg, "Bristol Yamma and John Quamine in Rhode Island," *Rhode Island History* 73:1 (2015): 4–30: 20.

92. "The British Occupation: The Occupation of Newport," The Battle of Rhode Island Association, https://battleofrhodeisland.org/.
93. Bamberg, "Bristol Yamma," 23.
94. Bamberg, "Bristol Yamma," and Edward E. Andrews, "Duchess Quamino," *African American National Biography* (Oxford: Oxford University Press, 2013), online.
95. James E. Ferguson, *The Power of the Purse: A History of American Public Finance, 1776–1790* (Chapel Hill: Omohundro Institute of Early American History and Culture / University of North Carolina Press, 1961), 67.
96. Max M. Edling, *A Hercules in the Cradle: War, Money, and the American State, 1787–1867* (Chicago: University of Chicago Press, 2014), 24.
97. Michelle Craig McDonald, *Coffee Nation: How One Commodity Transformed the Early United States* (Philadelphia: University of Pennsylvania Press, 2025), 84–86.
98. Farley Grubb, *The Continental Dollar: How the American Revolution Was Financed with Paper Money* (Chicago: University of Chicago Press, 2023), 172.
99. John Adams to James Warren, Baltimore, Feb. 12, 1777, *Papers of John Adams,* vol. 5: 83, MHS, https://www.masshist.org/.
100. Grubb, *Continental Dollar,* 11, and Edling, *Hercules in the Cradle,* 24. Farley Grubb argues that the currency lost value only as the result of congressional decisions in 1779. Grubb, *Continental Dollar,* 11 and passim.
101. Edmund Randolph, Philadelphia, May 29, 1787, quoted in Grubb, *Continental Dollar,* 172.
102. Ferguson, *Power of the Purse,* 41.
103. Ferguson, *Power of the Purse,* 67.
104. Diary of Lieut. Anthony Allaire, "Memorandum of Occurrences During the Campaign of 1780," Thurs., March 16, 1780, in *King's Mountain and its heroes: history of the Battle of King's Mountain, October 7th, 1780,* ed. Lyman Copeland Draper (Cincinnati: P. G. Thomson, 1881): 484–515: 486.
105. Allaire, "Memorandum of Occurrences," 487.
106. Allaire, "Memorandum of Occurrences," 490–91.
107. Allaire, "Memorandum of Occurrences," 508.
108. Eliza Yonge Wilkinson, *Letters of Eliza Wilkinson During the Invasion and Possession of Charlestown, S.C. by the British in the Revolutionary War,* ed. Caroline Gilman (New York: Samuel Colman, 1830): 1–2.
109. Wilkinson, *Letters,* 2.
110. Wilkinson, *Letters,* 4.
111. Nicholas Rowe, *Tamerlane: A Tragedy* (London: Jacob Tonson, 1702), Act I, Scene 1, 10.
112. Wilkinson, *Letters,* 28–30, 31.
113. Wilkinson, *Letters,* 42, 24.

Chapter 10: A Rock in Gibraltar

1. James Horsbrugh Diary, vol. 1 (June 21, 1779–Oct. 5, 1780), Add MS 50256, 148, BL.
2. Ferreiro, *Brothers at Arms,* 193, and Roy Adkins and Lesley Adkins, *Gibraltar: The Greatest Siege in British History* (New York: Viking, 2017).
3. Helen Duff to her brother, Gibraltar, Jan. 29, 1778, in Alistair Tayler and Henrietta Tayler, eds., *The Book of the Duffs,* 2 vols. (Edinburgh: William Brown, 1914), vol. 2:316.
4. Francis Carter, *A Journey from Gibraltar to Malaga* (London: T. Cadell, 1777), 230–31.
5. Carter, *Journey,* 230–31.
6. John Drinkwater, *A History of the Late Siege of Gibraltar* (London: Horizon Books, 2013), 40.
7. Thirty-five thousand French and Spanish soldiers and sailors plus five thousand British soldiers. "Military History: The Great Siege of Gibraltar," National Museum of Gibraltar, https://www.gibmuseum.gi/.
8. Gibraltar Census of 1777, National Archives, Gibraltar, https://www.nationalarchives.gi/.
9. Duff, *Book of the Duffs,* vol. 2: 316.
10. Ferreiro, *Brothers at Arms,* 112–16. This pledge later complicated the peace settlements. Andrew Stockley, *Britain and France at the Birth of America: The European Powers and the Peace Negotiations of 1782–1783* (Exeter, UK: University of Exeter Press, 2001), 118–19.
11. R. H. Vetch and W. Johnson, "Sir William Green, First Baronet," *Oxford Dictionary of National Biography* online.
12. Drinkwater, *History of the Late Siege,* 25.
13. Miriam Green, "A Lady's Experiences in the Great Siege of Gibraltar (1779–1783)," ed. E. R. Kenyon, *Royal Engineers Journal* (1912), part 1, 41.
14. Green, "Lady's Experiences," 42.
15. Green, "Lady's Experiences," 118.
16. Captain John Spilsbury [12th Regiment], *A Journal of the Siege of Gibraltar, 1779–1783,* Sept. 25, 1779, entry, B.H.T. Frere, ed. (Gibraltar: Gibraltar Garrison Library, 1908), 6, 21, 26; Drinkwater, *History of the Late Siege,* 59.
17. Spilsbury, *Journal of the Siege,* 10; Drinkwater, *History of the Late Siege,* 59.
18. [Anonymous], "Considerations with regard to the Invasion and Defence of Ireland in case of a Rupture with France," Add. MS 33118, Pelham papers, Fo. 32, 1, 6, BL.
19. Add. MS 33118, Pelham papers, fo. 32: 1, 2, BL.
20. Aug. 5, 1779, Pantheon Minutes.
21. Add. MS 33118, Pelham papers, fo. 33: 16. BL.

22. Add. MS 33118, Pelham papers, fo. 33: 105–6, BL.
23. Patrick Geoghegan, *Trinity College Dublin: The College Historical Society Oratory and Debate, 1770–2020* (Dublin: Hinds/The Lilliput Press, 2020), 21.
24. Vincent Morley, *Irish Opinion and the American Revolution, 1760–1783* (Cambridge: Cambridge University Press, 2002), 223–37, and Padhraig Higgins, *A Nation of Politicians: Gender, Patriotism, and Political Culture in Late Eighteenth-Century Ireland* (Madison: University of Wisconsin Press, 2010), 73–83.
25. *Dublin Evening Post*, July 31, 1779, quoted in Higgins, *Nation of Politicians*, 83.
26. *Finn's Leinster Journal*, Dec. 15, 1779, quoted in Higgins, *Nation of Politicians*, 78, 99.
27. *Hibernian Journal*, April 5, 1779, quoted in Joel Herman, "Imagined Nations: Newspapers, Identity, and the Free Trade Crisis of 1779," *Eighteenth-Century Ireland / Iris an dá chultúr* 35 (2020): 51–69, 64.
28. Higgins, *Nation of Politicians*, 100, 154–56.
29. John MacDonald, *Autobiographical Journal of John MacDonald, Schoolmaster and Soldier, 1770–1830*, ed. Angus Mackay (Edinburgh: Norman MacLeod, 1906), 42–43.
30. J. H. Carpenter to Sir Francis Henry Drake, Tavyton [Devon], Aug. 29, 1779, in Elizabeth Eliott-Drake, *The Family and Heirs of Sir Francis Drake*, 2 vols. (London: Smith, Elder & Co., 1911), vol. 2: 313–14.
31. British population in 1776 from "1570–1750 Estimated Population," https://1841census.co.uk/.
32. Andreia Durães and Vicente Pérez Moreda, "Population of the Iberian Peninsula in the Early Modern Period: A Comparative and Regional Perspective," in Leonor Freire Costa et al., eds., *An Economic History of the Iberian Peninsula, 700–2000* (Cambridge: Cambridge University Press, 2024), ch. 11.
33. Peter McPhee, "France in the 1780s," in *The French Revolution 1789–1799* (Oxford: Oxford University Press, 2001), 4–23.
34. "Special Edition: America's Independence: 250 Years Ago: The Boston Tea Party (1773)," December 16, 2023, census.gov/.
35. Benjamin Franklin, *Observations Concerning the Increase of Mankind, Peopling of Countries, &c*, in [William Clarke,] *Observations On the late and present Conduct of the French, with Regard to their Encroachments upon the British Colonies in North America* (Boston: Printed and Sold by S. Kneeland in Queen-Street, 1755), *Founders Online*, National Archives, https://founders.archives.gov/.
36. [Allen,] *Oration upon the Beauties of Liberty*, 14.
37. Ezra Stiles, *A Discourse on the Christian Union* (Boston: Edes and Gill, 1761), 112.
38. Adam Smith, *An Inquiry into the Nature and Causes of the Wealth of Nations by*

Adam Smith, ed. Edwin Cannan (London: Methuen, 1904), vol. 1, ch. 8: "Of the Wages of Labour," https://oll.libertyfund.org/.

39. Julian Hoppit, "Political Arithmetic in Eighteenth-Century England," *Economic History Review* 49:3 (Aug. 1996): 516–40: 519.
40. Charles Davenant, "An Essay Upon the Ways and Means of Supplying the War," in Charles Davenant, *The Political and Commercial Works of that Celebrated Writer Charles D'Avenant, LL.D.*, 5 vols. (London: R. Horsfield, 1771), vol. 1: 1–82: 73.
41. Sylvana Tomaselli, "Moral Philosophy and Population Questions in Eighteenth Century Europe," *Population and Development Review* 14 (188): 7–29: 27.
42. Lydia Syson, *Doctor of Love: James Graham and His Celestial Bed* (Richmond, UK: Alma Books, 2008), 36.
43. Thomas Short, *A Comparative History of the Increase and Decrease of Mankind in England* (London: W. Nicoll, 1767), 27.
44. Short, *Comparative History*, 26, 25, 54.
45. Roy Porter, "The Sexual Politics of James Graham," *British Journal for Eighteenth-Century Studies*, 5:2 (Autumn 1982), 199–206, and his "Sex and the Singular Man: The Seminal Ideas of James Graham," *Studies on Voltaire and the Eighteenth Century*, 228 (1984), 3–24; Barbara Brandon Schnorrenberg, "A True Relation of the Life and Career of James Graham, 1745–1794," *Eighteenth-Century Life* 15 (November 1991), 58–75; and Syson, *Doctor of Love.*
46. Henry Angelo, *Reminiscences of Henry Angelo*, 2 vols. (London: Henry Colburn and Richard Bentley, 1830), vol. 2: 61–62.
47. *The Morning Chronicle, and London Advertiser*, July 22, 1780, 3.
48. Angelo, *Reminiscences*, vol. 1: 127–28.
49. Capitalization original. James Graham, *Advertisement* (London[?]: N.p., 1780[?]), 1–2.
50. James Graham, *A Lecture on the Generation, Increase and Improvement of the Human Species* (London: M. Smith, 1780[?]), 59.
51. Graham, *Lecture*, 58 (electricity), 62–63 (visualization), and 61–62 (threesomes), 29, 22, 28, 37.
52. Graham, *Lecture*, 8.
53. Graham, *Lecture*, 7.
54. Graham, *Lecture*, 4.
55. Graham, *Lecture*, 3.
56. Graham, *Lecture*, 7.
57. *Maryland Gazette*, Jan. 25, 1770.
58. *New-York Gazette, or Weekly Post-Boy*, Aug. 20, 1770, and "Baltimore-Town Oct. 16, 1773," *Maryland Journal*, Nov. 13, 1773.

59. James Delbourgo, *A Most Amazing Scene of Wonders: Electricity and Enlightenment in America* (Cambridge, MA: Harvard University Press, 2006), 117–18, 154–55.
60. Wiederhold to Gilsa, New York[?], May 4–7, 1782, *Krieg in Amerika*, 327–28.
61. Kate Davies, *Catharine Macaulay and Mercy Otis Warren: The Revolutionary Atlantic and the Politics of Gender* (Oxford: Oxford University Press, 2006).
62. Syson, *Doctor of Love*, 99.
63. Graham, *Lecture*, 23, 14.
64. *The Manual Exercise* (Monaghan, n.d.), quoted in Higgins, *Nation of Politicians*, 198.
65. Abigail Adams to Mary Cranch, New York, June 27, 1790, in Stewart Mitchell, ed., *New Letters of Abigail Adams, 1788–1801* (Boston: Houghton Mifflin Company, 1947), 52.
66. Short, *Comparative History*, 28.
67. Smith, *Inquiry*, vol. 1, ch. 8.
68. Mary Fissell, *Pushback: The 2,500 Year Fight to Thwart Women by Restricting Abortion* (New York: Seal Press, 2025), 70, 71, 119–22. James Boswell and Casanova both used condoms: "armour" and "redingote anglaise." James Boswell, *London Journal, 1762–1763* (London: Penguin Classics, 2010), 215, 182, 186–87, 237; Jean-Jacques Amy and Michel Thiery, "The Condom: A Turbulent History," *European Journal of Contraception & Reproductive Health Care* 20:5 (2015): 387–402: 392, 393, 401.
69. George Fisher, *The American Instructor: or, Young man's best companion* (Philadelphia: B. Franklin and D. Hall, 1753), 366; Molly Farrell, "Ben Franklin Put an Abortion Recipe in His Math Textbook," *Slate*, May 5, 2022, and Fissell, *Pushback*, 119–21.
70. *Whitehall Evening Post*, Jan. 50–7, 1769; *The World* (London), Sept. 24, 1788.
71. Cornelia Hughes Dayton, "Taking the Trade: Abortion and Gender Relations in an Eighteenth-Century New England Village," *William and Mary Quarterly* 48:1 (1991): 19–49.
72. Susan Klepp, *Revolutionary Conceptions: Women, Fertility, and Family Limitation in America, 1760–1820* (Chapel Hill: Omohundro Institute of Early American History and Culture / University of North Carolina Press, 2009), 8; Nora Doyle, *Maternal Bodies: Redefining Motherhood in Early America* (Chapel Hill: University of North Carolina Press, 2018), 2; Laura Drewett, "'Fatal Secrets' and the Silent Contraceptive Revolution of Eighteenth-Century France: 'C'est le secret du vinaigrier'?" *Population* 76:4 (2021): 621–44: 621.
73. Francesco Cinnirella, Marc Klemp, and Jacob Weisdorf, "Malthus in the Bedroom: Birth Spacing as Birth Control in Pre-Transition England," *Demography* 54 (2017): 413–36.
74. Klepp, *Revolutionary Conceptions*, 6.

75. Angus McLaren, *A History of Contraception: From Antiquity to the Present Day* (Oxford: Basil Blackwell, 1990), 180.
76. Sejanus in *London Chronicle* 19 (Feb. 13, 1766), 149, quoted in Morgan, *Prologue to Revolution,* 134.
77. "First Blacks of Portsmouth, Part 1," SeacoastNH.com, http://www.seacoastnh.com/.
78. Morgan, *Gentle Puritan,* 290, 310.
79. Stiles, *Diary,* vol. 2: 272.
80. Divorce case, Newport and Violet Freeman, RG 003: Records of the Judicial Department, New Haven County, Superior Court, Papers by Subject 1712–1900, Divorce, box 665. Thanks to Susan Bigelow at the Connecticut State Library for this reference.
81. Akeia A. F. Benard, "Appendix I: Database of Names," from *The Free African American Cultural Landscape: Newport, Rhode Island, 1774–1826* (Ph.D. diss., University of Connecticut, 2008).
82. [Esther De Berdt Reed,] *Sentiments of an American Woman* (Philadelphia: John Dunlap, [1780]).
83. George Washington to Esther Reed, Bergen City [N.J.], July 14, 1780, *Founders Online,* National Archives, https://founders.archives.gov/.
84. *New-Hampshire Gazette,* November 6, 13, and 20, 1761.
85. Sword, *Wives Not Slaves*, 146, 183.
86. "First Church of Scarborough Admissions and Baptisms, 1763–1789," *Maine Genealogy Archives,* https://archives.mainegenealogy.net/.
87. *Virginia Gazette (Purdie),* March 15, 1776.
88. Rachel Hope Cleves, *Charity and Sylvia: A Same-Sex Marriage in Early America* (Oxford: Oxford University Press, 2014), 2.
89. Jen Manion, *Female Husbands: A Trans History* (Cambridge: Cambridge University Press, 2020), 95.
90. Robert Kent Donovan, "The Military Origins of the Roman Catholic Relief Programme of 1778," *Historical Journal* 28:1 (1985), 79–102: 90.
91. To J[ohn] S[pink], Esq. Charles Street, June 6, 1780, in Ignatius Sancho, *Letters of the Late Ignatius Sancho, An African,* 2 vols. (London: J. Dodsley, 1782), vol. 2: 172.
92. Thomas Holcroft, *A Plain and Succinct Narrative of the Late Riots and Disturbances in the Cities of London and Westminster and Borough of Southwark*, ed. Garland Garvey Smith (Atlanta: Emory University Library, 1944), 24.
93. Holcroft, *Plain and Succinct Narrative,* 27–28.
94. *Morning Chronicle,* July 22, 1780, 3.
95. Sancho, *Letters,* June 6, 1780, 174.
96. Lord George Gordon, *Innocence Vindicated, and the Intrigues of Popery and its Abettors displayed,* 2nd ed. (London: R Denham, [1783]), part 2: 20.

97. *The Morning Post, and Daily Advertiser,* June 9, 1780.
98. McNeill, *Mosquito Empires,* 191; J. W. Fortescue, *A History of the British Army,* 12 vols. (London: Macmillan, 1902), vol. 3 (1763–1793): 339–41; O'Shaughnessy, *Men Who Lost America,* 177–85; Brown, *Reaper's Garden,* introduction.
99. Mulcahy, *Hurricanes and Society,* 77–82.
100. Fortescue, *History of the British Army,* vol. 3: 338.
101. Prince Golam Mohammed, *History of Hyder Shah,* 262.
102. Prince Golam Mohammed, *History of Hyder Shah,* 262.
103. Major James Mackenzie of the 73rd Foot [to Rt. Hon. Charles Jenkinson, Secretary of War], Nov. 3, 1780, Papers of the Earl of Cromartie, Centre of South Asian Studies, Cambridge University, https://www.s-asian.cam.ac.uk/; Conway, *War of American Independence,* 151–52.
104. Iqbal Husain, trans., "The Diplomatic Vision of Tipu Sultan: Briefs for Embassies to Turkey and France, 1785–86," in Irfan Habib, ed., *State and Diplomacy Under Tipu Sultan* (New Delhi: Tulika Books, 2001), 19–65: 48; Rosalind O'Hanlon, "Kingdom, Household and Body History, Gender and Imperial Service Under Akbar," *Modern Asian Studies* 41:5 (2007): 889–923: 914–16; and Ali Anooshahr, "The King Who Would Be Man: The Gender Roles of the Warrior King in Early Mughal History," *Journal of the Royal Asian Society,* series 3, 18:3 (2008): 327–40: 333–34.
105. "The Battle of Pollilur, India, Seringapatam, Early 19th Century," sothebys.com.
106. Jean-Marie Lafont, trans., "The *Mémoires* of Lieutenant-Colonel Russel," in Habib, *State and Diplomacy Under Tipu Sultan,* 82–110: 99.
107. M. P. Sridharan, "Tipu's Letters to French Officials," *Proceedings of the Indian History Congress* 45 (1984): 503–8.
108. "Statement of Instructions for Negotiations with the King of France," Iqbal Husain, trans., in Irfan Habib, *State and Diplomacy Under Tipu Sultan,* 19–65: 42, 44.
109. Conway, *War of American Independence,* 157, and Linda Colley, *Captives: The Story of Britain's Pursuit of Empire and How Its Soldiers and Civilians Were Held Captive by the Dream of Global Supremacy* (New York: Pantheon Books, 2002), 209.
110. John Adams to Vergennes, Paris, July 13, 1780, *Founders Online,* National Archives, https://founders.archives.gov/.
111. Charles O'Hara to Duke of Grafton, "Camp near Wilmington Cape Fear River April 20th 1781," Duke of Grafton Papers, 423/191/S, Suffolk Record Office, Bury St Edmunds. Many thanks to Matthew Mulcahy for this reference.
112. Earl Cornwallis to Sir Henry Clinton, Wilmington, Aug. 29, 1780, and

Wilmington April, 23, 1781, *Colonial and State Papers of North Carolina,* vol. 15: 276–78, vol. 17: 1018–19, *Documenting the American South,* https://docsouth.unc.edu/.

113. O'Hara to Grafton, April 20, 1781, 11, 12.
114. Earl Cornwallis to Sir Henry Clinton, Wilmington, Aug. 23, 1780, and Sept. 19, 1780, *Colonial and State Papers of North Carolina,* vol. 15: 273–76, 278–82, *Documenting the American South,* https://docsouth.unc.edu/.
115. Dan L. Morrill, *Southern Campaigns of the American Revolution* (Baltimore: Nautical and Aviation Publishing Company of America, 1993), 157.
116. O'Hara to Grafton, April 20, 1781, 17, 14.
117. William B. Willcox, ed., *The American Rebellion: Sir Henry Clinton's Narrative of His Campaigns, 1775–1782* (New Haven, CT: Yale University Press, 1954), 226.
118. Rochambeau to Vergennes, July 11, 1780, as quoted in Eugena Poulin and Claire Quintal, trans. and ed., *La Gazette Françoise, 1780–1781: Revolutionary America's French Newspaper* (Newport, RI: Salve Regina University, and Hanover, NH: University Press of New England, 2007), xvii.
119. Poulin and Quintal, *La Gazette Françoise,* xvii.
120. Robert A. Selig, "A German Soldier in New England During the Revolutionary War: The Account of George Daniel Flohr," *Newport History* 65:2 (1993): 48–65: 49.
121. *La Gazette Françoise,* Dec. 15, 1780, in Poulin and Quintal, *La Gazette Françoise,* 60.
122. Scott, *British Foreign Policy,* 307.
123. Edward Gray, *American in the Tower: The Prison Narrative of Henry Laurens, the Law of Treason, and the End of the American Revolutionary War* (forthcoming).
124. Hanbury Parish Records, D 1528/1/4, Staffordshire RO, as quoted in Stephen Conway, *The British Isles and the War of American Independence* (Oxford: Oxford University Press, 2000), 202.
125. O'Hara to Grafton, April 20, 1781, 6.
126. Horsbrugh Diary, vol. 2 (Oct. 15, 1780–Jan. 15, 1782): 270–71, Add. MS 50257, BL.

Chapter 11: A Cabaña in Havana

1. The best work on Spain and Spanish America, especially Florida and Cuba, includes DuVal, *Independence Lost;* Ferreiro, *Brothers at Arms;* Schneider, *Occupation of Havana;* Gonzalo M. Quintero Saravia, *Bernardo de Gálvez: Spanish Hero of the American Revolution* (Chapel Hill: University of North Carolina Press, 2018); Gabriel Paquette and Gonzalo M. Quintero Saravia, eds., *Spain and the American Revolution: New Approaches and Perspectives*

(Charlottesville: University of Virginia Press, 2020); and Ada Ferrer, *Cuba: An American History* (New York: Simon & Schuster, 2021).

2. Francisco Saavedra de Sangronis, *Journal of Don Francisco Saavedra de Sangronis . . .*, ed. Francisco Morales Padrón, trans. Aileen Moore Topping (Gainesville: University of Florida Press, 1989), Feb. 28, 1781, 127; Gabriel Paquette and Gonzalo M. Quintero Saravia, "Introduction," in Paquette and Saravia, *Spain and the American Revolution*, 1–36: 21.
3. Schneider, *Occupation of Havana*, 67.
4. Ferrer, *Cuba*, 43.
5. Schneider, *Occupation of Havana*, 77–78.
6. Ferrer, *Cuba*, 45.
7. Saavedra, *Journal*, March 11, 1781, 131.
8. Joanne B. Freeman, *Affairs of Honor: National Politics in the New Republic* (New Haven, CT: Yale University Press, 2002), xxii.
9. Freeman, *Affairs of Honor*, xv, and Verónica Undurraga, "Honor," *Atlantic History*, in *Oxford Bibliographies Online* (2014), introduction, DOI: 10.1093/OBO/9780199730414-0247.
10. Freeman, *Affairs of Honor*.
11. Esteban de Terreros y Pando, *Diccionario castellano . . .*, 2nd ed. (Madrid: Viuda de Ibarra, 1787), from La Biblioteca de la Real Academia Española.
12. Pablo Piccato, *The Tyranny of Opinion: Honor in the Construction of the Mexican Public Sphere* (Durham, NC: Duke University Press, 2010).
13. Sonya Lipsett-Rivera, *The Origins of Macho: Men and Masculinity in Colonial Mexico* (Albuquerque: University of New Mexico Press, 2019), 6, and Robert C. Schwaller, "'For Honor and Defence': Race and the Right to Bear Arms in Early Colonial Mexico," *Colonial Latin American Review* 21:2 (2012): 239–66.
14. *Massachusetts Gazette and Daily Advertiser*, Feb. 17, 1784, and Alfred F. Young, *Masquerade: The Life and Times of Deborah Sampson, Continental Soldier* (New York: Knopf, 2004), especially 1–19.
15. Schneider, *Occupation of Havana*, 242.
16. María del Carmen Barcia, *Los Ilustres Appellidos: Negros en la Habana Colonial* (Havana, Cuba: Ediciones Boloña, 2008), 245.
17. Ferrer, *Cuba*, 55.
18. Schneider, *Occupation of Havana*, especially chs. 5–6, and Alex Borucki and José Luis Belmonte Postigo, "The Impact of the American Revolutionary War on the Slave Trade to Cuba," *William and Mary Quarterly* 80:3 (2023): 493–524.
19. Schneider, *Occupation of Havana*, 9, 270.
20. Saravia, *Bernardo de Gálvez*, 5.
21. Saravia, *Bernardo de Gálvez*, 18.

22. Manuel Danvila y Collado, *Reinado de Carlos III*, in *Historia General de España*, Antonio Cánovas del Castillo, general ed., 6 vols. (Madrid: Real Academia de la Historia/El Progreso Editorial, 1894), vol. 4: 201–2. See also Saravia, *Bernardo de Gálvez*, 136.
23. DuVal, *Independence Lost*, 120–21.
24. Bernardo de Gálvez to José de Gálvez, Oct. 16, 1779, Archivo General de Indias (hereafter AGI), Santo Domingo, 2586, as quoted in Saravia, *Bernardo de Gálvez*, 135.
25. J. Barton Starr, *Tories, Dons, and Rebels: The American Revolution in British West Florida* (Gainesville: University Press of Florida, 1976), 78–121.
26. "Diario formado por Don Esteban Miró . . . ," Feb. 10, 1780, AGI, Santo Domingo, 2543, and Cuba, 2, as quoted in Saravia, *Bernardo de Gálvez*, 175.
27. Paquette and Saravia, *Spain and the American Revolution*, 20.
28. Bernardo de Gálvez to José de Gálvez, Mobile, March 20, 1780, AGS 6912, EX 2, as quoted in Saravia, *Bernardo de Gálvez*, 174.
29. Stuart B. Schwartz and Matthew Mulcahy, "Natural Disasters in the Caribbean to 1850," in Morgan et al., eds., *Sea and Land: An Environmental History of the Caribbean* (Oxford: Oxford University Press, 2022), 187–252: 203, and Saravia, *Bernardo de Gálvez*, 190.
30. Saavedra, *Journal*, Oct. 15, 1780, 32.
31. Saavedra, *Journal*, Jan. 23, 1781, 107.
32. José de Gálvez to Juan Manuel de Cagigal, El Pardo, Feb. 12, 1781, AGI, Santo Domingo, 2082, in Saravia, *Bernardo de Gálvez*, 240.
33. James A. Lewis, "Anglo-American Entrepreneurs in Havana: The Background and Significance of the Expulsion of 1784–1785," in Jacques A. Barbier and Allan J. Kuethe, *The North American Role in Spanish Imperial Economy, 1760–1819* (Manchester, UK: Manchester University Press, 1984): 112–26: 113–16.
34. Saavedra, *Journal*, Feb. 2, 1781, 113.
35. Saavedra, *Journal*, Jan. 23, 1781, 108.
36. Saavedra, *Journal*, Feb. 4, 1781, 115–16.
37. Saravia, *Bernardo de Gálvez*, 196.
38. Bernardo de Gálvez, "Bernardo de Gálvez Diary of the Operations Against Pensacola," trans. Gaspar Cusachs, *Louisiana Historical Quarterly* 1:1 (1917): 44–84: 48 (March 10, 1781).
39. Paquette and Saravia, *Spain and the American Revolution*, 22.
40. Gálvez, "Bernardo de Gálvez Diary," March 10, 1781, 49.
41. Gálvez, "Bernardo de Gálvez Diary," March 17, 1781, 52.
42. Legajo 6853 (1789): Cuba: Tropa y incidencias (1788–1795), Archivo General de Simancas, Secretaria de Guerra Moderna, PARES, https://pares.mcu.es/.

43. Gálvez, "Bernardo de Gálvez Diary," March 28, 1781, 59; DuVal, *Independence Lost,* 200.
44. Saavedra, *Journal,* May 1, 1781, 164.
45. Gálvez, "Bernardo de Gálvez Diary," April 5 and 6, 1781, 63.
46. Gálvez, "Bernardo de Gálvez Diary," April 12, 1781, 63–64.
47. Saavedra, *Journal,* April 21, 1781, 153–54, and DuVal, *Independence Lost,* 209–10.
48. Saavedra, *Journal,* April 21, 1781, 153–54.
49. Gálvez, "Bernardo de Gálvez Diary," April 18, 1781, 66.
50. Saavedra, *Journal,* May 6, 1781, 168–69.
51. Diego Joseph Cavarro to S Fran Ayma de Monteil, Havana, May 12, 1781, "Documents Relating to the French participation in the American Revolution," Gen MSS 308, Box 1, Beinecke Library, Yale University.
52. Francisco de Miranda, "Miranda's Diary of the Siege of Pensacola, 1781," Donald E. Worcester, ed. and trans., *Florida Historical Quarterly* 29:3 (1950): 163–96: 189; May 6, 1781; Saavedra, *Journal,* May 6, 1781, 167–68; and Gálvez, "Bernardo de Gálvez Diary," May 6, 1781, 73.
53. Starr, *Tories, Dons, and Rebels,* 27, 28.
54. Howe to Germain, July 7, 1777, CO 5/594, as quoted in Starr, *Tories, Dons, and Rebels,* 57–58.
55. Chester to Hillsborough, Pensacola, March 8, 1771, in Eron O. Rowland, "Peter Chester, Third Governor of the Province of British West Florida under British Dominion, 1770–1781," in Dunbar Rowland, ed., *Publications of the Mississippi Historical Society* 5 (1925): 1–183: 34.
56. Starr, *Tories, Dons, and Rebels,* 57.
57. Hugh Mackay Gordon to Edward Winslow, March 20, 1779, Winslow Family Papers, University of New Brunswick Archives and Special Collections, online at https://web.lib.unb.ca/winslow/.
58. Campbell to Clinton, March 10, 1779, BHP, 1815, Reel 7, in Starr, *Tories, Dons, and Rebels,* 138–39.
59. DuVal, *Independence Lost,* 199, 205–6.
60. Peter Chester to the Earl of Hillsborough, Pensacola, March 9, 1771, in Rowland, "Peter Chester, Third Governor," 38.
61. Report of Congress with the Creek Indians, Oct. 29, 1771, in Rowland, "Peter Chester, Third Governor," 111.
62. Alexander Cameron to Lord Germain, Oct. 31, 1780, CO 5/82, in Starr, *Tories, Dons, and Rebels,* 177.
63. Saavedra, *Journal,* May 10, 1781, 184.
64. DuVal, *Independence Lost,* 206.
65. Miranda, "Miranda's Diary," May 8, 1781, 191, and Saavedra, *Journal,* May 8, 1781, 170–71.

66. Saavedra, *Journal,* May 11, 1781, 173, and Miranda, "Miranda's Diary," May 10, 1781, 192.
67. Saavedra, *Journal,* May 26, 1781, 191, and *Courrier d'Avignon,* July 27, 1781, 250, Presse18, Les gazettes européennes du 18e siècle, https://www.gazettes18e.fr/.
68. Saravia, *Bernardo de Gálvez,* 7–8.
69. Kimberly S. Hanger, *Bounded Lives, Bounded Places: Free Black Society in Colonial New Orleans, 1769–1803* (Durham, NC: Duke University Press, 1997).
70. Schneider, *Occupation of Havana,* 296–97.
71. Philip D. Morgan and Andrew Jackson O'Shaughnessy, "Arming Slaves in the American Revolution," in Christopher Leslie Brown and Philip D. Morgan, eds., *Arming Slaves: From Classical Times to the Modern Age* (New Haven, CT: Yale University Press, 2006): 180–208, especially 182, 187, 192.
72. Robert A. Geake with Lorén M. Spears, *From Slaves to Soldiers: The 1st Rhode Island Regiment in the American Revolution* (Yardley, PA: Westholme, 2016), 133, 15, 42.
73. Hanger, *Bounded Lives,* 119–20.
74. Schneider, *Occupation of Havana,* 299–302, and Hanger, *Bounded Lives,* 121.
75. Saavedra, *Journal,* July 18, 1781, 200–201.
76. *Royal (Rivington's) Gazette,* May 12, 1781 (New York).
77. George Washington to Joseph Reed, Morris-Town, May 28, 1780, *Founders Online,* National Archives, https://founders.archives.gov/.
78. William B. Reed, *The Life and Correspondence of Joseph Reed,* 2 vols. (Philadelphia: Lindsay and Blakiston, 1847), vol. 1: 375.
79. Hannah Farber, *Underwriters of the American Revolution: How Insurance Shaped the American Founding* (Chapel Hill: Omohundro Institute for Early American History and Culture/University of North Carolina Press, 2023), 74–76.
80. Alexander Hamilton to Robert Morris, April 30, 1781, *Founders Online,* National Archives, https://founders.archives.gov/.
81. Adam Jortner, *The Promised Land: Jewish Patriots, the American Revolution, and the Birth of Religious Freedom* (Oxford: Oxford University Press, 2024), 21, 85–87.
82. Ferguson, *Power of the Purse,* 126.
83. Reed, *Life and Correspondence,* vol. 1: 373.
84. Saavedra, *Journal,* July 31, 1781, 208.
85. Saavedra, *Journal,* Aug. 16, 1781, 211.
86. James A. Lewis, "Las Damas de La Havana, el Precursor, and Francisco de Saavedra: A Note on Spanish Participation in the Battle of Yorktown," *The Americas* 37:1 (July 1980): 83–99: 98.

87. June 20, 1781, in Stephan Popp, *A Hessian Soldier in the American Revolution* (Papamoa Press, 2018), unpaginated.
88. Ewald, *Diary of the American War,* 314.
89. Ewald, *Diary of the American War,* 336.
90. Sylvia R. Frey, *Water from the Rock: Black Resistance in a Revolutionary Age* (Princeton, NJ: Princeton University Press, 1991), 170.
91. Georg Daniel Flohr as quoted in Robert A. Selig, "Georg Daniel Flohr's Journal: A New Perspective," AmericanRevolution.org.
92. Popp, *A Hessian Soldier,* Oct. 16, 1781.
93. Flohr as quoted in Selig, "Georg Daniel Flohr's Journal."
94. Edward M. Riley, "St. George Tucker's Journal of the Siege of Yorktown, 1781," *William and Mary Quarterly* 5:3 (July 1948): 375–95.
95. Flohr as quoted in Selig, "Georg Daniel Flohr's Journal."
96. Riley, "St. George Tucker's Journal," 391.
97. Ewald, *Diary of the American War,* 335.
98. Ewald, *Diary of the American War,* 298, 426.
99. Wiederhold to Gilsa, New York, April 12–May 5, 1782, *Krieg in Amerika,* 320–23.
100. Ewald, *Diary of the American War,* 345.
101. Paul Hockings, "Anglo-Mysore Wars," *Encyclopedia of Modern Asia,* ed. Karen Christensen and David Levinson, vol. 1 (New York: Charles Scribner's Sons, 2002), 106–7.
102. British estimates—likely exaggerated—were forty thousand to fifty thousand. Adkins and Adkins, *Gibraltar,* 306; Paquette and Saravia, *Spain and the American Revolution,* 16.
103. Drinkwater, *History of the Late Siege,* 258.
104. Eliga Gould, *Crucible of Peace: The Turbulent History of the United States' Founding Treaty* (Oxford University Press, forthcoming).
105. Paquette and Saravia, *Spain and the American Revolution,* 24.
106. *Massachusetts Gazette,* Feb. 17, 1784.
107. "Treaty of Paris, 1783," "Milestone Documents," National Archives, https://www.archives.gov/.
108. Speech to Lord Sydney, Jan. 4, 1786, William L. Stone, *Life of Joseph Brant-Thayendanegea,* 2 vols. (New York: George Dearborn & Co., 1838), vol. 2: 253–54.
109. Barbara Graymont, "KOÑWATSIˀTSIAIÉÑNI (Mary Brant)," in *Dictionary of Canadian Biography,* vol. 4 (Toronto: University of Toronto / Université Laval, 2003), https://www.biographi.ca/.
110. Wiederhold to Gilsa, New York, April 6–10, 1783, *Krieg in Amerika,* 360–62.
111. Mary Beth Norton, *The British-Americans: The Loyalist Exiles in England,*

1774–1789 (Boston: Little, Brown, 1972); Maya Jasanoff, *Liberty's Exiles: American Loyalists in the Revolutionary World* (New York: Knopf, 2011); and Cassandra Pybus, *Epic Journeys of Freedom: Runaway Slaves of the American Revolution and Their Global Quest for Liberty* (Boston: Beacon Press, 2006).

112. Jasanoff, *Liberty's Exiles,* 6.
113. Jasanoff, *Liberty's Exiles,* 122, and Christopher Leslie Brown, *Moral Capital: Foundations of British Abolitionism* (Chapel Hill: Omohundro Institute of Early American History and Culture / University of North Carolina Press, 2006).
114. John Eardley Wilmot, Debate of Feb. 17, 1783, *Cobbett's Parliamentary History of England* (London: T. Curson Hansard, 1814), vol. 23, cols. 564–70: col. 564.
115. Speech of Lord North, Debate on Preliminary Articles of Peace, Feb. 17, 1783, *Cobbett's Parliamentary History of England,* vol. 23 (London: T. C. Hansard, 1814), col. 453. See also Sarah M. S. Pearsall, *Atlantic Families: Lives and Letters in the Later Eighteenth Century* (Oxford: Oxford University Press, 2009), and Jasanoff, *Liberty's Exiles,* 118–19.
116. Jasanoff, *Liberty's Exiles,* 121.
117. Jasanoff, *Liberty's Exiles,* 131.
118. Mary Beth Norton, "The Fate of Some Black Loyalists of the American Revolution," *Journal of Negro History* 58:4 (1973): 402–26 and her "Eighteenth-Century American Women in Peace and War: The Case of the Loyalists," *William and Mary Quarterly* 33:3 (July 1976): 386–409.
119. Joseph Galloway, *The Claim of the American Loyalists, Reviewed and Maintained upon Incontrovertible Principles of Law and Justice* (London: G. and T. Wilkie, 1788), v, 107.
120. Grace Galloway to Elizabeth Galloway, Nov. 27, 1778, Galloway Papers, Library of Congress.
121. Grace Growden Galloway, "Diary of Grace Growden Galloway (June 1778–July 1779)," ed. Raymond C. Werner, *Pennsylvania Magazine of History and Biography* 55:1 (1931): 32–94: 76.
122. Linda K. Kerber, "The Paradox of Women's Citizenship in the Early Republic: The Case of *Martin vs. Massachusetts,* 1805," *American Historical Review* 97:2 (1992): 349–78.
123. Anna Rawle to Rebecca Shoemaker, Sept. 20, 1780, Shoemaker Papers, Historical Society of Pennsylvania.
124. Richard Weaver to Lord North, c. November 1783, AO 13/79, 729–33ff., NA.
125. Stiles, *Diary,* Oct. 1, 1781, vol. 2: 558.
126. "The Child Jacob two years old last Month and bound to me till aet. 24," Stiles, *Diary,* vol. 3: 50–51. See also Contract with ES for indentured service by Newport, Violet, and their son, Jacob Freeman (MVP #806), October 8, 1781, and payment order for transportation for Newport, Violet, and their

son, Jacob Freeman (MVP #830), December 25, 1782, series 5, Additions to Stiles Bequest, Beinecke Library, Yale University. See also Sam Dinnie, "The Labor Behind the Learned: A Reexamination of Ezra Stiles," Newport Historical Society, Sept. 8, 2023, https://newporthistory.org/.

127. "Expediente sobre la queja dada por los oficiales del Batallón de Morenos libres de La Havana contra el subinspector Antonio Seidel" (1788–95), Archivo General de Simancas, Guerra Moderna, 6853, exp. 53, ff. 234–73; Schneider, *Occupation of Havana*, 299–302.
128. DuVal, *Independence Lost*, 218.
129. Borucki and Postigo, "Impact of the American Revolutionary War," 522.
130. Carlos Marichal, "The Spanish-American Silver Peso: Export Commodity and Global Money of the Ancient Regime, 1550–1800," in Steven Topik, Carlos Marichal, and Zephyr Frank, eds., *From Silver to Cocaine: Latin American Commodity Chains and the Building of the World Economy* (Durham, NC: Duke University Press, 2006): 25–52: 41–42.
131. Alejandra Irigoin, "Global Silver: Bullion or Specie? Supply and Demand in the Making of the Early Modern Global Economy," London School of Economics Economic History Working papers, no. 285 (September 2018), 16.

Chapter 12: A Mansion in Guangzhou

1. May-bo Ching, "Chopsticks or Cutlery? How Canton Hong Merchants Entertained Foreign Guests in the Eighteenth and Nineteenth Centuries," in Kendall Jackson, ed., *Narratives of Free Trade: The Commercial Cultures of Early US-China Relations* (Hong Kong: Hong Kong University Press, 2012): 99–116.
2. Philip Chadwick Foster Smith, *The Empress of China* (Philadelphia: Philadelphia Maritime Museum, 1984), 149–52, 183. On Sino-American relations and the Canton system, Smith, *The Empress of China;* Weng Eang Cheong, *The Hong Merchants of Canton: Chinese Merchants in Sino-Western Trade,* Nordic Institute of Asian Studies Monograph Series (Richmond: Curzon Press, 1997); Paul A. Van Dyke, *The Canton Trade: Life and Enterprise on the China Coast, 1700–1845* (Hong Kong: Hong Kong University Press, 2005); James R. Fichter, *So Great a Proffit: How the East Indies Trade Transformed Anglo-American Capitalism* (Cambridge, MA: Harvard University Press, 2010); Kariann Akemi Yokota, *Unbecoming British: How Revolutionary America Became a Postcolonial Nation* (Oxford: Oxford University Press, 2011); John R. Haddad, *America's First Adventure in China: Trade, Treaties, Opium, and Salvation* (Philadelphia: Temple University Press, 2013); and Dael A. Norwood, *Trading Freedom: How Trade with China Defined Early America* (Chicago: University of Chicago Press, 2022).

3. "Letter from Mr. Shaw, . . . addressed to John Jay, esq.," *The American Museum, or Universal Magazine* (Philadelphia, PA) 1: 3 (March 1787): 194–97: 197.
4. Paul A. Van Dyke, *Merchants of Canton and Macao: Success and Failure in Eighteenth-Century China* (Hong Kong: Hong Kong University Press, 2016), 11, 61, and Charles Constant, *Les Mémoires de Charles de Constant sur le commerce á la Chine,* ed. Louis Dermigny (Paris: École Pratique des Hautes Études, 1964), 411.
5. East India Company records, Dec. 20, 1781, as quoted in Van Dyke, *Merchants of Canton,* 92–93.
6. Valery M. Garrett, *Chinese Dragon Robes,* ed. Nigel Cameron and Sylvia Fraser-Lu, *Images of Asia* (Hong Kong: Oxford University Press, 1998), 11, 15, 17, 56–57, and Cheong, *Hong Merchants of Canton,* 162.
7. Garrett, *Chinese Dragon Robes,* 8–10.
8. Evelyn S. Rawski and Susan Naquin, "Review Essay: A New Look at the Canton Trade, 1700–1845," *Harvard Journal of Asiatic Studies* 78:2 (December 2018): 491–514: 504.
9. Japan and Russia had their own ports of access. Van Dyke, *Merchants of Canton,* 1.
10. Van Dyke, *Merchants of Canton,* 15.
11. Smith, *Empress of China,* 149, and Ping Chia Kuo, "Canton and Salem: The Impact of Chinese Culture upon New England Life During the Post-Revolutionary Era," *New England Quarterly* 3:3 (July 1930): 420–42.
12. Smith, *Empress of China,* 181.
13. Samuel Shaw, "First Voyage to Canton" in Josiah Quincy, ed., *The Journals of Major Samuel Shaw* (Boston: WM. Crosby and H. P. Nichols, 1847): 131–214: 174, 183–5.
14. Shaw, "First Voyage," 178, and Smith, *Empress of China,* 180.
15. John White Swift to his father, Canton, Dec. 3, 1784, in John W. Swift, P. Hodgkinson, and Samuel W. Woodhouse, "The Voyage of the Empress of China," *Pennsylvania Magazine of History and Biography* 63:1 (Jan. 1939): 24–36: 29.
16. "Letter from Mr. Shaw, agent for the owners of the ship Empress of China, in her voyage to Canton, addressed to John Jay, esq. New York, May 19, 1785," *The American Museum, or Universal Magazine* (Philadelphia, PA), 1:3 (March 1787): 194–97: 195, 197 (the gifts).
17. Yokota, *Unbecoming British,* 116.
18. Swift et al., "Voyage of the Empress of China," 29.
19. Smith, *Empress of China,* 172.
20. Norwood, *Trading Freedom,* 16–17.
21. Meg Roberts, "Caregiving, Crisis and Coercion in the American Revolutionary War," Ph.D. diss., Cambridge University, 2025.

22. Lawrence A. Peskin, *Three Consuls: Capitalism, Empire, and the Rise and Fall of America's Mediterranean Community, 1776–1840* (Cambridge: Cambridge University Press, 2024).
23. Smith, *Empress of China,* 14.
24. Edward G. Gray, *The Making of John Ledyard: Empire and Ambition in the Life of an Early American Traveler* (New Haven, CT: Yale University Press, 2007), 101–7.
25. *Pennsylvania Packet,* Aug. 21, 1783, quoted in Smith, *Empress of China,* 23.
26. Robert Morris to John Jay, Philadelphia, Nov. 27, 1783, in John Jay, *The Correspondence and Public Papers of John Jay,* ed. Henry Phelps Johnson, 3 vols. (New York: Putnam, 1890), 3: 96–97.
27. George Lupton to William Eden, Paris, July 23, 1777, in Benjamin Franklin Stevens, *Facsimiles of Manuscripts in European Archives Relating to America, 1773–1783,* 24 vols. (London: Malby & Sons, 1890), vol. 3, nos. 235–34: no. 259.
28. Jonathan Feld, "Navigating the Legal, Economic, and National Boundaries of the Incarceration of American Sailors at Mill and Forton Prisons, 1777–1783," M.Phil. thesis, Cambridge University, 2019, and T. Cole Jones, *Captives of Liberty: Prisoners of War and the Politics of Vengeance in the American Revolution* (Philadelphia: University of Pennsyvania Press, 2019).
29. John Green, "American Prisoners in Mill Prison at Plymouth, in 1782: Captain John Green's Letter," *South Carolina Historical and Genealogical Magazine* 10:2 (April 1909), 116–24, and John Green to Henry Laurens, Mill Prison, April 5, 1782, Henry Laurens Papers, South Caroliniana Library, University of South Carolina, https://digital.tcl.sc.edu/.
30. Smith, *Empress of China,* 55.
31. Shaw, *Memoir,* 10.
32. Shaw, *Memoir,* 92.
33. Shaw, *Memoir,* 99.
34. Shaw, *Memoir,* 100.
35. Alexander Hamilton to Robert Morris, De Peyster's Point, New York, April 30, 1781, *Founders Online,* National Archives, https://founders.archives.gov/.
36. Ferguson, *Power of the Purse,* 137.
37. Grubb, *Continental Dollar,* 224.
38. Jay Coughtry, *The Notorious Triangle: Rhode Island and the African Slave Trade, 1700–1807* (Philadelphia: Temple University Press, 1981), 92, and Farber, *Underwriters of the American Revolution,* 80.
39. Rufus King to John Adams, New York Feb. 3, 1786, in *The Life and Correspondence of Rufus King,* ed. Charles R. King, 5 vols. (New York: G. P. Putnam's Sons, 1894), vol. 1: 155.
40. Fichter, *So Great a Proffit,* 39.

41. I have used the timeline function on the Slave Voyages, Estimates: Trans-Atlantic Slave Trade, https://www.slavevoyages.org/assessment/estimates.
42. The only work on this topic of which I am aware is Christopher Leslie Brown, "The War for American Independence on the West African Coast," presented at the Annual Omohundro Institute of Early American History and Culture Conference in Poitiers, France, June 2024.
43. Fichter, *So Great a Proffit,* 35.
44. *Maryland Journal and Baltimore Advertiser,* vol. 12: 64, Friday, Aug. 12, 1785.
45. *Maryland Journal and Baltimore Advertiser,* vol. 12: 64, Friday, Aug. 12, 1785.
46. Phillis Wheatley, "LIBERTY AND PEACE, A POEM," in *Writings of Phillis Wheatley*, 141–43: 142.
47. Charles Dudley to Catherine Dudley, London, December 6, 1785, and December 5, 1787, Dudley Papers, Newport Historical Society.
48. Edward E. Andrews, "Duchess Quamino (c. 1739–29 June 1804)," *African American National Biography*.
49. "Channing letter," Updike, *Memoirs,* 100.
50. George G. Channing, *Early Recollections of Newport, Rhode Island, from the year 1793 to 1811* (Newport, RI: A. J. Ward and C. E. Hammett, Jr., 1868): 170.
51. *Greenman,* "November–December [1783]," xvi.
52. *Greenman,* 273, xvii.
53. *Providence Gazette and Country Journal,* Oct. 18, 1783.
54. *Providence Gazette,* Oct. 23, 1784.
55. *Greenman,* 273.
56. Michael Kwass, *Contraband: Louis Mandrin and the Making of a Global Underground* (Cambridge, MA: Harvard University Press, 2014).
57. Dull, *Diplomatic History,* 78.
58. Charles Rappleye, *Robert Morris: Financier of the American Revolution* (New York: Simon & Schuster, 2010), 416–17, 420, and Elizabeth M. Nuxoll and Mary A. Gallagher, eds., *The Papers of Robert Morris, 1781–1784,* 9 vols. (Pittsburgh: University of Pittsburgh Press, 1999), vol. 9 (Jan. 1–Oct. 30, 1784): 150–56.
59. Edward J. Larson, *The Return of George Washington, 1783–1789* (New York: HarperCollins, 2014), 38–50.
60. George Washington to Fielding Lewis, Jr., Mount Vernon, Feb. 27, 1784, *Founders Online,* National Archives, https://founders.archives.gov/.
61. Donald Jackson and Dorothy Twohig, eds., *The Diaries of George Washington,* 6 vols. (Charlottesville: University Press of Virginia, 1976–79), vol. 4: 14.
62. Calloway, *Indian World of George Washington,* 295, 298, and Larson, *Return of George Washington,* 47.
63. Blaakman, *Speculation Nation,* 16.

64. Lennox, *North of America,* 170.
65. Calloway, *Indian World of George Washington,* 301–5.
66. Seneca Chiefs to George Washington, Dec. 1, 1790, *Founders Online,* National Archives, https://founders.archives.gov/.
67. Thayendanegea to Sydney, Jan. 4, 1786, in William L. Stone, *Life of Joseph Brant-Thayendanegea,* 2 vols. (New York: George Dearborn & Co., 1838), vol. 2: 253.
68. Thayendanegea, in Stone, *Life of Joseph Brant,* vol. 2: 254.
69. John Jay to Thomas Jefferson, New York, July 14, 1786, *Founders Online,* National Archives, https://founders.archives.gov/.
70. Lennox, *North of America,* 172.
71. Calloway, *Indian World of George Washington,* 303.
72. "A Talk Delivered by old Corn Tassle, a Cherokee Chief, for the Governor of Virginia, in Chota, ye 12th of June, 1787," William P. Palmer, ed., *Calendar of Virginia State Papers & Other Manuscripts* (Richmond: n.p., 1884), vol. 4: 306.
73. Seneca Chiefs to George Washington, Dec. 1, 1790, *Founders Online,* National Archives, founders.archives.gov/.
74. Susan Sleeper-Smith, *Indigenous Prosperity and American Conquest: Indian Women in the Ohio River Valley, 1690–1792* (Chapel Hill: Omohundro Institute of Early American History and Culture / University of North Carolina Press, 2018).
75. Ferguson, *Power of the Purse,* 238, and Blaakman, *Speculation Nation,* 9.
76. John Adams to John Jay, Nov. 11, 1785, *Founders Online,* National Archives, founders.archives.gov/.
77. Ezra Stiles, *The United States Elevated to Glory and Honor* (New Haven, CT: Thomas and Samuel Green, 1783), 52.
78. Stiles, *U.S. Elevated,* 52.
79. *Maryland Journal and Baltimore Advertiser,* vol. 12: 64, Friday, August 12, 1785.
80. Rebecca Rawle Shoemaker to Edward Shoemaker, May 12, 1785, quoted in Yokota, *Unbecoming British,* 123.

Chapter 13: A Settlement in Sierra Leone

1. Susane (or Susana) Smith to the Governor, May 12, 1792, Sierra Leone Collection, Box 1, Folder 5, University of Illinois, Chicago.
2. "Half Pay Officer of 88th Rgt Infantry" to Pitt, "Spanish Main Nov. 25th 1784" CO 123/3, ff. 130–36, NA.
3. Mattias McNamara to Lord Germain, "Fort Lewis? Senegal August 5 1776," CO 267/16, NA; "Half Pay Officer of 88th Rgt Infantry" to Pitt, "Spanish Main Nov. 25th 1784" CO 123/3, ff. 130–36, NA; Diana Dalrymple undated

letter (annotated Sept. 17, 1785), PRO 30/8/128, ff. 67–68, NA; James Matra to Fox, No 4 Duke Street Grosvenor Square 7 Aug. 1784, Add. MS 47568, 240–46, BL, and CO 201/1, NA.

4. Gwenda Morgan and Peter Rushton, *Eighteenth-Century Criminal Transportation: The Formation of the Criminal Atlantic* (New York: Palgrave Macmillan, 2004).
5. J. Adair, Recorder of London, to Lord Sydney, 8 Feby 1785, HO 47/3 f. 96–99, NA.
6. Emma Christopher, *A Merciless Place: The Fate of Britain's Convicts After the American Revolution* (Oxford: Oxford University Press, 2010).
7. On Sierra Leone and its context, see Mary Beth Norton, "The Fate of Some Black Loyalists of the American Revolution," *Journal of Negro History* 58:4 (October 1973): 402–26; Ellen Gibson Wilson, *The Loyal Blacks* (New York: G. P. Putnam's Sons, 1976); James W. St. G. Walker, *The Black Loyalists: The Search for a Promised Land in Nova Scotia and Sierra Leone, 1783–1870* (New York: Holmes & Maiers, 1976); Lamin Sanneh, *Abolitionists Abroad: American Blacks and the Making of Modern West Africa* (Cambridge, MA: Harvard University Press, 1999), 22–109; Simon Schama, *Rough Crossings: Britain, the Slaves, and the American Revolution* (London: BBC Books, 2005); Cassandra Pybus, *Epic Journeys of Freedom: Runaway Slaves of the American Revolution and Their Global Quest for Liberty* (Boston: Beacon Press, 2006); Jasanoff, *Liberty's Exiles*, 280–309; and Rachel Herrmann, *No Useless Mouth: Waging War and Fighting Hunger in the American Revolution* (Ithaca, NY: Cornell University Press, 2019), 136–54, 178–99. On the U.S. Constitution and its context, see Woody Holton, *Unruly Americans and the Origins of the Constitution* (New York: Hill and Wang, 2007); Pauline Maier, *Ratification: The People Debate the Constitution* (New York: Simon & Schuster, 2010); Michael J. Klarman, *The Framers' Coup: The Making of the United States Constitution* (Oxford: Oxford University Press, 2016); and Mary Sarah Bilder, *Madison's Hand: Revising the Constitutional Convention* (Cambridge, MA: Harvard University Press, 2016).
8. Paine, *Common Sense*, paragraph 40.
9. Ronald Dworkin, "What Is Equality? Part 3: The Place of Liberty," *Iowa Law Review* 73:1 (1987): 1–54, and Allen, *Our Declaration*, 21–23, 275–76.
10. David George, "An Account of the Life of Mr. DAVID GEORGE from Sierra Leone in Africa; given by himself in a Conversation with Brother RIPPON of London, and Brother PEARCE of Birmingham," in John Rippon, ed., *The Baptist Annual Register for 1790, 1791, 1792, and Part of 1793* (London: Dilly, Button, and Thomas, 1793): 473–84: 483, and Gregory O'Malley, *The Escapes of David George: An Odyssey of Slavery, Freedom, and the American Revolution* (New York: St. Martin's Press, 2026).

11. Eric Herschthal, *The Science of Abolition: How Slaveholders Became the Enemies of Progress* (New Haven, CT: Yale University Press, 2021), 100–107.
12. Henry Smeathman to John Lettsom, Paris, Feb. 7, 1784, and July 16, 1784, in Thomas Joseph Pettigrew, ed., *Memoirs of the Life and Writings of the Late John Coakley Lettsom* (London: Nichols et al., 1817), 279–80, 271, and Herschthal, *Science of Abolition,* 108.
13. Deirdre Coleman, *Henry Smeathman, the Flycatcher: Natural History, Slavery, and Empire in the Late Eighteenth Century* (Liverpool: Liverpool University Press, 2018), 23.
14. Coleman, *Henry Smeathman,* 21.
15. Starr Douglas, "The Making of Scientific Knowledge in an Age of Slavery: Henry Smeathman, Sierra Leone and Natural History," *Journal of Colonialism and Colonial History* 9:3 (2008): 1–16; Herschthal, *Science of Abolition,* 100, 102, 105, 107; Wilson, *Loyal Blacks,* 140.
16. Wilson, *Loyal Blacks,* 141.
17. Henry Smeathman, *Plan of the Settlement to be made near Sierra Leone on the Grain Coast of Africa* (London: T. Stockdale, 1786), 8–9.
18. Granville Sharp letter to his brother, January, 1788, and Granville Sharp to Archbishop of Canterbury, "1 Aug. 1786," Prince Hoare, *Memoirs of Granville Sharpe, composed from his own Manuscripts, and other Authentic Documents in the Possession of his Family and of the African Institution* (London: Henry Colburn and Co., 1820), 260, 263.
19. Herrmann, *No Useless Mouth,* 180.
20. Wilson, *Loyal Blacks,* 86, 87, 92.
21. Boston King, "Memoirs of the Life of Boston King, a Black Preacher," *The Methodist Magazine* 21 (May 1798): 209–13: 209–10.
22. Brown, *Moral Capital,* passim.
23. *Public Advertiser,* Jan. 19, 1786, 3.
24. Henry Smeathman to Lords of Treasury, May 17, 1786, T 1/631, NA.
25. "Mr. Smeathman's Useful hints for those who intend to visit or settle in Africa and other hot Climates," in Coleman, *Henry Smeathman,* 253–57: 254.
26. Black Poor Committee minutes, Batson's Coffeehouse, June 7, 1786, T 1/632, NA.
27. King, "Memoirs," 264.
28. Wilson, *Loyal Blacks,* 148.
29. Norton, "The Fate of Some Black Loyalists," 414.
30. Pybus, *Epic Journeys of Freedom,* 113.
31. Capt. John Matthews, "Journal of my Particular Proceedings . . . ," Oct. 27, 1785, April 28, 1785–May 15, 1787, Box 1, Folder 1, Special Collections, Princeton University.

32. Thompson to Philip Stephens, July 23, 1787, Adm 1/2594, NA.
33. Schama, *Rough Crossings,* 320.
34. Jasanoff, *Liberty's Exiles,* 286.
35. Old Settlers at Sierra Leone to Granville Sharp, Sept. 3, 1788, Hoare, *Memoirs of Granville Sharpe,* 331.
36. Granville Sharp to Right Hon. William Pitt, June/July 1788, Hoare, *Memoirs of Granville Sharpe,* 328.
37. Exclamation mark original. Granville Sharp to Sierra Leone settlers, Nov. 11, 1789, Hoare, *Memoirs of Granville Sharpe,* 345.
38. Granville Sharp to Sierra Leone settlers, Nov. 11, 1789, Hoare, *Memoirs of Granville Sharpe,* 346.
39. "Sierra Leone Treaty of 1788," *Ardhi Initiative: An African Digital Humanities Project,* University of Nebraska, https://ardhi.unl.edu/.
40. Old Settlers at Sierra Leone to Granville Sharp, Sept. 3, 1788, Hoare, *Memoirs of Granville Sharpe,* 332.
41. Hoare, *Memoirs of Granville Sharpe,* 274.
42. Old Settlers at Sierra Leone to Granville Sharp, Sept. 3, 1788, Hoare, *Memoirs of Granville Sharpe,* 332.
43. Brown, *Foul Bodies,* 6, 111–12.
44. Granville Sharp, *A Short Sketch of Temporary Regulations . . . for the Intended Settlement of the Grain Coast of Africa,* 2nd ed. (London: H. Baldwin, 1786), 22.
45. Sharp's Memorandum of Aug. 1, 1783, Hoare, *Memoirs of Granville Sharpe,* 266.
46. Schama, *Rough Crossings,* 363.
47. Granville Sharp to Dr. Lettsom MD, Oct. 13, 1788, Hoare, *Memoirs of Granville Sharpe,* 320.
48. GS to Mrs — in New York, Jan. 12, 1788, Hoare, *Memoirs of Granville Sharpe,* 314.
49. Sharp, *Short Sketch,* 42–53, 15.
50. Wilson, *Loyal Blacks,* 141–42.
51. Stefania Galli and Klas Rönnbäck, "Land Distribution and Inequality in a Black Settler Colony: The Case of Sierra Leone, 1792–1831," *Economic History Review* 74:1 (2021): 115–37.
52. Mary Church, *Sierra Leone, or, the Liberated Africans, in a Series of Letters from a Young Lady to Her Sister in 1833 and 1834* (London: Longman & Co., 1835), 8.
53. Holly Brewer, "Entailing Aristocracy in Colonial Virginia: 'Ancient Feudal Restraints' and Revolutionary Reform," *William and Mary Quarterly* 54:2 (1997): 307–46, and her *By Birth or Consent: Children, Law, and the Anglo-American Revolution in Authority* (Chapel Hill: Omohundro Institute of Early American History and Culture / University of North Carolina Press, 2005).

54. Mathew Carey, ed., *Debates and Proceedings of the General Assembly of Pennsylvania* (Philadelphia: Carey & Co., 1786), 65.
55. Terry Bouton, *Taming Democracy: "The People," the Founders, and the Troubled Ending of the American Revolution* (Oxford: Oxford University Press, 2007), 33.
56. Bouton, *Taming Democracy,* 101.
57. Honor Sachs, *Home Rule: Households, Manhood, and National Expansion on the Eighteenth-Century Kentucky Frontier* (New Haven, CT: Yale University Press, 2015), 44.
58. Sachs, *Home Rule,* 45.
59. Edling, *Hercules in the Cradle,* 30.
60. *Providence Gazette and Country Journal,* Jan. 6, 1787.
61. *Providence Gazette and Country Journal,* Jan. 6, 1787.
62. Henry Knox to George Washington, New York, Oct. 23, 1786, *Founders Online,* National Archives, https://founders.archives.gov/.
63. Bruce Mann, *Republic of Debtors: Bankruptcy in the Age of American Independence* (Cambridge, MA: Harvard University Press, 2009).
64. Stephen Higginson to Henry Knox, Boston, Nov. 25, 1786, http://www.americanhistory.amdigital.co.uk/.
65. Knox to Washington, Oct. 23, 1786, and Henry Knox to George Washington, New York, Dec. 17, 1786, *Founders Online,* National Archives, https://founders.archives.gov/.
66. George Washington to Henry Knox, Mount Vernon, Dec. 26, 1786, *Founders Online,* National Archives, https://founders.archives.gov/.
67. John Jay to Thomas Jefferson, New York, July 14, 1786, *Founders Online,* National Archives, https://founders.archives.gov/.
68. George Washington to Henry Knox, Dec. 26, 1786.
69. Alexander Hamilton, "Federalist 15: The Insufficiency of the Present Confederation to Preserve the Union," *Independent Journal,* Avalon Project, Yale Law School, https://avalon.law.yale.edu/.
70. *Worcester Magazine* (June 1787): vol. 3:12.
71. See May 29, 1787, in *The Records of the Federal Convention of 1787,* vol. 1, https://oll.libertyfund.org/. Also Grubb, *Continental Dollar,* 172.
72. *Worcester Magazine* (June 1787), vol. 3:12.
73. David Waldstreicher, *Slavery's Constitution: From Revolution to Ratification* (New York: Hill and Wang, 2009), 19.
74. Taylor, *American Revolutions,* 381.
75. Grubb, *Continental Dollar,* 225–26, 224.
76. *United States Chronicle,* July 10, 1788.
77. *Connecticut Courant,* July 14, 1788.
78. *Connecticut Courant,* July 14, 1788.

79. David Menschel, "Abolition Without Deliverance: The Law of Connecticut Slavery, 1784–1848," *Yale Law Journal* 111:1 (2001): 183–222, and Sarah L. H. Gronningsater, *The Rising Generation: Gradual Abolition, Black Legal Culture, and the Making of National Freedom* (Philadelphia: University of Pennsylvania Press, 2024).
80. John Wood Sweet, "'More than Tears': The Ordeal of Abolition in Revolutionary New England," *Explorations in Early American Culture* 5 (2001): 118–72: 151–52, and Sean Wilentz, "The Radicalism of Northern Abolition," *New England Quarterly* 96: 1 (March 2023): 8–26: 25–26.
81. George Washington to John Francis Mercer, Mount Vernon, Sept. 9, 1786, *Founders Online*, National Archives, https://founders.archives.gov/.
82. "Mr. Wheeler," *United States Chronicle*, July 17, 1788, 3.
83. Richard Bell, *Stolen: Five Free Boys Kidnapped into Slavery and Their Astonishing Odyssey Home* (New York: Simon & Schuster, 2020).
84. Christy Clark-Pujara, *Dark Work: The Business of Slavery in Rhode Island* (New York: New York University Press, 2016); Calvin Schermerhorn, *The Business of Slavery and the Rise of American Capitalism, 1815–1860* (New Haven, CT: Yale University Press, 2015); and Seth Rockman, *Plantation Goods: A Material History of American Slavery* (Chicago: University of Chicago Press, 2024).
85. Granville Sharp to Benjamin Franklin, "Leadenhall Street, London, 10th June 1788," Hoare, *Memoirs of Granville Sharpe*, 252.
86. Samuel Hopkins, "A Discourse upon the Slave Trade, etc," in *The Works of Samuel Hopkins, D.D.*, 3 vols. (Boston: Doctrinal Tract and Book Society, 1854), vol. 2: 597–661: 620, 614, 619.
87. Granville Sharp to John Jay, March 7, 1789, Hoare, *Memoirs of Granville Sharpe*, 335.
88. Samuel Hopkins to Granville Sharp, "Newport Jan. 15, 1789," Hoare, *Memoirs of Granville Sharpe*, 341.
89. Granville Sharp to Samuel Hopkins, "Leadenhall Street, 25th July, 1789," Hoare, *Memoirs of Granville Sharpe*, 343–44.
90. Hopkins, "Slave Trade," vol. 2: 609–11.
91. Nicholas Guyatt, *Bind Us Apart: How Enlightened Americans Invented Racial Segregation* (New York: Basic Books, 2016), 12.

Conclusion

1. Cowie, *Freedom's Dominion*, especially 6, 415.
2. Franklin Roosevelt, "President Franklin Roosevelt's Annual Message (Four Freedoms) to Congress (1941)," National Archives, https://www.archives.gov/.

3. James N. Arnold, *Vital Record of Rhode Island, 1636–1850, First Series,* 21 vols. (Providence: Narragansett Historical Publishing, 1903), vol. 13: 513.

Acknowledgments

1. Benjamin Franklin to Don Gabriel Antonio de Bourbon, Dec. 12, 1775, *Founders Online,* National Archives, https://founders.archives.gov/.

Index

Page numbers in *italics* refer to illustrations.

Illustration Credits

Page ix: Item author's own. Photo credit Hannah Levy.
Page x: Smithsonian Institution Archives, RU000371 [77-8840-17A]
Page 18: National Library of France
Page 19: Courtesy of the Burton Historical Collection, Detroit Public Library
Page 39: Library of Congress, Geography and Map Division
Page 48: From the New York Public Library
Page 52: Library of Congress, Prints and Photographs Division, Cartoon Prints, British
Page 57: National Museum of American History, Smithsonian Institution
Page 59: Courtesy of HathiTrust, original at Duke University
Page 64: Library of Congress, Rare Book and Special Collections Division
Page 83: Library of Congress, Prints and Photographs Division, Cartoon Prints, British
Page 85: Reproduced with the permission of the National Library of Scotland
Page 89: Library of Congress, Prints and Photographs Division, Cartoon Prints, British
Page 94: Library of Congress, Prints and Photographs Division, Cartoon Prints, British
Page 95: Courtesy of the American Antiquarian Society
Page 98: Library of Congress, Prints and Photographs Division, Cartoon Prints, British
Page 106: The National Archives, UK
Page 126: National Portrait Gallery, Smithsonian Institution
Page 130: Library of Congress Prints and Photographs Division
Page 133: Library of Congress, Geography and Map Division
Page 153: Universität-und Stadtbibliothek Köln
Page 156: Prints, Drawings and Watercolors from the Anne S. K. Brown Military Collection, Brown Digital Repository, Brown University Library

Page 158: Music Division, the New York Public Library for the Performing Arts
Page 177: National Library of France
Page 180: John Hill Morgan, B.A. 1893, LL.B. 1896, M.A. (Hon.) 1929, Fund, Yale University Art Gallery
Page 182: Library of Congress Prints and Photographs Division
Page 197: Prints, Drawings and Watercolors from the Anne S. K. Brown Military Collection, Brown Digital Repository, Brown University Library
Page 203: McCord Stewart Museum, Montreal
Page 210: McCord Stewart Museum, Montreal
Page 229: National Museums Northern Ireland Picture Library
Page 233: Look and Learn / Peter Jackson Collection
Page 235: Yale University Library
Page 250: Library of Congress, Prints and Photographs Division
Page 256: Library of Congress, Geography and Map Division
Page 259: Library of Congress, Rare Book and Special Collections
Page 275: Courtesy of the Peabody Essex Museum. Photo by Jeffrey R. Dykes.
Page 283: Library of Congress, Geography and Map Division
Page 296: "Plan of Freetown," SLEO.0001.0001.0008.0000, Sierra Leone collection, Special Collections and University Archives, University of Illinois at Chicago

Insert

Page 1: National Museum of African American History and Culture, Smithsonian Institution
Page 1: With permission of ROM (Royal Ontario Museum), Toronto, Canada. © ROM.
Page 2: Collection of the Historical Society of Pennsylvania
Page 2: Digital Image © Museum Associates / LACMA (Los Angeles County Museum of Art). Licensed by Art Resource, NY.
Page 3: Gift of graduates to the University, Yale University Art Gallery
Page 3: Philadelphia Museum of Art: 125th Anniversary Acquisition. Alvin O. Bellak Collection, 2004-149-70.
Page 4: Library of Congress, Prints and Photographs Division
Page 5: Library of Congress Prints and Photographs Division
Page 5: The Menil Collection, Houston
Page 6: Pierre Charles Canot, *A General View of Quebec from Point Levy,* 1761, Engraving Printed in Black Ink and Colored by Hand on Laid Paper. Detroit Institute of Arts, Gift of Lillian Henkel Haass, 48.112.
Page 6: Trumbull Collection, Yale University Art Gallery
Page 7: From the New York Public Library

Page 7: Prints, Drawings and Watercolors from the Anne S. K. Brown Military Collection, Brown Digital Repository, Brown University Library

Page 8: Courtesy of the Lewis Walpole Library, Yale University

Page 8: © 2026 Museum of Fine Arts, Boston. Designed by: Pierre-Thomas LeClerc, French, about 1740– after 1799. Engraved by: Etienne Claude Voysard, French, 1746– about 1812. Publisher: Esnauts et Rapilly, French, 18th century. Gallerie des Modes et Costumes Français. 28e Cahier de Costumes Français, 22e Suite d'Habillemens à la mode en 1780. dd.168 "Habit à l'Insurgente..." French, 1779. Hand-colored engraving on laid paper, 36.2 x 4.1 cm (14¼ x 9½ in.). The Elizabeth Day McCormick Collection. 44.1445.

Page 9: Courtesy of the Pennsylvania Academy of the Fine Arts, Philadelphia. Charles Willson Peale, *Baron Frederick William von Steuben,* 1780. Oil on canvas, 29 15/16 x 24 15/16 in. Deposited by Mrs. Maria L. M. Peters, 1881.1.

Page 9: Harvard Art Museums / Fogg Museum, Bequest of Grenville L. Winthrop

Page 10: From the New York Public Library

Page 11: Prints, Drawings and Watercolors from the Anne S. K. Brown Military Collection, Brown Digital Repository, Brown University Library

Pages 12–13: The Picture Art Collection, Alamy

Page 12: National Gallery of Canada. George Romney, *Thayendanegea (Joseph Brant),* 1776. Oil on canvas, 127 x 101.6 cm. Transfer from the Canadian War Memorials, 1921. National Gallery of Canada, Ottawa. Photo: NGC. Accession No: 8005.

Page 13: The Picture Art Collection, Alamy

Page 14: Yale University Library

Page 14: Courtesy of the Peabody Essex Museum. Artist in Guangzhou, China. Panoramic view of Guangzhou with the Foreign Factories, about 1800. Opaque watercolor on paper, 24½ x 47 in. (62.23 x 119.38 cm) H x W. Anonymous gift, 1975. E79708.

Page 15: Göteborgs Stadsmuseum

Page 15: Philadelphia History Museum at the Atwater Kent / Courtesy of Historical Society of Pennsylvania Collection / Bridgeman Images

Page 16: Princeton University Library, Department of Special Collections

Page 16: The Royal Society

About the Author

Sarah M. S. Pearsall is an award-winning historian with degrees from Yale, Harvard, and Cambridge, where she also taught for nearly a decade. She is a professor in the Department of History at Johns Hopkins. She wrote this book as both a National Endowment for the Humanities Public Scholar and a Distinguished Fellow in the American Revolution at the British Library.

Arctic Ocean
Asia
North America
Québec City, Canada
Six Nations, or Haudenosaunee Confederacy
Bkejwanong (Detroit)
Havana, Cuba
Atlantic
Basseterre, St. Christophers (St. Kitts), Leeward Islands
Pacific Ocean
Equator
South America
Southern Ocean
Antarctica